The Mark of Cain

The Mark of Cain: Guilt and Denial in the Post-War Lives of Nazi Perpetrators

KATHARINA von KELLENBACH

OXFORD
UNIVERSITY PRESS

OXFORD
UNIVERSITY PRESS

Oxford University Press is a department of the
University of Oxford. It furthers the University's objective
of excellence in research, scholarship, and education
by publishing worldwide.

Oxford   New York
Auckland   Cape Town   Dar es Salaam   Hong Kong   Karachi
Kuala Lumpur   Madrid   Melbourne   Mexico City   Nairobi
New Delhi   Shanghai   Taipei   Toronto

With offices in
Argentina   Austria   Brazil   Chile   Czech Republic   France   Greece
Guatemala   Hungary   Italy   Japan   Poland   Portugal   Singapore
South Korea   Switzerland   Thailand   Turkey   Ukraine   Vietnam

Oxford is a registered trade mark of Oxford University Press
in the UK and certain other countries.

Published in the United States of America by
Oxford University Press
198 Madison Avenue, New York, NY 10016

ISBN 978-0-19-993745-5

A copy of this book's Cataloging-in-Publication
Data is on file with the Library of Congress.

1 3 5 7 9 8 6 4 2

Printed in the United States of America
on acid-free paper

*This book is dedicated to memory of the
Jews of Pinsk.*

Contents

Acknowledgments

THIS BOOK BEGAN with an ambitious sabbatical proposal to examine Christian discourses of forgiveness that received a fellowship from the Alexander von Humboldt Stiftung in 2000, which allowed me to spend a year at the Evangelische Theologische Fakultät at Humboldt University in Berlin. I spent the year digging through various church archives without quite knowing whether I would find anything or what exactly I was looking for. I benefited from my many conversations with historians and theologians in Germany. When I returned for my subsequent sabbatical in 2007–2008, once more generously supported by the Alexander von Humboldt Stiftung, I enjoyed the Evangelische Theologische Fakultät's palatial new quarters in Berlin-Mitte. In 2006 I juggled my duties as department chair with a three-month fellowship at the Center for Advanced Holocaust Studies (CAHS) at the United States Holocaust Memorial Museum (USHMM) in Washington, DC. The Charles H. Revson Foundation Fellowship for Archival Research at USHMM provided a wonderful atmosphere of scholarly exchange among various disciplines, and its library and archive staff are the best in the world. It would be impossible to thank all the people who have been important to this project from the CAHS, but I must single out Victoria Barnett, as well as my former student Paul Rose, who works as a researcher for exhibitions. Steven Feldman provided encouragement during the final phase of preparation of the book manuscript as the museum's Book Publications Officer.

Over the years, I received several faculty development grants from Saint Mary's College of Maryland, which enabled me to travel to different archives and to present at scholarly conferences. I am especially grateful to my colleagues at Saint Mary's College who participated in faculty summer writing workshops and provided invaluable feedback on early drafts of these chapters from different disciplinary vantage points. I want to thank Robin Bates, Professor of English, and Jacky Paskow, Professor Emerita of French, who believed in the project when I despaired. Celia Rabinowitz, Director of the library at SMCM, is not only a good friend but can always be relied upon to drop everything in order to track down some obscure reference. Among the many archivists I encountered, I want to thank Stefan Flesch, Director of the Archiv der Evangelischen Landeskirche im Rheinland in Düsseldorf, who granted me access to the Schlingensiepen papers, although they had not yet been registered. I am grateful for the forbearance and assistance of archivsts in the Evangelische Zentralarchiv Berlin, the Landeskirchliches Archiv in Nuremberg, the National Archives at College Park, MD, the Institut für Zeitgeschichte in Munich, and the United States Holocaust Museum.

At various stages, I had the opportunity to present these materials in lectures and conference settings, including the American Academy of Religion (thank you, Oren Stier and Laura Levitt, who cochaired the "Religion, Holocaust and Genocide Group" at the AAR with me) and the Christian Scholars Group (CSG), whose collective wisdom in matters of Jewish-Christian relations is unsurpassed. I want to thank my friends Shulamit Magnus, Carleen Mandolfo, and Susanne Scholz for their expertise and companionship throughout these years. Detlef Siegfried accompanied this work with his critical eyes as a historian across the wide distance between us. Hilary Earl graciously agreed to read the second chapter despite her hectic schedule. Björn Krondorfer and Norbert Reck are my long-term collaborators and companions in this quest of developing a perpetrator theology, which emerged from our conversations about Jewish-Christian and Jewish-German dialogue in the aftermath of the Holocaust. The first fruits of these labors appeared in German publications that we coedited or cowrote, which created a network of third-generation German theologians committed to the exploration of the implications of the Holocaust for Christian theology. Many of them have become friends, including Tanya Oldenhage, Jürgen Mannemann, Britta Jüngst, Paul Petzel, Rainer Bucher, Lucia Scherzberg, Lydia Koelle, and Antonia Leugers.[1] Björn Krondorfer, our daughters Zadekia and Tabitha Krondorfer, and my mother Brigitte von Kellenbach have all endured long periods of my misery and ambivalence and have supported me steadfastly as I struggled to bring this manuscript to fruition.

The experience of traveling to Belarus with the Nosanchuk family in 2002 has provided a moral and emotional compass for this work. While the Nosanchuk family returned to their ancestral hometown to commemorate their dead at different sites of mass graves, I followed the trail of my uncle Alfred Ebner and his codefendants, who stood trial for these massacres in West Germany. We, who had traveled from Israel, Canada, Cuba, the United States, and Germany, were cordially welcomed by the townspeople of Rubele, a small village where the Nosanchuk family had operated the grain mill. The entire village of wooden houses had been burned to the ground and the surrounding forests of the Pripyat marshes deforested during the German occupation. The villagers had suffered greatly under Nazi occupation, but some locals had also collaborated in the murder of their Jewish neighbors. As we gathered at the mass grave and shed tears in each other's presence, we came to realize that this history not only divides our communities but that it can also bring us together. By virtue of race, religion, nationality, and politics, our communities were affected and implicated in different ways by this absurd evil, but we do not have to bear the burden of memory separately and in isolation from each other. On the contrary, our future on this planet may very well depend on our ability to commit to the battle against the racism, antisemitism, nationalism, and ethnic hatred that threaten to erupt into genocidal violence in times of crisis and transition. The ideologies that convinced otherwise normal people to massacre thousands, actions that can only be considered insane when seen from the outside, cannot be underestimated. This virus remains virulent not only in Europe (cf. Yugoslavia) but also in any number of African countries (Rwanda, Sudan, Congo, Nigeria) and in Asia (Indonesia, Sri Lanka, Tibet). The Holocaust is an important case study of the power of antisemitism, racism, and nationalism but it also provides lessons for turning painful histories into common ground from which to shape different futures.

The Mark of Cain

Introduction

NOT TOO LONG ago, I received an e-mail from someone unknown to me from the Netherlands. He had googled his last name and wanted to know why my website chronicling the murder of the Jews of Pinsk in Belarus had come up. Could one of the members of Police Battalion 306, whom I mentioned by name, be his grandfather? E-mail is a dangerously quick medium, and since I happened to be sitting at my computer, I answered immediately: "If you send me your grandfather's first and last name and his birthday, I can double check the court records and find out." I received a response right away and checked my files. Within a couple of minutes, I could confirm to the young man that it was indeed his grandfather who had been sentenced to four years in prison for the mass murder of 16,200 Jews in Pinsk by the Regional Court in Frankfurt am Main in 1973. Then I added, "Did you know this?" and held my breath. I heard nothing.

It is in such moments that the ordinary world of good and evil collapses. Although we have become habituated to knowledge of atrocities, it remains unimaginable that someone whom one knows intimately could have been involved in the killing of tens of thousands of human beings, mostly women and children, in a mere three days (between October 29 and November 1, 1942). Such knowledge is unbearable. The closer one is related to a perpetrator, the more intolerable it becomes.

The next morning I received his response e-mail. No, he wrote, he had known nothing about this, but had questioned his father about it that very evening. His father first denied any connection and claimed that this must be a case of mistaken identity. Then he argued that the Frankfurt proceedings were nothing but a "show trial," and that his grandfather had merely been a soldier caught up in postwar vindictiveness. I e-mailed back and pointed out that his grandfather had not been prosecuted as a soldier of the Wehrmacht (German army) but as a member of Police Battalion 306, whose specific assignment included the killing of Jewish civilians. I also cautioned him to be careful as he approached his father, as well as his grandmother, who was still alive. I advised him to familiarize himself with the trial records before he engaged in conversation in order to prevent defensive denials and protective quarrels.

I am a veteran of such family battles and spent several years in archives to disprove the webs of lies, deceptions, and evasions that were spun by close family members to conceal my own uncle's history. This history is dangerous. Fathers will not hesitate to lie to their children. My father both told outright fabrications and bullied me into silence whenever I raised questions about the husband of his cousin, whom he still admired. Alfred Ebner, born in 1913, had risen through the ranks of the SS and become a powerful and successful man. My father, born in 1925, was prevented from joining the SS by my grandfather (who believed that the SS would put his son at too much risk). My father enlisted in the Wehrmacht as soon as he turned eighteen in 1943 and fought in the German retreat all the way from the Crimea into the Bavarian heartland, where he was captured by U.S. armed forces and interned.

The school dropout and unemployed Alfred Ebner had joined the SS in 1931 and was sent to the Ordensburg Vogelsang for political leadership training. The Ordensburg was created as an elite Nazi training school for aspiring SS men who were supposed to take on political and administrative leadership roles. In 1941, Ebner was appointed deputy area commissioner of Pinsk, Belarus, as part of the civil administration of the Reichskommissariat Ukraine. There he was put in charge of the Jewish population, the majority in this district city. In the spring of 1942, Ebner established the ghetto and forced 18,300 Jews to move into 240 houses within one day. According to a handwritten registry, the majority of ghetto inhabitants were women and children, since the Second SS-Cavalry Regiment had already killed most men in September 1941. Ebner oversaw the slave labor recruitment and systematic starvation of the ghetto inmates, and he directed their mass executions over the course of three days between October 29 and November 1, 1942. He later joined the Wehrmacht and was officially denazified by the U.S. Army in 1946. He was the best man at my father's first wedding and, again, at his second marriage to my mother in November 1959. On January 1, 1962, Alfred Ebner was arrested and indicted before the Stuttgart Regional Court. This initial arrest was followed by two trials, prison stays, and releases on bail throughout the 1960s. The trial was eventually moved before the Frankfurt regional court, where, in 1971, Ebner was declared incompetent to stand trial for medical reasons. Thus, he was never convicted, and by 1978 all proceedings were officially discontinued. He died in 1987, a free man.

Alfred Ebner's legal troubles and the events in Pinsk were never openly discussed in my family—at least not with me or anyone else in the younger generation. There were bits and pieces, though, and I vividly remember the moment when I was given a newspaper article that contained the number of 30,000 Jewish victims. I must have been eleven (in 1971) or thirteen (in 1973) when this newspaper article circulated around the table announcing the discontinuation of Ebner's trial for health reasons. I already felt suspicious of his acquittal and could not quite join in the celebration. I remember my confusion: who were these Jews? (At that time, I had never met a Jew.) How did one man kill 30,000 people? Where did this happen? What did this mean for our family, especially since he was sitting—apparently healthy—among us? Had he killed one person, he would have been considered a murderer; had he killed ten, a serial killer. But 30,000? This seemed beyond comprehension and therefore meaningless to my family. The staggering number put him beyond moral censure. My questions could not be answered and were never discussed in the family. Even the attempt to inquire further resulted in angry harangues about the arrogance of the young, their lack of understanding and judgmental hypocrisy. Without information, and feeling completely isolated, I eventually forgot the whole affair.

Like the young German man whose e-mail I received from Holland, I would need an external trigger to retrieve this memory. In my case, the impetus came from Holocaust survivors and their children, who befriended me when I arrived as an exchange student in the religion department of Temple University in Philadelphia. They educated me about the Holocaust and told me their stories of brutality, loss, and survival. Their knowledge was specific and their memory of times, places, people, and events was excellent. They knew who had denied them, hidden them, and brutalized them and their families. Their recollections were often detailed and precise. My lack of knowledge, I began to realize, was not at all innocent. My ignorance was rooted in guilt and protected the anonymity of perpetrators. Most extended German families somehow cope with the presence of perpetrators in their midst. The violence of racist policies affected all Germans and generated guilt, often unacknowledged and usually dismissed or denied. But the experience of guilt has actually grown over time with increasing political, cultural, and personal distance from National Socialist ideology. Its shadow haunts German families. The ghosts of the past reappear whenever National Socialist crimes are exposed and perpetrators uncovered. The accused could be well-known public figures or unknown family men who had lived unremarkable lives. While the Holocaust is omnipresent as a cultural and political metaphor of evil, its agents have been shrouded and hidden until recently.

As long as we can keep mass murder at a distance—committed by someone else, different and removed from us—its knowledge is bearable. But if the perpetrator is one's own uncle or grandfather, that seems unfathomable. The mind and heart desperately want to shut such knowledge out. In this way, factual knowledge of history collides with emotional and moral understanding. Evil hits too close to home for comfort. Therein lies the root of denial, exoneration, and historical revisionism. Every so often, I still hear a small voice in me that wants to question whether the deeds of which Ebner was accused could possibly have happened. In order to prove it to myself, I spent considerable time in archives to examine court records and the documents of the Nazi civil administration of Pinsk. I also met with survivors of this area and their children from Israel and the United States. In 2002, I joined the Nosanchuk family to travel to Pinsk and Stolin in Belarus. Among the Nosanchuk family were two survivors: one had served in the Soviet army, the other had immigrated to Palestine before German occupation. There was also the son of a deceased survivor who was hidden in a village before joining the partisans. He later testified in the trial against Alfred Ebner. I needed all of these intellectual and emotional experiences and all of these conversations to learn to accept the truth of this history.

I wonder how the young German man from the Netherlands was able to process the information I had sent him. His grandfather was sentenced to four years in prison; my uncle's trial had been discontinued for health reasons after more than a decade of court proceedings. These were just two men who stood trial in West German courts. In total, three trials in West Germany dealt with the murder of the Jews of Pinsk.[1] They resulted in prison terms for the accused, none of which were severe enough to satisfy anyone's sense of justice. We continue to speak of "the Holocaust" as if it was one singular event, but the crimes committed in the Pinsk region alone are overwhelming. The murder of six million Jewish men, women, and children happened in many places and under very different conditions. Each murder was particular and committed by a specific person. Historian Konrad Kwiet estimates that 500,000 German men and 5,000 women were actively involved in the various killing programs of National Socialism. Half a million Germans carried guilt for the murder of innocent civilians, foremost Jews, but also Roma and Sinti, homosexuals,

Jehovah's Witnesses, and political prisoners. People were convicted of all sort of crimes and incarcerated in the sprawling slave labor camp system. Eleven million civilians died in the camps and killing programs implemented by National Socialism.

The Jews of Pinsk were not deported to one of the six extermination camps specifically set up to kill Jews: Auschwitz, Majdanek, Treblinka, Sobibor, Chelmo, and Belzec. Instead, they were shot at the outskirts of town in the surrounding forests and buried in trenches. Their voices were almost completely erased. Only a handful survived and could testify. There was very little information about the Jews of Pinsk, but their memory is kept alive by Zionist immigrants to Palestine and to the United States, as well as by Jewish Soviet veterans and deportees.[2] Their world vanished and their way of life has been destroyed forever. All that is left are mass graves scattered across Belarus and Ukraine. As of 2011, the French Roman Catholic priest Father Patrick Desbois has identified over 900 unmarked mass graves in an estimated 2,000 locations across Belarus and Ukraine.[3] These numbers are overwhelming. Such crimes cannot be expiated by judicial punishment alone.

But the trials served several important functions. They collected important historical information and allowed survivors to testify. The International Military Tribunal in Nuremberg (IMT) and the various national military and criminal proceedings, as well as the criminal trials in East and West Germany, provide a treasure trove of historical evidence: witnesses were interviewed, defendants were interrogated, and the sites of murder were documented and brought to public attention. Many of these trials were covered widely in the national and international media. With each sentencing, the twisted logic of National Socialism was repudiated and the victims were vindicated, their memory restored. Especially the West German trials during the 1960s created public debates over the legality of state-sanctioned mass murder. Despite the often outrageously lenient verdicts and the painfully conflicted reasoning, each trial increased public awareness of the brutality and criminality of National Socialism and nudged the public discourse toward acknowledgment of the immorality and inhumanity of National Socialist ideology.

But what about the hearts and minds of perpetrators and the intimate world of their families? Did they learn to accept punishment as just recompense for culpable wrongdoing? There is no adequate payment for the moral debt arising from the brutal murder of 16,200 (as the German courts alleged)—three days in the work of Police Battalion 306. These numbers alone speak to the incongruity of the magnitude of crimes and the limitations of human forms of recompense and resolution. Even the death penalty did not relieve the children of perpetrators of feeling haunted by guilt as they struggled with the moral burden incurred by atrocities committed by their fathers.[4] The Holocaust leaves a moral remainder that threatens to crush anyone who finds himself or herself personally connected.

The magnitude of harm suffered and done makes memory unbearable for both survivors and perpetrators as well as their families—though for different reasons and with different results. Survivors of the Shoah became witnesses who vowed "Never to Forget." Their testimony was always based on traumatic memories, and I know many survivors who cannot eat or sleep after sharing their stories. There are also survivors of the Shoah who have resisted speaking of their experiences with their families, and whose children suffer from the silence. But as a community, Jewish survivors were committed to bear witness, to document meticulously, and to chronicle conscientiously, irrespective of the emotional, physical, and economic costs of such memory.

The perpetrators, on the other hand, were committed to forgetting, erasing, and burying the guilt of the past. They developed evasive, vague, and deceptive stories and engaged in elaborate schemes to obscure and hide their true biographies. Perpetrators and their descendants experience an internal compulsion to conceal the truth and to hide the shame. Descendants are often driven by fear of "guilt by association,"[5] which turns this knowledge into a shameful and burdensome secret.[6] These feelings of shame and fear are not rational. On the rational level, everyone agrees that a father's sins cannot and should not be visited upon the children and the children's children. In public, there are mutual assurances that nobody can be held responsible for acts committed by someone else, certainly not someone generationally removed. But on the emotional level and in private, the histories of our families and communities hold us captive. We cannot be released from their hold on us by time alone. Time does not heal all wounds. In some cases, traumatic events that happened decades and centuries ago can continue to reverberate in the political, cultural, and religious life of cultures: Turkey, for instance, is still held hostage by its undigested history of genocide of the Armenians; white U.S. Americans continue to be in the grip of unresolved feelings over slavery and racism; and several European countries are paralyzed by conflicted emotions over the Holocaust and antisemitism.

Evil that is not suffered but perpetrated causes guilt. Guilt is more than a feeling, it is an objective reality. There are some who are guilty without feeling any guilt (and we will meet many of them in this book), and then there are others who feel guilty although they have committed no wrong. Any act of wrongdoing creates a moral debt that is owed to the victims. We often conceive of guilt as a burden, from which one should eventually be released or redeemed. A debt can be paid off and a liability can be forgiven. In spite of traditional Christian soteriological claims, there are some burdens of guilt that cannot be removed by either forgiveness or punishment. Almost seventy years have passed since the Shoah was ended on the military battlefield, but the stain of the murder of European Jews has not been purified. Is there an appropriate sacrifice that would atone for such an enormous crime? Truly horrific traumatic histories, such as the Holocaust, cannot be expiated, purified, or washed away.

I will argue in this book that the desire to declare closure on such a past is a form of escapism. Instead, I suggest that it is preferable, and in fact liberating, to learn how to shoulder the legacy of perpetration and to acknowledge the reality of the agents of collective evil. Analytic philosophers have recently rediscovered the power of narratives in understanding evil.[7] In *Rethinking Evil*, philosopher Maria Pia Lara argues that stories "offer a better approach to evil than abstract or formal theories"[8] because they "relate concrete and compelling experiences of evil, and they...have the power to shape our moral perception of evil over historical time."[9] In this book, I am taking up her suggestion to relate concrete experiences of doing evil. I want to introduce particular evildoers in their own words and ask how they explained their actions to their clergy, lawyers, and families. Did they ever come to see the wrong of their actions? Or did they, like my uncle, refuse to accept moral accountability? As an entry into this story of coping with genocidal violence, I will present the biblical narrative of Cain as a paradigm for the central role of memory in the process of moral recovery for communities of perpetration.

I

The Mark of Cain

here in this carload
i am eve
with abel my son
if you see my other son
cain son of man
tell him that I

<small>DAN PAGIS, *"Written in Pencil in the Sealed Railway-Car"*[1]</small>

WHAT IS LEFT hanging and unsaid in Pagis's poem, is where this book begins. What were the conversations with those who carried out the killings? To find out I turned to the archives of prison chaplains who visited defendants and convicts in prisons as they awaited their trials and served their sentences. The story of Cain, the firstborn son of Adam and Eve, is evocative of the long-term effects of guilt in the lives of murderers. With a few sparse lines, the Genesis account outlines Cain's murder of his brother Abel in a fit of jealousy and outrage over God's alleged favoritism. His attempt to hide the deed is futile, and he is punished by God. But he is allowed to live and is protected from retaliatory violence by a mark. Cain's mark is a public signifier of his guilt. It protects him and prevents the erasure of memory. There is no miraculous purification of guilt in the story of Cain. No sacrifice cleanses the stain of Abel's blood. No ritual absolves Cain from the guilt of the past. Instead, God's protective mark imposes radical transparency and links Cain's redemption to memory. Truth-telling becomes the basis of moral and spiritual recovery. Cain lives a successful and productive life as a married man, father, and founder of a city as he grows into the memory of fratricide and (re)gains moral integrity.

Let us look at the biblical account: Cain is the firstborn son of Eve and Adam. He murders out of jealous rage because he felt wronged and humiliated when his younger brother's sacrifice of the "firstlings of his flock and of their fat portions" (4:4) was accepted by God, while his own "offering of the fruit of the ground" (4:3) was shown "no regard." The biblical text gives no reasons for God's unequal treatment of these two sacrifices. Later commentators have argued that Abel had chosen the best of his animals and sacrificed the choicest meats, while Cain kept the better part of his harvest for himself. But the biblical text itself gives no clues for such evaluative judgments. Cain's "countenance fell" and he got "very angry" (4:5). As if to taunt him, God asks Cain, "Why are you angry?" and warns him that "sin is lurking at the door; its desire is for you but you must master it" (Gen. 4:6–7).

The perpetrator sees himself as the victim of an injustice. Because his sacrifice has been rejected, Cain turns his rage against his brother. From Cain's perspective, Abel deserves a thrashing, because he has upstaged his brother and is guilty of treachery. He has swindled his way into God's good graces and cheated his brother out of well-earned respect. Cain feels justified in his rage. The Hebrew name of Abel, *hevel,* announces Abel's unworthiness.

> All it means is "breath" or "vapour," and not breath which gives life, but breath in the sense of transience, transitoriness or worthlessness. (It is the same word which Ecclesiastes uses to indicate transience or vanity, הבל.) Abel's name strongly suggests that in the eyes of other people he does not amount to much.[2]

Abel's name, *hevel,* means vanity and futility (Eccles. 1:2); his nothingness foreshadows his annihilation. He is the primordial victim, who possesses no human dignity in the eyes of the victimizer. His name prefigures the universal phenomenon of "blaming the victim." The victims deserve the fate that has befallen them. Their dehumanization must be merited. Victims are suspect. The fact of their violation undermines their respectability and moral worth. The shame of humiliation and degradation adheres to the victim rather than the perpetrator.

After the murder, Cain is confronted by God: "Where is your brother Abel?" Cain's defiant retort diverts attention from what happened out in the killing fields, where Cain had lured his brother in a blind rage over God's lack of appreciation. His rejoinder, "Am I my brother's keeper?" has become a classic retort. Brothers, biblical exegetes tell us, do not "keep" brothers; human beings only "keep" sheep. The *New Interpreter's Bible* notes that the Hebrew verb "to keep" is never used to describe responsibility for another person.³ Cain's reply suggests that God should have kept an eye out for Abel. Cain redirects blame and tries to implicate God, his parents, or anyone else who might have watched out for Abel. His evasive denial and attempt to cast a wide net of complicity is classic perpetrator behavior. His retort expresses his emotional detachment and indifference toward his brother. "This reply," Claire Elise Katz argues, "indicates that he is unable to assume responsibility for the death of his brother, but it also implies Cain's detachment from humanity in general. Cain has no attunement to an 'other,' or at least no attunement that he is able to access."⁴ He is disconnected and unwilling to assume account-ability for the effects of his actions.

Cain grumbles about the severity of his punishment and defends his life. The Hebrew word for "crime" is also the word for "punishment": His crime (avon) befits his punishment (avon). But he is not killed. Rather, he is cut off from the land, from his parents, and from God, because he had severed the bonds of brotherhood. His punishment affects Cain on three levels: profes-sionally, socially, and spiritually. First, Cain is cut off from the soil, which secured his livelihood. The farmer and "tiller of the ground," who sacrificed the fruits of the earth to God, is uprooted. The soil (ha adamah) that received the blood of his brother no longer nourishes him and "will no longer yield…its strength" (Gen. 4:12) to Cain. Second, Cain is displaced socially and culturally as he is forced to relinquish the security of family, home, and community. And third, Cain is driven "from the presence of YHWH" and lives henceforth alienated and at a distance from God. This triple punish-ment initiates transformative processes that force Cain to reinvent himself professionally, socially, and spiritually in the decades that follow the crime.

The mark of Cain is not part of the punitive program despite centuries of misinterpretations of the mark as a stigma. Cain is not stigmatized and forced to live as an outcast. The mark serves as his protection as he is granted his life. Cain settles in the land of Nod, literally translated as "Wandering" (4:12, 14). In this new place, he marries, fathers a son, builds a city, and becomes the founder of the arts, music, and culture. It is this mixed blessing of punishment and protection, of exposure and provision, that pushes Cain along the road of moral growth. This is not a straight path that progresses easily from crime to redemption. Rather, Cain learns to bear the memory of guilt and to integrate its presence into his identity. He learns to master the "sin lurking at the door" that caused him to disre-gard the human dignity of his brother. His new relationships are built upon his ability to honor the memory of his victim.

Cain's struggle with guilt is public and communal. His marriage facilitates his reintegration into the social life of human communities. As a patriarchal text, the Bible gives no clues about the woman who suddenly appears without a history of her own. Presumably, she is not the daughter of Adam and Eve (and thus inaccessible to Cain by virtue of incest prohibitions). We are also not told how she reacts to the man who bears the mark of guilt. Apart from the fact that she is bound to Cain by sexual intercourse and becomes the mother of his son, we must fill in the gaps in their relationship. The biblical text and our patriarchal philosophical and ethical traditions do not generally give much attention to the deliberations and choices of women. Wives are supposed to stay in the background of his/story, without voice, will, or command over their own lives, or that of their husbands. But the quality of her companionship has the power to move Cain toward moral maturation. Moral recovery occurs within families and communities. The moral interventions of wives, in particular, facilitate perpetrators' settlement into male social roles of provider and protector. The response of Cain's wife is unrecorded in the biblical text but should be considered critical for Cain's moral recovery. While only Cain can be held accountable for fratricide, the ways in which the wives of perpetrators facilitated or blocked the moral and spiritual transformations of their husbands should be considered.

Cain's son, Enoch, remains voiceless like his mother. Cain names the city he builds after his firstborn son: Enoch. The shared name symbolizes Cain's commitment to the future. Enoch links Cain's past to his future. City life may promise some anonymity to Cain, but the protective mark of his past violence accompanies him. Sooner or later Cain must explain its significance to his son. What intergenerational conversations occurred in this household? "The talk" may have occurred early in Enoch's childhood; or perhaps later, after Enoch had already ventured beyond the confines of family life and realized that something was different about his father. In all likelihood, Enoch took the mark for granted and assumed that all fathers were thus marked. At some point in his development, however, Enoch must have noticed the mark or must have been made rudely aware of his father's distinctive past. Enoch, we may assume, loves his father unconditionally. Like all children, he is grateful to his father for his life, and for the care and protection he received in his house. Enoch's desire to admire, respect, and cherish his father might be boundless, but at some point he had to begin wrestling with the ambivalence of his roots. Enoch's life unfolds in the shadow of the mark of Cain. Did Enoch ask frankly and innocently, "Hey Dad, what's up with the mark?" Or had he already learned through nonverbal cues to approach this topic gingerly? Had he queried his mother before he dared to approach his father? How did Cain cushion the news that he had bludgeoned Enoch's uncle? The imagined "talk" tests Cain's credibility and authority as a father. A Cain who has grown to regret and who can mourn his wrongdoing can help the son cope with its traumatic repercussions. But a Cain, who retreated into denials ("It's nothing, Son"), resorted to evasions ("You don't understand that") or aggressive rebuffs ("Don't you dare to judge me"), transmitted the task of dealing with guilt and of seeking atonement to the next generation.

Many people associate the mark of Cain with a permanent stigma of shame and interpret it as a punitive symbol that permits a community to humiliate, discriminate, and harm outcast criminals. The mark of Cain has come to mean a curse that follows Cain into exile as an "outward sign of an inward blemish" in a reversal of customary definitions of sacramental grace. Read through the lens of the Greek concept of *stigma*, the mark of Cain is fraught with cruel and repressive implications. It has been used in the course of history as a divinely endorsed invitation to marginalize and penalize individuals and communities.

Dik Van Arkel titled his social history of Christian anti-Judaism *The Drawing of the Mark of Cain,* although he makes no biblical reference in the book itself.[5] For most people, the mark of Cain is synonymous with exclusion, discrimination, and humiliation of marginalized and stereotyped populations. Beginning with Ambrose and Augustine, the story of Cain was used to delegitimize Jews as the older brother who had killed Christ and was forced to become a "wandering people" marked by the sign of circumcision.[6] This interpretation climaxed in Pope Innocent III's mandate, promulgated at the Fourth Lateran Council in 1215, that Jews wear badges on their clothing to become distinguishable in Christian lands. The mark of Cain played not only an ignominious role in the history of Christian anti-Judaism but was also used to justify racism and colonialism. Black skin became the mark of shame that legitimated the capture, trade, and enslavement of African peoples and the colonization of nonwhite populations by European Christians.[7] As a divine stigma, the mark of Cain invited and justified the mistreatment of vulnerable minorities (or majorities in the case colonization), who were considered guilty of some past violation and deserved to be subjugated.

This racist and antisemitic history powerfully speaks against the restoration of this story as a paradigm for perpetrators in the aftermath of genocide. We certainly do not need any more reasons to stigmatize, ostracize, and dehumanize fellow human beings. Given the close association of this story with oppressive politics, we may be well advised to "forget" the mark of Cain. I am nevertheless drawn to the mark as a symbol of the liberating power of memory. Despite the danger of interpretations of the mark as a stigma and sign of disgrace that might cause retaliatory harm, I read the Genesis text as a benevolent sign that protects Cain from retributive violence.[8] It is neither a substitute for, nor an addition to, punishment. Cain is stripped of home, professional identity, and proximity to God. He had felt secure and certain in his home, his status, and his relation with God, all of which had contributed to his false sense of entitlement, invulnerability, and indifference to his brother. God's mark, rather than a badge of shame, is intended to provide an opportunity for renewal of his moral integrity and the restoration of his human dignity. Its public nature means that Cain's ability to speak about his past openly serves a crucial function. In my reading, the mark of Cain encapsulates the task incumbent upon perpetrators. Cain's success as a human being is measured by his ability to resist the impulse to bury, forget, and cut off the past. Cain's crime does not end his life. He lives on and gets a second chance, but only because he does not erase the guilt of his past. His life as city builder and father of toolmakers, artists, and musicians depends on his ability to respect the memory of his brother and to accept his responsibility.

What does this mean for Nazi perpetrators and their communities? The mark of Cain suggests a strategy of open engagement with perpetrators that is separate and distinct from their punishment. Their punishment (*avon*) should befit the crime (*avon*). The simple biblical formula, however, is difficult to apply in the context of modern genocides since they exceed human possibilities of justice. National Socialists set themselves as masters over life and death. They arrogated the power to decide on a *Final Solution to the Jewish Question* and initiated a purgation of the national body politic of racial, social, religious, medical, and political "impurities." No punishment can ever be equivalent to such idolatrous presumption and genocidal intent. After 1945, the Nazi elites were (at least in theory) removed from power and authority. They were made to face internment, interrogation, judgment, and punishment, including in some cases the death penalty. None of these punitive measures were ultimately satisfying as recompense for the enormous suffering and destruction wrought by their hands. There remains a fundamental incongruity of *avon* as genocidal crime and *avon* as limited punishment. Because it is impossible to

punish agents of mass violence adequately, we must develop different reg-
iments for atoning such guilt.

Individual and Collective Guilt

Genocidal atrocities challenge traditional legal definitions of culpability
because genocidal perpetrators do not primarily act out of personal base
motives. Traditional law codes define a crime as an individual act that is
motivated by personal intentions to fulfill desires such as greed, hatred, or
lust. A criminal is defined as a person who acts intentionally and breaks a
law "for emphatically *his or her* reasons, reasons not involving group membership."[9] Such "person-to-person evildoing" guides how we think about
perpetrators and how we respond institutionally in courts of law, pasto-
rally in religious communities, and communally as families and societies
to the eruption of violence in communal life. "Collective evil, by contrast,"
argues Norwegian philosopher Arne Vetlesen, is "where the individual
agent from the very start sees himself as acting *on behalf of his group*, and
so genuinely in his capacity as a group member" (emphasis in original).[10]
Far from breaking the laws of the state, genocidal agents claim to act on
behalf of the community. In collective evil, Vetlesen argues,

> the agent thinks, feels and acts in a manner *giving primacy to his
> relationship (bond) with his co-actors over his relationship with his vic-
> tims.* To put it simply, for such an agent the only relationship that he
> recognizes as placing demands on him (not least moral ones: duties,
> obligations, entitlements) is his relationship with fellow group
> members. (Emphasis in original)[11]

Collective evil obliterates personal conscience and replaces it with a powerful collective cohesion and corporate identity. Ideology supplants
personal moral agency and blocks the perception of the humanity, value,
and personal identity of victims. Time and again, Nazi perpetrators on
trial stressed the corporate nature of the violence and portrayed themselves as servants of the state and obedient agents of superior instructions. They refused to concede individual "intent" or "motivation"
throughout the decades of their prosecution before international and
national courts. "I *know* my husband," wrote the wife of a convicted
member of a police battalion, "and realize that this did not happen because
of base motivations, as they claim nowadays so easily and simply, but

because of a situation that we today, 24 years later, are no longer capable of approximating or comprehending, not even my husband" (emphasis in original).[12] Perpetrators and their families vehemently rejected any insinuation of having killed out of malice or evil intent; they always emphasized the corporate structure of their actions.

Hannah Arendt likened this kind of evil to a fungus: "Evil possesses neither depth nor any demonic dimension. It can overgrow and lay waste the whole world precisely because it spreads like a fungus."[13] The metaphor of a fungus captures the fact that atrocities are committed by collectives. State-sponsored mass murder is not committed by individuals but organized by collectives in pursuit of ideologies that dehumanize and target minorities. Such violence is legitimized ideologically and authorized by law. Protestant theologian Dietrich Bonhoeffer, who was executed a week before Allied victory, also grappled with the peculiar nature of his enemy. He described the phenomenon of National Socialism as "stupidity," which he considered to be "less a psychological than a sociological problem."[14] It is not the "people who have isolated themselves from others" but "individuals or groups of people inclined or condemned to sociability."[15] In his letter, "After Ten Years," written in 1942, Bonhoeffer characterized evil as stupidity:

> Stupidity is a more dangerous enemy to the good than malice. One may protest against evil; it can be exposed and, if need be, prevented by use of force. Evil always carries the germ of its own subversion in that it leaves behind in human beings at least a sense of unease. Against stupidity we are defenseless. Neither protest nor the use of force accomplishes anything here; reasons fall on deaf ears, facts that contradicts one's prejudgment need not be believed.... In all this, the stupid person, in contrast to the malicious person, is utterly self-satisfied and, being easily irritated, becomes dangerous by going on the attack. For that reason, greater caution is called for when dealing with a stupid person than with a malicious one.... [Stupidity] is in essence not an intellectual defect but a human one. There are human beings who are of remarkably agile intellect yet stupid, and others who are intellectually quite dull yet anything but stupid.... In conversation with him, one virtually feels that one is not dealing with him as a person, but with slogans, catchwords, and the like that have taken possession of him. He is under a spell, blinded, misused, and abused in his very being.

Having thus become a mindless tool, the stupid person will also be capable of any evil and at the same time incapable of seeing that it is evil.[16]

Bonhoeffer's analysis, written in 1942 from his prison cell, is quoted at some length here, because his observation about the peculiar character of Nazi evil continued to hold true in the postwar world. When agents of the Nazi state defended their actions, they used platitudes and clichés, and their phrases were devoid of original thinking and personal insight. The deliberate absence of individual intent, of emotional involvement, and of personal motivation distinguishes their writings and characterizes their peculiar criminality.

Bonhoeffer's notion of stupidity and Arendt's metaphor of a fungus tried to capture the new phenomenon of collective evil. After 1945, courts of law as well as religious institutions struggled with this new reality of guilt that was not the result of individual choice and action but of deliberate abdication of personal responsibility. By and large, perpetrators of atrocities do not torture and kill for personal gain or satisfaction, and they try hard not to break the law. In general, they do not lose control over their desires and succumb to envy, lust, greed, or anger. Rather, they enforce the law and they actively deny personal moral agency and claim ignorance, impotence, and dependence. Hannah Arendt coined the term "banality of evil" for this phenomenon. Similarly, philosopher Susan Neiman notes:

Jurisprudence views heinous crimes as those done with malice and forethought. Both of these components of intention were often missing in many agents who carried out the daily work of extermination....At every level, the Nazis produced more evil, with less malice, than civilization had previously known.[17]

For the experience of Nazi perpetrators, the refusal to acknowledge personal responsibility and the absence of remorse is central. Bonhoeffer himself gave up fighting stupidity with reason and vowed to "never again try to persuade the stupid person with reason, for it is senseless and dangerous."[18] "Only an act of liberation," he came to see, "not instruction, can overcome stupidity. Here we must come to terms with the fact that in most cases a genuine internal liberation becomes possible only when external liberation has preceded it. Until then we must abandon all attempts to convince the stupid person."[19] Bonhoeffer became disillusioned and realized that National Socialism had to be defeated by military force, which is why he joined the conspiracy to assassinate Adolf Hitler. Only external liberation brought about by the sword would be able to stop the mass murder of Europe's Jews in the midst of the National Socialist reign of terror.

But Bonhoeffer also realized that evil cannot be conquered by force alone. As a Protestant theologian, he envisioned deliverance from evil as an internal change or, in the language of Lutheran theology, as an act of grace. Stupidity is a blindness of the heart, a deformation of the will, a stubborn obduracy that must be touched and transformed by God's power of grace. Repentance, liberation, or deliverance from evil is initiated by an undeserved act of divine forgiveness, an external intervention to soften a stubborn heart. In Protestant theology, this process is elaborated in the doctrine of justification (from the Latin *justificationem*—to make just again). "What must I do to be just again," asked Martin Luther famously in despair over his inability to lead a righteous life. It was over this question that he parted ways with the Roman Catholic Church and its indulgence practices.

Against a religious merit system, whereby a person "worked" herself out of sin and damnation, Luther posited the notion that one could not save oneself through effort. No merit, no repentance, no amount of good works could ever make up or atone for one's guilt. Only God could overcome sin and evil and change the heart of the wicked. God delivers the sinner from evil by sending his Son to die for the forgiveness of sins in an act of unconditional love. It is unconditional, because no one can earn God's love or deserve it on the basis of good behavior. Repentance is the result of unconditional forgiveness, not its precondition. It cannot be achieved by human effort but is received in faith as a gift of grace. In Lutheran theology one is saved by faith in Christ's atoning sacrifice and not by effort and meritorious works.

The letters and diaries of Nazi perpetrators certainly confirm that repentance is not easily accomplished. Their hearts and minds did not turn contrite overnight with the collapse of National Socialism in 1945. Rather, they clung obdurately to their ideological convictions—even as some of them converted to Christianity and used the Christian language of sin and salvation, of guilt and redemption. But despite their rebirth in the Christian faith, they did not acknowledge remorse for the crimes of National Socialism. The historical records of their religious life question the efficacy of traditional Christian stories that conceptualize forgiveness as a momentary outpouring of divine grace. Instead, reconciliation should be understood as a path and lifelong project involving many twists and turns. The experience of those guilty of participation in atrocities suggests that we need new stories to think about the mechanisms of deliverance from evil.

The Christian Story of Sin and Redemption: The Prodigal Son

Christianity's central stories are about sin and redemption. When I began my archival research on perpetrators' moral and spiritual struggles, I assumed that I would find individuals whose conversions would exemplify the Christian paradigm of guilt and forgiveness. I was imagining contrite perpetrators, willing to renounce the evils of Nazi anti-semitism and ready to embark on born-again lives of faith and penitent service. But I did not find such biographies that would neatly conform to this model of spiritual rebirth and ideological conversion. Nevertheless, this was the hope with which Christian pastors entered the internment camps and prisons, where Nazi functionaries awaited their trials before Allied military tribunals in the immediate aftermath of Germany's defeat in 1945. These pastoral caretakers (*Seelsorger*) offered a gospel of new beginning to those willing to submit to God's merciful judgment. They hoped to prepare these men (they were mostly men) to confess their trespasses and to accept the grace of Christ's sacrifice for the forgiveness of sins. Those yearning for renewal and rebirth would be granted reprieve in Christ and be released from the bondage of sin if they submitted to faith in Christ.

One prominent biblical narrative that sums up the paradigm of guilt and forgiveness is the parable of the prodigal son. The story tells of a young man who squandered his inheritance. When he hit rock bottom, he resolved to return to his father's house and to ask for forgiveness. As he approached his home, his father welcomed him overjoyed and prepared a feast to celebrate his return. The father received him unconditionally—to the dismay of the elder brother, who had served his father faithfully and had never been rewarded with a big party. The punch line of the parable is the father's explanation that "we had to celebrate and rejoice because this brother of yours was dead and has come to life, he was lost and has been found" (Luke 15:31–32). The prodigal son encapsulates the message of a gracious father who welcomes the sinner back into the household without reprimand or precondition. The father's love is willing to forgive and to forget, a paradigm that became central to Germany's efforts to rehabilitate and reintegrate Nazi perpetrators.

But one of the problems with Luke's story in the context of postgenocidal societies is that perpetrators of state crimes do not seek forgiveness. They repudiate any suggestion of wrongdoing, because they feel innocent and are convinced that they acted in the interest of the father (i.e. the state). There is no need to return to the father's house as a remorseful penitent because in their minds, genocidal agents never left the house of the father. Instead, the Christian story of sin and redemption as told in the parable of the prodigal son was used to suspend perpetrators' punishment and to accelerate their reintegration and the restoration of postwar German society.

By listening attentively to what perpetrators were actually saying, one realizes that the paradigm of unconditional forgiveness cannot be the right starting point for moral recovery and redemption. Instead, we need stories that express the circuitous and complicated processes of moral transformation and ideological disentanglement. We need religious stories because the realms of politics and law cannot address guilt and forgiveness in postgenocidal societies without the conceptual and ritual tools of the religions of the world. Religious terminology has regained relevance in the emerging discussions of transitional justice. For instance, the Roman Catholic sacrament of penance, which ritualizes the Christian practice of reconciliation through the tripartite process of *contritio cordis* (cordial contrition), *confessio oris* (oral confession), *and satisfactio opere* (acts of satisfaction) lends itself to transitional procedures in societies emerging from systemic human rights abuse. It informs Truth and Reconciliation Commissions, in which agents of violence are given the option to confess truthfully in exchange for amnesty and acceptance of some form of reparation or satisfaction. Religious traditions provide important narratives and rituals to facilitate the healing of nations.

Cain as Counternarrative

I am proposing the story of Cain as a counternarrative to the parable of the prodigal son. In contrast to the prodigal son who is quickly forgiven and welcomed back into the house of the father, Cain is sent away from the house of the father and bidden to rebuild his life in open conversation about his life. While the story of the prodigal son links forgiveness to erasure of memory, Cain's story associates redemption with transparency and remembrance. In the story of Cain, repentance is moved from an internal affair of the heart (*contritio cordis*, the contrition of the heart) to the public realm of conduct and communication. Cain learns to bear up under the weight of guilt as he communicates its lessons to family and community. The story of Cain projects the process of atonement across a lifetime. There are no quick solutions but a multitude of daily interactions and practices of small steps that change perspectives, modify attitudes, and repair relationships.

The counternarrative of Cain articulates more accurately the history of Germany's struggle to "come to terms with the past" (*Vergangenheitsbewälti-gung*). While individual perpetrators failed, time and again, to accept personal responsibility for their actions, Germany's political culture has shifted dramatically. By and large, transparency, accountability, and commemoration have been embraced by individuals, families, institutions, and communities. In its political culture, Germany has accepted itself as a perpetrator nation, like few other states. Its governments have acknowledged moral obligations of repair and financial commitments to pay reparations. People, cities, businesses, and institutions have issued declarations of regret and extended gestures of restitution or initiated projects of commemoration. Significantly, these reparative and commemorative acts have been accelerating rather than declining as the distance from the mentality of perpetration has grown.

The story of Cain projects the process of redemption across a lifetime. In contrast to the prodigal son whose return to the father's house marks the end of the story of forgiveness, Cain's struggle with the legacy of fratricide proceeds through many stages that are shaped by his encounters with different people, places, and philosophies. Hence, Germany's moral recovery from National Socialism should be seen as a dynamic process across time that involved retributive justice and protection, reintegration and disempowerment of the old ideologies. For all of its flaws—and the book will discuss many—the German case of transitional justice worked: the leadership of Nazi Germany was held accountable by the International Military Tribunal, by military courts, and by national criminal jurisdictions. No matter how inconsistent, there were recurring attempts to remove the political, economic, and cultural elites of the Nazi state from power, to divest them of privilege and profits, and to undermine their political prestige. Germany was both politically ostracized and integrated into military and political alliances, albeit for reasons of the Cold War and as a divided country. The international community—in East and West—

remained vigilant and applied pressure on the political establishment to prosecute perpetrators and to confront complicity in Nazi crimes. Over the decades, there were multiple scandals involving particular people, properties, municipal and state governments, education, culture, businesses, museums, and the media. The cumulative effect of these controversies and debates has changed the political, social, religious, and artistic culture of the nation.

Germany today is no longer as haunted by the guilt of the Nazi past as it used to be. To the extent that the two German states were prevented from sweeping the events of the Third Reich under the rug, individuals and communities were forced to "come to terms" and to accept the legacy of perpetration. Transparency removes the sting of guilt. As long as guilt has to be hidden as a shameful secret, it turns into a paralyzing burden. But when the facts of wrongdoing can be acknowledged and its victims mourned, its recollection loses the power to haunt and terrify. This is why the mark of Cain is correctly read as a sign of grace.

The redemptive power of truth becomes apparent over time. In the beginning, the prospect of "branding" Nazi perpetrators by exposing their misdeeds publicly struck most Germans as cruel and vengeful. Many believed that such disclosures would only serve to humiliate and ostracize people who were trying hard to leave their pasts behind. The concept of the mark of Cain elicits fear and resentment, and it is, no doubt, a dangerous idea. It is probably no accident that this story is rarely used for self-critical introspection or self-reflective analysis. Usually, the mark of guilt is affixed to the forehead of the Other. The tendency to "take the speck out of your brother's eye" while overlooking "the log" in one's own (Matt. 7:4) has long inhibited any creative exploration of the story of Cain.[20] This includes Nazi defendants, who quoted and reflected on the story of Cain, but always to ponder the war crimes committed by Allied forces, most prominently the American use of the nuclear bomb in Hiroshima[21] and the aerial bombing raids on civilian cities.[22]

A best-selling book published in the 1960s by investigative German reporter Hans Herlin appeared under the title *Kain, wo ist dein Bruder Abel? Die Flieger von Hiroshima und Nagasaki* (Cain, Where is Your Brother Abel? The Flyers of Hiroshima and Nagasaki).[23] Herlin wrestled with the topic of guilt through the lens of American pilots following the story of Major Claude Eatherly, who had been committed to a mental institution in Waco, Texas, and was later tried for a robbery attempt in 1959. Herlin makes the case that there are high psychological costs for those directly involved in the mass death of civilians. He cited psychological expert testimony during Eatherly's court trial that diagnosed a "guilt complex": Eatherly wanted "punishment, in a desperate attempt to perform acts of atonement."[24] He was acquitted in the robbery trial but continued to speak publicly against the nuclear arms race. The publication of Herlin's book might have been the source for the erroneous passage in German public school textbooks published in the 1970s that reported of the suicide of one of the American pilots—a patent falsehood, as it happened. Paul Tibbets, the pilot of the *Enola Gay*, which dropped the bombs killing 150,000 people in Hiroshima and 75,000 people in Nagasaki, remained unrepentant to his death: "I am proud to have planned all of that out of nothing and that everything worked so well. I wanted to do that" (quoted in the *Süddeutsche Zeitung* in his obituary in 2007).[25]

Interestingly, all of Herlin's books were translated into English and published in the United States except for his book on Cain.[26] It seems obvious that the German reading public was fascinated by the guilt of American pilots, while the American public was more intrigued by German (and Japanese) atrocities. In both cases, the figure of Cain confirms the prejudice that depravity lurks at the doorsteps of someone else's house. Such a use of the mark of Cain—as a stigma to denounce, demean, and brand one's (former) foes—is contrary to my intentions. It should never be read as a shameful "bloodstain" that defiles a person. If the mark were a sign of defilement, it would require purification and removal. But it is meant to provide protection, which turns the public proclamation of guilt into an integral aspect of Cain's redemption. Its removal is neither required nor salutary. Cain cannot be released from guilt by erasure of the memory. Rather, it is only perpetrators' truthful engagement with atrocities inflicted on victims, whether they be in Auschwitz, or Hiroshima, on American slave plantations, or in South African townships, that can provide release from the moral remainders of history. As long as perpetrators remain ideologically convinced of victims' lack of human worth and dignity, there can be no remorse or repentance. Such histories haunt. As long as the "stupidity" of antisemitism, racism, anticommunism, nationalism, and militarism reign supreme, no sense of culpable wrongdoing can emerge. Time itself does not change attitudes. But open engagement, public debates and private conversations, and reparative acts of reconciliation do.

Can Cain Be Saved?

Although this is not a book in systematic theology, it is concerned with "salvation." The Latin root of the term salvation stems from *salve*, meaning health or healing. In this book I do not merely *describe* the moral state and spiritual condition of perpetrators but also intend to *prescribe* appropriate steps toward renewal, restoration, health, or salvation. In other words, I want to combine the descriptive skills of the historian with the normative discourse of the theologian. Guilt and redemption, remorse and reconciliation, repentance and forgiveness, atonement and expiation are terms rooted in the religious traditions. Religions have developed various prescriptions and restorative pathways intended to heal the wounds incurred by sin, oppression, alienation, violence, and violation of moral and religious law. For such recuperative remedies to work, the diagnosis has to be correct. But what exactly did the symptoms of guilt look like in the minds and hearts of Nazi perpetrators in the postwar world?

The following biographical case studies can be read as diagnostic reports on the state of mind of individuals who awaited trials for atrocities committed in the name of the Nazi state. While no one (but God) can know the innermost recesses of another's soul, it is possible and important to listen carefully to what people are saying. The archival materials used for these diagnostic portraits come from church and state archives that maintain collections of documents and correspondence between Nazi convicts and clergy who visited them in internment camps and West German prisons. As professionals, prison chaplains were committed to probing questions of ultimate meaning and morality with criminals of all kinds, but Nazi convicts were in a category all of their own. They were different, often better educated and more eloquent, and they were generally more resistant to acknowledging culpable wrongdoing than ordinary prisoners. The tools at the disposal of prison chaplains often proved ineffective in the case of these educated, self-assured, and remorseless defendants. The Christian message of forgiveness failed to penetrate the ideological armor of killers sanctioned by the state.

Contemporary Christian teachings privilege forgiveness and reconciliation over moral discernment and judgment. At the risk of overgeneralization, one can say that for many Christians, forgiveness constitutes an ethical imperative that is given precedence over accountability and justice.[27] To give but one example, the American Protestant theologian Gregory Jones argues in *Embodying Forgiveness* (1995) that forgiveness should always be the principled Christian position and that this does not require contrition or recognition of wrongdoing. Jones quotes from the Gospel of Luke: in the account of Jesus' last moments on the cross, Jesus explicitly exempted the Roman soldiers from accountability: "Father,

forgive them, for they do not know what they are doing" (Luke 23:34).
Jones takes this to mean that Jesus forgave even those (especially those?) who are
ignorant and unaware and "without requiring prior repentance."[28] Jesus, he
argues, "diverge[s] from Israel's understanding and practices...[because]
he both claimed divine authority to forgive sins and offered forgiveness
without necessarily presuming prior repentance."[29] Apart from the anti-
Judaism implicit in this interpretation, such a one-sided embrace of forgiveness releases the Roman soldiers from moral obligation to critically
analyze their participation in imperial violence and colonialist exploitation. Forgiveness in such theological accounts is perceived as an injection of divine grace that magically touches and transforms the heart of
hardened soldiers, such as the Roman executioners. Instant conversion
follows such miraculous transformations, and the sinner comes to
renounce his Old Adam and to see the Way. While Nazi perpetrators
shared the religious sentiments of such conversion experiences, they
generally refused to embrace remorse or recognition of culpable
wrongdoing.

When moral agents are forgiven without knowing what they have
done, moral transformation and political change are slowed down or
obstructed altogether. Martin Luther King recognized the danger of permanently tipping the "balance of opposites" inherent in God's attributes
"of tough-mindedness in his justice and wrath and his tender-heartedness
in his love and grace":[30]

> Nothing in all the world is more dangerous than sincere ignorance
> and conscientious stupidity...somewhere along the way, the church
> must remind men that devoid of intelligence, goodness and consci-
> entiousness will become brutal forces leading to shameful crucifix-
> ions. Never must the church tire of reminding men that they have
> a moral responsibility to be intelligent.[31]

Martin Luther King knew perfectly well that the evils of racism, the politics
of subjugation, and the laws of segregation could only be overcome by
political analysis and moral judgment. He understood that racist emotions had to be fought by clearheaded analysis and recognition of the
moral effects of racist violence on perpetrators and victims alike. King
echoed Bonhoeffer's insight that the willfully stupid person is more dangerous than the depraved. Both became passionate voices for critical discernment and political analysis.

The call for intelligence is a call for openmindedness, sound judgment, and love for truth. It is a call for men to rise above the stagnation of closedmindedness and the paralysis of gullibility. One does not need to be a profound scholar to be openminded, nor a keen academician to engage in the assiduous pursuit for truth.[32]

Nazi perpetrators were purposefully and tenaciously obtuse, their writing convoluted, their recollections deceitful, and their thinking twisted. Reading their accounts requires critical distance and moral judgment. While it is important to take their perception of reality seriously, it is equally important to recognize and adjudicate the deceptions and falsehoods. Nazi perpetrators were manipulating their audiences, whether that audience was prison chaplains, family members, courtrooms, or the media. The most persistent deformation in their recollections is the near total absence of the victims. In most cases, documents written by perpetrators censor all information concerning their former responsibilities, positions, and assignments in the Nazi hierarchy. Victims are rarely acknowledged, their suffering occurs virtually never. To ascertain the charges brought against them, one must consult a different set of archival materials, namely the documents and witness accounts presented in the trials. There is a significant gap between the remembrance of perpetrators and the testimony given to the judges in the courts. These discrepancies, denials, and evasions define the predicament of perpetrators and constitute the symptoms of guilt.

Release from guilt can be measured by a person's ability to bear the reality of victims' suffering, a reality that is deliberately concealed by ideologies that dehumanize and degrade the victims. Such ideologies change slowly, incrementally, and as a result of persistent scrutiny and political pressure. Without moral judgment, political discernment, and social change, agents of the state do not consider the infliction of lethal force an act of culpable wrongdoing, no matter how heinous the violence. Remorse cannot be presumed but may occur as a result of political transformation and moral rehabilitation. It is for this reason that public scrutiny and critical engagement, symbolized by the mark of Cain, can be seen as integral parts of recovery.

The empirical evidence presented in this book suggests that this happens rarely. But we cannot abandon the task. While the biblical Cain could be banished to the land of Nod, we have run out of remote places where those who carry grave guilt can be deported. Increasingly, our world has grown together so closely that we will not be able to give up and write off anyone in the global family. We cannot execute or imprison the thousands who require the medicine of retribution. Hence, we must develop different strategies that heal past hurts and that detoxify the poisons of hate and of guilt. That is why the mark of Cain, the path of radical transparency, commends itself. When the first generation fails to accept the challenge, its descendants inherit the task.[33] But there is an inexplicable imperative toward *at-one-ment*, or a coming back together, that can be trusted.

An Outline of What Follows

The second chapter sets the stage for the political situation in Germany immediately after the Nazi state surrendered unconditionally and its organizations were declared illegal. Millions of people were displaced, and hundreds of thousands of Germans were detained in prisoner of war and internment camps. The churches emerged as the only organized and morally credible organization that spoke publicly on behalf of and to the German people. This chapter examines the churches' contradictory messages about guilt that vacillated between calling on the Christian "solidarity of sin," condemning "collective guilt," and resisting the "selective" prosecution and condemnation of individual Nazi officials. Sermons and study groups in internment camps as well as official church declarations tried to navigate the toxic politics of "collective guilt" by affirming the universal condition of human sinfulness and introducing a vague sense of shared guilt that allowed individual perpetrators to reject personal responsibility. Implicit in these early debates about guilt was the expectation that any sincere confession would generate forgiveness and release from the guilt of the past. Hence, the well-known Protestant Stuttgart Declaration of Guilt was followed by the less well-known, indeed secret, Memorandum of the Evangelical Church in Germany on the Question of War Crimes Trials before American Military Courts,[34] which denounced the International Military Tribunal in Nuremberg as "victors' justice" and called for the immediate release of all prisoners held in the Allied Military Prison in Landsberg/Lech.[35] The same churchmen who had acknowledged German wrongdoing and the solidarity of guilt now demanded amnesty and reprieve for the convicts of Nuremberg and Dachau.

The third chapter examines the "last words" of men sentenced to death by the international and American military trials who were hanged in War Crimes Prison (WCP 1) Landsberg between 1945 and 1951. U.S. military authorities recorded their last words, and the Protestant prison chaplains maintained detailed logs on each death candidate. The vast majority of prisoners stepped under the gallows affirming their innocence "before God." Christian expressions of faithful piety stood alongside the denial of personal responsibility. Among the 285 recorded executions in Landsberg, there were only three unambiguous declarations of regret. These three men, who had been transferred to Landsberg from other prisons, had been sentenced to death for individual crimes such as robbery, assault, and murder. An examination of the recorded "last words" vividly demonstrates the difference between those whose violence broke criminal law and those whose cruelty upheld the law, albeit a perverted and genocidal law. Overall, the prison chaplains failed to grasp the peculiar moral challenges of Nazi criminals and understood their primary task as pastoral counselors to be helping convicts achieve peace of mind rather than recognition of culpability for atrocities. The religious practice in Landsberg/ Lech did little to challenge the ideological convictions of those who were being prepared to face the highly ritualized public spectacle of the gallows.

The fourth chapter contrasts the professional ethos of General of the Waffen-SS Oswald Pohl, chief of the SS Economic and Administrative Main Office (Wirtschafts- und Verwaltungshauptamt), with the criminal reputation of Klara Pförtsch, a former concentration camp inmate who was sentenced to death for beating fellow inmates as a prisoner functionary. Oswald Pohl framed his prison experience in terms classic to theodicy and asserted that he had been "purified … in the purgatory of extreme abandonment." His Roman Catholic prison chaplain, Father Morgenschweis, praised him for his saintly piety and character and published his conversion narrative as *Credo: My Path to God*.[36] Pohl was responsible for the economic affairs of the SS-run concentration camp universe and claimed reconciliation and purification of sin and "guilt," a term he only used in quotation marks. By contrast, Klara Pförtsch, who was also on death row in a French prison, was considered a *vraie bête humaine* (true human beast) by the French military court in Rastatt. She was the only appeal case whom Pastor Sachsse, the "Plenipotentiary for Political Prisoners in the French Zone," refused to support. Arrested in 1936 as a member of a communist resistance group, she was recruited into camp service as *Lagerälteste* (camp elder) in Ravensbrück, Auschwitz, and Dachau. While Pohl claimed that suffering turned him from sinner into a saint, the degradation and suffering endured by Pförtsch changed her from political activist into subhuman beast. This chapter questions the nature of guilt and the role of punitive suffering in its purgation.

The fifth chapter traces the sacrificial language of Nazi perpetrators across time. In the Christian tradition, the blood of the sacrificial lamb washes away the sins and expiates guilt. Sacrificial language permeated the self-portrayals of Nazi perpetrators in postwar prisons and camps. The language of sacrifice reversed the indignity of criminal convictions and the agony of the gallows with transcendent meaning and purpose. Suffering endured for altruistic reasons in pursuit of higher goals is ennobling. Perpetrators in the immediate postwar period framed their punishment in language related to three subthemes: first, the Passion narrative, which turned executions into voluntary sacrifices for the future resurrection of Germany; second, the biological language of the seed, which is planted to ensure future fertility and rebirth, by which they asserted immortality through the eternal cycles of nature and the nation; and third, the military language of heroic sacrifice on the battlefield, by which they offered their lives in expectation of vindication in the future. But by the 1960s, the language had changed because the unity of collective purpose had splintered. Perpetrators no longer volunteered for sacrifice but felt offered up against their will by an ungrateful nation. They felt abandoned and resentful of the German state that moved to sacrifice them. Nazi perpetrators still felt innocent, but could no longer communicate this without resorting to antisemitism and Nazi ideology that had lost credibility.

The sixth chapter analyzes the moral lessons contained in a seventy-seven-page, handwritten letter for a son's seventeenth birthday in 1966. Artur Wilke, who served ten years in prison for the killings of Jews in Minsk/Belarus, tried to preserve his paternal authority and moral integrity by reflecting on the "truth of the mistake." Wilke was trained in theology and classics, and he extensively quoted from the Latin Vulgate in order to impress his son with his learning and sincerity. There is no information about the son's actual response or later biographical development, but we can extrapolate his reaction from the conflicted responses of members of the generation of 1968. The German second generation received parental love alongside political counseling, tainted by failure to acknowledge culpable wrongdoing and moral corruption. The parents' evasions forced the children to choose between, on the one hand, complicity in pervasive deceptions and, on the other hand, betrayal of filial loyalty and intimacy, a moral dilemma that shaped the coming of age of that generation.

The seventh chapter examines the moral complicity of wives. Women who had married SS men during the Third Reich had to undergo rigorous testing of their biological and political fitness before they received permission to proceed with wedding plans. Hence, SS wives were usually politically committed and supportive. They were encouraged to visit their husbands during deployments or lived close to concentration camps, ghettos, and occupation sites.[37] Loyalty and steadfast support were the hallmark of the National Socialist wife. After 1945, this value system carried over to the Christian duties of a wife. Wives were expected to stick by their husbands—and the vast majority did. I found only one wife who experienced shock and moral qualms when her husband was arrested and tried for crimes he had committed as an SS man in Auschwitz. She had married in 1953 and been unaware of his past. Pastor Hermann Schlingensiepen argued passionately against her wish for a divorce. Their correspondence prompts consideration of divorce as a moral choice for women to prod their husbands toward moral change and transformation.[38]

The last chapter follows two clergymen, one Roman Catholic and one Lutheran, who faced public exposure over their participation in killings in the Third Reich. Their stories show why forgiveness and moral integrity should not be linked to forgetfulness and dissociation from the past. In 1969, the magazine *Der Spiegel* reported that the newly ordained Roman Catholic auxiliary bishop Matthias Defregger of Munich had given orders to execute seventeen civilian hostages in an Italian village in 1944. Defregger, supported by Cardinal Döpfner, claimed that he had truthfully confessed his sins and received absolution before his ordination to the priesthood in 1949. Defregger denied responsibility and was acquitted in court. The ensuing public debate provided opportunities to consider the Christian sacrament of absolution, penance, and moral obligation toward the victims. The second clergyman, Pastor Otto Zakis, had joined the SS when he was sixteen years old. He was assigned to Buchenwald and the death camp of Majdanek. When he was deposed in preparation for the Majdanek trial in 1972, he spoke of having imposed various forms of penance on himself. He reported himself to the French police and wanted to testify truthfully. He belonged to the youngest cohort of perpetrators and was able to regain the respect of Jewish witnesses who appreciated his truthful testimony in the Düsseldorf trial. Of all the perpetrators in this study, Zakis came closest to the truthful acknowledgment of the suffering of victims.

This book is a plea for open engagement with legacies of perpetration and with the agents of atrocity. Cain lives among us. He cannot be banished and deported, ostracized and incarcerated for the rest of his life. He should not be abandoned and hidden behind veils of indifference. We should not avert our eyes and reintegrate him by erasing the memory of his past. The price for such "rehabilitation" is high. It not only coerces the victims to forgive and to forget, but also paralyzes perpetrators in defensiveness and denial. True reconciliation can only arise where the truth of the past can be born communally and across the chasm of hate and violence. As long as the past has to be censored and airbrushed out of fear of offending victims or perpetrators, communities remain caught in the clutches of guilt. The story of the mark of Cain serves as a paradigm for such radical openness. Especially in instances of state crimes, such public exposure compels critical conversation and communal scrutiny that stimulates changes in public policy, personal behavior, education, and culture. Release from guilt is not the result miraculous divine interventions but the fruit of faith in human beings' ability to change and to embrace responsibility in the face of the suffering of others.

2

Guilt Confessions and Amnesty Campaigns

*And the question whether the German people will ever be
released from the subjugated life of a marked nation throws
millions into bitterness and despair.*

(February 10, 1947)[1]

LESS THAN TWO years after the military defeat of Nazi Germany on May
8, 1945, the newly reconstituted national council of the Evangelical Church
in Germany (EKD) complained bitterly that the nation was still marked
with guilt for crimes committed during the reign of National Socialism
between 1933 and 1945. The memorandum, distributed to all Protestant
ministers in Germany, denounced Allied campaigns of "denazification"
designed to classify various levels of complicity and responsibility for Nazi
crimes. The request to be relieved from the burden of guilt was symptomatic of the desire to move forward by closing off the past. Guilt, it was
understood, had to be confessed in order to be forgiven. Therefore, guilt
confessions became the foundation upon which the churches launched
amnesty campaigns, built rescue networks, and assembled opposition to
denazification programs.

World War II claimed the lives of over 50 million people. But the "guilt
question" that would occupy Germany for decades thereafter was not
about unleashing this war by invading Poland in 1939—though it did that.
In contrast to the infamous Versailles Treaty of 1918 that imposed "war
guilt" (*Kriegsschuld*) for World War I on Germany, the moral burden haunt-
ing Germany in the aftermath of the Third Reich was the murder of eleven
million civilians who were enslaved, starved, and tortured in its vast
concentration camp system, including six million Jews who were systematically slaughtered in the "Final Solution of the Jewish Question," today
known as the Holocaust or the Shoah.

Brief Historical Overview

National Socialism promised the rebirth of the Aryan master race (*Herrenrasse*), victory over the German nation's external enemies, and triumph over its internal threats. In its ideology and practice, National Socialism was committed to conquest and defeat of all "elements" deemed decadent, inferior, and dangerous to the supposed purity and supremacy of the Aryan race. The vision of internal purification and external colonization was spelled out in the twenty-five-point party platform on which the NSdAP was voted into power during democratic elections in 1933.[2] Territorial expansion and war against the "Jewish materialist spirit" were part of this political program, though few could have envisioned the actual nightmarish execution of this agenda. Few imagined that point 18, "We demand that ruthless war be waged against those who work to the injury of the common welfare," would eventually become reality in programs designed to kill the physically weak, the racially impure, and the politically suspicious. The practical implementation of these programs would evolve by trial and error, and with the thoughtful involvement of scientists, legal scholars, administrators, industrialists, police, and security forces, as well as business and military leaders. The gradual exclusion of Jews, newly defined as "non-Aryans," from citizenship and all spheres of economic, cultural, and social life of the nation involved all sectors of German society.[3] Every institution was implicated in boycotts, discrimination, expropriation, humiliation, and eventually deportation of German Jews. Long before any mass killings started in "the East," German schools expelled Jewish children, movie theaters denied entry, professional associations cancelled memberships, notaries signed the transfer of "Aryanized" property, and neighbors applauded the flight into exile of their Jewish fellow citizens. With the invasion of Poland, two million Jews came under the control of the Nazi state. The level of violence intensified as ghettos were established that crowded Jews into fenced-in sections of town, where they were forced to perform slave labor and subjected to systematic starvation. Random cruelties and arbitrary executions became the daily bread of ordinary men,[4] deployed to the east by the SS, the police, the civil administration, and the military. The invasion of the Soviet Union in the summer of 1941 saw another escalation in the war against the Jews[5] with the deployment of *Einsatzgruppen* that would trail the front lines, drive Jews out of villages and towns, and conduct mass shootings, turning trenches, ravines, and stone quarries into mass graves.

Several perpetrators in this study were members of the *Einsatzgruppen*, of the SS, and of police battalions who had volunteered for service. While the first concentration camp in Dachau was built immediately after Hitler's ascent to power in 1933,[6] extermination camps were an innovation born of the mental and emotional fatigue observable among the men of the *Einsatzgruppen*. Six death camps were built for the express purpose of streamlining and industrializing the killings: Auschwitz, Chelmno, Majdanek, Treblinka, Belzec, and Sobibor, each surrounded by factories and satellite camps for the efficient exploitation of Jewish slaves before their deaths in gas chambers. The conditions in these places defy imagination, and survivors have struggled over the decades to find words to express and communicate the hellish realities created there. We use a singular word, Holocaust or Shoah, to refer to the vast array of places and events in which six million Jewish men, women, and children were killed across Europe. Jews were killed in transition camps in France, starved to death in trains from Greece, beaten to death in the Netherlands, shot in Belarus, gassed in Poland, worked to death in Austria. Each death constitutes its own unique crime. Each murder was committed by a particular individual. In the midst of the massive carnage of World War II, the single-minded pursuit of the annihilation of the Jewish people stands out. Sometimes Jews shared the brutal concentration camp conditions with homosexuals marked by a pink triangle, Jehovah's Witness wearing a purple triangle, criminals marked in green, so-called asocials (alcoholics, prostitutes, homeless people) in black, communist and socialist prisoners wearing a red triangle, and Roma and Sinti people, known as Gypsies, with the letter Z sewn to their uniforms. But only Jews, who wore a variety of signs, but often a yellow star, were targeted for systematic extermination. Eleven million civilians died in camps and murder campaigns designed to purify the Aryan nation, and to rid the German *Volk* of its internal and external enemies.

These murders became the focus of guilt discussion in postwar Germany. Remarkably, those most directly engaged in Nazi violence were also the most adamant in the denial of any political, moral, or criminal guilt. The perpetrators themselves remained ideologically committed to the notion that these eleven millions victims somehow deserved their mistreatment. In their eyes, these victims had no claim to human dignity and humane treatment, because they were seen as subhuman, dangerous, and expendable. Their abjection confirmed their lack of human worth. Not all perpetrators were directly involved in physical brutality. Some, like Adolf

Eichmann, fainted at the sight of blood, and made sure to keep the corporeal violence of their administrative measures at a safe distance. Others, like the CEOs of the chemical company IG Farben, directed the construction of factories surrounding Auschwitz staffed by laborers recruited from the camps. To determine their levels of guilt required the creation of new legal categories and new approaches to theories of evil.

Our moral and legal traditions focus on violence as relational acts that involve the presence of malicious intent. The law reserves the highest degree of culpability for those who physically harm someone out of greed, lust, or anger. The moral conundrum of Nazi crimes arises because the two aspects of this definition have been severed: those who intended the crimes weren't bodily present, while those who physically inflicted the harm claimed to have no personal motivation to do so. This division of labor confounds the moral imagination: We have no problem considering the policeman who is physically splattered by the blood of his victims after a day of executing thousands of Jews guilty, but does he carry more responsibility than the administrator (*Schreibtischtäter*) who ordered the execution from his faraway desk in Berlin? We recognize the culpability of Dr. Mengele, who physically performed sadistic medical research in Auschwitz and selected Jews for the gas chambers in cold blood, but the blame of anthropologists and medical researchers who ordered body parts from Auschwitz for autopsies and research purposes in distant Vienna seems less immediate. The corporate nature of these crimes gives rise to conflicted moral responses and legal paralysis. Such moral confusion was at the root of Nazi perpetrators' self-defense and exoneration. They pointed to the moral and legal implication of others. Subordinates blamed their superiors, while the leadership pointed to the proverbial "bad apples" among the foot soldiers. They shared an unwavering unwillingness to accept personal responsibility.

Under the leadership of the United States, the Allies had already decided by 1943 to initiate criminal proceedings against the leadership of Nazi Germany (and of imperial Japan) in specially convened courts of law. The International Military Tribunal at Nuremberg (IMT) developed and applied a new code of international law, which created new legal categories, such as "crimes against peace," "war crimes," and "crimes against humanity." The new code explicitly disallowed exoneration on the basis of having "followed orders" and declared that "participation in a common plan or conspiracy" was sufficient grounds to convict individual defendants.[7] Exculpatory arguments on the basis of having acted "on orders" were excluded from the inventory of the defense. Article 6 of the Charter of the International Military Tribunal targeted "leaders, organizers, instigators, and accomplices participating in the formulation or execution of a Common Plan or Conspiracy to commit any of the foregoing crimes [and] are responsible for all acts performed by any persons in execution of such a plan."[8] The IMT set out to address the corporate nature of crimes committed on behalf of the state by picking twenty-four high-ranking functionaries from the military, political, economic, and propaganda establishments. They were tried between November 20, 1945 and October 1, 1946. These representative leaders were held personally accountable for decisions made as heads of organizations and government agencies to prepare the war and to implement the subjugation, exploitation, and extermination of subject populations. The Nuremberg Principles governing these Allied proceedings were designed to ascertain individual responsibility for corporate, political, and administrative decisions.

Between 1946 and 1949, the United States carried out twelve follow-up or subsequent trials in Nuremberg on the basis of Allied Control Council Law No. 10 against 177 main "war criminals," including medical doctors, jurists, industrialists, members of the Einsatzgruppen, the SS *Wirtschafts- and Verwaltungshauptamtes*, the SS Racial and Security Main Office, and the Wehrmacht. These trials were different from the IMT because they were conducted by the four Allied victors (France was given a seat at the judges' table and jurisdiction over its own territorial sector) in their respective occupation sectors. They are known as NMT or Subsequent Nuremberg Proceedings and are to be distinguished from the IMT.[9] Another 257 trials involving 800 defendants took place in Dachau and are known as the Dachau trials.[10] "The total number of convicted NS perpetrators in the Western Allied zones including Nuremberg was 5,025; the death penalty was imposed on 806 defendants."[11] Of those, 486 persons were executed. The vast majority of the death sentences were commuted to life in prison. For a number of political reasons, including the strenuous opposition of the German churches, the prisoners were amnestied and eventually released. By 1958, the convicts held in War Crimes Prison Landsberg, chosen for its proximity to Nuremberg in the south of Germany, under American military administration, had been set free.

Within Germany, opposition to these trials programs focused on two aspects in an effort to undermine their credibility. First, the IMT and NMT confounded "war crimes" with "crimes against humanity." Second, the new international code applied only to the defeated Axis powers of

Germany and Japan (excluding Italy) and explicitly exempted Allied military personnel from the reach of its statutes.

The IMT collected and processed an extraordinary amount of evidence (between eight and nine million documents, by an estimate of main prosecutor Benjamin Ferencz),[12] but the conflation of war crimes with crimes against humanity muddled its moral message. The Holocaust, for instance, was not tried separately. Instead, genocidal mass killings by the *Einsatzgruppen* (mobile killing units) and of SS personnel in concentration camps were tried alongside German civilians who mistreated U.S. pilots and received the death penalty for violating the Geneva Conventions' protection of POWs. In the Landsberg prison, high Nazi functionaries, SS men, and German civilians convicted for retaliatory killings of U.S. flyers were all lumped together awaiting their executions. German critics of the IMT never tired of objecting to the exemption of carpet bombings of German cities from the reach of the Nuremberg Principles. The exclusive application of the new law to the conquered nations became the source of endless debate and opposition. Equally contested was the Nuremberg Laws' imposition of individual accountability on agents who claimed to have acted dutifully and conscientiously on behalf of the state and within the chains of military command. Resistance to this legal course of action was not limited to Germany but generated discussion in the United States as well. For instance, a habeas corpus petition before the U.S. District Court, District of Columbia, drawn up by a Washington, DC, law firm and signed by lawyers Wallace Cohen and Frank Reel, argued that

> numerous decisions of courts in the United States and elsewhere recognized that, while, in principle superior orders are not a valid defense to a violation of law, obedience to an order, which is not on its face illegal, relieves the solider of criminal liability. This rule reconciles the conflict between a soldier's military duty to obey his superior without being held criminally responsible.... If the soldier, as a reasonable man, could not be expected to know that the order was illegal, then he is protected from criminal liability.... Any other view would place an impossible burden on every military subordinate.[13]

German opponents of the IMT cited this American lawsuit to make their case that the IMT created new legal standards that contradicted age-old military rules of conduct as a means to demoralize and discredit the vanquished. "Military opposition to the trials was the earliest form of concerted protest in the USA," notes historian Donald Bloxham. "The IMT was attacked repeatedly in the *Army and Navy Journal* for the indictment of General Staff and High Command. That organ, a non-official Washington based publication...considered that the only legitimate subjects for trial were individuals who had gone beyond the remit of their orders to commit or condone outrages."[14] Some of these objections, as we will see in the next chapter, were valid and could have been averted if the IMT had more consistently distinguished between "war crimes" and "crimes against humanity" and applied rules regulating military conduct equally to the victorious and the vanquished armies.[15]

A vastly greater number of Germans were affected by the Allies' mass internment policy than by the IMT proceedings against the political, military, and economic elites. All National Socialist organizations were banned, including the Nazi party, SS, Gestapo, SD (Security Service), BDM (Organization of German Girls), and the NS-Frauenschaft (NS-Women's League). The "Law of Automatic Arrest" for members in any of these organizations resulted in the internment of approximately two hundred thousand men and women.[16] Housed in former concentration camps or in newly established makeshift camps, the men and women awaited hearings before *Spruchkammern*, hastily established panels that would assess their level of participation in Nazi programs. *Spruchkammerverfahren* were proceedings designed to ascertain varying level of complicity and impose sanctions appropriate to the degree of culpability on the basis of character witnesses, often drawn from camp survivors, clergy, or neighbors. Quickly these *Spruchkammerverfahren* turned into spectacles of hypocrisy as internees secured testimony confirming their morally upstanding character and disposition. A wide variety of Nazis shared the uncertainty of life in these internment camps, ranging from SS concentration camp guards, who were arrested upon liberation, to high-ranking functionaries and ordinary housewives active in the NS women's league. While the panels proceeded with all deliberate speed, the sheer numbers overwhelmed the system. Some internees languished in camps for several years. In any case, it was this population that became the special concern of Germany's Roman Catholic and Evangelical churches as they dispatched clergy to set up congregations, to provide moral support and practical assistance, and to organize Christian (re)education programs.

Evangelization in Internment Camps

By May 1939, six years into the reign of National Socialism, 94 percent of the citizens of Nazi Germany maintained membership in one of its two state churches.[17] These *Volkskirchen* were established after the long and bitter battles following the Reformation and consisted of the Roman Catholic Church and the Protestant Church in Germany (EKD), the national umbrella organization of Lutheran, Reformed, and United regional churches. There also existed several Free Churches (*Freikirchen*), as well as some newer religious movements, including Jehovah's Witnesses, that would be targeted by the Nazi regime. And then there were the Jews, who had lived in German territories since the Roman Empire and whose history is long, culturally and religiously rich, and often bitter. By 1933, there were 500,000 Jews living in Germany, about 1 percent of the overall population.

National Socialism was more than a political movement. It advertised itself as a Weltanschauung, an ideology that claimed and suffused all of life. Some of the most dedicated (or "fanatic," as they would call themselves) National Socialists believed that total commitment to this Weltanschauung conflicted with membership in a retrograde belief systems such as Christianity. Allegiance to Christianity with its Jewish Old Testament and slavish morality of compassion for the weak constituted an impediment to the revolutionary battle for the survival of the fittest. The Roman Catholic Church was denounced for its requirement of submission to an Italian pope, while the Protestant Church was faulted for its internal divisions between its Lutheran, Reformed, and United wings and its resistance to a streamlined hierarchy under one state-appointed German *Reichsbischof*. "Starting in late 1936, many Nazis began a movement within the party known as *Kirchenaustritt*" (church exit).[18] First, it was Catholic Nazis who felt compelled to leave the Roman Catholic Church, and then their Protestant comrades dropped their membership in the German state church (*Volkskirche*). But Nazism did not advocate atheism. On the contrary, the führer, Adolf Hitler himself, invoked the power of God in many of his speeches, and he strongly condemned atheism.[19] Nazism called its blend of neopagan and Christian beliefs and rituals "positive Christianity" and invented the category *gottgläubig* (God-believer) for legal and statistical purposes. By May 1939, a nationwide census revealed that 3.5 percent of the population professed allegiance to this new movement. Religious affiliation was broken down into the following categories: "54% of Germans considered themselves Protestant and 40% considered themselves Catholic, with only 3.5% claiming to be neo-pagan 'believers in God,' and 1.5% unbelievers."[20] Departure from the Christian churches was never mandatory, and many high-ranking Nazi party leaders retained their church membership, including Hermann Göring, Joseph Göbbels, Emil Kaltenbrunner, and Adolf Hitler himself.[21] By the census of 1941, 10.2 percent of people living in Berlin, 7.5 percent in Hamburg, 6.4 percent in Vienna, and 6.0 percent in Düsseldorf checked the box for *gottgläubig*, indicating their withdrawal from the state churches. Among members of the SS organization, this number was considerably higher. By 1939, a quarter of all SS members defined themselves as *gottgläubig*. Although *Kirchenaustritt* was never compulsory, many SS members reported substantial pressure to renounce allegiance to rival faiths and communities. In a questionnaire administered by the American prison administration in Landsberg, prisoners were asked to check their religious and denominational status and to explain their choice: Willie Eckert noted on his form that he left the Protestant Church "for professional reasons."[22] Another dropped out of the Roman Catholic Church out of "professional compulsion,"[23] while a third claimed that this was "demanded by the SS."[24] Others admitted that they became *gottgläubig* "out of conviction,"[25] or because the "Protestant Church was so splintered."[26] In some internment camps, up to 50 percent of the interned SS men declared *gottgläubig* as their religious affiliation.[27] A Protestant minister in the Bavarian camp of Moosburg, located in the American occupation zone, noted that "about half displayed an anti-Christian attitude."[28] This specific group of men was known as the "third confession,"[29] a new denomination that competed with the Protestant and Roman Catholic state churches.

In 1945, both churches jumped at the opportunity to evangelize among this pool of potential converts to Christianity. The missionary campaigns presented Christianity as the alternative to National Socialism and highlighted the churches' difference from and immunity to Nazi ideology. National Socialism was presented as a secular aberration and result of the Enlightenment, an *Abfall von Gott*, or abandonment of the Christian God.[30] The political and moral collapse of Germany was seen as the logical result of the rejection of the Ten Commandments in the Bible. But the eternal truths of Christianity had now been proven right by history. The return to Christianity would protect against the false teachings of secularism that had irrevocably led to human degradation and wholesale slaughter. While this message was not entirely false, it certainly was also not completely true.

The much-invoked resistance of the churches turned out to have been much less principled than the official narrative allowed. The churches were much more receptive and appreciative of the anticommunist, antisemitic, nationalist, and law-and-order policies of National Socialism than they cared to remember after 1945. Historians have now roundly rejected the self-serving story line that formed the basis of these early evangelization campaigns.[31] This message actively overlooked the failure of Christianity not only on the personal level but also on the institutional and doctrinal levels. It was not only individuals who had actively served in killing programs while remaining Christians in good standing. The institutional leadership was similarly complicit in many aspects of the Nazi state, most notably with respect to the persecution of Jews. But in the early enthusiasm to convert repentant Nazi sinners, soul-searching, and critical examination of the historical record was not at all on the agenda.

Instead, the churches claimed the mantle of a resistance movement to National Socialism. The Roman Catholic Church pointed to its vocal opposition to the euthanasia program and recalled the powerful sermons of Bishop von Galen, who denounced the murder of handicapped children and adults. The Protestant churches emphasized the Church Struggle (*Kirchenkampf*) and the formation of an underground church, the Confessing Church (*Bekennende Kirche*), which was founded when the Aryan paragraph was applied to church employees. The Aryan paragraph mandated that anyone with Jewish grandparents be dismissed from public service. Applied to the church, this paragraph interfered with internal church governance and undermined the theological meaning and efficacy of baptism. In protest, many congregations severed their ties with the state, which had traditionally collected church taxes, financed theological university training, and administered employment contracts and retirement benefits. Except for three "intact" Lutheran regional churches (Bavaria, Württemberg, Hannover), the Protestant regional churches split, and congregations pledging allegiance to the Confessing Church went underground. Among a very small minority within the Confessing Church, this early resistance to the application of the Aryan paragraph extended to the protection of Jews. A very small minority! These activists, as well as individual Roman Catholic priests and religious monks and sisters, risked their lives in the battle against Nazism. They endured harassment, police surveillance, arrest, convictions, imprisonment, and death in concentration camps for their opposition to

Nazi policies. Their heroic resistance should not be forgotten or diminished. But it was only part of the story. On the whole, the churches colluded and compromised, and they failed to defend the victims of dehumanizing policies and extermination. The extent of institutional collaboration has only recently been documented for the euthanasia program,[32] the employment of slave laborers, anticommunism, and total war against the Soviet Union,[33] as well as the persecution and killing of Jews.[34] It is historically more accurate to speak of the exceptional bravery of individuals and the acquiescent collusion of the institution. But in 1945, clergy emphasized the churches' immunity to Nazi propaganda and refashioned Christianity into a resistance movement, a narrative that was widely accepted by the German public as well as by the international community.

Church leaders quickly garnered the support of Allied occupation authorities and set up pastoral programs for detainees in internment camps.[35] They hoped that the collapse of National Socialism would open the hearts of hardened *gottgläubige* Nazis, who would become receptive to the good news of Christianity. Pastor Adolf Dresler, for example, recounted in his reflective report on his internment camp ministry between August 1945 and August 1947 that "in light of the immediate shock of the collapse, many interned in the camp Altenstadt, especially those from the countryside, were willing to continue church life or to return to it. Worship services were well attended."[36] Pastor von Eickstedt listed several motivations for reconversions to Christianity:

> inner emptiness, gnawing worry, great insecurity.... What weighed most heavily was the total collapse of everything that one had heretofore considered great and holy, the loss of the homeland, the humiliation of the *Volk*, now disgraced and torn apart, the breakdown of all ideologies that had sustained life, the questioning of all moral values, which had provided inner confidence—in short, this radical rupture that threw everyone into a completely new existential situation.[37]

Protestant and Roman Catholic clergy competed over the fallen souls of the interned.[38] Protestant pastors noted with dismay that Catholicism proved more attractive to former SS men because "it was simply there...unperturbed in the chaos of the world, a cell of order in midst of disorder.... The impressive assuredness of the Catholic Church in the camp was profound, and equally so the great insecurity and disappointment of the Protestants, since the Evangelical Church was nowhere to be seen."[39] Protestant clergy strove mightily to close this gap and quickly established congregations to serve as a solid rock in the turbulent times of transition: "That in the midst of chaos and amid all this confusion, the church appeared and proclaimed an indisputable truth and strove for unity (which was noted greatly) stirred many people's interest."[40] Christian congregations aimed to replace the broken collective of the *Volk* that had reigned supreme in Nazi ideology. Now that the unity and authority of the totalitarian state was bankrupt, the church could be offered as an alternative. But this strategy proved risky, as the ministers well understood. For instance, Dresler warned: "After party and state collapsed, many believed, they could place their hope in the substitute of the church. They would have been willing to follow her if they could be assured of external help and an improvement in their situations similar to that of the party and the state."[41] When these expectations did not come to pass, they spoke of "disappointment and failure" and turned their back on Christianity. Such a simple replacement of one ideology for another failed to generate any change.

This first burst of missionary activity was intense but short-lived. According to a 1947 report on internment camp ministry, "The wave of returns [to the churches] occupied the camp chaplains during the first one and a half years most intensely. This movement seems to have largely subsided. The missionary time in this sense has come to a close in light of the current situation of the interned."[42] In his study of reeducation campaigns in British internment camps, historian Heiner Wember observed a similar timeline: "The wave of reentries remained strong until the end of 1946 and then diminished noticeably."[43] The massive "rechristianization of society" that had been hoped for by church leaders did not come to pass. Church historian Besier points out that the "movement to return into the churches reached its height in 1946; by the year 1949 a total of 43,000 returns into the various evangelical state churches was dwarfed by the exit of 86,000."[44] By early 1947, camp ministers registered with some disappointment: "The camp congregations are still relatively large and their spiritual life is very intense. But the great missionary opportunity, which occurred as a result of the impact of collapse and imprisonment, seems to be over."[45]

Religious Life in Internment Camps

The congregational life in the Moosburg internment camp in the American occupation zone in southern Germany was chronicled by Dr. Klaus von

Eickstedt in a booklet published in 1948 and now available online.[46] *Christus unter den Internierten* was written as a retrospective for "comrades and brothers" and sheds light on the religious life and political discussions in the camp. There were twelve thousand internees in Moosburg, two-thirds of them political functionaries, while the rest were military officers, members of the SS and the SD (Security Service), the Gestapo, and the higher civil service, among them three to four hundred women.[47] Von Eickstedt was an inmate himself who felt energized by the challenges of creating a provisional church under adverse conditions. Described in 1948, the events were very vivid in his memory, and he radiated pride in the church's many accomplishments. He celebrated the growth of a viable Christian fellowship and the depth of its theological debates. Spurred into action by the vitality and visibility of the Roman Catholic Church, individual Protestants started seeking each other out. The first minister who volunteered was quickly ruled out by the members because he was a dedicated "German Christian," the Nazi wing of the Protestant Church in Germany. Then Pastor Wilhelm Rott came forward. Like other ministers commissioned by the Protestant Church for service in internment camps, Pastor Rott was an internee himself. Unlike other interned clergy, he had been trained by Dietrich Bonhoeffer in the underground Confessing Church seminary of Finkenwalde and had become an active member of the underground Confessing Church. Arrested by the Gestapo, he was sentenced to a year in various prisons and then entered the Abwehr (Intelligence Service), like his mentor, Dietrich Bonhoeffer. His deployment as a soldier with the intelligence services in Athens led to his arrest by U.S. military authorities, and he was transferred to the internment camp Moosburg in Bavaria. There he built a group of Protestants who moved to engage in "goal-oriented missionary work that targeted those circles who were standing apart but were somehow searching."[48]

Von Eickstedt described a story of growth and excitement, as the men sought to break the isolation, boredom, and anxiety of camp life and embarked on an experiment in community building. Among twelve thousand inmates, Eickstedt recounted, they found only two Bibles and a few hymnals. They depended on donations of New Testaments from a Swedish volunteer[49] and smuggled in full Bibles (including the Old Testament), as well as prayer books and hymnals. They invented their own order of service and elected presbyters representing different barracks.[50] A men's choir was formed and delivered moving musical performances of Protestant church hymns. Soon 100–150 men met for daily morning prayers,[51] and on Good

Friday they ran out of bread and wine serving the Eucharist to an unexpected number of 700–800 men. They organized lectures on "pantheism," Christian social ethics, and the Ten Commandments and arranged debates on German Christianity, paganism, and different conceptions of God. Internment camp administrators generally supported religious life by providing space for assembly and allowing men from different cell blocks to gather in provisional chapels. There were occasional incidents of vandalism, derision directed toward "turncoats," and threats of future retaliation emanating from the SS barracks, and von Eickstedt was well aware of "marginal individuals" (*Randexistenzen*)[52] and members of the "third confession" who held tight to their National Socialist convictions. But the congregational life was growing, providing spiritual support, intellectual stimulation, and political commentary—until the question of guilt was broached.

In October 1945, the Protestant Church issued the Stuttgart Declaration of Guilt (Stuttgarter Schulderklärung) to an international delegation of ecumenical Christians. It was not intended for release to the German public, but news of the church's acknowledgment of German guilt spread quickly and caused outrage among the detainees in internment camps. In the camps, it "provided the desired trigger to discharge all of the repressed rage."[53] The Evangelical Church, it was claimed, had conceded Germany's "collective war guilt," which enraged not only hardened Nazis but even the Christian faithful. "If Niemöller really said this, then I despair of the leadership of our church,"[54] responded one parishioner quoted by von Eickstedt, declaring in resignation that "it was altogether impossible to speak to non-Christians about guilt, not about personal guilt of individuals, and even less about the guilt of a group, of a party, of the government, let alone of a people."[55] A solid wall went up whenever the topic of guilt was brought up: "The guilt question was the stone of contention, the starting point of the propaganda hostile to the church unleashed by anti-Christian circles and it became the bugle call for the attack on the Evangelical congregation."[56]

Pastor Martin Niemöller became the lightning rod for many of these discussions on guilt. One of the initiators and cosigners of the Stuttgart Declaration of Guilt, he traveled extensively across southern Germany to preach in internment camps. Niemöller had been a member of the conservative upper crust of German society and comfortable in its nationalist, antisemitic, and antidemocratic circles. Born in 1892, he had enrolled in seminary in 1919 after a full tour of military service as U-boat commander in the Great War.[57] Niemöller vehemently opposed the Versailles Treaty, the revolutions of 1918, and the Weimar Republic. He voted for Adolf Hitler in 1933. His collision course with National Socialism began with his assignment as pastor of the Annengemeinde in Berlin-Dahlem, a wealthy suburb of Berlin. The state's appointment of the Nazi puppet Reichsbischof Ludwig Müller and the imposition of the Aryan paragraph on church employees spurred his opposition. He became a founding member and president of the Confessing Church (*Pfarrernotbund*: Ministers' Emergency League). Arrested in 1937, he was tried, convicted, and sentenced to seven months in prison in March 1938. After the expiration of this unexpectedly mild prison sentence, he was transferred to the concentration camps of Sachsenhausen and then to Dachau as the "personal prisoner" of Adolf Hitler. When the SS evacuated Dachau on April 26, 1945, he was almost executed. Captured by American military forces on May 3, 1945 in Austria, he was shipped to an internment camp in Naples, Italy. He was released only after going on a hunger strike. On June 24, 1945, he was reunited with his family after having spent eight years in captivity.

Niemöller is best known for the poetic rendition of his personal confession of guilt, which summarizes his standard sermon he delivered before many captive audiences in internment camps:

> When the Nazis came for the communists,
> I was silent because I was not a communist.
> When they came to arrest Social Democrats,
> I was silent because I was not a Social Democrat
> When they came to get the trade unionists, I was silent because I
>   was not a trade unionist.
> When they came for the Jews, I was silent because I was not a Jew.
> When they came for me, there was no one left who could protest.[58]

Oftentimes, his sermon included the dramatic retelling of a visit to his former prison cell in the concentration camp of Dachau a few months after his liberation.[59] In October 1945, his wife had asked to see his cell and the couple received permission from the American guard to enter his former cell, number 32. Upon leaving, they walked through an open door and accidentally found themselves in the crematory, where former inmates had affixed the following sign: "238,756 human beings were cremated here during the years 1933–1945." While his wife grew faint by his side, Niemöller was not shocked by the numbers. Instead, he felt a "cold shower running down his spine" when reading the dates: 1933–1945. In that moment, he told his audience, he realized that his alibi of political blame-lessness covered only the period of his imprisonment between 1937 and 1945. No one could hold him accountable for crimes committed by his government while he was a prisoner (which included Kristallnacht, the nationwide pogrom against synagogues and German Jews in November 1938). But he felt responsible for his government's politics of dehuman-ization while he was a free man and citizen. Dramatically, he would ask himself in his speeches: "Where were you between 1933 and 1937? While people were cremated here, did you not know anything?"[60] He would then acknowledge that he had, of course, read about the arrests of active Communists in 1933 in the newspapers and had quietly congratulated himself for how easily "we got rid of this threat against God."[61] He recounted hearing about the "mercy killings" of mentally retarded patients in 1935 and thinking that it might be "most merciful to kill these people in a painless manner." He concluded these admissions of guilt with the exclamation: "1933–1937...the wanted poster of God had already found me."[62] Niemöller tried to model two essential ingredients of a confession of guilt: first, it needs to be personal, and second it must be historically precise and factually specific. That is why he insisted on exact dates and particular victim groups in whose ill-treatment he felt personally impli-cated. By anchoring his sermons in his own failures, he sought to elicit self-reflection and reciprocal confessions. He actively took on the moral obligation to pay for the debt of guilt, although he limited his personal obli-gation to the period between 1933 and 1937 before his incarceration. He believed that his example could animate others, who had been more actively involved, to follow his path.

On July 1, 1946, Niemöller visited the central women's internment camp, Camp 77, in Ludwigsburg. His itinerant ministry was sponsored by American military authorities as part of their reeducation program. By the summer of 1946, Niemöller's reputation as a "zealot and fanatic,"[63] a "judge and prosecutor,"[64] preceded him. Rumors of his insistence on guilt and repentance and his contribution to the Stuttgart Declaration of Guilt—the latter caricatured as an acceptance of Germany's "war guilt" or "collective guilt"—overshadowed his reception among the internees. Some prisoners greeted the news of his coming with comments like "The pig is coming"[65] and "Too bad they didn't gas him."[66] The invitation to address female internees occurred suddenly and unexpectedly. He had only two hours to prepare his remarks to the women, following his main visit to the men's camp, Hoher Asperg.

Niemöller's address was interrupted repeatedly by angry protests that turned the camp into "an excited beehive."[67] To calm the waves of indignation, the resident Protestant camp chaplain encouraged the women to record their misgivings and reactions on paper.[68] Based on their handwritten comments as well as their written summary of Niemöller's sermon, we can reconstruct their rhetorical strategies of guilt denial. While Niemöller spoke at length about the victimization of particular groups of people, such as the sterilization of the handicapped and the killing of six million Jews, his audience primarily responded to Niemöller's challenge of "personal responsibility." This point seemed to touch a raw nerve among the female internees of Camp 77, and they protested its implication in many letters:

> Why should one take upon oneself a burden of guilt for something that one has not personally committed? ... Most among us have performed our work with the greatest idealism and extreme sacrifice, oftentimes in the area of social work. Many tell themselves: once I am allowed to leave the barbed wire behind, I will continue to live with exactly the same principles. I have always only desired and accomplished the good; I have wanted to assist my people and I will continue doing so.[69]

Niemöller had not asked anyone to accept responsibility for acts they had not committed! On the contrary, he had challenged his listeners to follow his example and to conscientiously review their own history of consent and contribution to various Nazi policies. He insisted on historical precision and personal accountability. The respondents deliberately misheard him and used the term "responsibility" differently. They asserted that they had always accepted their duties and performed them "responsibly," with the best of intentions and great willingness to sacrifice their own well-being for the common good. They deliberately reframed the term "responsibility" and emphasized their personal virtues, such as idealism, sacrifice, and desire to do good—how could anyone condemn such noble values? Such rhetorical questions obscured the connection between their idealism, sacrifice, and hard work and the overall goals of National Socialism. Their idealism and hard work had served criminal objectives, such as ethnic supremacy and racial purity. It was precisely their loyal dedication and devoted assistance to the annihilation of racially, politically, sexually, and medically deviant human beings that was at stake. His audience fervently denied any link between Nazi values and Nazi crimes:

It was very hard and onerous for us women to hear him speak of our lives as being without responsibility. Many women have accepted and performed this work, and I am thinking here especially of the social aspects of women's work, because they felt responsible and because they knew that this work would be done well, and even done compassionately, if they performed it.[70]

One woman accused Niemöller of failing to recognize that she had never "shirked" responsibility but had been "virtually crushed...by the burden of responsibility that was put on their [women's] shoulders."[71] Or as Kirchenrat Schieber, the regional church official for internment camp ministry, put it, "Their thoughts always revolve around one argument: We have only fulfilled our duty and always wanted the good."[72] Such innocence and well-meaning intentions could create the impression that the U.S. military authorities had falsely imprisoned hundreds of innocent housewives, matrons, and social workers. The reality was, needless to say, radically different: Up to one third of the detained women's population in Camp 77 consisted of women who had worked for the SS as female guards in various concentration camps. In January 1947, a report prepared by Kirchenrat Schieber describes the following composition in Camp 77: Among the 1,023 prisoners, 50 percent belonged to the upper ranks of the NS Women's League and BDM (Bund Deutscher Mädchen); 20 percent were SS-Helferinnen (SS associates) and the remaining 25 to 30 percent were considered "special cases" (Sonderfälle), "among them camp guards of the National Socialist concentration camps (more than 300). Among them very bad elements."[73] Hence almost half of the interned women were either SS associates or "special cases" arrested in connection with guard duties in various concentration camps. All of the arrested female camp guards of Ravensbrück and many from Auschwitz had been transferred to Camp 77. In her historical analysis of the denazification of women in internment camps, Kathrin Mayer confirms these numbers and cites statistics for October 1946: a total of 1,506 women were incarcerated there, of whom 30 percent (30.8 percent) had belonged to the NS Women's League, 34 percent belonged to the SS (as SS associates who were trained and deployed as guards in concentration camps), 4 percent were arrested for membership in the Gestapo, 11 percent (11.2 percent) as leaders of the BDM, and 2 percent (2.1 percent) were party functionaries (6.8 percent were listed as miscellaneous and 7.2 percent as foreign).[74] When the women claimed ignorance and innocence, they were being deliberately evasive. For instance, one writer asserted aggressively, "That such terrible things happened in concentration camps, we regret deeply, but we are prepared to testify, again and again, and under oath that we did not know anything about these atrocities."[75] Another woman declared that "the crimes in the concentration camps were only revealed to me during my fourteen months of internment,"[76] and she failed to question the connection between her own political commitments and the belated revelations of the hellish conditions in the camp system. In the rush to deny knowledge, the respondents did not accept Niemöller's challenge to assume personal responsibility.

The women's responses anticipate the denial strategies that would come to dominate German discourses for decades: an aggressive denial of any knowledge of atrocities; overgeneralizations that assigned blame to unnamed and unknown others; universalizing strategies that decried the inhumanity of mankind; reductive strategies that would blame "excess brutality" (*Exzessstaten*) on a few bad apples and exonerate respectable servants of the state. Let's sample some of these rhetorical tactics. For instance, one woman defended the purity of her conscience by implicating not only the national collective but all of humankind:

> We do not feel our conscience troubled in the manner suggested by the speaker, and if we carry any guilt, then it is one that is carried not only by our German people but—one may say so—by all peoples.[77]

Such a position concedes that unspecified crimes may have occurred but rejects personal culpability on the view that misdeeds are being committed everywhere and by everybody. Another letter similarly admitted that "terrible things"[78] and "horrendous deeds" (*Greueltaten*)[79] took place but asked that "the transgressions of a few irresponsible elements [*verantwortungsscheue Elemente*] should not be blamed on everyone in the collective [*Gesamtheit*]."[80] "If the question of guilt is raised," another letter summarizing several statements complained, "one should only approach this from a large perspective [*von ganz grossen Gesichtspunkten aus*] and should never generalize singular examples [*Einzelbeispiele*]. For us the past time is too much of a personal experience."[81] Such contradictory arguments played off the "larger picture" against personal experience and blocked any consideration of moral agency. The writers not only denied personal involvement but personal knowledge of injustice and cruelty. At most, these respondents were willing to admit the possibility of a few bad apples, who were most certainly unknown to them or who belonged to subordinate ranks in the lower echelon of society. Niemöller had tried to cut through these defenses by insisting on personal moral agency, historical precision, and individual accountability, but he was foiled by internees' deliberate use of vague formulations and sweeping generalities. His model for a confession of guilt was confounded by conservative forces resisting change. The Stuttgart Declaration of Guilt, which Martin Niemöller had initiated and with which he became publicly identified, is indicative of the slow co-optation by vague collectivist expressions of contrition. The Protestant churchmen attempted to articulate remorse on the basis of a "solidarity of guilt" that failed to be specific and avoided giving precise examples of collusion and complicity. This ambiguity and elusiveness played into the hands of perpetrators' rhetoric of denial and evasion and was effectively co-opted to serve the protection, amnesty, and restoration of perpetrators to power and status.

The Stuttgart Declaration of Guilt

The Stuttgart Declaration of Guilt satisfied a condition set by international representatives of the Ecumenical Council of Churches. On their tour through the defeated Germany in October 1945, they required a statement before resumption of relations with the German Protestant Church. German church representatives obliged and opened their statement with a sincere apology affirming solidarity of guilt for wrongdoing:

> We are all the more grateful for this visit, as we not only know ourselves in a great community of suffering with our people but also in solidarity of guilt. With great pain we say: By *us* infinite wrong was brought over many peoples and countries.[82]

The concept of "solidarity of guilt" was a double-edged sword. On the one hand, it constructed a fictitious unity among a people who had both suffered and become guilty, which created a bridge across the different factions of perpetrators, bystanders, resisters, and victims. The "we" suggested a harmony designed to obscure internal divisions. The interned noted with relief that the church leaders disavowed their isolation and ostracism. When the text of the Stuttgart Declaration became available in Moosburg, the internees commented: "At least they did not arrogantly distance themselves from everything."[83] The "solidarity of guilt" von Eickstedt reported impressed the "reasonable and considerate elements in the camp ... as noble and decent."[84] But the statement's inclusiveness could also be used to shield individuals behind veils of collective abstractions. Unlike Niemöller's sermons, the statement was neither personal nor specific. The statement's lack of specificity allowed the manipulation of the historical record. For instance, the church leaders omitted any reference to particular victim groups and were silent on the Jews. Instead, the Stuttgart Declaration spoke of "infinite wrong" and assigned blame to "our people," who were supposed to accept a "solidarity of guilt." They also insinuated that the church had consistently warned against "the spirit" of National Socialism.[85]

> That which we often proclaimed in our communities, we express now in the name of the whole church: Yes, we fought in the name of Jesus Christ for many years against the spirit that found its horrendous expression in the National Socialist regime of violence; but we accuse ourselves of not testifying more courageously, of not praying more faithfully, of not believing more joyously, and of not loving more fervently.[86]

The declaration glossed over internal political conflicts among the more conservative-leaning and progressive voices within the Protestant Church. All the signatories of the Stuttgart Declaration claimed to have been active in the resistance against National Socialism. But their resistance had taken quite different paths. While Pastor Martin Niemöller had spent eight years in concentration camps, Bishops Theophil Wurm (Baden Württemberg) and Hans Meiser (Bavaria) had remained in office, negotiating with government authorities. Their ecclesial leadership positions had carried certain risks: they had been intimidated, put under surveillance, and sometimes arrested, but their experience was quite different from Niemöller's. After 1945, Martin Niemöller and his Swiss colleague Karl Barth pursued more radical institutional change in the aftermath of the catastrophic failure to stop the murderous policies of National Socialism. But the more conservative bishops wanted quick reconstruction, the restoration of proven structures, and the speedy rehabilitation of traditional elites. As a consensus document, the Stuttgart Declaration of Guilt covered up these conflicts. The result was a failure to be specific. They could not agree on naming precise victim groups, particular crimes, or identifiable perpetrators. This inability to articulate specific acts of wrongdoing, to name the culprits, and to identify the victims undermined the statement's efficacy in spurring moral and political transformation. Instead, the "new beginning" envisioned by the Stuttgart Declaration remained vague and was supposed to flow from "the spirit of peace and love" rather than "violence and revenge":

> Now a new beginning is to be made in our churches. Based on the Holy Scripture, focused with complete sincerity on the One Lord of the church, they have begun to cleanse themselves of the influences alien to faith and to restructure themselves. We hope that the God of Grace and Mercy will use our churches as his tools and give them authority to proclaim his word and to effect obedience to his will, among ourselves and our whole people. That we may consider ourselves sincerely connected in this new beginning with the other churches of the ecumenical community fills us with great joy. We hope to God that the joint service of the churches may control the spirit of violence and revenge, which wants to become powerful again nowadays throughout the world, and that the spirit of peace and love comes to rule, in which alone tormented humanity can find healing. Thus we request in an hour in which the whole world needs a new beginning: *Veni Creator Spiritus!* (Come, spirit of creation!).[87]

The juxtaposition of "the spirit of peace and love" over against "the spirit of violence and revenge" became the foundation of church leaders' vigorous amnesty campaigns. Their close alliance with former elites becomes evident in their characterization of criminal trials as "violence and revenge" rather than as "justice." For victims, justice is about vindication and restitution. Only perpetrators experience justice as violence and revenge. The Declaration's denunciation of justice as violence and revenge reflected the fears of perpetrators who stood to lose power and prestige at the hands of Allied tribunals. The authors of the Declaration did not stand unambiguously with the victims, but expected them to renounce claims to justice. While the church leaders might have spoken out of genuine fear for the future viability of the German state in the face of visions such as the Morgenthau Plan that proposed to permanently dismember, deindustrialize, and demilitarize the region, their concerns took the side of the interned who faced prosecution and an uncertain future.

The verbal ambiguities of the Stuttgart Declaration that privileged "peace and love" over "justice" eventually shaped political action. Several excellent historical studies have pointed to the Protestant and Roman Catholic churches as prime organizers and coordinators of the opposition to legal prosecution and punishment of Nazi perpetrators.[88] In public and confidential memoranda, Protestant and Roman Catholic bishops denounced the Allied trials as "victors' justice" and criticized their legal principles and judicial procedures.[89] They coordinated defense counsels, funded solidarity committees, orchestrated amnesty campaigns, and provided financial and logistical support to secretly assist high-ranking perpetrators, including Eichmann, in evading capture and fleeing across the Alps to Rome.[90] Prison and camp chaplains complained about prison conditions and interceded on behalf of individual defendants and convicts. Church administrators advised clergy and congregants against testifying before Allied courts and denazification panels (*Spruchkammern*).[91] These obstructions of the legal process had several roots, including entrenched nationalism and resentment of foreign interference, as well as church leaders' close personal ties to the aristocratic and bourgeois elites who faced charges in Nuremberg. But it was the Christian theological linkage of guilt confession with absolution and Christian affirmations of forgiveness that were most often cited as reasons for amnesty appeals. The claim was made that those willing to admit to wrongdoing should be released from the burden of guilt and allowed a new beginning.

The Secret Memorandum by the EKD on the Question of War Crimes Trials

As church officials geared up the defense for interned and convicted defendants, they referred back to the Stuttgart Declaration of Guilt as evidence of their own successful moral rehabilitation. In 1949, the newly constituted Council of the Protestant Church submitted a secret Memorandum of the Evangelical Church in Germany on the Question of War Crimes Trials before American Military Courts to High Commissioner John J. McCoy.[92] The Memorandum criticized the prosecution of German nationals as "victors' justice" and presented a bound collection of appeals and legal documents to show "legal deficiencies" of the International Military Tribunal at Nuremberg as well as subsequent proceedings in Dachau. The Memorandum called for a complete review of the procedures and verdicts by "neutral" judges and argued for the immediate release of all convicted prisoners held in Allied military prison WCP 1 in Landsberg. The translation into English and the printing costs for this bound volume were financed by a donation from IG Farben, the chemical company that maintained factories outside Auschwitz using cheap slave labor. One thousand copies of this 160-page collection of documents were printed and distributed confidentially to authorized persons in a numbered edition. It has never been published. The bound document contains letters and statements by Roman Catholic and Protestant bishops and reports and affidavits by defendants, their lawyers, and sympathizers. Although the introduction and epilogue acknowledged that the information provided by defendants and lawyers, including allegations of mistreatment, "may in some cases be incorrect" (3, 149), these claims were used as basis for the churches' "repeated requests...for a detailed legal reexamination" (20).

> In conclusion we wish to call attention in the name of the righteous and merciful God to the fact that the highest expression of justice is not necessarily sentence and punishment. As servants of God we ask that in suitable cases mercy be shown....In the name of humanity we ask for an act of mercy for the young, the aged and the sick. (23)

The Memorandum was signed by none other than Martin Niemöller, who at the time served as president of the Protestant Church of Germany. While he was not the author of this remarkable amnesty plea,[93] he was willing to lend his name because he endorsed the Christian prioritization of forgiveness over justice.[94] Remarkably, the council of the EKD was willing to support the radical request that all "the prisoners of Landsberg be given parole, that is, that they be released from prison under the usual conditions" (22). WCP Landsberg housed, among others, all high-ranking leaders of the National Socialist regime who had been convicted by the IMT in Nuremberg. Three years later, they were supposed to go free.

The moral authority to demand their release derived from of the church's previous confession of guilt. The most public spokesmen for clemency and amnesty, such as Bishop Meiser, had co-signed the Stuttgart Declaration.[95] The Memorandum itself cited the Stuttgart Declaration as proof of moral authority to demand clemency in 1949:

The objection that the church itself is not without guilt is invalid. In 1945, we confessed before the whole world: "Through us immeasurable suffering has been brought.... We accuse ourselves that our profession of faith was not more courageous, our prayers more faithful, our faith more joyous and our love more burning. Now we shall begin anew in our church. Founded on the Holy Scripture and with eyes solemnly turned to the sole Lord of the church, the church will set about purging itself of foreign influence and bringing its house in order. In the name of the God of mercy and loving kindness, we hope that He will use our church as His instrument and give us authority to propagate His word and procure obedience to His will. (4)

Whatever sense of contrition had spoken through the Stuttgart Declaration in 1945 was now turned into a strategy of empowerment and opposition to the Allied prosecution. The church had released itself from moral debt and felt entitled to demand the right to purge "itself of foreign influence." Significantly, the English translation of the Stuttgart Declaration included in the Memorandum shifted the definition of "foreign influence." While in 1945 the purification from foreign influence referred to the "alien" ideology of National Socialism, it now applied to the imposition of foreign standards of justice. Where the original Stuttgart Declaration had tried to signal humility and willingness to accept correction, the Memorandum used the same text to insist on the right to set the terms of justice.

The desire to begin anew without looking back also shaped the statement issued by the Roman Catholic bishops' conference meeting in Fulda in 1948, which was included in the Memorandum. They complain that the "German youth was ready to confess past mistakes and errors, hoping to begin a new life where not force but right should be guides."[96] However, they continued, the spectacle of "power politics...made the demoralization of our people unavoidable" (40). The German people had lost all "confidence in justice" because of the "internment, the way and manner of denazification," and the bishops observed that "the Nuremberg law-courts condemn Germans according to a right until now unknown in Germany and to which the nations applying it against Germany are not willing to submit" (41). In the bishops' view, people were demoralized by attempts to remove National Socialists from power, however haphazardly implemented, not by the crimes themselves. The vague readiness "to confess past mistakes" substituted for precision and fact-based truth-telling.

Retributive justice was categorically rejected by the Protestant com-
pilers of the Memorandum, who quoted from Paul's letter to the
Romans. They used Paul's polemic against the law to underscore the
preeminence of forgiveness over justice in the Christian tradition and
theologized sin and guilt as a collective condition and universal experience. In their selective quotation from chapter 3, they tried to impress
on the American recipients of the Memorandum that every human
being would be considered sinful in the eyes of God and that no human
being should feel authorized to sit in judgment of another. The
theological universalization of guilt served to undermine the need for
precise discernment of individual culpability. If individual guilt cannot
be determined, then the search for justice is futile and destructive. The
passage from Paul was placed as a prologue to the introduction to the
Memorandum to suggest that individual guilt should be absorbed into
the universal state of human sinfulness:

Romans 3

(10) None is righteous, no not one; (11) no one understands, no
one seeks for God. (12) All have turned aside, together they have
gone wrong; no one does good, not even one.... (17) And the way of
peace they do not know.... (21) But the righteousness of God has
been manifested apart from the law and the prophets; (22) the righteousness of God through faith in Jesus Christ for all who believe.
For there is no distinction, (23) since all have sinned and fall short
of the glory of God; (24) they are justified by his grace as a gift,
through the redemption, which is in Jesus Christ, (25) whom God
put forward as an expiation by his blood, to be received by faith.[97]

The body of the Memorandum deals exclusively with legal matters, and
the editors did not provide a theological commentary to this biblical
passage. But these verses in the prologue seem intended to undermine
the Lutheran doctrine of two kingdoms that had traditionally separated
the realm of law, politics, and justice from the realm of the grace and
redemption. In other words, in Reformation history, the "righteousness of
God" had not ordinarily invalidated the workings of the law in the courtroom. Normally, conservative churchmen were known to uphold law and
order in society. But in the context of Nazi war criminals, the churchmen
found it expedient to question the strict application of the law. The quote
from Romans conveys a warning that no one should consider himself

above reproof and that the Allied military had not known the "way of peace" any more than its German counterpart. Why, they asked in the main text, should Allied military personnel be exempted from the strictures of the Nuremberg Principles, which were only applied to the defeated nations of Germany and Japan? They cited the aerial bombings of cities and the expulsion of millions of Germans from the east and insisted that "it is a well-known fact that ... war crimes were not committed by Germans only" (20). The Allied powers "placed themselves above [the law] ... by allowing war crimes and other inhumanities committed within their jurisdiction to go unpunished" (20). The new international law, they asserted, was fundamentally unjust as long as it was applied only to "the vanquished" (20). It was little more than an instrument to humiliate the powerless and to exonerate the victorious and the powerful.[98] "But who among us is without sin?" the authors asked rhetorically in the introduction. Those who sat in judgment of German war criminals were no better than the hypocritical men in the Gospel of John who set out to stone an adulterous woman. The solidarity of guilt created vague webs of complicity that undercut any possibility of judgment.

A second point conveyed by the selection from Romans 3 is the notion that righteousness is a matter of faith rather than of moral conduct. Those who believe in Christ's sacrifice are justified—made just—and hence, exonerated. The blood of Christ purifies, quite "apart from the law." The law, the realm of moral judgment and pursuit of justice, has been suspended by Christ's sacrifice, which paid the wages of guilt. The primacy of faith over law was frequently applied in clemency pleas, where personal testimony about the sincerity of Christian piety and character witness (*Leumundszeugnisse*) was supposed to vacate and undo the factual record of wrongdoing.

The Memorandum contained numerous depositions testifying to the religious sincerity of defendants. One example involved the Bavarian bishop Hans Meiser, who pleaded on behalf of his friend Wilhelm von Ammon and asked that his "case be re-examined with a view to a considerable mitigation of his penalty and a speedy release" (52). Von Ammon was convicted to ten years in prison in the Jurists' Trial of the IMT. In his amnesty plea, dated August 30, 1949, Bishop Meiser testified as follows:

I have known Mr. von Ammon personally for many years as a man of calm and modest disposition, of irreproachable character

and sincere and Christian convictions, who has proved his loyalty to the church, even throughout the time of Nazi-rule and
anti-church strife, by his active participation in congregational
Church life.[99]

The gist of such arguments insinuated that a person's Christian commitments to congregational life somehow mitigated his professional involvement in atrocities. In von Ammon's case, his conviction stemmed from
his role as legal consultant who helped draft the notorious "Night and
Fog" orders that legalized the extrajudicial arrest and "disappearance" into
night and fog of anyone suspected of opposing German occupation.
Beginning in December 1941, this order was responsible for the deaths of
approximately seven thousand people, mostly in France. As a young
attorney for the Reichsjustizministerium in 1935, he was also involved in
writing the infamous race laws defining Jewish racial descent, although
that fact was not brought to the attention of the court in Nuremberg.
Meiser submitted the following legal brief, which had been prepared by
von Ammon's defense team. Defense lawyers became very adept at shifting liability from the collective to the individual, and back again, until
culpability lost all meaning and could no longer be assigned to particular
persons or institutions:

> Von Ammon's official position differed in no way from the position
> held by hundreds of other officials in the German Ministries. Like
> all of them he had to administer a certain category of matters within
> the frame of existing laws according to the directives of his supe-
> riors. Within this category his functions were not left to his own
> initiative, but were dependent on precise political decisions of the
> supreme authority.... To extend the criminal responsibility to sub-
> ordinate organs of the Government has, however, in other cases
> intentionally omitted in Nuremberg. A charge of such collective
> responsibility should be avoided, and the responsibility should be
> limited to the Government organs having ordered such unlawful
> measures on their own initiatives. (52–53)

The solidarity of guilt became a tool of exoneration. On the one hand,
the legal brief advised that "collective responsibility should be avoided,"
but, on the other hand, von Ammon should not be held personally
accountable for any of his actions, which "hundreds of other officials"

similarly performed. Collective culpability mitigated individual responsibility, and the solidarity of guilt erased personal accountability. The real culprits were never available. They had no names. The language of perpetration obscured agency and failed to name specific "government organs" that might have "initiated" "unlawful measures" or von Ammon's precise role and rank in these bureaucracies. Von Ammon had used his legal expertise and professional position to write Jews out of citizenship in the Nuremberg Laws, the handicapped out of the right to life in the euthanasia laws, and opponents of German occupation out of human rights in the "Night and Fog" laws. He was not a harmless cog in a vast government machine, nor a bland civil servant. But by 1951, he was paroled and released from WCP Landsberg. He was employed by the Protestant Church in Bavaria and served as director of church administration (*Landeskirchenstelle*) responsible for the legal and financial affairs of the church until his retirement in 1970. His rehabilitation and restoration to respectability, power, and prestige was the result of Christian understandings of forgiveness that swept away precise knowledge of deeds and erased the memory of its victims. This paradigm of guilt and forgiveness came to be known as *Stunde Null* (hour zero) or *Schlussstrich* (line of closure) in German political history.

The Stuttgart Declaration of Guilt became an important document in dividing the guilt of (pre)history from the birth of the new future. After a very short internal struggle, both churches moved quickly to distance themselves individually and institutionally from the crimes of National Socialism and dedicated themselves to the reconstruction of the bombed-out country. With German cities in ruins, the country occupied by foreign military powers, the people mentally exhausted, spiritually demoralized, and politically broken, church leaders set their hopes on a quick transition from a guilty past into a reconciled future.

3

Faith under the Gallows

SPECTACLES OF INNOCENCE IN WCP LANDSBERG

Together, with few exceptions, they [the death candidates]
knelt on the cold stone floor of the prison basement to
receive the Holy Eucharist, always at 6:00 AM on the
morning of the day of execution. Did they felt guilty about
the crimes for which they had been charged? Most of them
did not.

(PASTOR AUGUST ECKARDT, *Christmas 1985*)[1]

THE LUTHERAN PASTOR August Eckardt remembered the hangings
and shootings in the War Crimes Prison complex of Landsberg in
Bavaria as the most harrowing aspect of his prison chaplaincy.
Altogether, American military courts handed down 806 death sentences, of which 486 were carried out. The majority of these executions
occurred in WCP 1 Landsberg, with the last seven men hanged on June
7, 1951. There are only estimates for the overall number of executions
carried out in all four Allied jurisdictions. Historian Richard Evans
reckons that there were somewhere between 437 and 756 executions in
the Soviet zone and 398 executions in the British zone, which imposed
537 death sentences.[2] Norbert Frei provides different numbers: 268 for
the U.S., 240 for the British, 104 for the French, and 756 for the Soviet
Zone.[3] The number of court-imposed executions amounted to fewer
than two thousand people and pales by comparison to the overall death
toll in internment and POW camps from malnutrition, disease,
exposure, and lack of medical care, especially immediately after the war
and in the Soviet Union. But these executions were hotly debated,
reviewed repeatedly by appeals panels, and intensely scrutinized in the
national and international press.

The Prison Chaplains in WCP 1

Prisoners in American custody were given access to pastoral counseling, first by the American military chaplains, Pastor Henry Gerecke and Pater Sixtus O'Connor, and later by German clergy. Father Karl Morgenschweis worked continuously as Roman Catholic chaplain in the Landsberg prison between October 1932 and his retirement in August 1957.[4] The Lutheran pastors August Eckardt (June 1948–May 1949)[5] and Karl Ermann (July 1949–June 1951)[6] were specifically assigned to the prison and paid by the Protestant-Lutheran Church in Bavaria. Neither Pastor Eckardt (born 1912) nor Pastor Ermann (born 1911) had been members of the NSdAP. According to Pastor Eckardt's denazification papers, he had joined the SA in 1933 and remained a member until June 1935.[7] In November 1934, he declared allegiance to the Confessing Church and ran against a pastoral candidate belonging to the Deutsche Christen (German Christians, the Nazi wing of the Protestant Church) in the general church elections. He held pastoral positions as youth minister and hospital chaplain before enlisting in the Wehrmacht in 1940. He served in France and Italy and was wounded twice, but there was no a priori reason to suspect him of political collaboration with National Socialism. But he soon ran afoul of the U.S. military prison administration, which complained in April 1949 that "these clerics are inclined to mix politics and religion to such a degree that politics over-shadow the religious results."[8] He was relieved of his duties and replaced by Pastor Ermann, who took office in July 1949. The prison chaplains visited the cells, engaged prisoners in conversations, and recruited them for worship services and choir practices.[9] They also maintained contacts with families, lawyers, and, despite prison regulations, the press.[10] Both Eckardt and Ermann were removed from their positions because they sided with the convicts and became politically active in the solidarity movement.[11] They violated prison rules, smuggled out letters, and funneled information to various support organizations, including the authors of the secret Memorandum of the Evangelical Church discussed in the previous chapter, and the clandestine Stille Hilfe, which provided legal assistance, raised funds, and established political and professional networks for former Nazis.[12] The pastors maintained extensive, alphabetically arranged records on the prisoners, including letters to families and correspondence with colleagues and church administrators, which are located in the Landeskirchliche Archiv in Nuremberg. Further information comes from chronologically organized records of death row inmates in fourteen boxes marked "Executee Files" housed in the National Archives and Records Administration in College Park, Maryland.[13] These documents provide windows into the prison chaplains' conversations with convicts who faced the death penalty.

Pastor Eckardt noted in his retrospective reflections in 1985 that the spiritual and mental preparation for the gallows dominated his work: "The most significant task consisted in the pastoral preparation for the impending hour of death. Uplifting testimony of steadfastness, joyfulness in faith, and willingness to die belong to the most gripping experiences of this service."[14] The executions were highly ritualized events. Observers recorded the last words of convicts on their way to the execution site and directly under the gallows.[15] Army photographers were on hand to take pictures of the men, alive and dead. The first shot shows the convict, with bound hands and feet, often looking straight into the camera. They are flanked by two U.S. soldiers whose faces are sometimes scratched out to protect their identity. The second photograph is a full view of the body, shot from above, after the condemned had fallen through the trap door. Corpses were laid out, in the first executions usually naked, but later clothed, in a wooden coffin filled with sawdust. These photographs were taken, according to Ray Martin, "as proof of execution"[16] and included in the Executee Files.

Prisoners could also be tied to a wooden board and carried up to the gallows.[17] Pastor Eckardt described the case of Eugen Ziehmer, who had fasted for seven days prior to the hanging and was too weak to walk up by himself. Tied to the board, Ziehmer appeared to Eckardt

> like an animal [Stück Vieh] or a piece of furniture as he was carried up the narrow staircase from the basement. They had to be careful to get the stiff board around each corner. After a few more steps, the thirteen stairs go up to the gallows with the trapdoor. It is not expected that Ziehmer will say another word. But all of a sudden, he is completely awake: "Greet my homeland, my wife and my children. I am innocent and have nothing to do with this whole thing. Those who are, in fact, guilty are sitting in this house with term sentences. I am the victim of professional criminals. God help me.[18]

Ziehmer, like the vast majority of convicts, affirmed his innocence under the gallows. Approximately half of the 285 executed prisoners in WCP 1 Landsberg issued last statements, and almost all of them insisted on their innocence. We don't know what the other half was thinking or why they refused to respond when prompted for their last statements. Those who spoke addressed the attending clergy ("Father" or "Pastor"), the "prison director,"[19] or "the Americans."[20] Of the 133 last statements that I transcribed from fourteen boxes of Executee Files, only three unequivocally express verbal regret for killings that led to their convictions.[21] The overwhelming majority affirm their innocence and repudiate their guilty verdicts.

The prison chaplains played an ambiguous role in these spectacles of guilt denial. On the one hand, Pastor Eckardt tried to challenge the National Socialist Weltanschauung of his charges. He had been warned to expect what his predecessor, Pastor Werner Hess, called a "psychosis of blamelessness" (*Psychose der Schuldlosigkeit*). Werner Hess was himself a convict who was sentenced to six months for transmitting an order to form a gauntlet to beat a downed American pilot by an incensed German crowd in Dorsten, Germany.[22] A second lieutenant in the Wehrmacht, Werner Hess had never been a member of the Nazi party, and he began to informally counsel fellow inmates while imprisoned in Landsberg. After his release, he contacted Eckardt and advised him about the "peculiar atmosphere of tension, nationalism, and prison-induced psychotic exaggeration"[23] that would await him in Landsberg. Hess told Eckardt to look out for "horrible tales about their trials.... [B]ut eventually you will get a feeling for the credibility and the distortion of the real events."[24] Hess himself had experienced Landsberg "as a unique opportunity to seriously discuss the intellectual and spiritual errors of the Hitler regime."[25]

Despite this excellent advice, the Protestant prison chaplains seemed to fall for the deceptive evasions created by some of the convicts. The chaplains challenged their ideological values and religious convictions but were remarkably naive when it came to the coded cover-ups for atrocities. For instance, in his diary Pastor Eckardt simply accepted the story of Adolf Ott, who was convicted for leading an *Einsatzkommando* (mobile killing squad) in March 1942, and failed to try to distinguish historical fact from fiction:

> I was surprised to hear that whole areas behind the front could not be kept under control by German troops. The area of Briansk was held by partisans. During the Aktion Eisbär, a cleansing operation, they could not engage the enemy for ten days, because the partisans were hiding so cleverly.... Whenever one of the saboteurs was caught, they

were instantaneously executed [*standrechtliche Erschießungen*]. Among them were sometimes also Jews, although on the whole the area was considered to be "Jew-free" [quotation marks in orig.]. During his activities in the east, Ott supervised approximately 80–100 killings [*Erschießungen*], among them approximately 20 persons of Jewish descent.... Ott was under the impression that he was serving as a witness during the trial and not as a defendant. These admitted 80–100 shootings became "executions" of hundreds of people each. This is how these incredible accusations came into being.[26]

Eckardt faithfully echoed Ott's defense strategy in the courtroom, claiming "that he had not killed any Jews because there were none left when he arrived in Russia in January 1942."[27] In court, this "line of defense...was a complete failure,"[28] especially since he was caught in contradictory statements. But the prison chaplain was willing to trust Adolf Ott's self-proclaimed innocence. As a staunch German nationalist, Eckardt could not, or did not want to, accept the evidence of genocidal mass killings that was so clearly laid out before his eyes. Given his diary entry above, Eckardt rather matter-of-factly accepted the declaration that an area could be presumed "Jew-free" without inquiring how such a thing could come to pass, or why this could have been a legitimate goal. After all, it was the *Einsatzgruppen*'s sole responsibility to "cleanse" eastern territories of their Jewish inhabitants in systematic massacres. Pastor Eckardt did not challenge or contest Adolf Ott's denial of culpable wrongdoing.

Eckardt was much more suspicious when it came to religion and neo-pagan ideology. It was in this area that he engaged the inmates critically and refused to accept their value and belief systems. His diary recounts several long conversations with Otto Ohlendorf and Dr. Werner Braune, both of whom were sentenced to death in the Subsequent Nuremberg Proceedings (NMT) Einsatzgruppen Trial. Unlike Ott, whose death sentence was commuted to life and who was released from Landsberg in 1958, Ohlendorf and Braune were hanged in Landsberg on June 7, 1951. Eckardt was drawn into theological discussions with these men who were educated and passionate about their faith in National Socialist doctrine. He wrote that "whenever I turned the key to his [Braune's] cell, I had to be prepared to spend the next 2–3 hours in discussion."[29] Braune, the former commander of Einsatzgruppe 11b, subscribed to a theology that held that God must be detected in the laws of nature and should not be sought in revealed scriptures or doctrinal traditions. Eckardt recounted that for him, man is the measure of all things. Whatever makes sense to me in my conscience, that which corresponds to my essence [*Wesen*] and appears appropriate to my being [*artgerecht*], must be the divine presence inside of me. From this follows logically that God is also the source of evil because God put the inclination to do evil inside me. Since I am his creature, why would God not want me to be this way?

I object: Where is the space for genuine responsibility? How can there be a compelling obligation to follow the commandment of God, if I only accept as obligatory what is already commensurate with my being [*wesensgemäß*]? ... Does this not turn God into the sole carrier of responsibility or, to put it more crassly, into the real criminal?[30]

These theological debates raised important points. For Braune, God was synonymous with the natural law of the survival of the fittest. He espoused the Nazi understanding that the battle of the races for domination and the eradication of the weak, the decadent, and the redundant were part of the divine order of the universe. In his view, conquest and extermination were willed by God and written into the laws of nature. Compassion for the needy and justice for the weak were contrary to this conception of the divine as manifest in biology and nature. In the end, Eckardt failed to convince Braune to abandon this theology, but he challenged his worldview and engaged critically with his value system. Eckardt upheld the notion of a transcendent God, external to nature and beyond human control and cognition. He argued for the revealed nature of divine law, which imposes commandments to institute justice beyond and contrary to nature. For Eckardt, the ethical obligation to protect the vulnerable and to enforce justice for the powerless was rooted in the revealed God of faith. After three hours, as Eckardt was leaving his cell, Dr. Braune concluded that he would never be able to accept a scripture like the Old Testament, which he considered to be racially foreign (*artfremd*) and for which he felt an "instinctive contempt."[31] Braune did not reconvert, but was accompanied to the gallows by Eckardt's successor, Pastor Ermann, anyway.[32]

When Eckardt visited Otto Ohlendorf in his cell, he met with a man who was a similarly fervent believer in National Socialism. Again his diary recounts complex theological discussions that were supposed to challenge Ohlendorf's faith in a God present and knowable in the cosmos. "I cannot believe in Christianity any longer," said Ohlendorf, because it lost its relation to creation, and because it does not speak about the love, the justice, the good, the true and the beautiful placed by God inside human beings, and that life as willed by God should follow these natural basic inclinations [*Grundanlagen der Schöpfung*]. The divine spark inside of us should be awakened and developed.[33]

This list of supposedly instinctual human values provoked Pastor Eckardt to insert a parenthesis in which he noted dryly: "(And this is said by someone who has been charged with the liquidation of 90,000 Jews)."[34] His parenthetical remark about the charges also echoes Ohlendorf's own court strategy. Unlike most other defendants in the NMT, Ohlendorf was talkative and shocked the courtroom into stunned silence with his frank discussions of the "Final Solution of the Jewish Question."[35] Ohlendorf was in charge of Einsatzgruppe D between June 1941 and June 1942, when it systematically mass-murdered Jews along the southern end of the eastern front. During his trial in Nuremberg, Ohlendorf spoke frankly of the methods involved in the *Einsatzgruppen* killings and the overall number of 90,000 Jewish victims. He was known for his truthful testimony, which may explain Eckardt's note. Historian Hilary Earl attributes Ohlendorf's apparent honesty to his "Nazified conscience" along with his "arrogance and sense of mission," which is "why he never tried to hide his actions."[36] It is conceivable that Eckardt and Ohlendorf discussed the legitimacy and meaning of these massacres openly. But Eckardt's diary does not record any such conversation. His diary usually glossed over the charges of atrocities themselves and focused on the theological questions. He objected to statements about the immanence of God in nature, which he believed undercut human freedom and responsibility. He defended the revelation of law by a transcendent God as source of human accountability and choice. He thereby put his finger on the theological and ethical distortions of the Nazi Weltanschauung, but he did not address the specific antisemitic and racist reasons for the killings. In his diary he never questioned why an area could be presumed "free of Jews" or whether Jews should have a rightful place in the universe rather than face eradication like invasive species that did not fit the divine order of nature. Ohlendorf continued to believe that it was possible to "obliterate evil" (*das Böse ausschalten*) as long as one followed God's foundational order (*Grundordnungen Gottes*) as gleaned from nature and history. In Ohlendorf's thinking, "Nature and history are the sources of revelation for the elements of God's effectiveness."[37] Pastor Eckardt, like so many Protestant theologians and churchmen, battled the biology and social Darwinism of Nazi morality but let the central dogma of antisemitism slip by.[38] He concentrated on the more abstract theological truth claims rather than the specifics of the dehumanization of particular people who had been written out of the moral universe of Nazi perpetrators and were considered undeserving of human rights.

Peace in Their Hearts

The impending executions shifted the focus of pastoral care to the spiritual and emotional preparation for this final ordeal. Since these executions were public events, the pastors wanted the men to show "manly resoluteness" (*männliche Standhaftigkeit*) in the face of death.[39] In their condolence letters to wives, family members, and fellow clergy, the pastors invariably emphasized the calm resolve and serene composure of the convicts during their last moments.[40] Their pastoral care aimed at "inner peace" rather than the turmoil of remorse. For instance, Pastor Eckardt reported in a condolence letter that the final celebration of Holy Communion "strengthened his resolve by imparting the internal conviction of the forgiveness of sins."[41] The last celebrations of the Eucharist were intended to generate peace and closure. To the wife of a convict he wrote: "By laying on hands I could proclaim the forgiveness of sins and affirm his eternal salvation in the name of God, thereby leading him to the threshold over which God's mercy transports a believing soul from the temporal into the eternal realm."[42] In Eckardt's mind, the final dignity of passing "the last test upright and manly"[43] seemed to have taken precedence over the potential disintegration that accompanies contrition. Sudden remorse might have undermined the emotional and psychological stability of the men who tried to take the last walk with "manly bearing"[44] and to exchange "manly good-byes."[45] The assurance of peace and eternal forgiveness was bought at the price of denial, which seemed not to concern Eckardt: "When he, today, this morning, desired and received Holy Communion, it confirms to me that he will pass on from this life in peace and reconciled with God."[46] These final rituals of forgiveness intended to provide consolation rather than moral and spiritual confrontation with the omissions and commissions of a misguided life. "On the morning of his death day he participated in the celebration of Holy Communion...and was given the gift of the peace of God and a reconciled conscience [*versöhntes Gewissen*]."[47] Though we cannot know what was said in those last intimate moments of pastoral conversation (they are, after all, protected by the seal of the confessional) or peer into the depth of another person's heart and soul, we can note that these final rituals calmed, soothed, and strengthened men in their ideological convictions and their rejection of remorse.

Pastor Eckardt felt more eager to challenge offenses in the area of sexual conduct and private life. When he asked rhetorically in his diary: "How can such transgressions be purified before God?"[48] he was speaking of adultery and not of genocide. Eckardt used the language of "repentance and return" (*Buße und Umkehr*) in the case of Peter Merker not for guilt incurred during his service as an SS guard in Buchenwald but for keeping a "concubine" (*Nebenfrau*) with whom he had a child: "Is he a man who is willing to commit to repentance and return, irrespective of the costs and without consideration that he would have to forever abandon his deepest longing?"[49] A fair number of SS men had maintained multiple sexual relationships or followed the call to father racially superior children with several women.[50] And the pastors were much more inclined to challenge guilt in the context of sexuality than mass death. Eckardt could not decide whether to ask Merker to abandon the second woman along with his illegitimate child in order to return to the first wife, from whom he felt estranged. But he expected repentance, regret, and contrition in the area of private morality, while he rarely used this language in conversations about Nazi crimes.

The Case of Hans Hermann Schmidt: Manly Composure

The separation of guilt into public and private spheres of behavior is particularly obvious in the case of Hans Hermann Schmidt, who was among the last seven "red jackets" (as the death candidates were known in the press for their red uniforms) hanged on June 7, 1951.[51] Schmidt's biography demonstrates some of the rhetorical strategies used to circumvent feeling morally responsible or criminally liable for Nazi atrocities. Schmidt's chaplain, Pastor Ermann, spoke of his guilt only in the context of private sins—not with reference to his role as deputy commander (*Adjutant*) of Buchenwald. The language of guilt applied to private affairs and was rigorously rejected in the area of public conduct and professional behavior.

Hans Hermann Schmidt served as deputy commander of Buchenwald, the SS-run concentration camp where more than 250,000 people from all over Europe were held between 1937 and April 1945. It is estimated that more than 56,000 prisoners were killed in the camp located outside Weimar, many of them starved to death during the last months, when the mortality rate reached 5,000 prisoners every month.[52] Schmidt served as the chief "legal officer" and was in charge of all penal actions, including all executions. In the absence of the *Kommandant*, Schmidt was put in charge of the entire camp operation.[53] In his last words, Schmidt affirmed his innocence, as had the other six convicts who had stepped under the gallows before him.[54] His statement was prepared in consultation with Pastor Ermann, who had replaced Eckardt in July 1949. For his memorial sermon held three days after the executions, Ermann used this version of Schmidt's last words, which differs slightly from the version recorded by the prison personnel:[55]

> Colonel, I want to use this moment to emphatically protest the conviction that led to this death sentence. Before the face of God, before whom I will stand in the next moment, I affirm that I am innocent of the crimes with which I have been charged. I declare that I have done nothing else than what you, sirs, are doing right now: I have executed orders that had been legally given to me. I die as the last of the Landsberg death candidates. I die innocent.[56]

Ermann integrated the last statements into his sermon in order to preach about the convicts' obedient submission to the will of God and their heroic acceptance of their fates. He commended their "upright and obedient walk to their last destination" and claimed that it radiated "energy and strength" to the "loved ones at home and all of us who are connected with them."[57] None of them had expressed contrition. But for Ermann, obedience to the will of God was not principally tied to recognition of culpable wrongdoing or regret for participation in atrocities. On the contrary, he argued that

> even during their last hours before they stepped into God's presence, they fought accusations that contradicted the truth and resisted the contention that their actions should be considered ordinary crimes since they occurred under the hard compulsion of military necessities. They gave witness to this truth until they drew their last breath.[58]

When this sermon became public, Bishop Hans Meiser called Ermann into his office in Munich and criticized him for the apparent glorification of the convicts, his misuse of the Bible, and the complete absence of remorse.[59] Bishop Hans Meiser, himself a staunch nationalist conservative, asked Ermann to "consider the possibility that after two years of service in Landsberg, [he] was in too great a danger of identifying with the perspective of the prisoners and of becoming too involved in their struggle for justice instead of attending to pastoral tasks."[60] Ermann was given an ultimatum and forced to tender his resignation by June 26. He left Landsberg on June 29, 1951.

Hans Hermann Schmidt did not conceal the scope of his activities because he considered his use of lethal force legitimate. He had punished inmates who had misbehaved. Schmidt never denied his responsibilities as deputy commander and acknowledged "that all executions except those performed at the horse stables were carried out by this accused as adjutant and legal officer, including the giving of the order to fire."[61] Schmidt had convinced himself that he operated conscientiously within legitimate structures set up by governmental authorities. He argued that since he had not designed the conditions in Buchenwald he could not be held responsible for its exorbitant death rate, which he blamed on starvation and disease caused by the advancing enemy armies and the collapse of order toward the end of the war. Pastor Ermann seemed to concur with this view. In a letter to his colleague, Pastor Schloemann, who was slated to conduct funeral services for Schmidt in his hometown of Höxter, Pastor Ermann defended Schmidt's apparent lack of contrition:

> Herr Schmidt rejoined the Protestant Church in 1948 out of sincere conviction and remained faithful to this belief to his end. During those three years there was scarcely a worship service in which he did not participate. He was an attentive listener to the word of God.... He did not treat confession as mere lip service but was cognizant of much guilt and omission in his life of which he spoke openly. But he could not come to an affirmation of the guilt ascribed to him by the court even though he examined his conscience thoroughly. His appointment as deputy commander [*Adjutant*] in Buchenwald did not occur on his own initiative, and he is unaware of any cruelty since he performed only tasks required by military obedience. I can imagine that you are shocked by the last words of Herr Schmidt. Should one not understand them as a lack of

remorse? But I know Herr Schmidt well enough to know that he denied only the legal criminal guilt, which he did not want to accept and which he could not accept. His guilt before God he confessed truthfully in both his last celebration of the Confession and of Holy Communion, and he received the forgiveness of his sins with a desiring heart.[62]

What is most striking in this paragraph is Ermann's assertion that Schmidt was "unaware of any cruelty" in Buchenwald. This lack of awareness testifies to the narrowing of perception that screened out the pervasive cruelty inflicted within the institutional framework of the camp. Pastor Ermann separated individual "guilt before God" of which Schmidt was aware and to which he confessed contritely from the brutality perpetrated in the pursuit of professional assignments. Morality was reduced to the private realm of personal affairs.

In their reviews of amnesty cases, High Commissioner John J. McCloy and General Thomas T. Handy struggled with this logic. When General Handy ruled against commuting Schmidt's death penalty in January 1951, he maintained: "It is quite improbable that any of those who were in the camp for a few days could have believed that any of the beatings or killings were legitimate. It must have been apparent to them that the entire operation was contrary to universally accepted standards of human conduct."[63] The awareness of cruelty or lack thereof became critically important. Such a line of reasoning, however, would make culpability dependent upon a person's belief system. In other words, if someone believes in the legitimacy of killings, they should be considered innocent. Only a person who becomes aware of cruelty could legitimately be punished. Schmidt himself, for obvious reasons, steadfastly maintained his sincere belief in the legitimacy and conventionality of his work. He claimed never to have committed an act of violence on his own volition or out of "base motifs" such as anger, greed, or lust. General Handy disagreed and ruled that Schmidt had "gone beyond his duties" and had acted on "his own initiative" in the absence of camp commander Pister.[64] From the perspective of victims and survivors of Buchenwald, it mattered not at all whether Schmidt went beyond his duties. The distinction between personal intention and actual performance is irrelevant to those who suffer atrocities. From their perspective, whether someone acts out of personal malice or tortures in a dispassionate and professional manner is negligible. Where punishment depended on the internal state of the perpetrator, the reality of victims was lost. Schmidt's mere presence and administrative leadership function in Buchenwald was implicated in the murder of up to 5,000 people per month and the abject suffering of countless thousands more. Justice cannot be made dependent on perpetrators' perception of cruelty, or lack thereof, as Pastor Ermann maintained.

The deliberate disassociation of private morality from public agency further confounded the consciousness of culpability. Schmidt was perceived as a nice and respectable man in his private life not only in the eyes of the prison chaplain, but also in his hometown and by his family. As early as August 1947, his home pastor, Pastor Schloemann, had submitted a "petition for review" signed by sixty-six residents of Schmidt's hometown of Höxter to the deputy judge advocate's office.[65] His mother Käthe and his wife Margot submitted several amnesty appeals and confirmed this split sense of morality.[66] The sense of innocence that was staged in the executions in Landsberg percolated through the families and the wider German public. A number of rhetorical strategies blocked the "awareness of cruelty" and obstructed the recognition of culpable wrongdoing. Schmidt's defense lawyer, Froeschmann, outlined some of the arguments that would exonerate perpetrators and facilitate their unchallenged reintegration into postwar German society. In his eulogy delivered at Schmidt's memorial service in Landsberg/Lech on June 10, 1951, Froeschmann said:

> In order to judge a man correctly, one has to put oneself in the situation in which he found himself. Hans Schmidt did his *duty* as *soldier* and *civil servant* in a job to which he was reluctantly assigned by an adverse fate, always striving to ameliorate the suffering of the unfortunate prisoners. He did not gloss over the hideousness he had to observe unwillingly. But he felt personally free from any guilt. He fought against falsehood and distortion, and the knowledge of his blamelessness gave him the strength to believe that his fate could be averted until his bitter end. Thus he died as a sacrificial victim of a distressing and disastrous time, which likes to clothe its mistakes in the mantle of a legitimate law. From such actions no peace and reconciliation can grow between the peoples.... Comrade Hans Schmidt, your wife, your son, and your daughter are the visible legacy of your faith in the German people. Your faith must become truth. Germany shall live even if we have to die.[67] (Emphasis added)

The "knowledge of his blamelessness" proclaimed by Froeschmann was erected on the basis of several rhetorical tropes. First, there were the omissions: Froeschmann deliberately passed over references to the particular places of Schmidt's "job" or his specific title (*Adjutant*) and assignment (penal officer). No mention was made of concrete measures taken by Schmidt or of his actual power in the camp hierarchy. Second, there were the grammatical passive constructions: perpetrators did not choose but were appointed by an "adverse fate." In this view, they did not compete for tasks, they did not clamor for approval, and they did not strive to impress their superiors with ideological trustworthiness and competency. Third, specific names were erased: it was an "adverse fate" that assigned Schmidt to Buchenwald, not a particular supervisor or SS official. Such passive constructions void moral agency and conceal personal choice. Fourth, there was no commission of violence: the victims were obliquely referred to as "unfortunate prisoners," whom Schmidt allegedly had tried to help. Reluctantly, Schmidt was forced to "observe" "hideousness," but any brutality was notably committed by someone else.[68] Code words about the "soldier" and "civil servant" who performed his "duties" replaced historical facts and explicit descriptions of tasks. The nature of the "guilt," from which Schmidt knew himself to be "personally free," remained shadowy and unnamed. Such veiled allusions created the illusion of innocence and turned perpetrators into passive and innocent bystanders who deserved everyone's compassion.[69] These rhetorical tropes focused on the professionalism of the "hard compulsion of military necessity" which had, in effect, numbed the senses of the accused and anesthetized their conscience against the suffering of others.

Froeschmann's eulogy articulated the mentality of perpetration characterized by the absence of precise facts, personal agency, and empathy for the victims. In order to perform atrocities, perpetrators had to steel their hearts and focus their minds on expertise, efficiency, and ambition in order to "do their jobs" and to overrule their doubts and compassion. They suspended sensitivity to the pain and suffering of others and vigorously filtered out the sensual perception of smells, sounds, and sights of wounded and starving bodies, of terrified eyes and agonized faces. Their professional ethos as soldiers, police officers, medical doctors, and prison guards required them to overcome empathy. One could argue that their "sin" did not consist in too much emotion, but in too little. They had disciplined themselves and submitted to "higher" principles that demanded that the anguish of fellow human beings be screened out.

Unlike ordinary criminals who succumb to selfish desires and yield to emotions such as lust, greed, and anger, these perpetrators felt above reproach. This mentality of diminished humanity was at the core of what prison chaplains should have confronted. But they seemed to have colluded with the codes of evasive half-truths that failed to dispel the rationality of atrocity. Therefore, feelings of regret or remorse remained out of reach for the convicts.

By the time Pastor Ermann wrote his memorial sermon, he had deeply plunged into the "psychosis of blamelessness." Quite possibly, the proximity of death and execution had fortified the bonds of empathy between convicts and chaplains. But the chaplains' identification with the political position and moral predicament of the Landsberg prisoners undermined their ability to assist their moral recovery and human growth. The chaplains prioritized mental stability and emotional composure under the gallows over the mental anguish of remorse. Their pastoral care facilitated final spectacles of heroic courage and manly resolve and limited confrontation and critical engagement with the ideological and moral delusions of perpetrators. The chaplains must have been aware that those who vigorously denied culpability and believed fervently in their own innocence endured the last moments with confidence and conviction. By contrast those were distressed by doubt and plagued by a guilty conscience had trouble facing death calmly and with a peaceful heart.

The Case of Werner Raabe: Tears of Remorse

Pastor Eckardt described only one instance in which a prisoner broke down crying during his confessional conversations. In his condolence letter to the father, Eckardt acknowledged that Dr. Werner Raabe was "overwhelmed by anguish over the entire enigma of such events" and "did not try to play down the magnitude of his transgression."[70] Dr. Raabe arrived in Landsberg from a prison in Berlin where he had interacted with a different prison chaplain, Pastor Harald Poelchau. Poelchau was well known for his political activism and commitment to the Confessing Church in Berlin. He had personally hidden Jews and supported members of the conspiracy against the regime, who were imprisoned by the Gestapo. His memoir, *Die letzten Stunden: Erinnerungen eines Gefängnispfarrers* (1949), is a tribute to those who were executed during the Third Reich for their opposition. Given Poelchau's background, could it be possible that his earlier involvement in the political resistance and clandestine aid to Jews affected his pastoral care in such a way that it put greater moral pressure on Dr. Raabe? Did Poelchau succeed where the prison chaplains in Landsberg failed? In a letter to Eckardt, Poelchau described his difficulties in nudging Dr. Raabe toward a more honest confrontation with his deed:

> You can believe me that it was definitely not easy to break the ice that surrounded this man when I first visited him. But slowly, over time, Raabe attached to me in a special way ... throughout the entire year I had the impression that Raabe carries around something that is directly related to the crime (robbery?) about which he did not talk with anyone, not even with his mother. I could not shake the impression that he took a secret into the grave that he did not divulge for incomprehensible reasons.[71]

Poelchau seemed to have applied all the skills of a prison chaplain in order to pry open Raabe's heart and to prod him toward repentance. With empathy and kindness, as well as suspicion and critical scrutiny, Poelchau tried to enable Raabe to come to contrition on the basis of a truthful acknowledgment of what had happened.

Truthful knowledge and contrition are essential steps in the process of repentance according to Lutheran doctrine as spelled out in the Augsburg Confession of 1530. This creed defined repentance as a three-step process: "One is contrition, that is, terrors smiting the conscience through the knowledge of sin; the other is faith, which, born of the Gospel, or of absolution, believes that, for Christ's sake, sins are forgiven, comforts the conscience and delivers it from terrors. The good works are bound to follow, which are the fruits of repentance."[72] The reformers used words such as terror, pain, and horror to describe the affliction caused by knowledge of wrongdoing. They were fully aware of the devastating emotional and psychological costs of the realization of guilt. Remorse is costly even under normal circumstances, but it may be life-threatening in the aftermath of atrocity and mass violence, as Martin Niemöller recognized:

> If a person were to acknowledge [such wrongdoing], could he live another moment, could he find another hour of sleep, would he not have to depart into the night like Judas and hang himself? That is why people hang themselves when they come to realization of their responsibility.[73]

Dr. Werner Raabe had, in fact, attempted suicide. He was diagnosed with "reactive depression" and put on medication in June 1948.[74] In his letter to the father, Waldemar Raabe, Pastor Eckardt wrote: "He was so shaken up, as you know that he intended to end his life of his own accord, in the Prison Lehrter Strasse [Berlin]. This attempt was destined to fail. In the hours of our meetings I had opportunity to gain insight into the inner transformation granted to him by the grace of God during the year of his imprisonment."[75] Raabe's incarceration, depression, and suicide attempt engulfed the rest of his family: both his mother and his father were hospitalized at different points during his imprisonment, trial, and transfer to Landsberg. In contrast to most other Landsberg prisoners on death row, Raabe did not declare his innocence under the gallows. Although he objected to the death sentence, he declared his love of America, asked God to protect his relatives, and said: "Long live America, long live Germany. I am ready."[76]

He was executed on January 9, 1949, at the age of twenty-seven, in the War Crimes Prison 1 Landsberg. But he was not a war criminal. Instead, he had killed an American soldier during a botched black market transaction. The young dentist had battered an American GI with an ax on the Tempelhof airfield when the latter demanded more than the agreed-upon 30,000 reichsmarks for 312 cans of chocolate sauce.[77] Raabe's crime, then, corresponded to classic definitions of crime. Motivated by "base motives" such as greed or fear (the defense lawyer had pleaded self-defense), he had broken the law and killed a man. As a criminal, Raabe faced immediate censure by the community whose laws he had broken. The court, the chaplains, his family, and he himself all recognized the wrongful nature of this act. Raabe's remorse was not the result of Poelchau's superior pastoral skills or greater political acuity but a product of the different nature of the offense. While Raabe may have objected to the severity of the sentence, no one doubted that he had broken the law.

Besides Raabe, there are two other men whose last words indicated regret. Neither of them, I realized eventually, was executed for Nazi atrocities. Their statements are worth quoting, not only because they express unambiguous remorse, but also because they complicate the moral picture in Landsberg. One of the men was Paul Rübsamen, who was tried in Dachau and said shortly before his execution on July 15, 1947:

> Good-bye, American buddies. I regret once more here at the scaffolds in front of God that I had to carry out a criminal order, but

I hope God is with me. I wish to express once more in front of my American comrades that I deeply regret having shot one American soldier.[78]

Rübsamen was convicted for having "willfully, deliberately and wrongfully encourage[d], aid[ed], abet[ted] and participate[d] in killing of an unknown member of the United States Army, who was then an unarmed surrendered prisoner of war of the then German Reich."[79] He received the death penalty for failing to take a downed American pilot into custody and protecting him from a mob of "local citizens" who demanded his death. During his trial Rübsamen testified that he was sorry he was swayed by the crowd to commit the act on September 27, 1944,[80] and his last statement under the gallows reiterated his sincere contrition over his failure to stop the retaliatory violence.

The third statement of remorse comes from Jaroslaw Werbinski, who said on May 27, 1947: "I am sorry to have made such a wrong step. I hope that God in heaven will pardon me for the fault I did."[81] Werbinski was convicted by a U.S. military court in Munich on charges on murder, assault, and robbery. He was executed by firing squad, which was considered a privilege that was accorded only to non-German nationals. Werbinski was a Polish citizen. With him were twenty-nine other Polish convicts who were executed by firing squad in Landsberg, according to the list of executed prisoners from March 4, 1950.[82]

These three men were the exceptions among the 133 last words from the Executee Files. They expressed remorse, and they were not Nazis. They had no ideological basis to justify their actions. Although all these men took a life, the act of killing is processed entirely differently depending on the context. Those who committed individual crimes used the vocabulary of regret, wrongdoing, guilt, and forgiveness. But those implicated in atrocities did not. Therefore, the moral and ritual language of the prison chaplains failed to penetrate their armor. Without the terror of contrition that smites the conscience, there can be no deliverance. Nazi perpetrators defied the traditional terminology of guilt and forgiveness, crime and punishment, because they refused to see the problem.

Moral Ambiguities: The Executions in Landsberg

Despite its name, WCP 1 was not reserved for war criminals. Dr. Werner Raabe and Jaroslaw Werbinski were duly sentenced in military courts for breaking the law, while Paul Rübsamen was convicted in the Dachau trials for violating the Geneva Conventions. There were different categories of prisoners in WCP 1 Landsberg, and their last words cannot be analyzed exclusively in light of politically motivated crimes. The moral condition of the inmates in Landsberg was more complex, and in some cases the prison chaplains were not wrong when they protested the legitimacy of these sentences. Pastor Hess commented on the situation in his letter to Eckardt:

> Nowhere else have I confronted the fragility of human conceptions of guilt as much as here in Landsberg, where you will encounter some who consider murder justifiable, while others designate obvious combat situations murder.... You will deal with those who are definitely innocent by virtue of human law and who suffer because of the injustice done to them; while others among them are children of Satan and horrible murderers. The fact that they sit side by side seems to me, theologically speaking, a clear indication that justice cannot be merely a human affair but must ultimately rest in the hands of God.[83]

Hess's assessment was, in fact, an accurate description of the moral ambiguities facing the prison chaplains. Some prisoners were hanged although they were not guilty of atrocities, while others were released although deeply implicated in heinous policies. Three categories of prisoners were executed alongside ideologically committed Nazi perpetrators in Landsberg: foreign displaced persons, kapos and former concentration camp inmates, and German officials and civilians who retaliated against downed U.S. pilots.

Many of the Polish nationals executed in Landsberg were freed slave laborers and displaced persons (DPs) who came into conflict with military law that tried to impose order in the war-ravaged and starving country. By March 1950, the U.S. had executed twenty-nine prisoners by firing squad, an execution method reserved for non-Germans. In the British zone, the majority of executions involved non-German convicts, as Richard Evans establishes in the following statistic: "From July to December 1945, 56 Germans and 67 Poles (52% of the total) were sentenced to death. From January to June the figures were 35 Germans and 73 Poles (65%), in the second half of the same year, 33 Germans condemned and 57 Poles (61%)."[84] These Polish nationals had been freed from concentration camps or slave labor arrangements and organized street gangs and black market schemes that brought them into conflict with the occupation authorities.

> [They] roamed the countryside in search of food and booty. After years of cruel exploitation by the Germans and subjection to injustice and lawlessness of the Nazis, many displaced persons considered that they had every right to get their own back, and saw nothing wrong in carrying arms [which carried the death penalty in all military zones of occupation] now that they were on the winning side.[85]

Very few of the foreign nationals executed in Landsberg left last statements, possibly because of language and translation issues. Those who did protested their death sentences as unjust. For instance, Metschislaw Kowalczyk was transferred from the U.S. military court in Aalen, which handled criminal cases, and pleaded in his last words: "I already saw liberty and I want our country to be free. I have been brought to Germany by force and I waited a long time for liberation by the Allies. I have never expected that I'll meet such a fate. I hate to die in Germany."[86] Similarly, Dimitrios Kosturos, who was convicted in U.S. military court in Wetzlar, complained: "I am Greek prisoner of war. I have fought in the front line against Italian Fashism [*sic*].... It is a pity that the Americans are to shoot today on the 14 February such a prisoner of war who so long was kept in German Prisoner of Warship [*sic*]. But I am not afraid of the bullets which are going to hit me, for I am going to see my brother 'Engel' and my father God."[87] These prisoners were duly convicted of breaking the law, but in light of their traumatic experiences and the chaos of postwar Germany, execution seems an overly severe sentence.

The second group would receive more understanding and leniency in the contemporary world: former concentration camp inmates who had been pressed into service by the camp administration. They are known as "prisoner functionaries," because they were recruited with the promise of more food and greater privileges in return for controlling, guarding, and terrorizing their fellow prisoners. These prisoner functionaries also proclaimed their innocence when they stepped under the gallows. For example, former inmate Julius Straub, who had been imprisoned in Flossenbürg since 1940, declared before his execution: "It is an honor for me to die innocent. I am ready."[88] Former Mauthausen and Gusen inmate Karl Horcicka stated: "Greet everybody for me. Greet my people and tell them that I am innocent."[89] Rudolf Fiegl, a kapo from Mauthausen, said: "No, I haven't anything more to say but that I am dying innocent."[90] Should we differentiate their affirmations of innocence from the last words delivered by the SS guards of these same camps? Did the extraordinary physical brutality that was attributed to these men warrant the death penalty?[91] In the wake of Primo Levi, many have struggled with the moral conundrum of the "gray zone" of coerced complicity in atrocities.[92] Primo Levi felt deeply conflicted over "the death sentence of the sadistic *Kapo*, decided upon and executed without appeal, silently, with the stroke of an eraser."[93] He commented on kapos who were killed immediately upon liberation, but he also cautioned against their sentencing in courts of law and argued that kapos ought to be measured by a different set of moral standards than those who volunteered for SS service and reaped the benefits of career advancement and profit associated with concentration camp assignments.

Finally, there were German civilians and civil servants who were executed for killing U.S. pilots after they had parachuted to safety from airplanes en route to and from bombing missions over German cities. Around seventy death row candidates were convicted for violating international laws of conduct in war and the Geneva Conventions. Downed U.S. pilots were, of course, combatants, and some of them were killed in retaliation by angry mobs. For instance, Margarete Witzler was sentenced to twenty-five years in prison for "inciting a mob to kill U.S. fliers," a sentence she served in Dachau as a war criminal.[94] Many of those who were executed for mistreatment of U.S. pilots also proclaimed their innocence:

JOHANN SCHNEIDER: "I just want to say that I am dieing [sic] innocent. What I did does not justify such a sentence. God knows that I am not guilty and he will take revenge on those who execute me. I am ready."[95]

JOHANN SCHMITZ: "I just want to say, that I am not guilty. God stay with me in my last death struggle."[96]

CHRISTIAN MENRATH: "Americans, it is out of the question for me to assure you once more here in the last minute of my innocence. I had time enough to do that. But it didn't help me. You may kill my body, but not my spirit, for it will continue to live within my children. Hangman, do your duty!"[97]

RICHARD FRITZ GIRKE: "I protest against this execution of my sentence. As an officer I have done my duty for my people and my country when taking military orders to have those terror fliers executed, who shot women and children on open roads."[98]

Some killings of U.S. pilots were spontaneous, while others occurred as a matter of policy. Certainly the treatment of Soviet POWs was an integral element of the "war of annihilation" waged against the Soviet Union. The cases involving U.S. pilots were more isolated and sometimes involved civilians. Such retaliations can be understood in the context of crimes committed out of rage and revenge rather than ideology. The indiscriminate treatment of this category of prisoners fueled solidarity movements and united disparate sectors within the German public in opposition to the prosecution of war crimes. The growing sympathy benefited high-ranking Nazi perpetrators and led to growing public endorsement of clemency campaigns that demanded commutation of the convictions. In fact, by 1958, the Landsberg prison closed, and all prisoners were released.

Awkward Continuities: The Executioners in Landsberg

The executions in Landsberg also created disturbing parallels with the practices and policies of the Nazi state. There was the employment of the old hangmen who were released from prison and rehired.[99] There were the old gallows and guillotines that were recommissioned. Even the crematories were reactivated, as Dr. Roy A. Martin, the U.S. Army doctor who certified the death of executed "main war criminals" in October 1946, reported.[100] These continuities raised troubling questions, and the Landsberg prisoners knew just how to manipulate this in order to claim the moral high ground. They obviously had an immediate interest in stopping the executions to save their own lives. But they also began to question the legitimacy of lethal violence as a tool in the hands of the state.

The prison chaplains were challenged about their presence during executions and asked whether their participation lent sacred authority to the proceedings. Pastor Eckardt was advised by his predecessor to defend his accompaniment of convicts from the beginning: "You will see much heroism, and one must not deprive these people of their last protective shelter," Pastor Hess insisted.[101] The chaplains categorically defended the duty of prison chaplains to provide this service to the *Todgeweihte*, the death candidates. But Pastor Eckardt also spoke up for prisoners who refused to participate in the execution of others. When prisoners objected to their recruitment by American prison administration and were punished with solitary confinement for their refusal to build a shooting range for the execution of Polish prisoners, Pastor Eckardt intervened on their behalf:

> In all these cases, when tasks need to be performed in connection with executions (I could mention other examples), one should ask whether it would not be smarter to have these jobs completed by employees rather than by prisoners, among whom are some who have been given heavy sentences for their participation in or indirect contributions to executions.[102]

Hans Hermann Schmidt, for instance, addressed his executioners directly in his last words: "I declare that I have done nothing else than what you, sirs, are doing right now: I have executed orders that had been legally given to me."[103] In the photograph of him under the gallows, he is flanked by two U.S. soldiers whose faces have been scratched out. Although the executions in Buchenwald were quantitatively and qualitatively incomparable, the parallels and continuities were disturbing. The irony of applying the death penalty to punish people who were found guilty of executing people was not lost on the prisoners in Landsberg.[104]

Allied Law No. 1 tried to undo the legal perversions of the Nazi penal system by declaring all Nazi verdicts null and void. But it retained the death penalty, which was the law of the land in the United States, France, Great Britain, and the Soviet Union. General Dwight D. Eisenhower signed Law Number No. 1 for the Allied Supreme Command in Germany, which read:

> No cruel or excessive punishment is permitted. The death penalty is abolished except for offenses which were punishable by death according to a law which was either in force prior to 30 January 1933 or has been promulgated by the Military Government or sanctioned by it.[105]

One unintended side effect of the executions in Landsberg was the abolition of the death penalty in the newly founded Federal Republic of Germany. Conservative politicians, who were intent on saving the convicts of Landsberg, joined forces with political progressives and agreed to ban the death penalty from the new constitution. When the Basic Law (Grundgesetz) of the Federal Republic of Germany went into effect in May

1949, the death penalty was renounced. "A Gift of the Nazis," proclaimed a reviewer of *Rituals of Retribution*, Richard Evans's study of the history of death penalty in Germany. Evans shows that the defense of Nazi perpetrators contributed significantly to turn conservative supporters of law and order as well as popular opinion against the death penalty. Once the Federal Republic of Germany abolished the state's power over life and death of its citizens, the Allies' continued use of capital punishment created internal contradictions that augmented charges of hypocrisy.

The chaplains strengthened the fortitude of convicts in preparation for their last ordeal and helped them reach a false sense of peace. The peace they proclaimed to prisoners in the last rituals of reconciliation was based on denial of culpable wrongdoing. The dignity of their last moments depended on a false sense of manly courage that appeared preferable to bitter tears of remorse. Invariably, the peaceful heart was built upon the repudiation of regret. Two more examples show the correlation of dignity and denial. Robert Ley, former National Socialist minister of labor, reassured his children in his last letter from his cell that he had found reconciliation with God:

> I am reconciled with God. I have sought his grace and his mercy and have prayed ardently to receive it. I have read the Holy Scripture and have faith that Christ, the Lord, died also for me at Golgotha. I am not desperate but rest calmly in God, my guide and my redeemer. His will be done.[106]

He then committed suicide in defiance of the scheduled execution, which he denounced as an injustice. The reconciliation with God was possible because he refused to even consider the possibility of culpability. The same scenario happened several years later during the execution of Adolf Eichmann. He insisted that his wife, Vera Eichmann, be given a message via the American prison chaplain, William L. Hull, that he had died in peace: "Tell my wife that I took it calmly and that I had peace in my heart, which guarantees to me that I am right."[107] The peace that Eichmann felt in his heart at the moment of his death was proof positive for him that his lifelong commitment to National Socialism could not have been false. His courage and composure nevertheless impressed Pastor Hull, an American Pentecostal from the Zion Apostolic Mission in Jerusalem, who accompanied Eichmann to the gallows. When Eichmann was hanged on May 13, 1961, Hull reported that he "died courageously. He did not break down, he did not weaken ... this one thing is clear: he died boldly."[108] The performance of dignity was possible because Eichmann protected his sense of integrity and self-worth by shoring up his ideological principles and by putting up protective shields against the possibility of remorse. Strength and manly comportment took precedence over moral discernment. Executions promise quick solutions to the punishment of the guilty, but they do little to change ideologies. On the contrary, they harden the heart and stiffen the neck of perpetrators and their families. They leave the task of critical engagement and detoxification of poisonous ideologies to the descendants.

4

Cleansed by Suffering?

THE SS GENERAL AND THE HUMAN BEAST

*In the purgatory of extreme abandonment I was purified
towards true faith in God.*
OSWALD POHL, *Credo: Mein Weg zu Gott*[1]

THE LANGUAGE OF purification envisions guilt as a stain, an imaginary blot on the soul that can and must be cleansed. According to our religious traditions, guilt is cleansed by way of suffering. Penance and penitential practices have laid the groundwork for the modern institution of the penitentiary, and secular criminal law has elaborated the notion that retributive suffering in prison serves to reform and rehabilitate wayward criminals.[2] In the aftermath of the Holocaust, the Christian rhetoric of purgatory and hell occurs quite frequently. As places of punitive suffering in the afterlife, hell and purgatory provide a language to consider the meaning and goals of suffering. Irrespective of their belief in heaven, hell, and purgatory, survivors and commentators invoke these metaphors to probe the meaning and limits of suffering. Can suffering ever be said to purify the soul, restore the culpable, or relieve the burden of guilt? Or does suffering invariably dehumanize, degrade, crush, and demoralize its victims without hope for redemption? Is there a difference between affliction in purgatory and torment in hell?

General of the Waffen-SS Oswald Pohl used the language of purgation to interpret his punishment in Landsberg and to assert his faith in redemption as a result of "the purgatory of extreme abandonment." He chronicled his conversion to Roman Catholicism in a booklet titled *Credo: My Path to God*, where he credited his incarceration, trial, and conviction with finding "true faith in God." Pohl projected confidence in his redemption and his purification of guilt. Of course, a closer reading of his autobiography reveals his utter denial of culpable wrongdoing, as well as his chaplain's complicity in guilt denial. But his suffering and its perception by the prison chaplain and the wider German public contrasts sharply with the extreme abandonment endured by survivors of the hell that he oversaw.

Oswald Pohl: "I Never Killed Anybody"

As General of the Waffen-SS and chief of the SS Economic and Administrative Main Office (Wirtschafts- und Verwaltungshauptamt) in Berlin, Pohl was the official responsible for the "program of extermination by labor." He oversaw the economic aspects of the enslavement, expropriation, and industrial use of millions of people in the concentration camp system. From the outset, beginning in February 1934, Pohl's career of administering the financial affairs of the SS included the concentration camp of Dachau.³ He was a close personal friend of Heinrich Himmler and, in the words of Auschwitz commander Rudolf Höß, "the most willing and obedient executioner of the wishes and plans of RF-SS [*Reichsführer of the SS*] Heinrich Himmler."⁴ He administered the establishment and operation of factories in and around the concentration camps, the creation of brothels to reward productivity,⁵ the collection and use of gold dental fillings, glasses, shoes, clothes, and the hair of murdered Jews as well as of other inmates who succumbed to the working and living conditions in the camps.⁶ Death by starvation and ruthless exploitation of labor fed the coffers of the SS economic empire under his leadership.⁷ After the war, Pohl was convicted in the Subsequent Nuremberg Trials against members of the SS Economic and Administrative Main Office that occurred between January 13, 1947, and November 3, 1947. He received the death sentence and was among the last seven men hanged in Landsberg on June 7, 1951.

Pohl came under the tutelage of Father Morgenschweis, the Roman Catholic prison chaplain who rebaptized him and conducted the celebration of the Eucharist on February 12, 1950. According to Morgenschweis, Pohl's conversion "occurred exclusively under the influence of the grace of God"⁸ and without consideration of possible effects on averting the death penalty. "The desire originated with him ... when he heard God's summons for his soul to return home."⁹ In his foreword to Pohl's *Credo*, Father Morgenschweis described his obligation to

> paint a portrait of Pohl as I know him from my immediate interactions ... as well as on the basis of my knowledge of human nature

[*Menschenkenntnis*] derived from twenty years of working in prisons. Pohl is an officer from head to toe, an officer in substance and character, in his internal and external bearing and behavior, a man full of energy, will power, and determination, a man of high cultivation of the mind and heart, upright, straight, and genuine. He now demonstrates these qualities as a Catholic, filled with deep and living faith, with burning love for Christ in the Eucharist and for the church.[10]

Oswald Pohl's spiritual autobiography, *Credo: Mein Weg zu Gott*, was published under church auspices in 1950 and circulated widely.[11] According to Morgenschweis, it was "written by [Pohl] himself,"[12] but this is unlikely. The style and content of this seventy-five-page conversion narrative presuppose considerable theological training, which Pohl could not have acquired in prison. It is more likely that *Credo* reflects Father Morgenschweis's theological and pastoral agenda, for which Pohl supplied the biographical background.[13] In his foreword Morgenschweis summarizes Pohl's intention: "to publicly renounce his prior religious and ideological creed and his former life as well as to publicly profess his allegiance to the Catholic Church."[14] In the competitive missionary atmosphere, Pohl's conversion to Roman Catholicism constituted a victory. His baptism and confirmation in the Protestant Church was declared invalid, and he was given a second baptism *sub conditione* by Father Morgenschweis, a more widespread practice in Italy and Austria than in Germany.[15] Pohl had left the Protestant Church in 1936, disillusioned by the "disgusting infighting of the Evangelical Church between 'German Christians,' the 'German faith movement,' the 'Confessing Church' and other 'contesting groups' presented to the faithful."[16] He embraced the SS religion of "believer in God" (*gottgläubig*) and claimed that "authentic religious sentiment...was not suffocated under the black uniform"[17] of the SS.

Like his Protestant fellow prisoner Hans Hermann Schmidt, Pohl's religious life was characterized by the quest for inner peace. Father Morgenschweis reported that

a deep inner calmness and equilibrium poured into him after his conversion, and he completely submits to God and carries his uncertain fate with meekness and peace. I always find him in such holy and profound joy and bliss reminiscent of Saint Paul, who calls out (Cor. 7:4): "I am greatly encouraged; in all our troubles my joy knows no bounds."[18]

Morgenschweis presented Pohl as a deeply pious man who was immersed in prayer and Eucharistic devotion. Such inner peace, as shown in the previous chapter, was built upon rigorous suppression of remorse. Usually, whenever Pohl's text approaches the consideration of "guilt," the term is placed within quotation marks. His section on guilt begins with the following rhetorical question:

> Although I never killed anybody, or asked or encouraged anybody to so, and although I energetically opposed inhuman behaviors [*Unmenschlichkeiten*], if I was informed of them, as can be proven [*nachweisbar*]—did this acquit me of "guilt"?[19]

At the outset, Pohl categorically rejected personal responsibility for the approximately eleven million people who died in the camp system under his control. Instead, he tried to assign blame for these murders to unnamed subordinates and illusive bad apples who failed to inform him of inhuman conditions in the camps. As much as possible he sought to distance himself from the ruthless realities in the camps. His powerful post in Berlin insulated him from the corporeality of death and destruction. He, like the interned women in Camp 77, claimed ignorance and proclaimed his innocence on the basis of his physical distance from the daily brutality of the camps. This rhetoric, for all its crude delusion, did not fail to impress his audience, beginning with his smitten prison chaplain.

Pohl seemed to have recognized that he would be required to shoulder some guilt and proceeded to admit "co-responsibility" (*Mitschuld*) for the moral corruption of National Socialism. However, he located culpable wrongdoing in the ideological collapse of National Socialism upon its military defeat. He vigorously denounced the treachery and disloyalty of his comrades who dared to testify against him in court:

> Now that I was imprisoned and henceforth prevented from observing their actions in the external world, I observed all the more sharply the selection [*Auslese*] of those who testified as witnesses and defendants in the Nuremberg trials. Where was the proud courage of conviction that thundered through the German *Gaue* [regions] and with which high and highest leaders manifested their

untouchable and infallible position? Where was the professed ideal that "Loyalty is the mark of honor" (Hindenburg) and "Your honor means allegiance" (Himmler)?[20]

The failure of his colleagues and subordinates to stand firm on Nazi principles after the defeat convinced Pohl of the bankruptcy of NS ideology. He was "gripped by horror over such moral depravity" when he saw "the 'heroes' who gave tortured testimony as 'principal witness' against their own comrades."[21] Their betrayal and spinelessness, he maintained, was not rooted in individual moral failing but the result of ideological shortcomings: "That this 'Weltanschauung' would end up in such a moral and ethical swamp is not merely the fault of human beings...but caused directly by flaws in the ideology itself."[22] The "moral failure of the elite of National Socialism" is attributed in *Credo* to the "renunciation of commitments that are rooted in the depth of the soul and strive toward transcendence; they were replaced by fictions. The person was torn from transcendent commitments, and the meaning of his life was redirected toward this-worldly affairs" (45). This, he wrote, is "my co-responsibility, hence 'guilt.'"[23] But even though he misnamed the central evil of National Socialism and explicitly excluded the murder of millions, Pohl could not bring himself to acknowledge guilt without the use of quotation marks: "That I did not recognize my error in a timely manner makes me no less 'guilty' or even blameless."[24]

Pohl mostly regretted having lost the war. He was, however, not willing to denounce his "honest, devoted, idealistic, and enthusiastic service not for the party but for my fatherland, which I solely saw and in whose victory I believed until the catastrophe."[25] The catastrophe referred to Nazi Germany's military defeat, not the murder of millions. The enslavement and extermination of people whose property, work, and bodies produced the wealth that Pohl administered was not mentioned. Not even once. There is only one veiled allusion to the extraordinary nature of violence: Pohl acknowledged that "not much remained hidden from me, even if I did not participate in it personally—much against which healthy sentiments would have doubtlessly rebelled under normal circumstances."[26] Such vague hints about the "apocalyptic forms" of the "methods of violence of National Socialism" were immediately discounted with a reference to the "conscience of the all too many who remained silent although they were not deaf-mutes."[27] He tried to implicate a silent majority for failing to speak up, knowing full well that anyone who dared to do so could be incarcerated and killed. Like the women in Camp 77, Pohl implicated not only the German collective but the entire world.[28] By universalizing guilt, he tried to exonerate himself.

The extent of Pohl's sense of contrition is clearly debatable. But he felt ready to move out of purgatory. He did not want to dwell on the evils of the past but wanted to talk about the "highpoint of my entire life,"[29] his experience of the sacrament of reconciliation. In glowing words he described his yearning for the Holy Eucharist and desire to receive "the seeds of divine revelation."[30] His first Communion "shook me to the depth of my soul. My eyes saw more lightness than ever before; they looked into a new world; marvelous visions passed before my inner eye."[31]

> The moment of conversion filled me with a yearning love. But it is this love, on which everything else depends, because it is the essence and goal of Christianity; everything else is a means toward this goal: Sermon and gospel, sacraments, fasting and prayer—all of those are designed to coach us toward love, to ignite love in us, to nourish and perfect it, to strengthen, purify, and fortify it: true love for God and our neighbor.[32]

Purified and fortified in the love of God, Pohl wanted to look forward without looking back. The love he claimed to have experienced did not entail contrition and recognition of guilt, but felt to him like a release from the burden of the past. He believed that his sins were cleansed miraculously when he "made his life's confession," which he vowed was truthful because "God cannot be deceived!" His confession and absolution worked like a miraculous stain remover and created a barrier between his old and his new life:

> I have made a resolute and clean break with my previous life. Whatever was good in it, I have taken as uplifting memories into my reborn life. Whatever was bad, that which caused the minus balance, my innumerable sins, I carried humbly before God in prayer and fasting. That he took them from me, I feel as his immeasurable grace in my life.[33]

The burden of his "innumerable sins" was mysteriously lifted as he claimed to be reborn into the church. While the Catholic dogmatic tradition can contest such reductionist claims of reconciliation, there is no evidence that Roman Catholic priests denied conversion and Communion requests by former Nazis over a perceived lack of repentance. Instead, confession and conversion served as "get out of purgatory free" cards that opened a way out of contrition.

FIGURE 4.1. Eleanore Pohl, "Between Faith and Doubt." (From Pohl, *Credo*, 27.)

The image in figure 4.1 was drawn by his second wife, Eleanore Pohl, and conveys this concept of reconciliation as a "resolute and clean break." The text box "Between Faith and Doubt" visually divides former militarism and intellectualism from the cosmic lightness and harmonious swirl of the heavens. Sin and evil are represented by books and the Enlightenment project of critical inquiry, as well as by the sword and military violence. The small man who ascends toward the heavenly light has left behind the chaos and violence emanating from book knowledge and "earthly wisdom." He has been purified and his load has been lightened. Such purification was accomplished by God's "rods of punishment" that whipped Pohl and "poured out over me all the wretchedness of life: denunciation, humiliation, physical and psychological abuse, the earthly court of justice, and the scaffold."[34] Pohl asserted that

> only in the gruesome ruins of this life did I recognize the will of God. I submitted consciously and willingly and confessed my guilt and all of my sins truthfully, and accepted all of the misery and my suffering as his test for my purification [Läuterung]. I affirmed them sincerely and took them into my life, because I realized that no suffering arises without guilt, and that all afflictions have their cause. Knowingly or unknowingly even I had become guilty, and not only as an SS general. Where I have erred, this error has become my salutary path toward truth.[35]

His penitential suffering, unfortunately, did not include lessons in compassion for the victims of the camp system. The language of purgatorial suffering concealed the existence of those who suffered the effects of his "errors" and wrongful actions. His purification remained self-centered, caught in delusion and deception. Whatever suffering Pohl endured (and it certainly did not compare to the suffering in the concentration camps), it did not succeed in extending his moral universe to include the degraded and dehumanized of the camps.

The "rods of punishment" failed to dismantle the validity of his political ideology or to purge his totalitarian thinking. On the contrary, Pohl repackaged his most deeply held beliefs in the language of Christianity, which filled "the vacuum left by the collapse of all ideals, not least those of the political Weltanschauung."[36] He praised those aspects of the Roman Catholicism that confirmed his totalitarian proclivities, his desire for hierarchy, and his submission to a Führer. What attracted him was the

> strong spirit of order and the authoritative leadership that characterizes the Catholic Church above all other Christian churches, which impressed me greatly; since order and unity, leadership and obedience resonate with military sensitivities. Even Paul took his

cues from the world of the army and sports in order to describe the reorientation of the inner world to Christ's new order.[37]

Pohl embraced the "clarity and internal cohesion of its faith truths, the security and firmness of its doctrinal system, the solemnity and beauty of its worship service, the significance and effectiveness of its sacraments" (60). None of this required that he wrestle with or dismantle his National Socialist presuppositions. The new Christian identity he fashioned was designed to prevent ideological disorientation as he installed Roman Catholic rites and doctrines to satisfy his need for clear command structures and unconditional obedience: "The deliverance from this moral and ethical morass of humanity will only happen by way of unconditional profession of faith to the triune God as the absolute measure of all ethical values."[38] The rigid, antidemocratic, and antipluralist principles underlying National Socialism were now proclaimed as Christian truths. In other words, his conversion integrated Christianity into his totalitarian, militarist, and hierarchical worldview rather than the other way around. In truth, Pohl did not want to change, and he made this quite clear in his last words in Landsberg. On the way to the gallows he was recorded shouting: "Long live Germany." While standing under the gallows he summed up his last testament:

> For more than thirty years I have served as a professional soldier, twenty-two years of which were with the marines [*sic*; should be translated as navy]. During this long period the Americans were not able to prove or lay at my feet that I had given any orders or initiated anything, which led to the persecution or execution of people, especially Jews. I die firm in the believe [*sic*] in God in three persons. God, have mercy on my family, my faithful wife, and free Germany from its bad friends.[39]

Pohl lied to the end. He had never set foot on a battleground during World War II, but claimed to have been convicted as a soldier. He had, in fact, "given orders" and "initiated" policies to kill Jews and non-Jews in the camps as their economic manager. But, and this is troubling, despite these outright lies, Pohl could count on numerous supporters who organized a nationwide amnesty campaign. His lack of truthfulness and defiant rejection of contrition did not diminish his popularity as a pious convert to Christianity. Many, including then-chancellor Konrad Adenauer, appealed directly to the pope, asking for a papal intervention to spare his life.[40]

If someone refuses to repent and dies without being reconciled, does he go to hell? Should he go to hell? When I asked this question, rather facetiously, during a lecture in the Akademie der Diözese Stuttgart-Rottenburg, I was taken to task by systematic theologian Jan-Heiner Tück. Subsequently, Tück developed his theological response and asserted a position of universal reconciliation in the eschaton of the messianic end times, in which even someone like Pohl will eventually have to be forgiven.[41] In the process, he characterized my question as "new infernalism"[42] and suspected that the "supporters of the new infernalism...[want] the postmortal annihilation of the perpetrators following on the heels of the historical annihilation of victims."[43] In contrast, he invoked an "eschatological hope in which...nobody will be left to eternal death."[44] While I am flattered to be credited as initiator of a new infernalist movement, I find my concern gravely mischaracterized.

Like Tück, I am aware of the dangers of writing individuals out of the moral community by wishing for their "annihilation." We should safeguard and protect the human worth and intrinsic human dignity of every human being, including heinous perpetrators. Pohl deserved the chance to change his ways. He was rightly given the opportunity to repent until he took his last breath. But he chose not to change his perspective on the suffering of victims and affirmed his abiding faith in the worldview of the SS in his last words. This failure, it seems to me, cannot be fixed posthumously. It is *this* refusal—even more than the original misdeed—that condemns him. His final rejection of remorse—as far as we human observers can ever determine this—cannot be undone. No one can be redeemed despite themselves, by divine fiat, as it were, in the eschaton.

A theological position that tasks God with patching things up in the afterlife violates basic Christian teachings on humanity's free will and human responsibility. Tück realizes that his notion that "everybody *without exception* will be saved"[45] potentially violates the "ethical gravity of human freedom" and that it, furthermore, coerces not only victims but also perpetrators into reconciliation. Neither victims nor perpetrators seem to have much choice in the matter. While this violates the moral freedom of perpetrators, it is an even more dramatic denial of the rights of victims, who were denied consideration and human dignity in the first place. Their original powerlessness is compounded by relentless pressure to grant forgiveness despite the lack of remorse on the part of perpetrators. Father

Morgenschweis already admonished those who had suffered harm at Pohl's hands: "May it [this book] reconcile those who still live in hatred over the injustice done to them by a system in which the former general of the Waffen-SS served. Today he serves God, Christ and his divine love in the world as a full Catholic."[46] His alleged redemption became the tool to compel victims to abdicate claims to justice and restitution. Pohl's release from the burden of guilt had not required asking consent of his debtors. Their degradation and dehumanization had been of little concern to Pohl or his chaplain. His victims were "still" living in hatred and struggled to move beyond the abjection they had endured. One of those was Klara Pförtsch.

Klara Pförtsch: "A Zeal to Do Evil"

In contrast to the pastoral care and political attentions enjoyed by Oswald Pohl, Klara Pförtsch received little support and no recognition. She left no written documents. Her case caught my attention because she was the only person whom Pastor Sachsse refused to endorse in his amnesty appeals before the French high commissioner. Pförtsch was called a *vraie bête humaine*, a true human beast, by the French military judges who sentenced her to death for her cruelty as a prisoner functionary (*Funktionshäftling*). The Nazis had arrested her in 1936 as a member of a Communist resistance group and transferred her to the women's concentration camp in Ravensbrück. There she was picked out of a lineup by the camp commander and recruited as prisoner functionary.[47] Later, Pförtsch was transferred to Auschwitz, where she rose to the rank of a *Lagerälteste*, female camp elder. In this privileged role, she enforced camp rules and administered beatings that brutalized her fellow prisoners. Pförtsch survived the hell of the Auschwitz, but she did not emerge cleansed.

The suffering endured by Pförtsch did not purify her but forced her to make immoral choices and to act within what Primo Levi has famously called the "gray zone." The camps overseen by Oswald Pohl were designed to crush the human spirit and to create conditions that would prove the depravity of those considered subhuman enemies of the Aryan nation. As filthy vermin, prisoners deserved no better. "To Each His Own" (*Jedem das Seine*) read the wrought iron gate at the entrance to the concentration camp of Buchenwald. Those who entered through these gates lost their claim to human dignity. Auschwitz survivor Primo Levi captured the

effects of these dehumanizing conditions, in his groundbreaking description of the gray zone.

> Coming out of the darkness, one suffered because of the reacquired
> consciousness of having been diminished. Not by our will, cow-
> ardice, or fault, yet nevertheless we had lived for months and years
> at an animal level: our days had been encumbered from dawn to
> dusk by hunger, fatigue, cold, and fear, and any space for reflection,
> reasoning, experiencing emotions was wiped out. We endured filth,
> promiscuity, and destitution, suffering much less than we would
> have suffered from such things in normal life, because our moral
> yardstick had changed. Furthermore, all of us had stolen....We had
> not only forgotten our country and our culture, but also our family,
> our past, the future we had imagined for ourselves, because, like
> animals, we were confined to the present moment.[48]

Such suffering is not purifying, such degradation is not uplifting. The
camps were hell and not purgatory, relentless and without possibility of
redemption. Suffering in hell is meaningless and crushes a person's spirit.
Not surprisingly, images of hell were often used by survivors to convey the
weight of lunacy, infamy, grime, and terror they had to endure. Martin
Niemöller, for instance, had this to say in 1946 about his experiences:

> I have been imprisoned for eight years. I never talk about my expe-
> riences on principle. I could tell horrible things....And when
> someone asks me: was it really that awful? I can only say that it was
> thousands of times worse....In former times, educated people
> laughed at the idea that there could be hell and damnation...but
> these [images from the sixteenth century] are child's play compared
> to the reality....Hell came to earth.[49]

As if to add insult to injury, the architects of hell remained seemingly
unaffected by the corrosive effects of these infernal conditions on the
human spirit. They were able to screen out the stench and filth and could
supervise the torture of people without losing much sleep over inflicting
such agony. It is profoundly puzzling and infuriating that atrocities wound
the very being of victims indelibly while the sanity and mental health of
perpetrators seem scarcely touched. Perpetrators enjoy the privileges of
power and propriety and surround themselves with the air of respectability.

The prison chaplains were not unaffected by this dynamic. They were impressed by the courtesy and personal conduct of men who concealed the depravity of their political projects. The survivors of hell, on the other hand, bore the marks of the ravages of violence and deprivation. They could not cover up the years spent in depravity. Father Morgenschweis praised Oswald Pohl for his military charisma and personal charm, while Klara Pförtsch's chaplain, Pastor Sachsse, was repulsed by the debilitating effects of her degradation.

Pastor Carl Sachsse, the Rhenish plenipotentiary for political prisoners in the French zone, treated Pförtsch differently from the SS men, Gestapo, and Nazi functionaries who received his assistance. He maintained files on 174 Nazi prisoners, who were all awaiting trials or serving their sentences in Wittlich, the French war crimes prison. According to historian Ronald Webster, these church offices played a "pivotal role...in securing the ultimate release of most of the convicted prisoners."[50] They argued on Christian pastoral grounds and praised mercy and compassion as supreme Christian virtues. They also reasoned on political grounds and maintained that the normalization of international relations would be aided by the speedy repatriation and reintegration of German nationals imprisoned for crimes committed during the Nazi period. Sachsse represented the interests of German prisoners in French internment camps and war crimes prisons between October 1945 and the official closure of the office in 1959. Webster concluded that these churchmen's involvement

> went beyond a merely spiritual concern to embrace an all-out personal effort ultimately to secure the release of even the most incriminated prisoners. These included men convicted of the roundup, deportation, and murder of Jews, as well as of "political prisoners," and of shooting numerous civilians in retaliation for what the Germans alleged were illegal partisan activities.[51]

It was all the more surprising to find that Sachsse could not be persuaded to intercede on behalf of Klara Pförtsch: "It seems entirely impossible that we petition on behalf of Klara Pförtsch. No other prisoner enjoys such a bad reputation as Miss Pförtsch."[52] Certainly, her gender played an important role, as did her class, her lack of education, and her former political affiliation with Communism. But more than anything it was the moral opprobrium of surviving the gray zone.

To reconstruct her story, one must rely on the words of others: the prison chaplain who felt morally conflicted about her, the military judges who condemned her, and former prisoners who defended her. What seems clear is that the suffering endured in the camps did not purify and uplift Pförtsch. While Pohl could claim that suffering transformed him from sinner into saint, Pförtsch was changed from political activist into a *vraie bête humaine.* She was condemned to death for *crimes de guerre* by the Tribunale de Ière Instance de Rastatt on November 9, 1949. On appeal the Tribunal Superieur de Rastatt of the French High Commission upheld her conviction on January 12, 1950. The judges called Klara Pförtsch a "veritable bête frappant" (a veritable battering beast) and could find "no extenuating circumstances in her favor."[53] But her life was spared, as Pastor Sachsse pointed out in a letter in 1952, not "because her crimes were deemed any less grave but solely because she is a woman and one does not like to execute women."[54] One year later, in 1953, Sachsse wrote that a deputy of High Commissioner André François-Poncet had urged him to remove Pförtsch's file from his documents after previewing the submissions because "he would only annoy the High Commissioner."[55] "I followed his advice,"[56] Sachsse admitted. A month earlier, in July 1953, he explained his reluctance to advocate on Pförtsch's behalf in a letter to the Landesverband Pfalz-Innere Mission:

I cannot make up my mind to submit the amnesty plea for Klara Pförtsch, and I am herewith returning it to you. I have petitioned three times for her and each time with embarrassing consequences. After the first time, François-Poncet introduced me to his guests during a social gathering as "Kirchenrat Sachsse who always lobbies for the worst offenders." He repeated the same characterization several times, with great graciousness but also with an unmistakable edge. The second time, I was advised by the deputy of François-Poncet, who leafed through the requests, to remove the petition for Pförtsch from the file; I would not accomplish anything by submitting it except annoy the High Commissioner. The third time I insisted, despite the deputy's repeated counsel against submission. Whether it was coincidental or not, for the first time none of my petitions were granted. Under these circumstances and for the benefit of the other prisoners, I request that you refrain from approaching me again with a petition for Pförtsch.[57]

Clearly stung by this unsavory introduction as "lobbyist for the worst offenders," Sachsse attributed his dubious reputation to his support for Pförtsch. Why her and not the other defendants for whom he went to bat? In his principled preference for forgiveness and amnesty, he did not usually make his support contingent on the nature of charges. Even the newly created Zentrale Rechtsschutzstelle (Central Legal Protection Office), established in 1950 in Bonn to coordinate and provide financial and legal assistance to Germans convicted of Nazi crimes, "considered the case of Klara Pförtsch particularly severe [*sehr schwerwiegend*]"[58] and refused to provide assistance.

We may assume that the mere fact of her gender caused outrage and consternation. Women who inflict physical harm break gender conventions. In general, women who are prosecuted for violent crimes are considered deviant.[59] Those who stood trial for Nazi crimes in postwar Germany can be grouped into three categories: informers whose denunciations led to the murder of their victims (so-called *Judasfrauen*),[60] nurses and medical doctors who participated in the euthanasia program,[61] and female SS associates who worked as concentration camp guards. Only the last category crossed the gender line. Most female defendants used "nonviolent" means, if one considers acts of betrayal, lethal injections, and secretarial services as nonviolent.[62] But female SS associates were trained as concentration camps guards in Ravensbrück, the women's concentration camp.[63] They received weapon's training, carried guns, and were outfitted with whips and dogs. They used these weapons as well as their hands for beatings.[64] After liberation, these women were considered particularly odious, and their cruelty stood out as exceptional.[65] And they were exceptional, as Kwiet's calculations shows:

> Some 500,000 males were recruited for mass shootings, gassings and other forms of killing. Fewer than 5,000 women might have been called on to act as guards, torturers and, occasionally, as killers. Some 3,500 women, largely recruited from the ranks of the BDM (League of German Girls) served as so-called *SS-Aufseherinnen*, female SS-supervisors, in concentration camps during the Second World War.[66]

The vast majority of genocidal violence is committed by men—a fact that is usually taken for granted and hence not further pursued. When Christopher Browning and Daniel Goldhagen undertook their analysis of ordinary executioners, the masculinity of their subjects was not examined. Feminist historians have only recently begun to trace the lives of women who were guilty of Nazi atrocities.[67] The archives of the women's camp in Ravensbrück, where all female SS guards were recruited and trained, confirms Kwiet's estimate of 3,500 female guards.[68] These overall numbers confirm that 99 percent of atrocities were committed by men.

Given these statistics, these women's abnormal gender behavior caused scandal and received extensive media coverage. "Again and again judges showed surprise that women could commit such crimes. . . . The behavior of women was seen as especially brutal because it violated gender norms."[69] The existence of female SS associates was shocking and scandalous. Such women received disproportionately higher sentences because their brutality violated the basic rules of civilization.[70] They were often likened to animals, *bête humaine*, "beasts"[71] or "witches."[72] Salacious reports about the "SS beast" Ilse Koch, wife of the camp commander of Buchenwald,[73] or about Irma Grese[74] were inflamed by sexualized and pornographic titillation.[75] The bestial character of female violence also shaped the memory of witnesses, who were particularly impacted by cruelty received at the hands of women. It was not uncommon for survivors to testify that the sadism of women exceeded the brutality of men.[76]

These gender dynamics became particularly evident in the Majdanek trial (1975–1981), where the longest sentences were imposed on female defendants. Majdanek was an extermination camp, where more than 300,000 people were killed between October 1941 and July 1944, among them 59,000 Jews. The trial involved six women and eleven men. The Regional Court of Düsseldorf convicted Hermine Ryan-Braunsteiner to life in prison and Hildegard Lächert to twelve years, while the men received prison terms ranging from three to ten years. Elisa Mailaender-Koslov examined the proceedings and concluded that gender expectations shaped not only the judges and the media but the witnesses themselves. In their testimony, the witnesses "remembered violence committed by women more often and more clearly. The shock elicited by female acts of violence among survivors and trial participants was notable."[77] The witnesses could identify the women accurately even decades after the events. Their recollections were less sharp and precise when it came to the men. Several of the male defendants were also acquitted for reasons of ill health or old age. Needless to say, the women held less power and authority in the administration of the camp. They were not even full members of the SS but subject to male control. Their convictions reflect the scandal of female violence. When "women deviate from this mold [of femininity, they] are likely to be treated the same as their male counterparts...[or] they may be punished even more harshly," argued criminologist Dana Britton.[78] Women who use lethal violence face stiffer sentences and harsher condemnation.

Klara Pförtsch was imprisoned alongside female SS associates, and Pastor Sachsse was quite aware that the French considered such women "truly horrific and cruel criminals."[79] In the case of female SS associate Irene Imort, a former Ravensbrück guard,[80] Sachsse noted that "the French feel extremely angry toward the guards in this particular camp [Neubremme], and they explained repeatedly that one could understand why *men* participated in such torture typical of concentration camps in the general war psychosis, but that one could simply not comprehend such behavior among *women*" (emphasis in original).[81] Although Sachsse shared this intuitive aversion, he was willing to proceed in the case of Irene Imort, as he explained in a letter to a colleague: "I have described these facts in some detail in order to allow you to appreciate how difficult it is to intercede on behalf of these women But I will try again in the coming days and have already made an appointment with François-Poncet."[82] Why would Sachsse be willing to "gladly assume that Miss Imort never participated in any such tortures"[83] but refuse to extend such benefit of doubt to Klara Pförtsch?

Pförtsch did not fit the expectations of a "good victim." Her years of systematic degradation left her physically broken and morally compromised. She was arrested in October 1936 on suspicion of "high treason," tried in Munich, and released in 1937. She was rearrested in 1938 and convicted of "high treason" by the notorious Volksgerichtshof in Berlin on November 19, 1940, and was sentenced to two years' imprisonment. After she served the two months that remained of her sentence after counting time served, she was not set free but sent to the women's concentration camp of Ravensbrück as a political prisoner wearing a red triangle in the spring of 1940. In May 1941, she was appointed "camp elder" of Ravensbrück, the highest function for a camp prisoner. She was moved to Auschwitz-Birkenau in October 1942 together with five hundred Jewish Ravensbrück inmates, who were killed upon arrival. She was registered in Auschwitz and was made *Lagerälteste* by SS Associate Mandel by March 1943. She contracted typhus and spent three months in the *Strafblock* (prison block) for breaking camp rules. In the fall of 1944, she was transported to the concentration camp in Geislingen, where she was again made

Lagerälteste. When she was liberated by the U.S. Army, she was in Dachau, again as *Lagerälteste.*[84] Pförtsch returned to her hometown, Hof, where she was recognized by survivors and arrested in December 1945. The American military court sentenced her to three years on December 21, 1945. When she was released on December 17, 1948, she moved to Leipzig in the Soviet zone. There she attended a meeting of former Ravensbrück inmates in the spring of 1949 and was recognized as "camp elder" and extradited to the French zone. The French military court in Rastatt indicted Pfoertsch for "war crimes" and charged her with "extreme cruelty"[85] as "camp elder" in Auschwitz-Birkenau. She was sentenced to death on May 29, 1949, for the murder of women who had to be sent to the infirmary after she had beaten them, where they were selected and sent to the gas chambers. The French court also held her accountable for participating in selections of Jewish women for the gas chambers.[86] Her death sentence was commuted to twenty years in December 1953. She was released in January 1957.[87] She had spent twenty-one years in various concentration camps, internment camps, and prisons. In 1962, she sued the state of Bavaria for reparations and recognition as a victim of Nazism, with the outcome unknown because the files have been shredded.[88] When she was deposed as a witness by prosecutors in 1963, 1968, and 1974, she lived alone and on welfare in a senior citizen home in Hof. Unlike Pohl, who claimed to have emerged cleansed from "the purgatory of extreme abandonment," Klara Pförtsch never entirely left hell behind.

"Diabolical Evil"

Feminist philosopher Claudia Card introduces the term "diabolical evil" to describe the predicament of victims who are forced into complicity with their own degradation and the victimization of others. She is one more secular voice who employs the terminology of hell and of the devil to grasp the modern nature of collective evil:

> Diabolical evil, on my view, consists in placing others under the extreme stress, even severe duress, of having to choose between grave risks of horrible physical suffering or death (not necessarily their own) and equally grave risks of severe moral compromise, the loss of moral integrity, even moral death. This is stress geared to break the will of decent people, to destroy what is best in us on any plausible conception of human excellence. For that reason it

YBP Library Services

VON KELLENBACH, KATHARINA

MARK OF CAIN: GUILT AND DENIAL IN THE POST-WAR
LIVES OF NAZI PERPETRATORS.
                                    Cloth   287 P.
NEW YORK: OXFORD UNIVERSITY PRESS, 2013

AUTH: ST. MARY'S COLL. STUDY OF SELF-REFLECTION &
SELF-PERCEPTION OF GERMAN WAR CRIMINALS.

   ISBN 0199937451   Library PO# FIRM ORDERS
                                     List   35.00 USD
   8395 NATIONAL UNIVERSITY LIBRAR   Disc   14.0%
   App. Date   4/30/14 HUMANITIES 8214-08 Net   30.10 USD

SUBJ: HOLOCAUST, JEWISH (1939-1945)--MORAL &
ETHICAL ASPECTS--GERMANY.
AWD/REV: 2013 COYB
CLASS D804.7   DEWEY# 940.5318   LEVEL GEN-AC

deserves to be regarded as diabolical. The devil wants company and is a willing corrupter, plotting others' downfall. This is how evil extends its power.[89]

The shift of the burden of guilt onto the prisoners in concentration camps was deliberate. The *Reichsführer* of the SS, Heinrich Himmler, decreed in August 1942 that all beatings in concentration camps were to be administered by prisoners.[90] The insidious camp hierarchy charged inmates with various functions as kapo, *Blockälteste* (block elder), and *Lagerälteste* (camp elder) and made them responsible for maintaining discipline within housing units. The Nazi hierarchy of racial worth was enforced by the camp pecking order: "Aryan" German and Austrian prisoners were given leadership functions over inmates from other nationalities; Jewish and "Gypsy" prisoners formed the bottom of this hierarchy and were the least likely to be pulled into such positions of "privilege." Political (red triangle) and criminal (green triangles) prisoners were most often entrusted with functions in the camp administration, while Jehovah's Witnesses (purple triangles) were most often recruited for personal services in SS households. The "prison self-administration" depended upon the collaboration of prisoners to enforce the hellish conditions. The most hated prison functionaries were those empowered by the SS administration to "keep order" in the prisoner blocks, food distribution, roll calls, and so on. But prisoners were also stationed as receptionists for new arrivals, collected and sorted their belongings, herded victims along to the gas chambers or into the camp grounds, distributed the meager food rations, set up roll calls, and administered punishments. Each of these assignments came with particular risks and benefits, which were not immediately apparent to those choosing to accept particular roles. But the administrators knew the benefits of forced collaboration. They intended to demoralize and undermine solidarity among prisoners. They knew that the involvement of victims in the dehumanization of others would break their will, destabilize their human dignity, and damage their moral integrity.

The postwar world judged Klara Pförtsch's undeniable descent into depravity harshly and extended little compassion to her. To the French judges, she appeared even more tarnished than the SS wardens, most of whom were set free by the early 1950s.[91] She was considered a *femme terrible*,[92] and she could not convince the judges that she had tried to save women by falsifying names on a selection list. To the judges, this confirmed her "criminal character,"[93] and her small act of sabotage of replacing names was discounted on the grounds that the overall number of victims had remained the same.[94] Pförtsch, the judges concluded, had not saved anyone. Instead the judges detected in Pförtsch a "zeal to do evil" (zèle malfaisant) and a "total lack of pity on the occasion of selections."[95]

Other prisoners understood her situation more keenly and came to her defense. In November 1949, "Jewish and non-Jewish, German and Austrian fellow inmates of Klara Pförtsch approached us with the request to initiate an appeal of her [death] sentence," wrote Herta Gotthelf, a board member of the Social Democratic Party, to the French high commissioner, François-Poncet: "I am convinced that you will come to the conclusion after careful consideration of the case that a human being who has herself endured years of most dreadful torture in Nazi prisons and concentration camps, does not deserve ... to be condemned like a regular war criminal."[96] Rosl Jochmann, a member of the Austrian parliament and prominent Ravensbrück survivor,[97] similarly argued in a letter to Pförtsch's defense lawyer in November 1949:

> I want to emphasize that I have always condemned the beatings and I don't want to conceal that I was often angry at Klara Pförtsch because of them, but she did not kill anyone in Ravensbrück, and it is also true that she helped many there. She succumbed to the horrible maelstrom [Fluidum] of this camp, this hell, and one must say that anyone put into her position, with her psychic preconditions, would not have acted much differently.[98]

Many of those who came to her defense had themselves performed as function prisoners within the camp administration and understood the nature of guilt accompanying the awful choices made under the duress of severe and constant threat of violence. Rosl Jochmann pointed out that Pförtsch had initially refused the camp commander's request to take over the administration of punishment, which consisted of twenty-five strikes on the buttocks, although he had offered her a single cell, the same food as the SS, reprieve from forced labor, and daily walks. Another woman, she noted, had paid with her life for the refusal to accept this assignment.[99] But Pförtsch eventually relented and betrayed her fellow prisoners. Still, Herta Gotthelf argued, Pförtsch was not "a typical concentration camp sadist but a woman who after years of prison and concentration camp detainment, after disease and psychological and physical abuse, was broken and finally beat prisoners during the few months that she served as camp elder."[100] Such objections did not sway the judges of the military tribunal.

As historian Annette Neumann has shown for Ravensbrück, it was not uncommon for prisoner functionaries to receive harsher sentences than SS guards.[101] Ex-inmates of the camps had to contend with several layers of prejudice. Most were not greeted as heroic survivors of hell, but watched with suspicion and dread.[102] Some of them were immediately rearrested as outcasts and likely criminals.[103] When Kirchenrat Schieber described the conditions in Camp 77, where Pförtsch was initially held after her arrest by U.S. military authorities, he distinguished between "decent women" and "unclean elements," who consisted of "a number of concentration camp prisoners of the previous NS regime, among them homosexuals, prostitutes, and social misfits [*Asoziale*]. Sometimes prostitutes who have been arrested from the streets are brought to the camp and are now living among the decent women."[104] He complained that "the decent women heralding from the first group consider it extremely disgraceful to be forced to live together with such unclean elements [*unsaubere Elemente*] and in public perception to be thrown into the same pot with them."[105] The systematic and prolonged brutalization of these concentration camp prisoners had turned some of them "indecent" (*unanständig*) and "disorderly" (*unordentlich*) and threatened to "damage the reputation of everybody constantly."[106] As a Protestant pastor, Schieber had much more in common with the well-dressed, well-nourished, well-behaved, and well-spoken Nazi women than with the Communist, Jewish, criminal, sexually deviant ex-prisoners who had been brutalized and degraded for years. It is not at all clear into which category he might have placed Klara Pförtsch.

While Allied military courts were generally determined to reverse these power dynamics, the French judges seemed to have participated in some of these prejudices. They saw that Pförtsch had enjoyed "the confidence of the SS"[107] but did not appreciate her vulnerability as a prisoner. Orli Wald, another prison functionary who survived Ravensbrück and Auschwitz, tried to convey the abjection of inmates who made choices under duress and at the mercy of SS personnel. In her letter to François-Poncet in April 1951, she pointed out that

Many prominent representatives of National Socialism have recently been granted reprieve....They belonged exclusively to those who stood in light and glory during Nazi times. But Klara

Pförtsch sank into the darkness that was spread by these men across the entire world....I beg your Excellency to consider in your assessment of the person of Klara Pförtsch that she never profited from the Third Reich, that she was never a camp guard but only a beaten political prisoner, whose only guilt consisted of not being able to resist the pressures of the hell of Auschwitz as a simple and primitive woman, and who has now spent 15 years in prison, enough to atone.[108]

Long before Primo Levi's "gray zone" and Lawrence Langer's "choiceless choice"[109] had entered popular vocabulary, Orli Wald tried to articulate the peculiar nature of Pförtsch's guilt. She became an early advocate for prisoner functionaries and lobbied not only for Pförtsch but also for Fela Dreksler,[110] a Polish Jewish survivor of Auschwitz as a prisoner functionary who served a ten-year sentence in French prisons.[111] What incensed women like Orli Wald and Rosl Jochmann was that a Nazi functionary like "Ilse Koch...was let go," while Pförtsch remained imprisoned.[112] They tried to find a language to speak of guilt accrued by those who had served as "the tool of others," but who "could not choose one's function, or the specific task one was commanded to perform, or the means by which one carried them out."[113]

Primo Levi called the confusion between victim and perpetrator a "moral disease" and a "sinister sign of complicity; above all it is a precious service rendered (intentionally or not) to the negators of truth."[114] His book *The Drowned and the Saved* remains unsurpassed in its moral clarity and compassion for those who struggled to hold on to human dignity and moral integrity in the camps. In his discussion of the *Sonderkommandos*, the special squads forced to operate the crematories in Auschwitz, Levi asserts that "no one is authorized to judge them, not those who lived through the experience of the Lager and even less those who did not."[115]

Nobody can know for how long and under what trials his soul can resist before yielding or breaking. Every human being possesses a reserve of strength whose extent is unknown to him, be it large, small, or nonexistent, and only through extreme adversity can we evaluate it....Therefore I ask that we meditate on the story of the "crematorium ravens" with pity and rigor but that judgment of them be suspended.[116]

He was among the first to show that the camps as an "institution represented an attempt to shift onto others—specifically, the victims—the
burden of guilt, so that they were deprived of even the solace of innocence."[117] Although he demanded suspension of judgments, he did believe
that those who succumbed to the violence "are the rightful owners of a
quota of guilt (which grows apace with their freedom of choice) and
besides this they are the vectors and instruments of the system's guilt."[118]
But he opposed their criminal prosecution, specifically in Israel, where
collaboration in genocide was criminalized in 1950. Except for Adolf
Eichmann, who was tried in 1960, this law applied exclusively to Jewish
camp functionaries living in Israel.[119]

Pförtsch's level of complicity can be measured by the accuracy of her
memory. Her recollections of her own victimization were crystal clear, but
her memory became fuzzy when she was asked to describe her own
actions or the responsibilities of particular SS associates to whom she felt
indebted. She remembered the name of the "piece of shit" (*Miststück*) SS
associate Margot Drexel, "who beat me so savagely that she busted my ear-
drum. I was beaten by her in Birkenau. She always beat without cause,
whenever she was upset over something or needed to let off steam."[120] She
also remembered the woman, a "professional criminal" [i.e., green tri-
angle] and block elder, who "administered the 25 baton strikes to the buttocks because I was caught smoking without permission."[121] But her
memory becomes selective and self-serving when she spoke of beatings
that she herself administered:

> It also happened that I had to beat inmates. I have done this when
> I caught a prisoner, who was known to steal recurrently. I recall in
> this context a strong Polish female prisoner who brutally robbed
> bread from Jewish inmates. This inmate I slapped. But I refrained
> from making a report.[122]

Several protective deceptions shape this account: Pförtsch "had to beat,"
although she acknowledged moral agency by affirming a choice in when
she applied physical violence. She stressed that she only beat for good reasons, and she picked an incident involving a true villain who was caught
victimizing the most vulnerable inmates. She also emphasized that she
only slapped and that she had not reported the infraction to the camp
administration in order to protect the inmate. Clearly, she was intent on
protecting herself from further charges.

At the same time, she was generally unwilling to denounce and betray SS associates, or incapable of doing so. When she was asked, "Do you know any of the following SS associates in Ravensbrück?" and handed lists of names, she answered: "Of these persons, I recall nobody. These names are completely unknown to me." When she did remember names, she usually defended them: "Of the named persons, I can only recall Maria Merkle. She was in charge of the kitchen in Geislingen. I cannot say anything negative about Merkle."[123] Or: "Among the group of the accused, I only know the SS associate Ruppert... She did not strike me as unpleasant [*ist mir nicht unangenehm aufgefallen*]. I never observed her abusing prisoners."[124] When she described the *Abendappell* in Auschwitz, where the number of prisoners who left for work in the morning had to match the number of returnees in the evening, which included the corpses of those who had been beaten or shot to death during the day, she said: "Who was responsible for these murders could never be investigated. In any case, it could have only been the SS. I never heard that female kapos beat inmates to death."[125] She not only defended the female SS associates but also the SS men. Asked about the SS guards in the concentration camp Geislingen, she said: "I cannot remember names after so many years. I was in Geislingen between fall 1944 and March 1945. I cannot say anything negative (*Nachteiliges*) about the camp director, Romann. I had no contact with SS men and cannot make any statements about these persons."[126] Her vague and defective memory is a sign of indebtedness to and complicity with her jailors. She could speak freely about her own victimization but was prevented from testifying accurately by her complicity and guilt.

Pförtsch had made a pact with the devil and paid dearly for her survival. As feminist critic Andrea Dworkin noted for women surviving domestic violence: "battery is a forced descent into hell and you don't get by in hell by moral goodness."[127] Choices made in hell do not strengthen moral character or cleanse the soul. They merely damage the psyche and ravage the person. Pförtsch aligned herself with power and used her privileged position as a "*Reichsdeutscher* inmate" and political prisoner to her advantage. Her betrayal of the humanity of others compromised her moral integrity and prevented her from transforming into a witness to atrocity.

The experience of guilt was shaped by these perpetrators' social position, class, political and professional power, gender, and religion. While Pohl was blinded by ideology, Pförtsch was coarsened by circumstance. Neither was able to experience release from guilt or reach out to their fellow humans in compassion and human solidarity. They remained cut off from human bonds of care and consideration. It seems hard to imagine redemption in the case of Oswald Pohl. He was drunk with power and shackled by his sense of Aryan supremacy. He knew how to control his environment and was able to cloak his depravity in confidence, good manners, and educated intelligence. This allowed him to sway the chaplain and to manipulate prominent members of the political elite and the general public, who rushed to his defense. The chances of hell freezing over appear more likely than Pohl ever acknowledging culpable wrongdoing.

The case of Pförtsch should alert us, once more, to the dangers of stigmatization. Instinctively, the stigma of guilt attaches to the most vulnerable, the psychologically and physically ravaged bearer of guilt. One of the least powerful perpetrators received the severest punishment, although there was little pedagogical merit in inflicting further imprisonment on someone who had already been brutalized beyond human endurance. Despite twelve more years in prison in the postwar world, Pförtsch did not side unambiguously with the victims. When called upon to serve as a witness against SS men and SS associates and to repudiate the racism and antisemitism that had facilitated her survival, Pförtsch hesitated and hedged. By her last deposition in 1974, she could still not muster the moral courage to break the bonds of complicity and to stand in solidarity with the victims. Pförtsch might have become a powerful witness to the perilous border between victimization and perpetration and the devastating effects of unrelenting degradation on the moral self, but she seemed unable to find the door to exit hell.

5

From Honorable Sacrifices to Lonely Scapegoats

*The goat shall carry all their iniquities upon itself into
some barren waste. (Lev. 16:22)*

IN THE IMMEDIATE postwar years, sacrificial language permeated the self-portrayals of imprisoned Nazi perpetrators. Those sentenced by Allied and foreign national courts expressed their willingness to surrender their lives for the survival and recovery of the German *Volk*. The old Nazi logic of the individual's complete submission to the collective remained intact, vindicating the prisoners' fate. By portraying the indignities of their criminal prosecution by victorious Allies as sacrificial suffering, perpetrators endowed their experiences with transcendent meaning and purpose. In claiming to suffer on behalf of others—in their own view "innocently," of course—they reversed the dishonor of their punishment. Their death was honorable as long as it was altruistic and of benefit to others. A sacrificial victim suffers for noble reasons and need not be ashamed of the experience. Humiliation and indignity become badges of honor and pride.

These sacrifices were framed as disciplined suffering dedicated to the future rebirth of the German nation. The collectivist ideology of National Socialism reigned unbroken and gave meaning to personal hardship. Three subthemes were built around the trope of sacrifice: First, the Passion narrative articulated the expectation that executions would contribute to the redemption and eventual rebirth of the German people. Second, the biological language of the seed provided a sense of immortality, as their deaths were integrated into the eternal cycles of nature and lead to rebirth in the future of springtime. Third, the military language of heroic sacrifice on the battlefield endowed their deaths with honor and bravery that would lead to triumph and vindication.

The Passion of Christ: Sacrifice as Atonement

Christ on the cross is an ubiquitous symbol for the ultimate triumph of life, goodness, and light over the forces of death, evil, and darkness. Nazi perpetrators appropriated the Passion narrative and presented their fate in light of the suffering of Christ, whose resurrection overcame the shame of his arrest, trial, torture, and execution. His triumph suggested that they might be vindicated in the future as well. Hans Frank, for example, placed the German nation into the role of the crucified Jesus.[1] Frank acted as governor-general of Poland and was convicted by the IMT in Nuremberg on October 1, 1946, and executed six days later in Nuremberg. While in prison, he reclaimed his Roman Catholic faith under the pastoral guidance of American military chaplain Father Sixtus O'Connor. He also completed his memoirs, *Im Angesicht des Galgens*, published on August 3, 1946, as his political testament. In these memoirs, he envisioned his execution as a voluntary sacrifice and contribution to atone for the crimes committed by Adolf Hitler.

> The Germany, however, left behind by Hitler is now experiencing its most grueling passion. It is scorned, flogged, and nailed to the cross. The Reich is buried. And now that I am contemplating my path with Hitler, I bow my head in remorse. There is nothing left for me than to pray to God on behalf of my people and my country and to do my penance as a contribution for atonement. And in eternity I serve you my fatherland... because I loved you above all else in the world.[2]

As far as Frank was concerned, the crimes were Hitler's sole responsibility. But Hitler's suicide left the German people to carry its burden. Frank offered himself in vicarious payment for this debt. "God," Frank declared in his closing remarks before the IMT on August 31, 1946, "has pronounced his judgment on Hitler, and has rendered judgment on him and the system, which we served in godless passion [*gottferner Geisteshaltung*]."[3] He was rather unspecific and vague when it came to his personal responsibilities as governor-general of Poland, where he had overseen the systematic killings of Polish intelligentsia, managed the establishment of ghettos for Jews in Poland, and initiated deportations to the death camps, all of which were located in Poland. Frank tried his hand at blanket expressions of remorse in sentences like, "We could not imagine at the beginning of our path that the move away from God would have such devastating, lethal consequences, and that we would inevitably sink ever deeper into guilt."[4] But the rhetoric of Germany's "grueling passion" suggested the nation's innocence. Its primary guilt consisted of having been misled and duped by a charlatan. The Germany that is "scorned, flogged, and nailed to the cross" was, in his view, essentially blameless. The national collective had become the innocent victim. In a reversal of the Christian passion narrative, in which one man, Jesus, suffers for all of humankind, the personified German *Volk* suffers for the atonement of the guilt of one man, Hitler.

> We celebrated Easter mass today....In taking on guilt, I demonstrated that our great suffering people is innocent of the terrible events. Somebody had to confess after all the other cross-examined defendants asserted innocence. I at least want to be able to look into the eyes of the Lord God.[5]

He framed his obedient acceptance of the task of atonement as an investment in the future of the nation, which remained his first and last love "in eternity." While Frank played with the possibility of remorse for culpable wrongdoing and discussed the Passion story within the context of atonement, others focused on the innocence of the crucified.[6] "One could compare," wrote Lucie Girke, the widow of a Landsberg convict, "his life to that of the Passion narrative. He, who was always kind, who saved others' lives when Darmstadt went up in flames without ever considering his own survival, who pleaded on behalf of people who had been condemned to death and fought with his superiors to save them, who always thought first of his comrades and never considered resting—such a man must die!"[7] Her husband's selfless service and altruistic nature was supposed to disprove the possibility of wrongdoing. Girke's invocation of the passion story gave redemptive meaning to death on the gallows.

Sacrificial Seeds

While the Passion of Christ operated within Christian vocabulary of sacrifice, the metaphor of the seed was rooted in the neopagan, nature-based sensibilities of the Nazi worldview. The natural cycle requires sacrifice and death for the renewal of life, a theme that was already used extensively by Adolf Hitler to justify the necessity of sacrifice. The seed as a symbol of death and resurrection was mapped onto Easter celebrations of the return of spring, in a biological readaptation of Paul's explanation of corporal resurrection in the letter to the Corinthians.[8] The metaphor of the seed was useful to navigate the crisis of transition as an expression of the hope that the deaths on the gallows would ensure Germany's triumphant rebirth in the future.

Prof. Dr. Karl Brandt, the personal physician of Adolf Hitler, was hanged in Landsberg on June 2, 1948, primarily for his leading role in the euthanasia program as *Generalbevollmächtigter* for the Sanitätswesen.[9] Brandt called himself a "pious pagan" and wrote: "Only a pagan dies joyfully. He knows that there is no death and no ending. He knows that everything, everything is cyclical, no matter what its appearance and form."[10] His own death, Brandt claimed, was a sacrifice demanded by powerful victors exacted as a tribute from the vanquished. He was unapologetic and proclaimed his Nazi faith to the end. He was buried by Protestant pastor Lonitzer, who based his funeral sermon on his last words, which were subsequently published. In his final statement, Dr. Brandt asserted:

> Power demands sacrifice. We are such sacrifices. I am such a sacrifice. But, therefore, there is no shame in standing under this gallows. I am serving my fatherland here dutifully and without reservation!... The scaffold of Landsberg is the symbol of inner obligation for all who are upright and straight.[11]

Sacrificial language allowed Brandt to reclaim control over the meaning of his life, as he dedicated his death to "my poor, my sacred homeland, my people," and endowed it with transcendent significance. He linked his individual fate to the destiny of the *Volk*, in which he felt "comfortable and safe."[12] Brandt saw himself rooted in the "blood and soil" (*Blut und Boden*) of the homeland to which his sacrifice was consecrated. His "desire and duty to serve my people" validated his death as a heroic offering on the altar of enemy power. Brandt remained loyal to slogans such as "Germany must live and even if we die" and integrated his experience into an ideology that framed such sacrifices as an integral part of the natural cycle that ensured future generativity.[13]

Many prisoners in Landsberg walked to the gallows affirming their faith in duty and service to the fatherland. For instance, Fritz Dietrich, convicted for killing American POWs in Italy, stated:

In the conviction that my death for my passionately beloved fatherland, for which I worked and fought my entire life, will ultimately
be of service, I go this last walk of sacrifice [*Opfergang*] with a proud
heart because I know that my sacrifice will contribute to fill the
measure of suffering that has been imposed by a cruel victor over
the German people without compelling reason.[14]

Dietrich's last words were prepared in consultation with Pastor Eckardt,
who encouraged such sacrificial patriotism and assured Dietrich's widow
in his consolation letter that "his death, a sacrifice, was not in vain."[15] But
what was the purpose of these sacrifices?

In some cases, the sacrifices did not nurture the future of Germany but
contributed to the vitality and strength of the victors. Julius Ludolph, an
SS administrator from the concentration camp of Mauthausen, said in his
last words: "We Germans have to die so that other nations may live."[16]
According to the logic of Nazism, the strong have a biological right to con-
sume and exploit the vitality of the weak, and the Allies' military victory
had given them the prerogative to exact sacrifices of German lives. Such
sentiments attest to the minds of men who had been dulled by their own
cruelty and inhumanity. The golden rule of "do to others what you would
have them do to you" (Matt. 7:12) had come back to haunt them.

Military Sacrifices

Military language is replete with sacrificial imagery because it ennobles
the deaths of soldiers on the battlefield. Many men in Landsberg saw their
deaths as extensions of war and staged the executions as dignified defeat
in battle rather than as the result of legitimate court convictions. The
hangings became public performances of patriotism and of loyalty to the
state. In his good-bye letter, Herbert Kunze immortalized his death
poetically:

> Goodbye my *Volk*, these sacrifices shine
> Like a light on your sacred altar
> Because those who die on the gallows of their enemies
> Are heroes of their *Volk* forever.[17]

His physical sacrifice on the gallows would transform into spiritual power
on the sacred altar of the nation and ensure his place in eternity. Such

sentiments placed the Allied prosecution within the continuity of the war and rigorously denied any legal legitimacy. Many last words in Landsberg express the notion that the hangings were deaths deserving of military honor: "In two world wars I was denied the honest bullet, but now I fall for Germany in this place."[18] Kunze and Heim had not fought on the battle-field but were convicted for killing downed American pilots on the home front. Certainly, the SS men in the concentration camps had not served as soldiers, but they too claimed the language of military sacrifice. August Blei, for example, a former Mauthausen guard, affirmed: "I die for Germany; long live Germany."[19] And his colleague from Mauthausen, Hans Hegenscheidt, said: "I'm dying as an innocent German. Long live Germany. I'll die for Germany as a German."[20] The language of military sacrifice confirmed the validity of National Socialism and explained con-victs' suffering within its ideological framework. Their affirmations of voluntary sacrifice were rooted in their faith in the *Volk*, which, so they hoped, would vindicate their deaths in the future when it would arise tri-umphantly. But the resurrection of a National Socialist Germany did not come about. The planted seeds did not sprout, and the sacrificial blood did not fertilize the postwar field.

Instead, various social, political, and economic developments were set in motion that unraveled the bonds of collective destiny and disproved the legitimacy of Nazi racism and antisemitism. By the 1960s, the sacrificial language of Nazi convicts mutated to the trope of the scapegoat. By the time the second wave of Nazi trials got under way in West Germany, defen-dants began to feel like scapegoats who were being singled out by an ungrateful nation. They no longer felt "comfortable and safe" but vulner-able and isolated, the victims of the collective's intent on self-exculpation.

Historical Excursus

In 1958, all remaining prisoners were released from WCP 1 Landsberg. As the Allied military occupation of Germany drew to a close, the prosecution of Nazi crimes entered a new phase. Three high-profile court cases renewed public interest and focused national and international attention on the genocide committed against the Jews, much of which had hap-pened outside of Germany's borders: the Ulm Einsatzgruppen Trial (1958), the Eichmann trial (1961),[21] and the Frankfurt Auschwitz trial (1963–1965).[22] In contrast to the previous approximately ten thousand Allied and German trials conducted between 1945 and 1958, these three trials focused on the Holocaust. Prior to 1958, the systematic killings of Jews had not been the primary issue of criminal prosecution.[23] While the Allied proceedings mixed war crimes with crimes against humanity, the German trials had been restricted to crimes committed on German territory and confined to the prosecution of those involved in the euthanasia program, the expropriation of Jewish property, and the Kristallnacht pogrom of 1938, as well as the wave of political denunciations that led to detention, torture, and incarceration in German concentration camps like Dachau. All extermination camps of Jews were located in Poland, and the *Einsatzgruppen* had operated on Soviet territory, which put them outside of the jurisdiction of German criminal courts in the transitional period after the war.

The Ulm Einsatzgruppen Trial was the first German criminal proceeding that ventured beyond German territorial borders and exposed the methodical mass executions in the Soviet Union, Belarus, Ukraine, and Lithuania. The Eichmann trial in Israel received intense media coverage in Germany and uncovered the cold-blooded bureaucracy and the extent of the Nazis' operations against Europe's Jews. The Frankfurt Auschwitz trial presented evidence and eyewitness testimony to expose the industrialized quality of mass murder and the heinous cruelty of the camp structures and technology. One million Jews were killed in this extermination camp alone, and the name Auschwitz has since become synonymous with the "Final Solution of the Jewish Question."

Media reports on these three trials contributed to the public's growing sense that the Jewish genocide constituted a particularly monstrous crime and that its perpetrators should be held criminally accountable. As reporters and commentators disseminated the factual information brought to light in these trials, the German public in East and West was drawn into moral and political debates over the extraordinary nature of these killings. The nature of genocidal guilt and its proper prosecution became the subject of heated political debates as the legal statute of limitations for murder and manslaughter was set to expire. In anticipation of the expiration of the fifteen-year statute of limitations on manslaughter in 1960, the Zentrale Landesjustizstelle, the Central Prosecution Office, was created in 1958 in Ludwigsburg. Specially hired prosecutors were charged with collecting evidence and coordinating prosecution efforts against Nazi perpetrators in the short period left before the statute of limitations for manslaughter would bar prosecutions. Despite heated political discussions, the statute of limitations on manslaughter was allowed to pass. After May 1960, no charges could be brought against so-called *desk perpetrators*, the political leaders, legal experts, administrative managers, and economic beneficiaries. The prosecution had to build murder cases, which narrowed the field to those who were physically implicated in killings. The defendants after 1960 were no longer members of the academic, economic, and political elite, but more or less "ordinary men" who had physically implemented the genocidal policies of National Socialism. The focus of the prosecution shifted from the cultural elite to the middle and lower management of genocide, the camp guards, executioners, and policemen.

The statute of limitations for murder was set at twenty years, which would have meant an end to criminal prosecution of Nazi perpetrators by May 8, 1965. This time, the deadline was averted by recalculating the date to 1949, the official founding of the Federal Republic of Germany. By 1969, after much discussion, the statute was extended to thirty years until 1979. In 1979, genocide was exempted altogether from any statute of limitations. These political debates over the statute of limitations kept the topic of criminal guilt in the public eye. Despite constant calls for closure, time worked against perpetrators as the nature of atrocities became public knowledge and shifted perceptions of moral, political, and criminal culpability over the course of the 1960s.

Perpetrators had begun to feel safe after successfully reintegrating themselves into the newly established German state(s). After the initial wave of international military and foreign national trials, their skills and expertise as teachers, judges, doctors, policemen, engineers, business leaders, and civil servants were needed and welcome in both the Communist East and the capitalist West Germany. As long as they were willing to publicly abdicate the ideology and politics of National Socialism, they were able to return to work. The fiction of the line of closure (*Schlussstrich*) and of hour zero (*Stunde Null*) had seemingly successfully sealed off the atrocities in the past. The postwar world was not what their comrades had envisioned in their willing sacrifices. But most former Nazis had made their peace, and they were willing to live innocuous lives and to abide by the new rules, whether these rules applied to the Communist GDR (German Democratic Republic) or to the capitalist FRG (Federal Republic of Germany). Their quiet transition was rudely interrupted when the second wave of Nazi trials hit. Unexpectedly, they found themselves exposed, arrested, and interrogated by state's attorneys and prosecutors. A memorandum on pastoral care for Nazi defendants in West Germany, drafted by Bishop Stempel, the Protestant plenipotentiary for "convicts of war," explained that the defendants had understood their evasion of justice and surreptitious assimilation into the Federal Republic as a triumph over the violence of their pasts:

> The men about whom we are talking see this as a positive accomplishment: They succeeded in going underground and persevered against their former military enemies in the postwar period. In some instances, this might have saved their lives. That they were able to reintegrate into civil [bürgerliche] society was seen as proof that they successfully defied the danger of sinking into antisocial behavior [das Asoziale] after everything that had happened.[24]

Stempel said that the men had been able "to cut the offenses [Untaten] out of the continuity of their personal development and individual biography. But now these interrogations burrow into the past, bring it back up, and force confrontation with it."[25] The criminal proceedings in West Germany foiled private and clandestine attempts of disowning the past. Furthermore, a younger generation of prosecutors refused to accept the commission of atrocities as political acts and began to approach mass killings as criminal offenses. This development startled and outraged defendants, who tried to defend themselves against criminal charges with reference to their political status as agents of the state. The 1960s were characterized by a verbal tug-of-war over the appropriate definition of culpability. On the one hand, the perpetrators themselves argued that they had acted "politically" as agents of the state and on behalf of the national collective. On the other hand, a younger generation in the churches, the justice system, and the media began to demand that individuals be held accountable for atrocities that they had committed personally.

Barbara Just-Dahlmann, a young public prosecutor, became a leading voice and advocate of the justice system's duty and competence to prosecute Nazi perpetrators as "ordinary murderers."[26] She belonged to a new generation of legal scholars and was an active lay leader in the Protestant church. She challenged the courts and the churches to stop the pervasive exoneration and protection of Nazi perpetrators. Instead, she argued in speeches and publications, that "95 percent of all Nazi defendants were not 'seduced.'...These murderers are not 'different' murderers (only more cruel and colder) than ordinary murderers."[27] Their crimes were not, she maintained, political transgressions for which every German citizen should feel guilty, but rather ordinary criminal offenses committed by felons who should be held liable for their actions. She insisted that traditional criminal law was sufficient and should be applied to the killers. The mass murders they had committed could be prosecuted on the basis of conventional criminal law and needed no new legal codes. Voices such as hers infuriated and threatened perpetrators who defended their actions as idealistic service and dutiful obedience to the orders of superiors.

These public debates in advance of the Nazi trials persuaded the council of the Protestant Church (EKD) to publish another *Wort des Rates der Evangelischen Kirche zu den NS-Verbrecherprozessen* on March 13, 1963, where the church reversed its previous support for leniency. In contrast to the secret memorandum of 1949, the council now demanded a "legal purification" of the past.[28]

> Within the limits within which human justice is possible, transgressions must be characterized as reprehensible and must be punished by a community for its own sake and well-being. A state can only consider an act of mercy after it has properly met the demands of justice. "Righteousness exalts a nation but sin is a reproach to any people" (Prov. 14:35).[29]

The memorandum reprimanded German judges for issuing excessively lenient sentences and for dismissing so many cases on the basis of old age, ill-health, and other concerns. It called on the courts to fulfill their judicial obligations and to carry out their "difficult task...as their office demands: 'for justice will return to the righteous' (Ps. 94:15)." Under the slogan "law must remain law," the memorandum attempted to draw a line between those who had participated in atrocities and those who had lent their political support to the National Socialist regime. The paralyzing veil of the "solidarity of guilt" that blended active executioners and political supporters, individual and collective culpability, was now renegotiated. In the sixties, the application of criminal law to individuals who were found responsible for killing civilians seemed appropriate. "Regular courts" were tasked with prosecuting individuals, holding them personally accountable for executions or for acting "especially cruelly."[30] There should be no blanket calls for amnesty, the church leaders argued, and gestures of mercy would only be permissible after justice had been served in courts of law. The 1963 memorandum, in short, reflected the growing political and cultural distance from the ideology of National Socialism and the growing public perception of the criminal nature of mass killings.

Perpetrators protested their demotion into criminality by turning to the metaphor of the scapegoat. In the biblical world, the scapegoat is offered for the atonement of the sins of the community. The sacrificial animal itself is blameless and must be without physical blemish. It is symbolically loaded with the guilt of the entire community and chased into the desert. Nazi defendants used this metaphor to express their sense of abandonment by the German collective and to charge their accusers and judges with hypocrisy. They denied any and all personal wrongdoing. But they admitted that crimes had been committed. The rhetoric of the scapegoat, as opposed to the sacrificial language of the immediate postwar period, acknowledges collective guilt as it denies individual culpability. The scapegoat motif established a victim discourse for perpetrators, who complained angrily about undeserved punishment and the injustice of being singled out for retribution. While the first wave of convicts portrayed their punishment as noble and heroic sacrifice on behalf of a nation at war, the second wave complained about their political abandonment and social isolation by an ungrateful nation. The ideological bonds of National Socialism began to fray as perpetrators lost antisemitism as a politically viable ideology and feared expulsion from the very collective that had authorized their actions.

Scapegoats of an Ungrateful Nation

Hermann Schlingensiepen, a retired professor of practical theology at the Kirchliche Hochschule in Wuppertal, reached out and befriended the defendants of the second wave of Nazi trials in West Germany. His archive contains hundreds of letters exchanged with men in custody waiting for their court trials and serving their sentences, as well as with their wives and families. Schlingensiepen, born in 1896, studied Protestant theology upon returning from military service in World War I, where he was severely wounded. After a short period in congregational ministry, he received his doctorate and was appointed professor of practical theology in Kiel. In 1932, he was appointed director of the Ilsenburg theological seminary that trained ministers for South America, where he quickly came into conflict with Nazi authorities over his international connections and decision to join the Confessing Church. He was arrested, interrogated, and forced out as director. He withdrew into congregational ministry until he was recalled as professor in 1945 to the university in Bonn. After a failed surgery for his war wounds left him paralyzed, he was forced to retire from his position as provost of the Kirchliche Hochschule in Wuppertal. Confined to a wheelchair, Schlingensiepen began to write letters. He felt compelled to engage Nazi perpetrators in moral and theological questions out of genuine pastoral concern, but also because he felt guilty himself. Like Pastor Niemöller, whom he admired greatly, Schlingensiepen accepted a vague Christian "solidarity of guilt"[31] and believed that those serving prison sentences "suffered as substitutes [*stellvertretend*] for those of us who without merit or worth were spared from sullying their hands with blood."[32]

His correspondence partners were both grateful and manipulative. Their letters no longer spouted heroic patriotism and pompous national pride but rage and bitterness. Although most of them received rather short prison sentences, were released for spurious medical reasons, or acquitted over legal fine points, they lamented their betrayal and abandonment. The scapegoat discourse negotiated the growing disconnect between perpetrators and the larger society: first, perpetrators emphasized their blamelessness by disputing the motivation of the crimes: had they acted out of professional and political idealism or for criminal reasons? Second, they tried to manipulate their interlocutors into accepting collective guilt for genocidal actions. And third, they tried with increasing desperation to articulate the reasons for murdering Jews without using the vocabulary of antisemitism and racial hatred.

Many letters in the Schlingensiepen archive passionately contested the unexpected classification of the authors as common criminals. Johannes Miesel, for example, a lawyer by training, maintained that someone "who was subjectively convinced to serve his people with his actions cannot easily accept when he is accused of personal failure and criminal guilt."[33] Miesel, a graduate in Protestant theology, philosophy, and law, had insisted that an order for the extrajudicial mass execution of more than one hundred freed and returning slave laborers be carried out in March 1945. He was first acquitted by the Regional Court of Hagen in 1959, where the judges seemed to concur with the argument that mass executions on consecutive nights were an appropriate measure to relieve "traffic congestion."[34] Miesel had transmitted and enforced an order by his superior who was outraged over a traffic jam (a *Schweinerei*, he yelled) caused by returning slave laborers (*Fremdarbeiter*) headed east who were blocking retreating

Wehrmacht soldiers and German refugees who were heading west in the chaotic last weeks of the war. The West German judges weighed the legality of "prophylactic shootings"[35] as a means to prevent theft and plundering by "starving and hardly dressed people." They conceded that Miesel and his codefendant Wetzling had acted on orders with the best interest of the state in mind.

What happened in Langenbachtal in March 1945 was this: Miesel communicated his superior's order to Wolfgang Wetzling, who proceeded to assemble execution commandos from among the Wehrmacht soldiers under his command. They commandeered a Russian student as translator who used a bullhorn to broadcast a free ride to laborers on the road. Those who volunteered were asked to board waiting trucks. Fourteen men and fifty-six women and one child came forward on the first night. They climbed onto the back of trucks and were driven to a secluded spot in the forests. There they were executed summarily and buried in trenches. On the second night, eighty men volunteered, and on the third night thirty-five men, twenty-one women, and one child were killed. It was an extraordinarily callous approach to crime prevention and traffic congestion.

It was only on appeal that Miesel was convicted to four years in prison for his role in these executions. He "objected passionately" and argued that "justice demands that a portion of the burden [of guilt] should be distributed communally.[36]" He felt deeply misunderstood, "deserted, expelled, ridiculed, banned and forsaken." No one, "not even a collegial court can reconstruct and empathize with the psychological situation at the 'time of the crime,' i.e. in the midst of the collapse of the Reich," wrote Miesel:

> Like the other convicts...I have experienced the terror and shame of prison, have gone through the depth of despair and disappointment...and feel like a scapegoat, who is further burdened by the other co-guilty [Mitschuldige] with their own portion of guilt, in order to be chased into the desert of contempt.[37]

There is no sign of remorse in Miesel's letters. Like earlier convicts in the Allied trials, Miesel showed no empathy for the victims and remained self-centered. His moral outrage was directed against the judges, his former colleagues. He accused them of dodging "co-guilt" (Mitschuld). He parsed out this alleged co-guilt by abstracting it from the particular incident:[38]

There is no other possibility than to divide the guilt proportionally among all those who are legally incorporated into joint liability—and that includes everybody...who did not become a martyr for truth, justice, and humanity, and is therefore...exempt.[39]

Only those who died as martyrs are exempted from culpability. Miesel was desperate to recollectivize responsibility in order to alleviate personal criminal liability. The scapegoat motif became the rhetorical tool to do so.

By the 1960s, defendants reminisced nostalgically about the time of the Allied military trials when the notion of the solidarity of guilt and of collective responsibility was generally accepted. A letter published anonymously in 1965 in the Protestant *Sonntagsblatt* pointed out that Allied military courts were much more lenient and compassionate "even if they imposed the death penalty" than were the West German courts today:

Those pardoned had no criminal record, did not have to pay for court proceedings and were often welcomed back cordially in their hometowns as late returnees from the war...and if they were civil servants...they received their public positions back....Today all of this is different. No solidarity or sense of co-responsibility [*Mitschuld*] exists among adult Christians for Hitler's ill-fated regime, and measured by the amnesty praxis of the Allies, our political state leaders can only be characterized as merciless, at least as far as I have had opportunity to observe.[40]

"Solidarity" and "co-guilt" were found to be lacking as West German courts examined individual choices within the framework of criminal liability. Witness testimony and evidence presented in the courts destroyed the veneer of political idealism, dutiful service, and absolute obedience that had previously disguised the violence. The disclosure of the cruelty in the camp system and the systematic murder of Jews eroded the fiction of "collective guilt." Not everyone had participated. There was a clear moral distinction between someone like Miesel, who had ordered women and children shot, and someone who had not. Miesel noticed this moral extrication of West German society and complained bitterly: "The convicts feel too little comradeship, co-responsibility, solidarity from the German public. All of a sudden, they are abandoned, expelled, ridiculed, banned, and deserted. Without a doubt, this is in part caused by influences of... former enemy propaganda on the mass media."[41] Although he suspected enemy propaganda, it was the fact that he was prosecuted and convicted by his own German colleagues that caused his consternation and distress. What demoralized him was the fact the very collective on whose behalf he claimed to have acted withdrew its approval. The language of the scape-goat tried to reconstitute the national community by drawing it back into co-guilt (*Mitschuld*).

"Who in Our Generation is without Guilt?" Collective and Individual Guilt

This question was raised repeatedly by perpetrators who wrote to Schlingensiepen. There is, of course, a truth hidden behind this question. Some who asked the question, like Martin Niemöller or Schlingensiepen, tried to initiate a process of introspection. But others, like Otto Bradfisch or Adolf Eichmann, raised the question in an effort to evade and deny personal responsibility. Otto Bradfisch tried to challenge Professor Schlingensiepen from his Bayreuth prison cell, where he was serving a ten-year sentence.[42] The regional court in Munich had convicted him as principally responsible for the murder of 80,000 Jews in Minsk, Biyalostok, and Stolin as commander of Einsatzkommando 8.[43] Bradfisch led up to his rhetorical question—who is without guilt?—by quoting a passage from the Sermon on the Mount from the Gospel of Matthew. Jesus' warning against the hypocrisy of judgment was a favorite quote among Bible-literate perpetrators. It cautioned anyone who might be inclined to pass judgment:

> For if you forgive men their trespasses, your heavenly Father also will forgive you; but if you do not forgive men their trespasses, nei-ther will your Father forgive your trespasses. (Matt. 6:14–15)

Such appeals to the New Testament bolstered the general postwar German solidarity of guilt and fortified the webs of complicity that paralyzed moral discernment and undercut criminal justice. Bradfisch manipulated Christian doctrines of original sin to question anyone's authority to hold him morally or criminally accountable. Men of a certain generation, like Hermann Schlingensiepen, were not entirely immune to these manipula-tions. Certainly most West German judges, whose own complicity as enforcers of Nazi justice remained unexamined and uninvestigated, were highly susceptible to such arguments. Schlingensiepen would have agreed that every German who had come of age during the Nazi regime had to shoulder co-responsibility for its crimes. But he believed that court proceedings and guilty verdicts were important tools to disassociate Germany from the evils of National Socialism. Once prisoners were convicted, however, he supported their early release because he saw little benefit in long prison sentences.[44]

Schlingensiepen's position was more in keeping with another passage from the New Testament that was often quoted by Nazi perpetrators. Adolf Eichmann, for example, used this verse from the Gospel of John: "Let him, who is without sin among you, be the first to throw a stone at her" (John 8:7).[45] Eichmann, of course, was not about to acknowledge wrongdoing but cited this verse to warn against the "scribes and Pharisees," that is, politicians, journalists, and judges who were guilty of complicity and hypocrisy. The story of the adulterous woman is a version of the scapegoat motif because she is condemned to suffer the consequences of male sexual double standards. Her stoning indicts her judges and stands as a warning against the dangers of unacknowledged anxieties and guilt feelings that are alleviated by punishing a vulnerable scapegoat. The woman's victimization, so goes the lesson of the story, could not bring about the purification of the conscience of a culpable community. Instead, Jesus challenged the accusers' alleged moral purity and then let the woman go: "Neither do I condemn you. Go your way, and from now on do not sin again" (John 8:11). These New Testament texts, quoted by men like Adolf Eichmann and Otto Bradfisch, served to denounce a society moving toward extrication from collectivist ideologies. Numerous commentators exhorted the German public against the dangers of exemplary convictions. They argued that scapegoating constituted a moral evil in itself because it promised to lighten the burden of a group by loading its guilt onto an individual. This mechanism was symptomatic of "a society that tries to justify itself," as a group of prison chaplains argued in an open letter opposing the EKD memorandum.[46] They warned that the community soothed its own conscience by picking random agents and blaming them for the excesses of the policies of National Socialism. "Self-justification" was the code word that decried the prosecution of individuals for the cleansing of the society. The prison chaplains warned that the sentences imposed on Nazi perpetrators would be little more than a "search for scapegoats that would eventually lead to the exculpation of our people."[47]

These New Testament passages also tapped into Christian anti-Judaism. The contrast between the Gospel of John's Jesus, who was willing to forgive a guilty woman, and the "scribes and Pharisees," who were judgmental and hypocritical, validated old anti-Jewish stereotypes. With his quotation, Eichmann could not only make a religiously compelling case against his trial and conviction, but he could also reinscribe the moral degeneracy of Jews and Judaism. He did not have to spell out the antisemitic implications because every biblically literate Christian listener would have understood its meaning. References to the "Pharisees" permeated letters that warned against hypocrisy and judgment in postwar Germany. For instance, a letter to the editor of the established *Juristenzeitung* cautioned:

> The call for the strict treatment of executioners at the frontlines, i.e., the shooting sites, smacks of Pharisaism; one believes one can get rid of the discomfort over one's own behavior [during the Third Reich] by calling the "real" murderers to harsh account; they are metaphorically sacrificed—especially with an eye toward foreign lands—for the atonement [*Entsühnung*] of society. Minimally, as long as the last so-called "desk perpetrator" has not been prosecuted (would we not have to draw the circle of the responsible even wider?)—which, in my opinion, will never be accomplished—we must warn against making more easily accessible executioners into examples.[48]

The Pharisees were the quintessential hypocrites, whose legalism and retributive justice was legendary.[49] In the long history of exegetical misinterpretation, the Pharisees were caricatured as an elitist group that imposed strict law codes on everyone and allowed generous exemptions for themselves. Biblical references to the Pharisees became a clandestine vehicle for antisemitic clichés in a changed political culture where antisemitism had become dangerous. Perpetrators abdicated the ideology of racial antisemitism but found vehicles to express their anti-Jewish resentments. For instance, Otto Bradfisch conceded that the extermination of Jews constituted an "erroneous, yes criminal policy of a German government." The man in charge of an *Einsatzkommando* responsible for killing 80,000 Jews tried to distance himself from the ideology that had made the Final Solution of the Jewish Question seem like a good idea. He could no longer defend its legality and legitimacy. Instead, he portrayed himself as a dupe of the government, who felt like a "lone scapegoat who is sacrificed for reasons of state expediency—restoration of foreign relations and prestige—onto which the guilt has been dumped conveniently."[50] His loneliness was a feature of the changed political atmosphere that would not allow him to use "eliminationist antisemitism"[51] as an explanation for his career decisions. Instead, he was forced to depict himself as a powerless victim of government authorities who betrayed him twice: first by commanding him to commit mass murder and then by removing the cloak of ideological validity.

Antisemitism

By the 1960s, accused NS criminals felt increasingly restrained from open appeals to antisemitism because it hurt their standing in the courts and in public opinion. They had not changed their minds but became very careful and intent on censoring their speech. The following three cases show their struggles to defend the legitimacy of their actions without appearing to be invested in Nazi antisemitism. Their growing inability to communicate the truths of their lives intensified their feeling of isolation, expressed in the metaphor of the scapegoat. Once antisemitism had been criminalized, any admission of "racial hatred" (*Rassenhaß*) led to higher sentences, which perpetrators took pains to avoid.

In 1960, the West German government passed a new law against *Volksverhetzung*, best translated as "hateful agitation of the people" against racial and religious minorities.[52] The law intended to curb a wave of antisemitic attacks and vandalism of Jewish grave sites. Subsequently, public expressions of hatred and contempt of Jews were muted. In 1961, the Roman Catholic Church in response to the Eichmann trial publicly read a prayer "for the murdered Jews and their persecutors" from all pulpits and asked for "forgiveness for an immeasurable sin."[53] During its *Kirchentag* in 1961, the Protestant Church likewise denounced antisemitism and acknowledged communal co-responsibility (*Mitschuld*) for the murder of the Jews.[54] There was a small but growing movement in the churches as well as the German public that condemned the hatred of Jews and Judaism as a false teaching.

In courtrooms across West Germany, frank expressions of antisemitic sentiments could be taken as an acknowledgment of racial hatred and result in higher convictions. When judges found evidence of racial hatred, they ruled that defendants exhibited an individual motivation to kill and that they were not merely following superior orders. Defense attorneys counseled their clients to avoid any mention of Jews or Judaism and to claim indifference and ignorance of the Final Solution. Therefore, defendants testified that they had remained completely unaffected by hatred of Jews and remained unaware of the antisemitic objectives of National Socialism. They stressed their dutiful obedience to superior orders and emphasized their friendly demeanor towards their victims.

But this forced perpetrators to explain their involvement in the murder of Jews without reference to its ideological basis. Words like "Jew," "Jewish," and "Judaism" became taboo. There are very few references to Jews in the hundreds of letters that make up the correspondence of Hermann Schlingensiepen. One exception is Dr. Erhard Kroeger, a former Nazi propagandist in the Baltic states, who requested "discretion" before he went on a rampage about the Jewish conspiracy that was allegedly out to get him. He was clearly aware that the public admission of his deep-seated hatred could prove dangerous to himself. Dr. Kroeger attributed his prison sentence of three years and four months for several mass executions of Jews in the western Ukraine with Einsatzkommando 6 to the conspiratorial machinations of a long line of enemies, including

> the German justice system with its police and prosecutorial apparatus spanning the whole world, supported by the Office of Foreign Affairs [Auswärtige Amt], the national Jewry in Israel, international assimilationist Jewry in the entire world (may I ask that you use discretion here...talk of its existence is currently in Germany prohibited, it is considered "antisemitic" and punishable). Further among the persecutors belong Bolshevism in all its varieties, the greatest part of the media, TV and radio, the dominant journals, and last not least, the Protestant Church in Germany. One can grow faint when faced with such a phalanx.[55]

Dr. Kroeger was exasperated by changes in the West German political and legal culture that earned him a criminal conviction for what he considered "political service" in an *Einsatzkommando*.[56] He "sharply rejected...the political justice of the Federal Republic," which "is stubbornly being twisted into criminal justice by those who want to 'come to terms'"[57] with the past. He did not deny that mass killings of Jews had taken place in Dnejepropetrowsk, Drobomil, Lemberg, Makejewka, and Winniza, but he categorically rejected the court's finding of personal criminal guilt. "Murder," this doctor of jurisprudence lectured in his twenty-page letter to the theologian Hermann Schlingensiepen, is committed only on the "basis of greed, lust for murder, to satisfy sexual impulses or other base motives."[58] The killings of Jews, on the other hand, were committed for legitimate reasons of state. Therefore "all these charges are based on distortions or lies and deception."[59] SS men did not kill out of "base motives" but rather out of reasonable assessments of the threats emanating from Jews, Kroeger instructed:

> Perpetrators are supposed to have acted out of a motivation of race hatred, and race hatred is a vile motive, they say. In fact, very few acted because of race hatred. The Jewish Question, more than 2,000 years old, is a convoluted tapestry of historical and religious, economic and ideological, this-worldly and transcendent threads that involves racial factors on the periphery. It was one of the great cognitive defects of National Socialists to raise the question of the Jews only on biological grounds, especially since a Jewish race does not exist biologically beyond doubt. Jews are, seen racially, a mixed people with divers characteristics....I must admit that I do not know what race hatred is supposed to be and whether it exists. As an indicator of "base motives" it is...vague.[60]

For Kroeger, the "Jewish Question" was a scientific problem that had nothing to do with emotions such as hatred or contempt. The legitimization of his killings depended on the credibility of this ideology, which in his mind, had nothing to do with "race hatred." He was willing to concede that there might have been some "cognitive defects" in the racial teachings, and, like Otto Bradfisch, he publicly distanced himself from the Nazi programs of antisemitic extermination. But he held tight to the Christian roots of the teaching of contempt of Jews and was appalled at the prospect that "opposition to the synagogue may be leveled and erased" and that "young people" may no longer "perceive the antithetical, antagonistic, and un-Christian principles of Judaism."[61] Kroeger understood that racist, biological antisemitism had lost credibility, and he retreated into Christian anti-Judaism. In the following paragraph he paired the alleged depravity of Bolshevist Russia with the Israel of the Old Testament despite the obvious time difference:

> There are two types of inhumanity: those that one is allowed to talk about and those that must remain unspoken. It seems obvious to suspect a connection between whether one belongs to the group of

victors or vanquished at a particular time. We may agree that
Bolshevist Russia as well as Old Israel, for which one finds ample
evidence reading the Old Testament, should be listed at the top of
the roster of inhumanity.[62]

Communists and Jews were still his enemies, but he had to take recourse
to theological writings to express his hostility. The language of Nazi antisemitism had become toxic and could no longer be used. Kroeger realized
his ideological marginalization and tried to recast his rhetoric. But he could
not give up antisemitism, because it justified the killings. He needed reasons that confirmed the legitimacy of his actions, even if no one else understood or respected him. This dilemma silenced and isolated perpetrators
beginning in the 1960s. They were far from acknowledging wrongdoing,
but they realized that they had become disconnected and alienated.

A similarly conflicted rhetoric spoke through the letters of the deputy
commander of Auschwitz, Robert Mulka. Mulka was tried in the Frankfurt
Auschwitz trial of 1963–1965. In his letters to Schlingensiepen he performed a tightrope act, condemning mass murder while justifying his
involvement in it. He conceded that "terrible things" happened and that
"ghastly orders" were given and executed. "I regret and condemn the events
of the past, from the depth of my heart as I even did back then, once
I received news of the details, as a human being and a Christian," he wrote.
Needless to say, since Mulka was personally in charge of some of the most
appalling atrocities in Auschwitz, he certainly received news of everything
on a daily basis. He was deputy commander between April 1942 and March
1943 and was responsible for setting up the infrastructure of death,
including the gas chambers and crematories. The court convicted him on
the basis of copious evidence, which he flat-out denied: "These are innu-
endos and probabilities that remained unproven." Instead, he felt perse-
cuted: "Unfortunately, I am being stalked, harassed, scorned, and threatened
by evil, false and hateful people, even in the press, radio and TV."[63] He also
expected pity for his alleged internal conflicts of conscience. As he described
the cognitive dissonance and his moral conflicts, he inadvertently admitted
the extent of his ongoing ideological investment in antisemitism:

I was in a permanent situation of conflict—was this MURDER for the
sake of MURDER, or were these measures in the context of the former
war effort. WITH THAT I wrestled, and it ruined me psychologically
and physically. (Emphasis in original)[64]

The very question is absurd. There is no moral confusion over the legitimacy of the industrialized murder of Jewish children, women, and men unless one is committed to antisemitism. The possibility that Jews might constitute a worthwhile enemy is only reasonable to someone who subscribes to such a belief. The assertion of psychological turmoil and physical strain, of inner conflict and moral dispute, was a widespread discursive strategy that generated considerable sympathy from German interlocutors as late as 1965. Perpetrators used the grammatically passive voice to describe an unenviable fate that had put them in places such as Auschwitz and forced them to endure moral hardship. Anyone else, Mulka tried to imply, would have similarly failed to decipher whether the gas chambers of Auschwitz constituted murder or necessary "measures...of the war effort." Who could have predicted, he seemed to say, that killing Jews would turn out to be wrong?

Mulka also strove to reimplicate the national collective and pleaded his own ignorance and impotence: "I did not become co-responsible for the later events in their totality [*spätere Gesamtgeschehnisse*], as did a large part of the German people, who became members of the NSdAP for personal reasons." Again, we should notice the shift from criminal responsibility to the political realm. Pointing out that he never joined the National Socialist party and acted only as "a German patriot," he blamed the political will of the people. He saw himself as "a little soldier" who should not be held accountable for politics and rejected expectations that he should have "recognized the illegality.... No, dear Herr Professor [Schlingensiepen], the WHOLE people was guilty for that, because no one resisted or dared to criticize what was happening."[65] The German people carried responsibility because they voted Hitler into power and joined the party.[66] They should be held accountable for "the events of the past," while he himself only executed the "will of the people." Therefore, Mulka believed, he deserved to be acquitted rather than be pushed into the role of scapegoat.

The trope of the scapegoat expressed perpetrators' growing sense of being left behind by a culture that embraced a different perspective and broke allegiance with nationalism and antisemitism. The reasoning that had justified mass murders and sustained a conviction of righteous blamelessness could no longer be communicated openly. While they were far from any admission of culpable wrongdoing, they were forced to acknowledge that they could no longer count on community support. They had not changed, but the collective that had legitimated their actions had. This created a sense of isolation and alienation that was expressed in the rhetoric of the scapegoat.

Eichmann in Exile

We can contrast these West German perpetrator discourses with the language of Adolf Eichmann, who was surrounded by a Nazi expatriate community in Argentina. Eichmann spewed triumphalist convictions until he was arrested by Israeli Mossad agents. In exile, his ideology could thrive unchallenged, and his sacrificial rhetoric remained heroic. In a series of taped interviews in 1957 that would later be turned into his memoirs, he spoke uncensored and confident in his community's support.[67] In the midst of like-minded comrades who gathered to listen to his interviews, Eichmann did not portray himself as a scapegoat. He was supremely secure in his antisemitism and affirmed freely that he would not

> play a Saul who turned into a Paul. But I must tell you that I cannot do that, because my innermost being refuses to say that we did something wrong. No—I must tell you, in all honesty, that if of the 10.3 million Jews shown by [statistician] Korherr, as we now know, we had killed 10.3 million, then I would be satisfied. I would say "All right. We have exterminated an enemy."[68]

During these interview sessions, where "drinks were served, Eichmann became moderately inebriated, and the atmosphere was sometimes rowdy,"[69] Eichmann asserted with absolute certainty that any investigation into his activities as *Referent* in the office of IV B 4 "would have to acquit me, even if they were to come together to condemn me."[70] Unlike Mulka, who was forced to negotiate the changed political atmosphere in West Germany by entertaining rhetorical questions over whether his activities in Auschwitz might be construed as murder, Eichmann was not plagued by doubt. In Argentina, he could speak freely, because his political ideology reigned unchallenged and its goals were uncontested. He prided himself on having evaded the Allied justice of vengeance (*Rachejustiz*),

> which would have demanded my life. But that would not have been so terrible because I would have given it freely for Germany. I would have probably become a welcome scapegoat who could have been loaded with the feelings of hate and revenge of the enemy, and I would have assuaged his unhappiness and craving for victims, which would have allowed other comrades to reach relative safety.[71]

Eichmann was still willing to surrender his life for the nation. While his comrades in West Germany were already protesting their abandonment, Eichmann was focused on the old enemies, the Allies and the Jews, who he suspected were plotting revenge. His bluster only faltered after his arrest and incarceration in Israel. When he began to interact with Israeli interrogators and an American Pentecostal minister, his ideological certitude crumbled. Israeli interrogators described him "as a bundle of nerves. The left half of his face twitched. He hid his trembling hands under the table. I could feel his fear.... It must have seemed less than likely to him that the Israeli police would treat him with extreme fairness."[72] He desperately tried to recast his image and remake himself into a conscientious and unsuspecting bureaucrat who fainted at the sight of blood and remained unaware of any inhumane practices spawned by his well-laid plans. In his concluding statement he said, "I am not the monster I am made out to be...I am the victim of a fallacy." And Hannah Arendt continued: "He did not use the word 'scapegoat,' but he confirmed what Servatius [his defense lawyer] had said: it was his 'profound conviction that [he] must suffer for the acts of others.'"[73] His West German defense lawyer Servatius was well aware of the pervasive use of the scapegoat in West German courtrooms. For obvious reasons, this did not have the same emotional pull in Israel as it did with the German public. But Hannah Arendt felt compelled to respond anyway. In her epilogue to *Eichmann in Jerusalem: A Report on the Banality of Evil*, she addressed Adolf Eichmann personally:

> Guilt and innocence before the law are of an objective nature, and even if eighty million Germans had done as you did, this would not have been an excuse for you.... You yourself claimed not the actuality but only the potentiality of equal guilt on the part of all who lived in a state whose main political purpose had become the commission of unheard-of crimes. And no matter through what accidents of exterior or interior circumstances you were pushed onto the road of becoming a criminal, there is an abyss between the actuality of what you did and the potentiality of what others might have done.[74]

Arendt drew a line between actuality and potentiality and defended punishment as an appropriate response to actually committed egregious violations of human rights. The fact that others may bear guilt equally, she maintained, does not undo the need for justice in the actual case. Eichmann was executed for his personal responsibility in the genocide. He was not an innocent scapegoat, although he died on the gallows on June 1, 1962, unrepentant, like most of the others. He was the last Nazi perpetrator to be executed, and he affirmed, once more, his innocence and claimed that he "had to obey the laws of war and my flag." He concluded: "Gentlemen we shall meet again soon; such is the fate of all men. I have believed in God [gottgläubig] all my life and I die gottgläubig."[75]

The prosecutions of Nazi perpetrators, for all their legal scrupulousness and rational objectivity, also served a ritual function of expiating the guilt. Eichmann paid the moral debt for the Holocaust in his own name, but also on the behalf of the collective that he represented. In that respect, he was a scapegoat whose death had symbolic and cathartic meaning. "The surrogate victim dies so that the entire community, threatened by the same fate, can be reborn in a new and renewed cultural order," writes René Girard in *Violence and the Sacred*. As opposed to a scapegoat, Eichmann was not innocent. But his trial and execution was exemplary. It provided substitutionary restitution to the victims and survivors and proxy expiation to the perpetrators. Justice in the aftermath of genocide has a symbolic, ritual quality, because it can never be applied consistently and uniformly. Those who do face justice, like Eichmann, Bradfisch, and Mulka, stand in as representatives of the community.

We may best conclude that the debate over the role of scapegoats in the expiation of collective guilt is not an "either-or" but a "both-and" situation. Atrocities are committed by individuals who act within collective structures. Such guilt must be atoned at both the individual and the communal levels. Those individuals who served sentences handed down by courts as a result of due legal process not only paid for their individual culpability in atrocities, but also served an exemplary role in the expiation of guilt. Their punishment was both deserved and substitutionary, as their penalization delegitimized the ideologies that had authorized the killings and forced others to reinvent their lives as they tried to slip away into anonymity.

6

"Understand, My Boy, This Truth about the Mistake"

INHERITING GUILT

THE IDEOLOGICAL ARMOR of perpetrators cracked in conversation with their children who began to ask questions when their fathers were suddenly arrested and convicted in the second wave of Nazi trials during the 1960s. While perpetrators lamented their abandonment by an ungrateful German government, they were infuriated by signs of disloyalty from their children. Intergenerational conversations were always conducted under the shadow of the past. The presence of guilt and its denial affected virtually all German families, those already involved in criminal prosecutions, those afraid of exposure, and those suspicious of what might be hiding in their parents' closets. The crimes of the past loomed over communications between the generations and turned them into uneasy balancing acts.

In the ancient biblical world, guilt was seen as a communal and intergenerational matter. Although the Bible itself repudiated the idea of intergenerational liability and insisted that crimes committed by the fathers could not be prosecuted or atoned for by the sons, the notion of communal and intergenerational culpability remains prevalent. It is expressed, for instance, in the description of God as one who is

> merciful and gracious, slow to anger, and abounding in steadfast love and faithfulness, keeping steadfast love for the thousandth generation, forgiving iniquity and transgression and sin, but who will by no means clear the guilty, visiting the iniquity of the fathers upon the children and the children's children, to the third and the fourth generation. (Ex. 34:6–7)

The notion that the "iniquities of the fathers" can be visited on the "children and children's children, to the third and fourth generation" is later rejected by the prophet Jeremiah, who envisioned a time when it would no longer be said that "the fathers have eaten sour grapes, and the children's teeth are set on edge" (Jer. 31:29).[1] Like Jeremiah, one would be hard pressed today to argue for tribal justice, where penalties can be exacted from clan members across generations. But the biblical notion of intergenerational transmission of guilt has recently reemerged as a topic of scholarly discussion in the interdisciplinary field of transitional justice. Psychologists, legal scholars, political scientists, philosophers, and sociologists examine the intergenerational processes through which societies emerge from dictatorship, war, and genocide. West Germany's transition from National Socialism and its central project of the extermination of Jews to democracy provides important lessons for both the long-term legal prosecution of agents of state terror as well as for nonjudicial approaches to guilt and forgiveness, truth and reconciliation.[2]

No one wished more fervently to reject the sour grapes of the fathers than Germany's postwar generation. In Germany, the global student rebellion of 1968 was sharpened by antagonism and resistance to the legacy of the Nazi past. The children's vigilance and rejection of "fascist" policies challenged Nazi perpetrators in both the public and the private realms of the family.[3]

Letter to a Son

In this chapter, I will explore a perpetrator's struggle to appear both sincere and blameless to his son. It is based on a seventy-seven-page letter written in 1966 by a convicted member of Sonderkommando 1005 to his seventeen-year-old son. Artur Wilke tried to impress his son with his moral integrity and honesty even as he rejected moral culpability for mass murder. His exculpation implicated his son in webs of complicity. Despite Wilke's stated goal, to sincerely diagnose "the truth of his mistake,"[4] he misrepresented the "errors" of his past and bound his son into guilt. In subtle and not so subtle ways, the parents' deceptive evasions infected and shaped conversations and relationships between the generations in Germany. As Wilke formulated the lessons of his life, he counseled his son to distrust authority, to avoid consumerism and capitalist democracy, to heed God's laws, and to embrace radical pacifism. The roots of his moral advice were deeply entangled in his own life experience of participation in the murder of Jews. He did not merely repress the memory of his culpability but formulated twisted moral lessons for his son that intended to bridge the widening cultural and political gap between them. The choice he faced was not simply between repression or remembrance. Rather, he was involved in complicated constructions of biographical memory designed to induct the children into his exculpation.[5]

While the 1968 generation desperately wanted to distance itself from the legacy of perpetration, some of the lessons of the fathers resonated deeply—though unself-consciously—with the generation's own politics. The children were not merely passive recipients of generational knowledge: they actively embraced and rejected, molded and mended, repaired and recovered tainted wisdom dispensed by their elders. As we reconsider the intergenerational transmission of guilt, the question becomes less *whether* the legacy of guilt exists than *how* it is passed from one generation to the next. Let me begin with a quote from Artur Wilke's letter:

> Understand my boy, you who know so much about the sincere and courageous wrestling of your father, that the truth about the mistake for which we had to pay such a high price... is of great value to us, even if it is the only thing of value, and only an immaterial value, which I can leave to you in such a way that you should not have to pay again for such criminal wisdoms, foolishly, innocently, and naively trusting your teachers who weren't the best—they were already ours![6]

Who is this man who wrote this letter? Artur Wilke, born in 1910 in Hohensalza/Posen, studied Protestant theology in Erlangen and Greifswald (with well-known theologian Adolf Schlatter)[7] as well as classics, archaeology, and philosophy. He joined the National Socialist party in 1931, dropped out in 1932, and reenrolled in the SA with his fraternity (*Burschenschaft*). He climbed the career ladder in the SS (which he joined late, on September 1, 1939) and in the security police SD, for which he started to work in the fall of 1938.[8] He was deployed with Sonderkommando 1005 to Minsk in Belarus, where he oversaw several mass killings of Jews in the area of the Pripyat marshes.[9] On May 21, 1963, the regional court in Koblenz sentenced him, for his "principal function" in six mass killings of at least 6,600 Jews, to ten years in prison.[10] Wilke wrote many letters, all of which are long and rambling expositions that include biographical details, political musings, and ideological justifications. His verbosity was noted by the judges in Koblenz who declared in their verdict: "Wilke is incapable of clear and straight thinking; he has a tendency to engage in escapes and excuses." The judges considered him a "fanatical and enthusiastic nationalist whose wrongheaded idealism was used and abused by the previous regime."[11]

The letter's intended recipient was Wolfdietrich Wilke, born in 1949. At that time, his father was living under an assumed name. In 1945, Artur had abandoned his first wife and three children and gone into hiding, assuming the identity of his deceased brother. He entered civil service as a teacher under his brother's name and remarried, allegedly with the "full consent of my [first] wife, who suffered from incurable cancer (which she knew), since my brother had been unmarried."[12] In his defense of bigamy, Wilke claimed that "it was important for her and for me to save the father for the children."[13] It is quite possible that she, indeed, supported him in this decision, since she was a politically tested SS bride (the issue of women's support will be explored more fully in the next chapter).[14] As an ideologically committed wife, she might have consented to this ultimate sacrifice and testified freely to her husband's death in order to facilitate his escape and continued reproductive success as the father of more children. She died in Rostock (GDR) in 1954.[15] After her death, Wilke proceeded to adopt his first three children as their supposed uncle.[16] Wolfdietrich, the fourth child, was born into the bigamist marriage. Wilke's second wife, Dr. Ursula Wilke, practiced as a medical doctor in the district of Peine in the northern part of West Germany. Wolfdietrich was deeply shaken by his father's arrest. His mother confided to Professor Schlingensiepen that "Wolfdietrich has unfortunately received a rather significant shock. There is no telling how all of this will affect him in his future life."[17] His father referred to him in another letter to Schlingensiepen as "our problem child"[18] and requested that the Schlingensiepen family allow him to visit their home in order to receive guidance and support during this crisis.[19]

The seventy-seven-page letter is undated. It begins with "My dear Boy!" and is signed "Your Father," but ends with an epilogue addressed to the "esteemed Herr Professor" (Schlingensiepen). It is part of the Schlingensiepen files in the Archive of the Protestant Church in the Rhineland (AEKIR), where I discovered the original. In his paragraph-long afterword, Wilke asked Schlingensiepen to take "the communication of this letter as an open and honest attempt to grapple with a confused and misguided faith.... This is a personal answer for a boy, my son, who would also like to maintain his good faith."[20] The intended audience of this text is therefore ambiguous. Wilke may never have intended to send it to his son, or he may have changed his mind at some point. Starting on page 13, under the heading *De Peccatis in Euangelio Secundum Matthaeum*, Wilke quoted long passages in Latin from the Gospel of Matthew. He received a Vulgate (the Latin translation of the Bible) when Bishop Stempel, the EKD plenipoteniary for war convicts (*Beauftragter für Kriegsverurteilte*) visited him in prison on August 23, 1966.[21] This allows us to date the letter to the latter part of 1966, the year in which his son turned seventeen. There is no archival information about Wolfdietrich's receipt of the letter and no record of how he might have reacted to his father's explanations.

The Mistake

At first sight the letter appears to be one man's honest accounting for his "mistakes," a term that appears eighty-three times. Wilke referred to "sin" thirty times, to its Latin version *peccare/peccatum* fifteen more times, and to "guilt" twenty-one times. Wanting to impress his son with his honesty, integrity, and scholarly erudition as a Latinist, he cited John 8:32, "*cognasce-tis veritatem et veritas liberabit vos!* You shall recognize the truth! And the truth will make you free."[22] But despite these titillating promises of the truth, his reflections on "mistakes" were slippery, abstract, and completely devoid of concrete references. His style was exasperating and convoluted. In order to provide a taste of his thinking and writing style, I will quote from the letter extensively, though I have occasionally simplified and shortened his long-winded sentences. The following paragraph is a good example of his confessional mode that is designed to deflect personal responsibility.

> The world in its dynamic life force and its inexhaustible wealth of possibilities is marked by sin and branded by its mistakes; it is sub-ject to error in its existing contradictions and to the flawed decisions of human beings in their judgments and actions. And these mis-takes become ever more ominous, the greater the offense against laws and commandments of humanity that are irrevocably valid for all humans. Human beings trespass, when they decide on the cross-roads, in the crossing of life's paths, at the crucifixes in a certain way because they did not see correctly, because they overlooked a love, and acted only in self-love, in reckless intolerance toward others!... one recognizes one's offense on a falsely chosen path with pain, where one had forgotten and disregarded God's commanded

path, and allowed oneself to be seduced by false counsel and sermons of self-righteous and violent authorities, and realizes that one
walked down the wrong path.[23]

Mistakes are described as general facts of life. They occur anywhere and
at any time. Despite the stated "pain of recognition," the writer did not
express remorse about mass executions of Jews. The reason for his conviction was not mentioned in the letter, although in another letter to a prison
chaplain he used code words that refer to "ghetto liquidations" and
"breaking the armed resistance of Jewish partisans."[24] No such explicit references occurred in the letter to the son. Wilke delicately avoided certain
terms: He mentioned "Jews" twice but only in the context of the New
Testament; the term "National Socialism" appeared never, and the name
Adolf Hitler was avoided, although there was one reference to the general
word *Führer*.

> Without the existence of the mistake that hurts, we would be ines-
> capably caught in our own stupidity. But the mistake always leads to
> guilt/debt [*Schuld*], and it has always been a mistake to go into debt.
> And among the great defaulters we have always experienced—*ut
> historia docet*—that they were never capable of regularly redeeming
> their debt (and never seriously considered it), that in the end they
> went into serious bankruptcy and had to be bailed out by the faith-
> ful (not the investors!) [Wilkes plays here with the words *Gläubigen*
> and *Gläubiger*]. Every mistake provides good advice, and it is partially
> up to us whether we merely keep our heads above water or fly with
> full sails into temptation; and the mistake serves as a lesson that
> going into debt is no cure [*Heilmittel*], and that we will eventually
> recognize the mistake, even if laypeople are confused, while the
> experts are debating among themselves and the specialists are
> uncertain.[25]

These semantic contortions were supposed to attest to a semblance of
moral rehabilitation. But despite the letter's prominent discussion of "mistakes," the author categorically denied individual moral agency and used
passive constructions throughout. He portrayed himself as a victim of grand
defaulters who exploited his naive idealism and left him behind, stuck with
the bill. The letter created a moral universe without actors, as Wilke dis-
owned personal agency and moral subjectivity. Nevertheless, he distilled
several lessons from the ruins of his life and imparted them to his son.

Lessons from a Broken Vision: "Do Not Trust Anyone"

> *Be well, my son: Do not expect...that those who praise*
> *and bless the laws of the times [Zeitgesetze] will show any*
> *pity or compassion, once they have been defeated along*
> *with their mistaken, false laws, when tomorrow they have*
> *lost their gamble and the hour of truth will have revealed a*
> *different truth: then they will sacrifice you.*[26]

Wilke felt betrayed and used as a scapegoat forced to suffer for the "mistakes" of others. He raged against false teachers (*Weisheitslehrer*), lawyers, judges, experts, and specialists who deliberately (mis)led naive followers like himself. His greatest mistake, Artur Wilke suggested, was his youthful idealism and naive trust. This misdiagnosis averted a critical analysis of the particular values and ideologies, such as antisemitism, that he had actively advanced. This misdiagnosis was then followed by a faulty prescription for a cure.

Wilke cited Jesus' healing miracles as paradigms for renewal and regeneration. The Christian sinner, he believed, could be healed miraculously by the forgiveness of sin. Faith in the curative powers of Christ's forgiveness would instantaneously renew the life of the sinner:

> John 5:14 *Ecce sanis factus est: iam noli peccare.* You have been healed
> (the mistake has been overcome); now do not repeat the mistakes,
> so that nothing worse happens to you. You should no longer believe
> what others have believed and what turned out to be a bad mistake
> and of great harm to yourself.[27]

The misdiagnosis of the "mistake" was compounded by the expectation that forgiveness could offer a quick cure. Such a view empties forgiveness of meaningful transformative substance and reduces salvation (healing) to a magic wand that consigns the harm done by wrongdoing to the dustbin of history. Wilke tried to store his "mistakes" safely away in the past and move into the future.

The son was counseled to resist repeating a mistake that was misnamed as youthful trust in authority. Wolfdietrich should beware of teachers who "will approach you with persuasiveness [*Überredung*] or loquaciousness [*Zerredung*] or legal coercion."[28] This was one of the suspicions that passed from the experience of Nazi perpetrators to their antiauthoritarian children who rebelled in 1968. While the generation of 1968 suspected the government precisely for its involvement and incomplete renunciation of Nazi politics, the deep wariness, disillusionment, and distrust in established authority of the older generation formed a bridge to the next generation. Wilke affirmed the need for vigilance toward authorities as an appropriate response to the debacle of his life: "Do not repeat the mistake," he told his son, "so that nothing worse happens to you."[29] Wilke saw himself as the primary victim of his mistake, and not the Jewish dead buried in mass graves of Belarus. He was concerned that his son should avoid "great harm to yourself," but said nothing about the need to avoid doing harm to others. Wilke remained preoccupied with his own predicament and expressed no empathy for the actual victims.

We do not know whether the son challenged his father's self-referential focus, but we do know that the German second generation was rather self-referential itself. For all the passionate debates about the effects of authoritarianism and fascism on German families, politics, and culture, there was often surprisingly little curiosity about the former victims of Nazism. The political, social, economic, and psychological reality of Jews, of Roma and Sinti, homosexuals, Communists, Jehovah's Witnesses, or the victims of euthanasia and sterilization programs remained long hidden behind veils of shame and silence.[30] It would take decades before the focus of postwar German discussions of the Nazi past would include concern and curiosity about victims and survivors, beginning with the broadcast of the Hollywood series *Holocaust* in 1978 that centered on the dramatic life story of one Jewish family.[31]

Democracy, Consumerism, and Youth Culture

Before his arrest, Wilke had rather comfortably been ensconced in capitalist West Germany. Married to a medical doctor, he had received tenure in the public school system and, no doubt, publicly professed allegiance to the new democratic state. But his loyalty was fragile and he remained wary of the crass materialism and consumerism that had taken root in the wake of the West German *Wirtschaftswunder*. Convicted for mass murder, he decried the decline in moral values he noted among the young:

> A young girl recently said: I don't believe in Jesus! I believe in the Beatles! ... Our modern, cultivated, and civilized devils are no longer as easily recognizable as the devil back in the desert [confronting Jesus].... But all of these insurance policies surely lead into the realm of the devil.[32]

He lamented the corruption of education and sexual morality, of the arts and public media, and he railed against schoolteachers who assigned authors such as "Sagan, Casanova, Ringelnatz, Sartre" and who discussed "free love."[33] He bemoaned that the hypothetical "little Fritz" and "little Erna" were being led astray and turned into "well-paid whores, business-savvy liars and cheats, or successful, winning politicians...who effectively twist the commandments of God."[34] In keeping with Nazi aesthetic that condemned "decadent art," he scorned modern art that "I must be too stupid to understand"[35] and objected to psychoanalysis, which "burrows through the filth and shame of people's past" in order to "put their noses into the shit bucket."[36] For all his willingness to adapt to and integrate into the postwar world, he remained alienated from the emerging consumerist youth culture described in *Miracle Years*,[37] which seemed to him mired in "profit thinking" and breeding all manner of "infidelity and adultery, perjury, mendacity, and betrayal of heaven and earth."[38] While he would never allow himself to be openly nostalgic, the contemporary world seemed to contrast with the *Good Old Days*,[39] when loyalty and fidelity still counted. He repackaged some of the core values of National Socialism in Christian terminology:

> Without fidelity you won't succeed in life. It binds and commits everything that is alive from the smallest to the greatest. There are certain commitments in life that no human spirit and no living heart can disdain. Every betrayal of fidelity destroys more than just itself. Without faith there is no life. The heavenly firmament is built on fidelity and faith in the here and now as well in as the beyond.[40]

The logical inconsistency of endorsing both distrust of authority and unwavering fidelity reveals Wilke's transitional status between ideologies and political systems. His letter is studded with contradictions as he struggles to bridge contradictory and competing values systems. Intentionally vague formulations patch up the fragments of his broken universe that perched precariously between Nazi and Christian discourses. According to Wilke, the democratic world worships at "altars of relative conceptions of truth."[41] "We paint and make poetry, philosophy, theology, law, and morality only in dialectic dubious ways."[42] Democracy struck him as a "cruel but ridiculous political game" in which two political parties engage in debate and "each demonizes the other."[43] Terms such as "relativism" and "dialectic" discredited the analytic search for truth. Critical thinking can only lead to questionable theories because they are not grounded in absolutes. Wilke remained attracted and attached to totalitarian thought, now anchored in absolute "rights and responsibilities, the laws and commandments of heaven."[44] God, it seems, moved into the position previously occupied by the führer.

In rebuilding his moral and ideological universe, Wilke traded Nazi authoritarianism for a conservative Christian theology that remained totalitarian and infused with pagan nature symbolism. Even those perpetrators who rejoined churches for purely political and practical reasons, like Adolf Eichmann, wanted their children baptized and brought up in the framework of a Christian rather than overtly Nazi worldview.[45] The children would be raised with a conservative Christian morality, and the Christian church would take the place of the nation (*Volksgemeinschaft*) or of the SS-Sippengemeinschaft. Christianity was seen as the last bulwark of conservative morality standing up to godless communism and capitalist individualism that marred the modern world.

Unconditional Submission to Authority

Wilke still yearned for absolute truth and absolute submission to totalitarian authority, but he recognized that Adolf Hitler had failed to deliver. Now he was ready to submit to God. "God's law knows of no conditional and subordinate clauses, no If and But; there is no subjunctive! His laws and statements are imperatives that are stated as commands!"[46] He searched for a secure ideological foundation that would provide him with firm footing to navigate the changes in political and moral value systems. Wilke asserted that only an absolute perspective could transcend shifting political fortunes. His disillusionment with human laws, values, and visions colored his counsel to his son.

> Most importantly, you should keep his laws and instructions...and God will be with you.... Do not be led astray by those who keep several other gods beside him as an insurance policy, and who arrogantly think they can play God...and can be better lawmakers than he. Distinguish conscientiously between God's laws and the laws in East and West, where each considers himself in the right but which can be twisted like American chewing gum and which can be changed and lifted by succeeding gods.[47]

Only God's laws, he submitted, are guaranteed to be unchangeable, clear, and unambiguous. Human laws are haphazard and subject to change. His sense of abandonment buttressed his cynical sense of ethical relativism. Lawmakers, he claimed, are apt to twist laws depending on the direction of shifting winds, while they themselves keep out of the fray on their safe perches of power, and force men like him to pay for their inconsistencies.

> In translating the wisdom of a word, one therefore needs to know the direction in which the priests faced. Where once, there was an originally unambiguous word and concept, we now have two standpoints and the exegetes and legalists can then interpret one and the same action as either a heroic deed or a crime.[48]

Crime or heroic deed—it all depended on the definition. Obviously Wilke lamented his rude fall from heroic glory into criminality as a result of regime change. But he also misdiagnosed the ethical problem: It was not ethical relativism, critical thinking, and legal sophistication that had taken him into the forests of Belarus to kill Jews. But since he failed to confront the wrong of executing unarmed civilians, he misnamed the moral task facing the son. In the end, Wilke's abstract discussion of the merits and demerits of the law skirted the issue of culpable involvement in genocide.

His moral absolutism becomes most apparent in his endorsement of radical pacifism. This odd convergence of perpetrator exculpation and antimilitarist peace activism is surprising. The link between Wilke's conservative antimilitarism and the motivations of more progressive, younger peace activists in East and West Germany may help to explain why the peace movement became such a powerful integrative force in postwar Germany. It absorbed old disillusioned warriors and young conscientious objectors, Nazi perpetrators and their rebellious children.

Pacifism

Why would a Nazi convict become a champion of radical pacifism? His ethical absolutism committed Wilke to the total repudiation of the use of deadly force under any circumstance, including war, self-defense, and capital punishment. He maintained passionately that any ethical or legal exception would open the door to hypocrisy. Those who debated ethical questions in the long tradition of "just war theory" were discredited by Wilke as mere *Schriftgelehrte* (scribes) "who think they must question eternally valid laws instead of providing an honest response to God's call."[49] Scribes, exegetes, and legalists were set to undermine the clarity of God's law and make it harder for the imaginary "little Fritz" to do the right thing. Instead, he counseled his son, he should live by unambiguous radical principles rather than by ethical deliberation.

> Examine the debate concerning murder and nonmurder [he refers to just war theory] as a sorry example of how the disciples of Jesus dispute and dissect his wisdom and truth in suicidal and traitorous manner to the detriment of the simple believers.[50]

What attracted Wilke to radical pacifism, I suspect, was the opportunity to fold genocide into the general devastation of war and to blur distinctions between ordinary soldiers and SS men. He styled himself a professional soldier who repeatedly requested redeployment to the front lines: "Again and again!—I only had the one thought, to join the fighting units like my brother and all of my friends....Again and again this was denied to me and I was told with bitter reproof that I was supposed to perform my duty wherever I was being ordered!"[51] Despite this implicit admission that he performed mass executions of Jews (or "partisans," as he would call them), Wilke quickly asserted that he followed orders like any other soldier.

The legal and moral line between "war crimes" and "crimes against humanity" remained blurry. This was evidenced by public debates over the correct terminology that would refer to Nazi trials and defendants. Within the Protestant Church, there were still those who spoke of "war crimes" (*Kriegsverbrechen*) and "war convicts" (*Kriegsverurteilte*),[52] while others insisted on the language of NS crimes (*NS-Verbrechen*)[53] or NS crimes of violence (*national-sozialistische Gewaltverbrechen*).[54] These linguistic conventions exposed the newly emerging consensus that the killings in which Wilke had been involved were in fact different from military violence. This rightly worried Wilke. His embrace of radical pacifism attempted to reinstate the moral ambiguity and treated every act of violence by the state on the same principle. This made any distinction between war and genocide elusive again. In general, those accused of Nazi crimes during the sixties were not members of the Wehrmacht, but of the SS, of the *Einsatzgruppen* and police battalions.[55] Although Wilke had not served in the Wehrmacht, he questioned all forms of military violence on the basis of the Gospel of Matthew:

> What is meant here by "honest weapons"? Nuclear weapons? Ordinary bombs? 9 millimeter or 7.6 millimeter? Chemical or biological weapons? Bombs from above? Land mines from below? Invisible ambush with malice? Or an eye for an eye? Suddenly on a sunny day or by night? Murder in darkness or by daylight? From a distance or in arm's reach? Faced with such horror and before God (whether one accepts him or not), how can one speak of killing with "honest weapons."[56]

Once ethical distinctions between the military battlefield and genocide have been erased, Wilke's hypothetical "little Fritz" is left genuinely befuddled. How should the little guy be able recognize the legitimacy of particular military orders given by proper authorities, let alone resist them? He maintained that the Christian tradition and Western political theory had long blessed various methods of mass killings, including "mass starvation, aerial bombardments, gas attacks, mass rape, and mass killings."[57] He pointed to World War I, where millions of Christians "murdered each other by the millions...maliciously [*heimtückisch*], brutally, without pity or compassion, individually and in groups, and in the end there was a nice [*schönes*], God-willed mass grave of 9.7 million dead."[58] This was

> emulated in World War II, where we experienced how far the idea can be taken that such divinely sanctioned murder is an ethical necessity rooted in nature, to which one must submit; that murder is necessary in order to fulfill God's will and to establish law, judgment, and freedom (peace and justice) and to establish political demands; that it is a necessary order to terminate enmity in the world by killings one's enemies. By the end we stood before the mass graves of 55 million people. Can this be topped in the third round, since all good things come in threes? In both mass murders, murder remained murder.[59]

Wilke applied the words "mass murder" (*Massenmord*) and "genocide" (*Völkermord*) eleven times, but always in the context of war, and specifically with reference to nuclear war. It was never used in the context of killing Jewish civilians. Consider the following excerpt, where Wilke berates church leaders for ethically condoning nuclear arms on the basis of just war theory:

> Aren't they already justifying the next implementation of mass murder in their own way, so that on the Day X the faithful will be there and willingly follow orders to implement the greatest and possibly last mass murder and genocide [*Massen- u. Völkermord*].[60]

West Germany's remilitarization and integration into the NATO alliance, but especially the debate over nuclear weapons in 1957–1958, led to mass demonstrations and a burgeoning peace movement. As historian Michael Geyer pointed out, "a significant element of the antimilitary movement . . . reflected a profound disenchantment with the state, an initial alienation from the state as protector and guarantor of security and personal integrity."[61] Wilke exemplified Geyer's concept of "injured citizenship" that characterized a generation betrayed and insecure about the credibility and authority of its government. Wilke felt abandoned and resentful of the West German state, and his pacifism allowed him to express his frustrations as it served his exculpation.[62] His principled opposition to all military service erased the line between the military and the specific operations of *SS-Einsatzkommandos*:

> What irony and cynicism characterizes those who elevate themselves as judges over a mistake in their past and proceed to condemn the fathers while trying to animate the sons to commit the same mistakes, because they continue to need someone (their *Einsatzkommandos*) whom they can sacrifice for their sacrificial goals, and they can nail others on the cross in order to reap profit without having to sacrifice themselves...and thereby they prevent those who genuinely want to recognize and honestly confess their sins and mistakes so that others may learn from them and may, for God's sake, not have to repeat them, but they may not, they cannot do so, because the old sins, the mistakes of yesterday may turn out to be necessary and the right way again tomorrow—into the hour of truth!![63]

Einsatzkommandos were mobile killing units deployed against civilian populations in the National Socialist effort to "cleanse" the newly conquered territories in Soviet Union of Jewish civilians and Bolshevist commissars beginning in June 1941. *Einsatzgruppen* were under command of the German Security Police (Sicherheitspolizei) and Security Service (Sicherheitsdienst) and not the Wehrmacht. They trailed the front lines behind the troops and conducted mass executions in villages, towns, and cities of Belorussia, Ukraine, and the Baltic area. Wilke had been in the employ of the SD (Security Service) since 1938 when he was sent to Minsk to conduct "cleansing operations" in January 1942. The conflation of *Einsatzkommandos* with military service was intended to muddy the ethical waters.

His pacifism reached a fevered pitch on the topic of nuclear weapons, a moral outrage perpetrated by Germany's former enemies, the United States and Soviet Union. The two superpowers were competing against each other in "preparations for mass murder in the present."[64] Wilke agreed with a majority of Germans who suspected that the superpowers had stationed nuclear weapons on German soil and would not hesitate to destroy Germany in the event of a nuclear war, when it would be turned into "nuclear theater."[65] Nuclear war, wrote Wilke, "is the next escalation of mass murder (the one tomorrow will justify all of the previous mass murders) and will lead to humanity's self-annihilation and the complete destruction of life on this planet."[66] Wilke told his son: "You come closer to the truth of my life when you learn and teach: *Si non vis bellum, para pacem* [If you don't want war, prepare for peace]."[67]

For the younger generation in Germany, born during and after a devastating war, such pacifist sentiments rang true. The military defeat, the destruction of cities in aerial bombings, and the mass expulsion from Germany's eastern territories had deeply scarred the entire population. Nuclear weapons, first tested on Germany's ally Japan, reinforced Germany's self-perception as a victim of ruthless military superpowers. Resistance to Germany's remilitarization in the 1950s, protests against the Vietnam War in the 1960s and against the deployment of nuclear weapons on German soil in the 1970s and 1980s, and opposition to the first Gulf War in the 1990s formed a constant and unifying cultural force. The younger generation was mostly unaware of the extent to which their pacifist sentiments and activism in the peace movement transcended the political spectrum and were shared by some Nazi perpetrators. Wilke's pacifist message and strident condemnation of nuclear weapons, within the German context, could be considered an extreme right-wing as well as a politically progressive position. Germany's constitution banned nuclear weapons, and few could genuinely approve of Cold War posturing of the

United States and the Soviet Union over the territory of a divided Germany. Pacifism resonated powerfully with veterans' war weariness and the younger generations' suspicion of militarism. But it also served the self-exculpation of perpetrators.[68]

God's Chosen People

Like Bradfisch and Kroeger, discussed in the last chapter, Wilke was keenly aware of the need to avoid racist, antisemitic stereotypes while writing from prison. He censored anything that might be interpreted as evidence of "race hatred" and instead quoted the New Testament. Based on the Gospel of Matthew, he argued that Jesus had condemned "people's tendencies (especially among God's chosen people) toward egoism, reckless and blatant selfishness that only loves dialectic, in order to play hanky-panky and push the world toward self-destructive uncertainty in an extraordinarily sharp manner."[69] The very word "Jew" had become taboo in West German parlance. But Jesus of Nazareth was still fighting the good fight against the "ferment" of the Pharisees who "seduce" and "confuse" the people.[70] Selfishness, greed, seduction, and hypocrisy were staples of Nazi antisemitism, now safely repackaged in the figure of the Pharisee. For Wilke, Judaism and Christianity constituted antithetical and alien (wesenfremde) religious systems. Predictably, he identified the Christian tradition with peace, love, and forgiveness, while Judaism was associated with war, vengeance, and retaliation:

> There exists an internal contradiction, which we openly experience when a Polish bishop (Kardinal Wischinsky) states: "We forgive!" while the Jewish rabbi of Holland declares: "We do not forgive and absolve!" Through the first speaks the Messiah Jesus of Nazareth, while through the other speaks the recently born Messiah Uriel-Ben-David-Blau. One should not be surprised by antisemitism and everything that happened over the course of 1,900 years....There is a great decisive question mark...behind the antithetical claims of two essentially alien Messiahs (Jesus Christ, on the one hand— Uriel ben David Blau [sic], on the other). Those who argue for legal sanctions dialectically and who pursue retribution incessantly only intensify feelings of revenge until the last, clearly predictable, consequence is reached. I do not think that this is in the spirit blessed by God.[71]

What is this "last, clearly predictable consequence?" It sounds like a threat, and could imply that the next outbreak of violence would (once again) be an act of self-defense, a mere reaction to the (Jewish) pursuit of retribution. In the world of perpetrators, the victim was the aggressor and the aggressor saw himself forced to act in self-defense. Such reversals are characteristic of perpetrators, in whose minds the Holocaust did not occur as the result of centuries of German Christian contempt of Jews, but rather as the inevitable culmination of Jewish malice and hatred:

> Many people of goodwill who have not shown any sympathy for antisemitism are now ready to embrace it, as the deeper divine ground becomes visible, as it rises up in them. Such comprehension easily leads to further conclusions, much as in an ongoing partisan battle, where each side exacts revenge and retaliation, because all guilt must be paid off on this earth.[72]

This is the one of the few times that the word "antisemitism" appears in the document. Counting himself among the "people of goodwill," Wilke provides an accurate description of the physical sensation that signaled the "rising up" of antisemitic hatred in the body.[73] As much as he censored his speech, his emotions could not be repressed completely. They were present below the surface and restrained by his precarious legal situation. While antisemitism had lost political credibility, the underlying scorn and revulsion was now transposed onto Jesus' struggle against the Jews. The Christian language of contempt could still be legally invoked and serve as replacement of the racist, political, and economic vehicles of Jew-hatred.

Throughout the 1960s, antisemitism was a persistent, if often unacknowledged, undercurrent of German politics and culture. A diffuse fear and resentment of Jews transcended political factions and united progressive children with their conservative parents. The unconscious reception of undigested antisemitism expressed itself in a spate of antisemitic incidents and vandalism by young people in West Germany.[74] Among the radical wings of student activists anti-Jewish suspicion morphed seamlessly into anti-Zionism and laid the groundwork for close working relationships of the Red Army Faction (RAF) with the Palestinian and Arab underground, including several trips for training purposes to Jordan and Syria.[75] Israel became the preferred target of diatribes against imperialism, capitalism, international banking, and oil exploitation, as well as against America.[76] The old wine of religious anti-Judaism was poured into new skins, including progressive theologies that highlighted Jesus' alleged antagonism to Jewish authoritarianism, legalism, militarism, patriarchy, and colonialism.[77]

But there was a growing minority that actively advocated for new Christian attitudes toward Judaism and demanded a repudiation of anti-Jewish stereotypes. Initiatives, such as the *Freiburger Rundbriefe*, founded by Roman Catholic Gertrud Luckner, who was incarcerated in Ravensbrück for her efforts to rescue Jews;[78] the International Council of Christians and Jews (ICCJ) founded in 1948–1949;[79] the annual "week of brotherliness" (*Woche der Brüderlichkeit*) instituted in 1952 by the German Gesellschaften für Christlich-Jüdische Zusammenarbeit, with over eighty local chapters;[80] the introduction in 1959 of Jewish-Christian dialogue as a permanent fixture of the nationwide gatherings of Protestant Christians in the Evangelische Kirchentag;[81] the formation in 1958 of Action Reconciliation (Aktion Sühnezeichen/Friedensdienste), which sent out young volunteers to serve as "signs of atonement" in countries that had suffered under Nazi occupation;[82] the adoption of "Nostra Aetate" in 1965 at the Second Vatican Council, which revolutionized Roman Catholic attitudes, liturgies, and teachings about Judaism.[83] All of these initiatives increased awareness of Christian anti-Judaism as a contributing factor to the Holocaust and focused attention on anti-Jewish teachings. The ease with which Nazi perpetrators reappropriated Christianity as a vehicle for contempt shows how urgently needed these initiatives and discussions were. Scholars have debated the developmental links between religious anti-Judaism and political, race-based antisemitism in the nineteenth century.[84] There is less awareness of the reabsorption of antisemitism into Christian theological language in the postwar world. Christianity, one could say, provided not only the cradle but also the retirement home for political antisemitism.

The Perpetrator as Victim

Perpetrators perceived and presented themselves as victims. These portraits were sometimes adopted defensively on advice of their legal counsel, who tried to maximize their chances of acquittal. But these victim discourses were more than an outward facade. They became an integral dimension of their identity. Artur Wilke consistently stressed his powerlessness and lack of agency, while struggling to project paternal authority over his son. He offered grandiose affirmations of his classical education and verbal dexterity, while the same time emphasizing his impotence as a naive victim of greater powers. He wanted his son to sympathize with him and join his defense against the overpowering forces that were threatening him. Wilke felt surrounded by external enemies who attacked and betrayed him. But he also felt the victim of his internal struggles.

In one passage, Wilke described this internal battle in a series of remarkably violent verbs. The paragraph is convoluted and hard to translate and was written for defensive purposes. Wilke complained that the judges had failed to take account of his internal state of mind and the psychic costs of his service as executioner. Grammatically, the object of violent action was his internal self, as he positioned himself as the ultimate victim of violence:

> It always depends on how one wants to paint the picture of terror [*Schreckensbilder*]—to appraise, judge, and condemn a complex, simple mortal on the basis of his external actions in his spiritual plight, who had to smother and kill his inner bewilderment and helplessness and drown out all his internal voices, who bludgeoned the best in himself—which threatened to rape and crush him, which he tried to overcome and surmount by committing incomprehensible acts, to prevent himself from stumbling in a situation, where he had been ordered to kill, been persuaded and told that it was good and necessary to kill one's enemies—in order to protect a higher legal good—such a man is condemned as an evil excess perpetrator—while the objective and rational jurist who remained "internally uninvolved" [*innerlich unberührt*]...and can't remember...is shown leniency.[85]

His soul had been violated. His inner being became the battleground of violent action with verbs such as smother, kill, drown, bludgeon, rape, crush, overcome, stumble. The rhetoric of violence is transferred from the physical infliction of harm to victims to the internal psychological drama. It was not the body of the victim, but the soul of the victimizer that took center stage. He resented the judges' refusal to grant him victim status and denounced their heartless imposition of punishment on a "poor man... whose heart had been torn apart."[86] The internal torment of perpetration supplanted the need for punishment, in his estimation. He had already been punished enough. Meanwhile, Wilke railed against his codefendants, who had remained "cool" and unaffected but still received lesser sentences.

He felt unfairly punished and the victim of double jeopardy. He saw him-self as "the most pitiful of all the victims," as he put it in a different letter addressed to Schlingensiepen. There he articulated the sense of victim-hood in one long-winded and convoluted sentence:

> Do we really want to lighten our load by prodding the least, who are probably the most pitiful of all the victims of this murderous order of an insane time, when most people (among friend and foe) served unbelief in belief, and whose conscience became numb and deceived, who were misled and raped, do we want to ask these most pitiful to issue a frank confession of their guilt, the most ter-rible ordeal of their life, in order to accuse and condemn them, so that we can play prosecutor and judge and arrive at a damning ver-dict, while we (the others), the majority of whom are unwilling and unable to profess their guilt and who are sheltered from the conse-quences, this extreme agony of being, yes, who prove daily that one can save oneself from this whirlwind by forgetting, silencing, denying, and forgiving one's own failures and one's own guilt rather than by acknowledging one's own past, while the nation is distancing itself from what it once embraced as faith and command.[87]

Such self-pity became an impenetrable wall that obstructed meaningful communication between perpetrators and their children. Wilke's inability to speak of the physical reality of the killings as an act of wrongdoing forced his son into complicity. Any question the son might wish to raise would be interpreted as a vicious accusation and assault on his agonized father. German intergenerational family communications were perme-ated by threats against traitors and *Nestbeschmutzer* (those who soil the nest). Filial fidelity demanded acquiescence and submission to the narra-tives of victimization. The contradictions, omissions, and fabrications of the historical record were smoothed over in the interest of harmonious family relations. This created an emotionally charged environment where autobiographical questions would regularly mushroom into full-blown fights. The parents' inability to speak truthfully about their role as willing executioners inducted the children into what Ralph Giordano called the second guilt.[88] As the flight from responsibility became paramount, perpe-trators inadvertently endowed the past with uncanny power. The more pressure was exerted on the children to side with their parents by "forgiving and forgetting" the past, the greater became the strains and constraints of intergenerational conversations in postwar German families. As the burden of guilt was pushed away, under the rug, and out of sight, it reappeared in waves that would convulse families and the society at large. As Wilke complained in exasperation:

> We are turning in a vicious circle...when human beings who have been sentenced in their mistakes and recognize and confess their error with deep regret, yes who have already forgiven their bad teachers who advocated the "beloved, God-given führer," when these teachers have metamorphosed into judges who sit in self-righteous judgment as representative authorities of "Christian politics" and condemn those same repentant sinners while they themselves perpetuate the same bad, pernicious teachings.[89]

Wilke experienced guilt denial as a vicious circle, out of which he saw no escape. Of course, he could not truly "recognize and confess" his own "error." Schlingensiepen realized that Wilke was not truly capable of grasping the key to release from the vicious circle of guilt. He asked the local prison chaplain to convey to "our deplorable friend" that he was so "profoundly disappointed by its main message and that I literally want to cry over it."[90] Schlingensiepen was disheartened by Wilke's "pathetic self-mirroring and self-pity" and feared that his defenses and evasions were beginning "to infect his wife and his children." If only Wilke would follow the example of "Paul, Luther, and Augustine and confess his soul [*selbst*] and his past with its irredeemable guilt unsparingly before God and humanity" and would "mourn the victims of his wretched deeds until the end of his life.... then he could praise the blood of Christ that cries louder than the blood of Abel, and louder also than the blood that he himself spilt."[91] Wilke's refusal to take "the bitter medicine"[92] implicated the son, who was, after all, the intended recipient of this tortured communication. Schlingensiepen concluded:

> What could Artur Wilke do for his wonderful boy in Stederdorf, who visited us last Pentecost, and how much would it mean to his wife and all of his children if he could tear himself away from himself and into the arms of God, who as the merciful [God] shows anger when we move away from him, but as the angry [God] shows mercy.[93]

The Children's Response

Conversations, such as this snapshot from the Wilke family, often ended with hard choices for the children: they could submit to their father's warped view of the world and join him in categorical denials of moral culpability; they could recoil from their father in moral revulsion and cultivate an identity of rebellious opposition; or they could accept the legacy of perpetration and take on the moral obligations of repair themselves. All three pathways are well trodden in West Germany.

In his study of German family dynamics during the eighties, psychiatrist Dan Bar-On found that many children of perpetrators fluctuated between the first and the second option. The first group joined in the denial of culpability because they could not imagine loving a parent capable of committing atrocities. The second group demonstrated their own moral integrity by distancing themselves from the guilt of the parents.[94] Both pathways are essentially escapist: the first group runs away by accepting false claims of innocence, while the second tries to break away by abandoning their parents. Both strategies are compulsive and rooted in the fear of guilt by association. The tortured memoir literature of children of perpetrators is testament to the futility of the flights from this legacy.

Renate Wald's recent auto/biography (2004) of her father, Robert Ley, is a good example of the first pathway. Ley was chief of the German Labor Front for the duration of the Third Reich and was sentenced to death in the Nuremberg IMT, which he preempted by committing suicide.[95] Known as a notorious antisemite and fervent follower of National Socialism, Robert Ley oversaw the dissolution and assimilation of unions into the Deutsche Arbeitsfront. Renate Wald, a noted feminist sociologist in postwar West Germany, seemingly submits to her father's version of the world. In her biography, she concluded that he "was not a criminal, . . . never inflicted any damage on a human being; instead, his work benefited and served as a blessing to Germans and foreign races [sic!]."[96] She turned her intimate experience of her father and desire to respect him as a generous and caring human being into proof positive of his inability to participate in National Socialist atrocities. Her love purified the father and justified her revisionist reading of history despite her professional career as a sociologist who was trained to evaluate data dispassionately. In his interviews with children of perpetrators, journalist Gerald Posener characterized this position thus: "By denying their fathers' complicity in monstrous crimes, they attempt to justify the pureness of their love. Since they refuse to acknowledge any criminal taint. they do not feel compelled to explain or excuse their feelings."[97] Among this group of children, some expressly condemned National Socialist ideologies and its practices even as they exonerated their own parents. There were others whose denial of culpable wrongdoing led them to embrace the political ideologies of their parents, and they turned to right-wing and neo-Nazi fringe politics. Gudrun Burwitz, for instance, who was born 1929, the daughter of Heinrich Himmler,[98] became a prominent spokesperson for the neo-Nazi movement and an important link between old perpetrator networks and younger sympathizers.[99] Certainly, one way to avoid feeling guilty for the atrocities of National Socialism was to assent and to agree with its under-lying principles.

The second pathway is exemplified by Niklas Frank, whose father Hans Frank was convicted and sentenced to death in the Nuremberg IMT as governor-general of Poland. His auto/biography of his father concluded with the vow: "I will be trying to leap away from you for the rest of my life."[100] Niklas Frank felt sullied by being born into the "dirtiest family."[101] In his attempt to "leap away from" the legacy of guilt, Niklas Frank's books excoriated not only his parents' political crimes but also their general lack of character, sexual deviance, and personal flaws.[102] Frank tried to escape moral contamination by posing as his parents' prosecutor and judge. He cursed his father and mother in an "extended chain of insults and invec-tives hurled at his father by a bitter and unforgiving narrator," as literary critic Erin McGlothlin shows.[103] In this "aggressive, violent confrontation with the father's legacy,"[104] the parents turn into moral monsters, whose dishonesty, greed, self-aggrandizement, and cowardice made them appear devoid of humanizing emotions of concern, kindness, and private decency. Frank criticized other second-generation memoirs for trying to separate a "loving daddy from the ice-cold desk murderer."[105] For Frank, the Nazi conscience that justified the murder of innocents permeated and contam-inated every aspect of life. His portrayals of his father and mother turned them into demonic figures whose lives appeared preposterous and almost outside the realm of the humanly possible.

But the turn away from the perpetrators is not yet a turn toward the victims. While many in the second generation hated the fathers, they remained suspicious and fearful of the victims. For instance, both Rolf Mengele, the son of Auschwitz medical doctor Josef Mengele, and Niklas Frank, dreaded the possibility of rejection, which compelled them to avoid meeting Jews:

"I am afraid," says Dagmar Drexel, "that if the people I meet know what my father did, they won't want anything to do with me." "I would like to go to Israel," remarks Niklas Frank, "but how can I go? I am ashamed to meet these people." "I *do* apologize to all the people for what my father did," says Rolf Mengele.[106]

Such anxiety arises from an overwhelming fear of contamination by guilt. The renunciation of the parents does not automatically lead to rapprochement and reconciliation with the victims. On the contrary, the flight from guilt by association intensifies distrust and suspicion of victims because they embody allegations of wrongdoing and trigger feelings of shame and embarrassment. As Ernestine Schlant noted in her analysis of German *Väterliteratur*, a literary genre that deals with the guilt of the fathers, "in almost all of these situations depicted in these novels Jews are peripheral."[107] Even Peter Schneider's novel *Vati*, the fictional account of Rolf Mengele's meeting with his father in Brazil, which explicitly criticizes the instrumentalization of the victims, "reproduces the latter, for the word *Jew* and the mention of Jewish victims are strikingly absent in the entire narrative."[108] While the second generation urgently tried to move away and out of the shadow of the fathers, they were often not able to reach out to the victims and to repair the rupture of genocidal violence.[109]

The third, and chronologically most recent, response to the transmission of intergenerational guilt accepts it as a peculiar burden that can be carried with dignity. These children oppose the evasive deceptions of the parents by engaging in meticulous historical truth- and soul-searching. Their historical research generates moral change and restores relationships with former victims. For these authors, guilt is accepted as a task that cannot be escaped or ignored. As they search for historical truth, its shadow loses its uncanny power to determine the present and the future. The precise knowledge of particular moral and political choices dispels the vague myths of innocence and victimhood. Though these authors are often not trained as historians, they are drawn to archival research in order to overcome the strategies of exculpation. Sometimes such children divest ill-gotten gains and inherited possessions before they reconnect with victims and their descendants.

For example, Beate Niemann, who was born in 1942, began her auto/ biography *Mein guter Vater: Mein Leben mit seiner Vergangenheit* with the long-cherished conviction that her father, Bruno Sattler, had been imprisoned unjustly in a Leipzig prison by the Communist government in East

Germany, where he died in 1972. Her legal quest to secure his rehabilitation after reunification in 1990 revealed the extent of his involvement in the Holocaust. She decided to pursue these historical clues and engaged in a complex historical project that taxed her courage and determination. She reflected on the impulse to avoid the truth and to deny her father's "cold consideration, ideology, and political conception that manifested in actions." She struggled with her incomprehension: "I can understand homicide committed in passion...but this is not what this is about. To sit behind a desk and plan genocide in order to execute it is something altogether different."[110] As she examined her resistance to these revelations, she came to accept the full extent of her father's compromised life. She confronted the desire to escape and run from powerful and vague guilt feelings. Instead, she committed herself to rendering his decisions as factually as possible in order to make his actions concrete and personal. Niemann turned the Holocaust from a vague event in the past that elicited diffuse guilt feelings into a particular and personal memory of her father.

This led her to a Jewish family in London, whose aunt "was sent to the East" in order to vacate the house in Berlin into which the Sattler family had moved.[111] Niemann was born in that house just before the Jewish owner was deported to the ghetto/camp of Terezin. After the war, the house was returned to surviving Jewish relatives. Before she met this Jewish family, Niemann sold all furniture whose origins she could not determine. These steps allowed her to overcome her fears of retribution, and she was able to reach out to those who had been directly wronged by her father. In that moment, she emerged from the shadow of her father's guilty legacy. Having chronicled her father's crimes and divested herself of unearned privileges, she had become genuinely free to meet anyone on her own terms. She lost her fear and was no longer compulsively driven by guilt feelings. She reclaimed her father as the particular, albeit broken, ground from which she would explore and experience the world. In accepting the Holocaust as a personal task, she was released from its fearful stranglehold.

Martin Pollack was born in 1944 as the son of Dr. Gerhard Bast, the *SS-Sturmbannführer* who headed the Gestapo offices in Graz and Linz, was a member of Sondergruppe 11a, and was involved in mass executions of Jews. In *Dead Man in the Bunker: Discovering My Father*[112] Pollack uses his father's life to explore the history of the German-speaking minorities in the border regions of the old Austro-Hungarian Empire. His father was killed in a robbery, trying to flee occupied Europe across the Alps into Italy in 1945. The son never met him. But in *Der Tote im Bunker* (2004) Pollack combined meticulous historical research into his family with an incisive analysis of the political allure of National Socialism for German minorities living among Slovenian and Croatian majorities. Trained in Slavic studies and Eastern European history, Pollack traced the history and political career of Dr. Gerhard Bast, as he battled with his paternal grandmother, who was appalled by his choice to study in Warsaw and specialize in Polish literature. When she demanded that he take a vow on his father's memory never to marry a Polish or Jewish woman, he broke off relations with her. He married a Polish woman. His grandmother died without ever speaking to him again, which he regretted as a sign of his former "self-righteous" and "immature" being.[113] His own life choices come into new focus as he retraced his father's steps through Slovenia, Croatia, Poland, Belarus, and Italy. When he discovered that his father participated in executions of Jews, Gypsies, and Polish hostages in Warsaw, he began to appreciate his grandmother's "incredulous expression" and her questioning "why of all things I should be interested in Poland, Polish language and literature, whatever might have me given that idea."[114] In such moments, personal, cultural, and political histories converge and the connections and continuities across the generations emerge.

The third pathway engages in historically detailed research and tries to shatter the deceptive veils of denial that conceal the historical specificity of parental lives. Such work requires determination, resilience, and "staying power coupled with the willingness, yes the courage, to be confronted with this family, which will inescapably remain one's own," commented Michael Wildt.[115] This constitutes an active approach to guilt based on an unflinching commitment to truth and courage to overcome self-centered fears of reprisals.

We do not know which of these three pathways Wolfdietrich Wilke might have taken. He might have joined his father's denial and submitted to these twisted biographical constructions. He might have angrily repudiated his father and distanced himself from his legacy. Or he might have accepted his father's broken life as a means to find pathways towards renewal. If he was able to resist the impulse to run from his father's guilt, he might have traveled to Minsk and the Pripyat swamps in Belarus to meet survivors and mourn the dead who are buried in mass graves. He might have overcome the fears of retribution and encountered people willing to build bridges across the abyss of the past—as I did. The future can only be built on the foundations of the past, which includes its atrocities.

7

"Naturally I Will Stand by My Husband"

MARITAL LOVE AND LOYALTY

WIVES ARE INTIMATELY implicated in their husbands' moral and political lives, although their agency is rarely considered. Marriages and families are important sites of moral debate, and the support of wives—or their opposition—is not negligible. Guilt for atrocities is not borne by individuals alone, but involves families and communities. Women serve at the front lines of moral discernment: they cajole and nag, they soothe and console, they excite and reward, they challenge and accept the justifications provided by the men in their lives. These informal interactions remain usually unexamined and are hidden with reference to the sanctity of the institution of marriage. But feminist scholars are committed to lift these veils of silence and to show that a woman's "I do" does not entail unconditional consent to a husband's choices. Women's voices should be taken into account as we explore the presence and expiation of guilt in the aftermath of the Holocaust.

Who were the women married to Nazi perpetrators, and how did they cope with their husbands' participation in atrocities after the war? Most of them appear to have stood loyally by their husbands, and their letters rarely express shock or moral revulsion. On the contrary, the majority of wives remained protective and defended their husbands vigorously despite their claims that they had been kept in the dark about the precise nature of their men's wartime assignments. To understand their reactions, one has to revisit the gender ideology and marital politics of National Socialism.

Patriarchy and the SS-Sippengemeinschaft
(Clan Community)

National Socialism was ideologically committed to patriarchy and, in principle, asserted that women were to submit to male authority at all times. As
a party, the NSdAP denounced the achievements of the women's movement
and moved swiftly to dismantle the gains of women's equal rights instituted by the democratic government of the Weimar Republic after 1918. In
Mein Kampf, Adolf Hitler considered revoking women's citizenship rights
altogether, because he believed that only men should count as full members of the state. Women would be considered subjects of the state once
they were married to male citizens. This plan did not go into effect out of
respect for war widows and the surplus of women who could not find mates
because of the devastating losses among young men during World War I.
While women retained the right to vote, they could not run for elected
office. The Nazi party advocated a conservative gender politics and relegated women to their traditional roles of *Kinder, Küche, Kirche* (children,
kitchen, and church). (Aryan) women were supposed to marry and bear
children. Soon after assuming power in 1933, the newly established Nazi
government legislated the removal of women from professional life and
the universities in the same laws that mandated the dismissal of Jews.
Women were removed from civil service (June 1933), from medical practice
(May 1934), and from legal professions (December 1935),[1] and a quota of 10
percent was imposed on women's enrollment at universities, along with
1.5 percent for Jews. Despite this initial purge of professional women, they
were soon recruited into the labor force in order to meet shortages in virtually all areas of the German economy. Once Hitler invaded Poland in
September 1939 and conscripted men into the Wehrmacht for military service at the front, the patriarchal rhetoric was radically adjusted to suit the
needs of a war economy.[2] The contradictions between patriarchal ideology
and social and economic realities, however, did not undermine the appeal
of the rhetoric. Instead, women's abandonment by their soldier-husbands
and ensuing independence and competence coexisted with the ideology
that women were in need of male rule and protection.

In principle, women were supposed to marry, raise children, and run
the household. They were in charge of the private realm of the family,
while men ran the public world of government, law, the military, and the
economy. The segregation of the public from the private world is a critical
feature of patriarchy, especially in the modern West. Men are seen as

political agents acting in public, supposedly ruled by rational thought and cold logic, while women take care of the emotional, sexual, and physical needs of men and children in the private world of love and devotion. This patriarchal division of labor has influenced much of our moral tradition and explains why transgressions of the heart and of the flesh are primarily associated with women, while matters of justice, war, and peace are properly considered the affairs of men. The family is a sacred haven of love, and women are its guardians, charged with keeping the harsh world of conflict and combat at bay. By assignment, wives are supposed to maintain innocence, purity, and goodness within the family, while men get their hands dirty in the harsh battles of a hostile world. This division into public and private, male and female, active and passive, cold and warm, rational and emotional is obviously fictitious, but nevertheless persuasive to men and women alike.

The institution of marriage was an integral part of Nazi ideology and practice, since its racial vision of Aryan rebirth required healthy reproductive rates.[3] Gudrun Schwarz has shown persuasively that the SS understood itself not (only) as a male fraternity but as a family institution or clan community (*Sippengemeinschaft*) that was dedicated to the creation of a racially pure and biologically superior master race (*Herrenrasse*).[4] All SS men were required to submit detailed marriage applications, which screened the medical, genealogical, and political background of prospective brides. The SS Race and Settlement Main Office in Berlin maintained comprehensive files containing documentation on the political, biological, and social fitness of potential marriage partners.[5] A marriage application could number in the hundreds of pages and included detailed religio-racial history, medical exams, especially for reproductive potential, skin color (choices include pink, ivory, olive), hair texture (straight, curly, kinky), and eye color (blue, gray, green, brown). Potential brides and grooms had to submit letters of recommendation evaluating political reliability as well as, in the bride's case, her love for children (*Kinderlieb*) and multiple-choice questions: Was she friendly or dominant (*herrschsüchtig*), domestic or vain, and frugal or wasteful? The wives of SS men were carefully vetted before they were officially inducted into the SS-Sippengemeinschaft. They felt committed to its code of ethics and to its role as an elite unit in the racial battle for biological and political supremacy.[6] They understood their role as running the household, raising children, and maintaining the mental, physical, and spiritual well-being of their husbands. Gudrun Schwarz names three areas of direct involvement of SS wives: First they lived with or visited their husbands at concentration camps and killing sites, thereby confirming the "normalcy" of professionalized killings.[7] Second, they profited directly from deportations and killings by moving into vacated houses or participating in the dispossession of jewelry, clothing, and furniture, and accepting the spoils of genocide as gifts. And third, many wives worked as secretaries, nurses, or administrators in the SS bureaucracy of genocide.[8] These wives saw themselves as an integral part of the battle to cleanse and renew the fatherland and vowed unconditional and eternal loyalty to their husbands in SS marriage ceremonies.[9]

The honor code of the SS was summarized in the slogan "My honor is my faithfulness." Submission, loyalty, and obedience were sacred values in the Nazi Weltanschauung. These values were valid not only in the public realm of men but also in the private world of women, especially in marriage. Loyalty bound men in absolute obedience to National Socialism and the führer and extended to women's conduct with respect to their husbands' careers and political activities. The SS ethos of loyalty became part of the marriage vows. A case in point is the lavishly celebrated and highly publicized wedding of Emmy and Hermann Göring, both members of the German Protestant Church.[10] The Görings were married by the Nazi-appointed Reichsbischof Müller, who belonged to the Nazi-inspired faction of the "German Christians" (*Deutsche Christen*) within the Protestant Church. By request, the sermon was based on their shared confirmation verse from Revelation 2:10: "Be faithful until death, and I will give you the crown of life."[11] The undying loyalty every SS recruit pledged to the führer was mirrored in the wife's relation to her husband. This wedding fused Christian terminology of the "crown of life," as envisioned in the Book of Revelations, to the SS mythology of Aryan national rebirth that demanded absolute obedience.

Although women could not become full members of the SS, they were officially inducted into the SS-Sippengemeinschaft as wives. Heinrich Himmler accepted one bride in a marriage ceremony (whose rituals were revised to fit the *gottgläubig* Nazi ideology) with the following words: "I admit you, Rosemarie Wengel, who will be known from today onward as Rosemarie Schallmeier [*sic*], into the community of the SS. I expect from you that you will be faithful and obedient to the SS, the movement and the führer, like any other SS man."[12] For Rosemarie Schallermaier marriage vows and political fidelity to the movement were linked. When her husband was executed in Landsberg on June 7, 1951, she did not go back on her oath of loyalty.

Private Morality

With the military defeat of Nazi Germany, SS wives faced a new, radically different political situation. Now they emphasized that they had lived entirely in the private realm of the family and had remained completely unaware of the political activism of their husbands. They emptied their loyalty of political content and reframed their love as apolitical, private virtue. They now argued that their personal knowledge of their husbands made the charges against them unimaginable and inconceivable. As they wrote appeals letters, coordinated defense strategies, and organized amnesty campaigns, the wives stressed their husbands' private morality and personal decency as husbands and fathers. For instance, Clara Schubert, whose husband received a death sentence in the Ohlendorf Einsatzgruppen Trial, pleaded with U.S. general Lucius D. Clay to let her husband go:

> My husband is so young and devoted to his son and to me with such love and tenderness that I cannot believe that he could have committed a crime of such magnitude, which would call for such a harsh penalty in expiation. I beg you, esteemed Herr General, especially in the name of our son who is four years old, and who already asks desperately for his father. It would be terrible to have to later tell this child the bitter facts about his father. Please, Herr General, give my husband and therefore us another chance to start over and to help rebuild, and grant our child his father.[13]

Such tropes of familial harmony and private morality were supposed to outweigh the evidence, as if a loving husband and devoted father could not also—concurrently—engage in mass killings. The wives emphasized their own vulnerability and powerlessness as they questioned the plausibility of the indictments. Clara Schubert succeeded in her appeal. Her husband's death sentence was first commuted to life and then shortened to "time served." He was released from Landsberg in a gesture of benevolence on Christmas Day, 1951. Such testimony to perpetrators' private virtue as fathers and spouses proved remarkably successful and reinforced the impression that Nazi families were, as Hermann Schlingensiepen noted, "surprisingly healthy families."[14]

If there were marital conflicts over the morality of mass murder, the wives kept them well hidden. To these wives, the prosecution for war crimes constituted "hatred and revenge" rather than justice. As one widow put it in her response to Pastor Eckardt's condolence letter from WCP 1 Landsberg:

> I lost a good, loyal human being; his love toward his children and toward me was indescribable. It was his goal to become an out-standing husband, a good and strict father to his children. Thus we lived happily and contented, our happiness shattered when they took our loved one away. I remain loyally by his side and share the sorrow, as I have shared the joys between us. Now he has become the victim of hatred and revenge.[15]

Although her husband, Ludwig Kluettgen, was not a member of the SS but was hanged for killing two downed American pilots, she also con-structs a narrative of family harmony and private happiness inexplicably wrecked by a vengeful justice system.[16] Berta Piorkowski, whose husband, SS-Obersturmbannführer Alex Piorkowski, was executed as commander of the Dachau concentration camp between 1940 and 1942, thanked Pastor Eckardt for his condolence letter in the following way:

> I am glad that you assessed my husband correctly. I had the best father [for my two children] and the most ideal husband. How could I ever forget him or replace him with a successor? One says that life goes on, but I have sacrificed my entire happiness. I would have preferred going to my death with my husband; I no longer value my life. But I have two children and therefore obligations and responsibilities.[17]

With her willingness to die together with her husband she articulated the absolute unity of purpose that was envisioned by the ideal SS marriage. It is noteworthy that Pastor Eckardt censored Piorkowski's last words in his condolence letter. He wrote: "His last words in the face of eternity were mindful of his *Heimat* and his family. They were: 'Long live Germany, long live my family. Be well, Herr Pfarrer, I am ready.'"[18] But the American mon-itors recorded one more, and quite disturbing, sentence: "My son, take revenge for me."[19] Did the minister delete this sentence because he was concerned that this particular family might actually take the call for revenge to heart? Without critical distance between husband and wife, father and son, such a binding final command was potentially dangerous. Although Eckardt was usually quite conscientious in conveying convicts' last words accurately to their families, he made a conscious choice to suppress this bequest, which he considered morally and politically objectionable.

Wives' emphasis on their husbands' personal kindness was supposed to mitigate and negate the possibility of official misconduct or professional wrongdoing. Their descriptions of happy family lives were a deliberate strategy to screen out the reality of atrocity. The maintenance of healthy families was deeply intertwined with the denial of the politics of violence, conquest, and genocide. The family constructed a bulwark to protect the men from the ravages of cruelty and inhumanity. Their happiness in the family stabilized their mental health and normalized a world that was sharply segregated between their private experience as fathers and husbands and their professional lives as cold-blooded executioners.

It is this nexus of private decency and public atrocity, female nurture and male violence, that must become the starting point of a feminist analysis of the moral implication of wives in genocide. The wives skillfully manipulated the private/public, female/male divide. The line between these two worlds was permeable, and neither the perpetrator nor his wife lived exclusively in one or the other of these parallel universes. But both went to great lengths to conceal its interdependence. Historian Claudia Koonz concludes in *Mothers in the Fatherland* that "Stangl, Höss, and untold thousands of men felt their very sanity depended upon preserving an island of serenity where love, tenderness and devotion reigned. A place to 'touch base' and reaffirm one's humanity in the face of brutal criminality.... Wives...kept their family apart from the masculine world of brutality, coercion, corruption and power."[20] This feat required determination, an understanding of the traumatic nature of their men's work, and a willingness to support the overall goals of National Socialism.

Their successful creation and maintenance of islands of innocence and virtue was used to build the cases for parole and amnesty in the postwar world. Women denounced the punishment of their husbands, which only hurt their innocent children. "I have married innocently," argued Adelheid Hans in a letter to Hermann Schlingensiepen in 1966:

> I believe that it is finally time to let us live. Everybody is always going on about what is happening in the rest of the world. Why should not Germany finally be allowed to come to calm and peace [*Ruhe und Besinnung*] as well? Prayer alone won't help us. I want my husband back since no one knows how long he will have to live. And we also deserve a couple of happy years.[21]

Her sense of entitlement required an active disregard for the factual record of her husband's life. SS-Hauptsturmbannführer Kurt Hans happened to lead Sonderkommando 4a when it conducted the largest one-time massacre of the Holocaust, namely the murder of 33,771 Jews in Babi Yar that occurred September 29–30, 1941. His wife pouted that he was sentenced to eleven years, although he only "belonged to an Einsatzkommando for eight weeks." Eight weeks might be a short time, but if that period included two days of killing 33,771 people, they cannot easily be discounted. Presumably, Adelheid Hans shared the indifference and moral disregard that characterized her husband's coping mechanism. She never mentioned the presence of victims and shielded herself (and her husband) from this knowledge.

A similar strategy was used by Susanne Lucas, who lobbied on behalf of her husband, Dr. Franz Lucas, who supervised selections to the gas chambers in Auschwitz in 1943, before he was transferred to Mauthausen and Ravensbrück, where he performed sterilizations on inmates, especially Roma and Sinti.[22] In her letter soliciting Schlingensiepen's support for her appeal's case, she claimed that "her husband was a personality of unblemished character, who found himself in a situation of fear and coercion that he could not master by himself and in which he was forced to execute inhumane orders."[23] Dr. Lucas had joined the SS in 1937 and reached the same rank as SS-Hauptsturmbannführer Adolf Eichmann. While he claimed in his concluding remark in the Auschwitz trial that "I was sent to do service in the concentration camp against my will," he cycled through various camps and ended the war as camp doctor in Ravensbrück. While witnesses testified that he often acted more humane and professional than his medical colleagues in Auschwitz, his time there seems misdiagnosed as a "situation of fear and coercion." The trial focused on his presence on the railroad ramp and his medical participation in selections. Dr. Lucas was forced to amend his categorical denial and to admit that he had participated. As wife of an SS doctor, Susanne Lucas was probably not unaware of Nazi racial science and her husband's role in cleansing the national body of undesirable elements. In her amnesty plea, she hoped for "his speedy reintegration into the living and work community of the German people [*Lebens- und Arbeitsgemeinschaft des deutschen Volkes*],"[24] language that reveals her exposure to SS ideology. Her husband had similarly expressed the confidence that he would receive a "verdict that will enable me to liberate myself from the entanglement [*von der Verstrickung zu lösen*] and enter a new path in my life [*neuen Lebensweg einschlagen*]."[25]

His hope would be fulfilled, as his sentence to three years and three months in prison was overturned on appeal in 1969.[26] Since he had lost his position that he had held since 1945 as chief gynecologist in a medical clinic in Elmshorst, he opened a private medical practice until his retirement in 1983. He died in 1994.

These wives defended their husbands unconditionally and did not publicly criticize or disagree with them. Should we have expected them to do so? Or are we to consider such spousal loyalty as morally neutral or indeed praiseworthy? For the prison chaplains, the wives' unconditional love was commendable, and Schlingensiepen praised

> the brave women who have married them without knowing anything about their past and who nevertheless stand by them loyally, [and] the innocent children who visit them with their mothers.... These women and these children cry out for them on behalf of their humanity and suffer from the fact that our people who have participated in their guilt have locked them up.[27]

He assumed that the women were ignorant and did not know. But does this adequately describe their situation? They themselves claimed that they had been unaware of what was happening in concentration camps and at execution sites. But in their letters to the chaplains they also showed little shock or moral repugnance after they were confronted with the evidence in the courts. Their muted reactions made their claims of ignorance unbelievable. Instead, their letters showed an eagerness to justify, minimize, and condone their husbands' deeds after the war, which strongly suggests that they had prior knowledge. We can safely assume that many of them knew enough of their husbands' assignments to conclude that they would be better off not knowing more of the sordid details.

Helene Greiffenberger's husband was convicted in 1962 by the regional court in Moabit / West Berlin for supervising mass executions of Jews in Belarus as deputy of Dr. Filbert's *Einsatzgruppe*. She first minimized the charges and then highlighted his personal morality and human decency in her letter to Hermann Schlingensiepen:

> From the newspaper report one gets the impression that my husband served in an important position. But my husband was only a civil servant, and in the Filbert command, he was deeply unhappy, because he was twice forced to accompany him (Dr. Filbert) to the

executions. I cannot imagine the person who would have resisted the pressure that existed back then. My husband has generally been known as a benevolent [*gutmütig*] and compassionate [*hilfsbereit*] person since his earliest youth. I am convinced that God has already forgiven him. I myself have been deeply religious since my earliest youth and feel deeply connected spiritually with my husband. We are all only puppets on the stage of life; essential is the love of God. Nothing could take away our steadfast faith, not even the severe suffering that we have had to endure.[28]

One looks in vain for an expression of shock over her husband's involvement in mass killings as a member of an *Einsatzgruppe*. Instead, the author concentrated on emphasizing her husband's lack of initiative and responsibility. The main point of this paragraph was to deny that he *done* anything as a responsible moral agent. He was "forced" and acted on orders, not willingly and intentionally, on his own initiative, or for his own reasons. Her portrait minimized personal agency and attributed blame to his superior, Filbert. The letter set up a triple defensive wall to prevent the possibility of culpable wrongdoing: first, she denied the severity of the guilt (civil servant, forced, unhappy, lack of resistance); second, she affirmed his personal decency and goodness (benevolent, compassionate); third she affirmed the notion that God had already forgiven him. These lines of defense were staggered as if to protect a beleaguered city. Once the first line is breached, the second wall will hold the assailants at bay a little longer: (1) nothing evil happened, but should there be proof that something bad did happen, then (2) this does not mean that her husband is a bad person, but should there be proof that he was not "benevolent" and "compassionate," then (3) God will have already forgiven him. Her spiritual union with her husband included him in a protective circle of female benevolence and innocence that was supposed to rule out any possibility of wrongdoing. Her vigorous defense implicated her in his guilt as an SS man.

Her way of invoking and speaking of God was characteristic of perpetrator theology. She assumed that divine love and forgiveness would "cover" the occurrences in the past, irrespective of what exactly had happened, why these events occurred, or whether there was any regret and contrition. Helene Greiffenberger affirmed a God who pulls the strings and a universe in which human beings are mere "puppets on the stage of life." As playthings of God, human beings possess little agency and cannot, in the end, act freely and responsibly. The evasion of moral responsibility is written into her theological construction and it is reminiscent of Wilke's discourse of the unconditional submission to God's rule.

Love becomes an all-domineering, exclusive trait of God in these perpetrator-centered theologies. The love of God drowns out the concept of God's justice. Over and over, perpetrators insisted that "love is set above justice according to the order of the gospel,"[29] a theological position with obvious political and legal ramifications. No less than Adolf Eichmann held that belief and shared the profound fatalism that characterized Helene Greiffenberger's theology.[30] In a letter to prison chaplain William Hull, Adolf Eichmann described his religious beliefs thus:

> I am just a small part of the total; only a small link in an endlessly long chain. I have the task to pass on with love and care that which has been entrusted to me (the spiritual values) so that it will continue to develop towards perfection. The eternal track of love carries this on, according to the will of the creator. This for me is the higher sense of my existence as a human being. In my conception God, *because of his almightiness,* is not a punisher, not an angry God, but rather an all-embracing God in whose order I have been placed. And this order (fate) regulates everything. All being and becoming— including me—is *subject* to this order. (Emphasis in original)[31]

The combination of fatalism and divine love that speaks through Eichmann's letter alleviates the need for critical self-reflection and circumvents unpleasant feelings of doubt or regret. It is also a reductive understanding of love. On this definition, love affirms, soothes, and cares, but it can never challenge, demand, or confront. Love that has been ripped apart from judgment becomes utterly saccharine and meaningless. For Adolf Eichmann, the love of God was the ultimate affirmation that he was right and that his life's project had been valid. He was not going to begin doubting that now: "I believe in the love of God and I still believe that God guides me....I have believed this way so long that I have no doubt concerning my beliefs. *I cannot let you put doubt in my heart at this late date*" (emphasis in original).[32] He angrily rejected Pastor Hull's nagging questions that were trying to get him to acknowledge wrongdoing: "I have nothing to confess, I have not sinned. I am clear with God. I did not do it. I did nothing wrong. I have no regrets."[33] Eichmann's faith was his loyalty and he could not admit any doubt or allow any upheaval.

As long as love is divorced from judgment, it is emptied of moral meaning. Such love becomes mere loyalty and it no longer discerns between right and wrong, good and evil. Love that never challenges and confronts does not contribute to personal growth or moral transformation. Perpetrator theology reduced faith to fidelity and diminished love to loyalty, a move that was mirrored in its conception of marital relations.

This God of love is toothless and "his" role is the equivalent to women's place. It is not by accident that the three Ks that characterized women's universe as outlined by Nazi ideology (*Kinder, Küche,* and *Kirche*: children, kitchen, church) included the church. Beginning in the nineteenth century, religion was increasingly removed from the world of politics and restricted to the sphere of women, where religious sentimentality and pious morality could be practiced. Religion became privatized and feminized, relegated to the affairs of heart and of soul, while men tended to the secular business of running the world. Christianity seemed most relevant for women, children, the weak and the vulnerable with its warm and fuzzy glow. It became the place to which men retreated after they had made the hard choices and fought the tough battles. In Claudia Koonz's words, "What you do is public, how you feel is private. This is the essence of a system that severs masculine from feminine,"[34] and one might add, the political from the religious. Instead of demanding the dissolution of the boundaries between public and private, male and female, and the "splitting of consciousness" that had allowed the genocide to proceed, ministers followed the same paradigm.

The proclamation of divine love unbounded by demands for justice inadvertently perpetuated the wifely support function and failed to disrupt the loyalties and denial strategies of National Socialism. Prison chaplains, known in German as *Seelsorger* (caretakers of the soul) found themselves in the role of women, as they were called to comfort the wary souls of wounded warriors. Some ministers joined the wives in testimony about the private morality and religious decency of perpetrators before courts and appeals boards. Their strategy upheld the false barriers between private and public, where the religious realm of God's love, goodness, and morality was aligned with the world of women but kept separate from the manly world of war and violence.

As prison chaplains worked to create safe havens in the midst of the harsh realities of the prison, they invoked the love and care of women to restore the emotional and mental sanity of inmates. As *Seelsorger*, they realized that prisoners needed lots of love and support, and they drew on their wives for help. For instance, in their thirteen counseling sessions with Adolf Eichmann in his cell in Jerusalem, Protestant minister William L. Hull and his wife (who attended as his translator and remains nameless in Hull's memoir) repeatedly deployed references to Eichmann's wife, Vera, in their attempts to pry open his heart. At one point in the conversation, Ms. Hull implored Eichmann, "You are blind and won't let God show you. I am here in the place of your wife and you are so full of pride and want so much to make a good showing at the end that you do not even consider your wife and children."[35] Implicit in Ms. Hull's argument was the assumption that the contemplation of his wife would move Eichmann toward compassion, empathy, and repentance. She assumed that Vera Eichmann remained ignorant of her husband's mission to exterminate Europe's Jews and was worried about the state of his soul. "Even your wife is concerned, if she believes as you say she is. She is just as concerned for your soul as we are."[36] But Eichmann knew her better and replied: "She knows that I am not guilty. She is not concerned."[37] He could count on her loyalty as a former SS wife and took her consent for granted. It was Vera Eichmann, after all, who facilitated his escape to Argentina and joined him there to bear him another, his fourth, son. After Vera visited Eichmann in his cell in Jerusalem, he appeared greatly calmed and reassured to the Hulls. "Eichmann spoke very highly of his wife. He seemed to think a lot of her. He looked well and happy. It seemed that his wife's visit cheered him up; he was much more friendly toward us."[38] Apparently, it did not occur to the Hulls that Vera Eichmann's visit had reinforced the moral guidelines of SS honor, loyalty, and bravery. Far from challenging his false sense of pride, she might have affirmed the ideological basis for his choices. Her visit could have contributed to a hardening of his heart rather than to any reconsideration. Asked what he would like Hull to convey to his wife shortly before his execution, Eichmann declared, "Tell my wife that I took it calmly and that I had peace in my heart, which guarantees to me that I am right."[39] Vera Eichmann stood by her man without challenging his political, moral, or religious convictions.

Prison chaplains did not consider that women's love and loyalty might not help their case because they invested such love with moral meaning. They believed that the love of women and the love of God constituted an intrinsic good. But any love that embraces evil, without contesting it, is false and immoral.[40] This is as true of the love of God as it is for marital love. While the love of God and the love of women are obviously not completely analogous, there are significant parallels. Consider, for instance, the recent publication of "The Theological Grounds for Advocating Forgiveness and Reconciliation in the Sociopolitical Realm," in which systematic theologian Alan Torrance makes his case that God is willing to forgive unconditionally. He compares God's love to the love of married women who are willing to forgive their wayward husbands in cases of adultery. I will cite this passage at some length in order to examine this analogy and to point out its flaws:

> When a woman makes it clear to her husband that she will con-
> tinue to love him and be faithful to him even if he is unfaithful,
> this inspires faithfulness. By contrast, the opposite scenario—
> where she says her love is contingent or conditional upon his
> behaving himself (and thus implies that it is contractual)—is likely
> to discourage faithfulness. Why? Because conditional commit-
> ments suggest that the partner is not really loved. That is because
> love is by nature unconditional. To recognize that a spouse's "love"
> is conditional is to find oneself doubting whether one's spouse
> loves one at all. As this is doubted, the sense of obligation is under-
> mined. The relationship becomes depersonalized, appearing
> "nominal" or merely "legal"—contractual indeed.... The thrust of
> what we are suggesting is that unconditional faithfulness both
> begets and sustains faithfulness.[41]

Torrance follows Martin Luther's argument that human repentance cannot be accomplished by strenuous effort but only by faithful acceptance of God's love and grace, which are unconditional. It is not by *works* but *faith* alone that "sin" (i.e., deeply rooted self-deception and alienation) can be uprooted. Torrance then applies this "analogy of the inner logic"[42] to the realities of patriarchal marriages. However, the analogy breaks down on empirical grounds because women's forbearance has served to buttress men's sense of sexual entitlement in most patriarchal societies. Women's unconditional faithfulness across the centuries has done little to actually affect or change male behavior. Torrance mistakes the power dynamics inherent in patriarchal marriage. There is a reason that the God of the Bible is always envisioned in the role of husband (especially in the pro-phetic books) and never as a wife. God is powerful and uses his power to "smite" any wife who would "play the harlot" until she returned to monog-amous faithfulness. In his metaphoric regendering of God's loving for-giveness, Torrance has inadvertently disempowered "him." But it is not only this gender inversion that is problematic in Torrance analogy, but also his categorical disconnection between love and judgment. Judgment sets conditions, justice demands, and the law mandates behavior change and compliance. All of these are not marginal but central biblical concepts. In the biblical world, love was never divorced from judgment. To declare the unconditional primacy of love over justice not only mischaracterizes the biblical God but also misreads the wily ways of women, who developed nonviolent means of confrontation and learned to negotiate for their husbands' compliance.

Divorce as a Moral Response

It is not that wives are morally expected to divorce husbands who are discovered to be complicit in grievous human rights violations and atrocities. But a feminist hermeneutic would insist that women are equally and independently obligated to confront ideologies and practices that are intrinsically inhumane and immoral. Women do not lose moral subjectivity upon entering a marriage contract but exercise moral agency in long-term committed conversation with their partners. Women who are married to perpetrators of atrocities are morally obligated to confront their husbands critically, to challenge their choices, and to oppose their ideologies. This includes the threat of separation as a moral response to a partner's sustained refusal to change and failure to make amends. Omission to do so constitutes a form of complicity on the part of wives that incurred guilt.

The prison chaplains understood the Christian (patriarchal) tradition as categorically opposed to divorce under any circumstance.[43] They expected wives to honor their marriage vows and to remain supportive of their husbands while imprisoned. Tucked among Pastor Ermann's documents from his time in WCP 1 Landsberg was the copy of a court verdict that denied a woman's request for divorce. The name of the couple was anonymized, and I assume that he used the court's reasoning to counsel men facing marital strife and threats of divorce. The civil court in Bielefeld ruled on April 2, 1948, that "the desire for divorce [*Scheidungsbegehren*] of the complainant is unfounded."[44] The court found that the accused's conviction for war crimes did not constitute "dishonorable [*ehrlos*] or indecent [*unsittlich*] behavior that would culpably dissolve a marriage." The judge ruled that the complainant had failed to provide any evidence of unbecoming conduct but had "merely pointed to the fact of his conviction by an American military court."[45] His conviction by an American court did not constitute sufficient reason to grant separation. On the contrary, the court concluded that the woman was bound by her ethical obligation to fidelity:[46]

> The court has not been convinced that this marriage was truly affected by the fact of his conviction. After full consideration of the situation in which the complainant has been placed as a result of the harsh prison sentence for her husband, one must also question whether the ethical obligation of fidelity toward the other spouse does not compel the view that this punishment must be accepted as an act of fate [*Schicksalsschlag*] that impacts both spouses in their marital union equally. And this question is answered in the affirmative by the court. This act of fate must be borne jointly by both spouses.[47]

An "act of fate"? Apart from the German court's evident ambivalence toward Allied war crimes prosecutions, their legal position required women to accept the convictions of their husbands as joint punishment. While this particular case may not have constituted a legal precedent that could claim validity for other divorce cases, the fact that Pastor Ermann kept a copy of the ruling in his files is remarkable. We may assume that he discussed this case with prisoners in WCP Landsberg.

The chaplains were sensitive to signs of estrangement between spouses and intervened quickly by contacting wives and inquiring about any strains. For instance, Pastor Eckardt wrote to Rosa Greil on July 11, 1948, that he was

> concerned that he [Michael Greil] had to tell me he had not received any news from you for some time. The last mail from you is dated May 5. Of course, I don't know from my position what might have happened to prevent you from writing. And I don't think that your husband has any reason to be concerned, but I noticed that he feels worried over your prolonged silence.[48]

Michael Greil joined the SS in 1940 and worked as foreman in the carpentry shop in the concentration camp of Dachau. He was sentenced to four years in prison because he reported minor infractions by his employees to the camp administration and they were subsequently brutally punished.[49] There is no response from Rosa Greil among the files of

Pastor Eckardt. Sometimes Eckardt contacted local ministers directly and asked them to visit resident families and to check on a wife who "has withdrawn from him for inexplicable reasons and has not written since July of this year. Since October 7, 1948, there is also no letter from the sister either."[50] In this case, he received an immediate response from the colleague, who assured him that wife and sister were simply overwhelmed by taking care of five children, and shortly thereafter their letters started arriving again. If women withdrew emotionally from their imprisoned husbands, the prison chaplains usually suspected the "intrusion of another man."[51] Separation was never seen as moral response, but always a violation of the sacred bonds of marriage.

Kirchenrat Sachsse, who worked with prisoners in French custody, warned one wife contemplating divorce that "marriage is not a human contract that can be canceled at any time. You have promised before God on your wedding day to stay with your husband 'in good and bad times and to keep the covenant of marriage loyally and indissolubly until death do you part.' ... You can only be released from this vow if your husband broke the conjugal faith or committed acts that would render marital harmony impossible. This is not the case."[52] "As a Christian," Sachsse rejected "divorce of any marriage on principle."[53]

Similarly, the 1963 EKD "Guidelines for Pastoral Care in the Aftermath of NS Trials" warned that wives might be "tempted by ill-considered actions and false reactions."[54] The memorandum advised ministers to lead "the wives of the arrested into the company of right [or righteous] women and mothers as well as those who are capable of praying with them and who can give advice and assistance in the many questions, not least with a view toward the right care for their husbands."[55] Although the document did not mention the possibility of divorce, it also did little to address the dangers of moral complicity when wives condoned their husbands' actions uncritically. Their Christian counsel was beholden to patriarchal conceptions of women's lack of moral autonomy.

While separation is not itself a moral good, neither is uncritical allegiance and unexamined loyalty. Married women were confronted with moral choices in their relationships with men guilty of grievous brutality. Their pretense and maintenance of happy family lives was not morally neutral but complicit. Their intimate connections with perpetrators implicated them in the moral struggles over change and repentance. Separation, and the threat of divorce, was a necessary tool for wives who felt overwhelmed by the gravity of the crimes and were determined to demand change.

Such women were a tiny minority. Usually, it was not those who had undergone the SS vetting process and married into the SS-Sippengemeinschaft but those who married after 1945 who faced moral scruples. I found only one set of letters in the archives of a woman who genuinely struggled with shock and moral revulsion over her husband's activities in Auschwitz. She had, in fact, been unaware, and her response to the revelations serves as a counterpoint to the other wives who claimed to have been ignorant but remained strangely unmoved by the postwar disclosures. Her letters provide an intimate glimpse into one woman's effort to comprehend the man she had married. She made the future of her marriage dependent upon her husband's ability to feel remorse and acknowledge culpable wrongdoing. While I have no information about the eventual outcome of her marital negotiations, her struggle provides clues for wives' critical engagement with the burden of guilt that might lead to moral transformation.

When Hermann Schlingensiepen contacted Hans Stark after his conviction in the Frankfurt Auschwitz trial on August 10, 1965, his wife Margaret responded "on his behalf...and in his name."[56] On August 20, 1965, Hans Stark had been sentenced to ten years in prison as SS-Untersturmführer in Auschwitz. In her second letter to Schlingensiepen in October 1965, Margaret Stark described her husband's sudden arrest and revelation of his past:

> I married in 1953 and in April 1959, my husband was arrested in Cologne. He was in school and was allowed to come back home accompanied by two gentlemen. He said to me: "I have to tell you something that you do not yet know. I was once in Auschwitz during the war and now I am being detained by these men." I stood there with the children and found no words. But it was unfortunately true. He had concealed it from me until this terrible day. He had never found the courage to inform me about his former life. I feel terrible about this and I have not been able to deal with this.[57]

It is significant that this woman met her husband after the war. She had not undergone recruitment into the SS-Sippengemeinschaft and apparently did not share her husband's ideological commitments. There is scattered evidence in the prison chaplains' files that marital trouble arose for convicts with younger wives and from second wives. One finds references such as prison chaplain Konrad Merkt's note to Schlingensiepen: "W. has problems with his second wife, who maintains silence, which drives him crazy. He seemed to have been 'good enough' for her only during the good times. The first wife and her children stand by their daddy."⁵⁸ Presumably, younger women felt more alienated because they had been less subjected to SS ideology and less exposed to the sites of mass violence. Older wives and first wives, on the other hand, were fully committed to the ideology of National Socialism and supported the professional ambitions and opportunities of their husbands.

Hans Stark had not disclosed his time in Auschwitz to his wife. Born in 1921, he joined the SS at age sixteen in 1937 and was trained in various concentration camps. He was stationed as SS guard in Oranienburg, Buchenwald, and Dachau before he was sent to Auschwitz in December 1940. He completed his high school diploma while taking a three-month leave of absence from Auschwitz. Upon his return, he was promoted and granted another leave to enroll in law school at the university of Frankfurt am Main. He was transferred to Dachau, spent some time in an SS school, and was deployed to military service until he was arrested by Soviet forces. He escaped from Russian captivity. By 1953, he was a teacher and a married man, desperate to restart his life by erasing his past. His silence came at a considerable emotional cost, and his wife confided to Schlingensiepen that she had sensed the presence of a secret:

> In confidence I can also tell you that this marriage was not harmonious. I sometimes despaired because I did not know what to make of him. I felt that something was not quite right, but I could not explain to myself what it was. I would ask that you never give my husband any indication of this. It would be terrible [*sehr schlimm*] otherwise.... A chasm opened inside of me, and I have no idea what will be when my husband is released from prison. When I visit him, I often have the impression that I have a complete stranger in front of me. I do not let him know this, and this makes it all the more difficult once I am alone again.⁵⁹

Her husband's decision to hide his past undermined the possibility of intimacy between the spouses. Many German men were traumatized by the commission of grievous acts of violence and were struggling to establish or maintain emotionally healthy relationships. They failed to bridge the gap between their gruesome wartime memories and their postwar married family lives. His unspoken and unacknowledged time in Auschwitz stood between them. Stark tried to erase a highly traumatic period from his life and, in the process, obliterated an integral part of himself. Although he seemed to have believed that his future could be opened if he succeeded in locking away the past, he could not establish intimacy with his wife. Once arrested and exposed, Frau Stark realized that her marriage had been a sham. What jeopardized the viability of this marriage was not only the sudden spotlight on horrific and repugnant acts committed in Auschwitz, but his inability to be truthful. Frau Stark questioned the survival of the marriage not primarily because of her horror, shame, or moral repulsion but because she could not talk to him. Schlingensiepen was concerned and counseled her to fight for her marriage:

> I understand the distress caused by your visits to your husband all too well, now that you have written to me. I am grateful and have noted with admiration the great loyalty with which many a woman who finds herself in your position stands by her man and holds onto him despite everything. I am certain that a great blessing accrues from such behavior not only for the unfortunate himself but also for his family, especially when it happens in prayer. Not a day passes in which I do not pray to God himself to give such blessings to you and your husband. It could very well be that when our prayers are heeded, the oppressive estrangement that is so clearly challenging [*anficht*] will disappear over time.[60]

Should we object to Schlingensiepen's recommendation because he endorsed unconditional loyalty?[61] As we have seen, most wives' loyalty strengthened their husbands' resolve. It was not their fidelity per se that was morally praiseworthy but their willingness to engage their husbands critically and emphatically. Schlingensiepen sometimes endowed women with innate moral goodness and praised their steadfast love without appreciating that this constancy could backfire and turn out to be devoid of moral substance. Like the Hulls, Schlingensiepen supposed that visits by wives would have a salutary effect on their husbands' moral development and political transformation. The notion that these women would innately tend toward "Christian and humane" rather than hard-core National Socialist values is rooted in patriarchal assumptions about female purity and innocence. In one instance, Schlingensiepen commended the wife of Joseph Klehr, who was also convicted in the Frankfurt Auschwitz trial, because her visits to Auschwitz and its satellite camp of Gleiwitz had "exerted a Christian and humane influence on you there."[62] He hoped that she would visit him in prison and continue to exert her benign power. At the trial, a Czech witness had characterized Klehr's wife as very "nice and decent" (*lieb und anständig*) and recalled overhearing a conversation in which she confronted her husband and forced him to deny rumors that "you gas women and children here."[63] He must have lied convincingly. Of course, it was true that he himself did not participate in the gassing of Jews, because he was responsible for killing non-Jewish inmates by injection with deadly phenol poison. According to Lifton, his wife and children were "permitted to live nearby for a period of time,"[64] and it is hard to imagine that she could have remained clueless. But in any case, the survivor testified that the pressure she put on her husband made a difference: "After this visit Klehr changed considerably."[65]

The situation of wives is characterized by guilt by association. Like the children of perpetrators, the wives could choose between three pathways. They could submit to their husbands' silences and evasions and join in their defense; they could renounce their husbands and divorce them, thereby preserving their own integrity by distancing themselves from the crimes of National Socialism; or they could engage in complicated battles of coming to a truthful recognition of harm doing. Very few wives have publicly reflected or written about their experiences. Those who wrote memoirs took the first path and styled themselves as proud defenders of their husbands.[66] The second group craved anonymity. Margaret Stark might be an example of the third path, although her story is entirely based on my conjectures. Her correspondence with Schlingensiepen allows some insights into her strategy to force her husband to acknowledge wrongdoing. She objected to Schlingensiepen's recommendation of unconditional loyalty and insisted that her husband had to change before she could imagine resumption of marital relations.

There is little precedent or guidance in the Christian tradition for her strategy, because the religious traditions are beholden to patriarchy with its denigration of women's moral agency and autonomy. Women's choices have rarely become the raw material for theological inquiry or ethical analysis. Ethics attends more often to the male world of violence and politics than to the mediated experience of women. While men commit the majority of violence, women are more than innocent bystanders or victims. The situation of wives was fraught with ethical dilemmas and laden with conflict. Margaret Stark tried to extricate herself from moral culpability as a secondary beneficiary of wrongdoing by insisting that her husband confront his past. She contemplated divorce as a moral response and considered her options for disengagement from the evil of Auschwitz. In her reply to Schlingensiepen, five months later, she reassured him:

> Naturally, I will stand by my husband and visit him as long as he is in this situation. I am only concerned about what will happen once he is released, that everything may go well. It is as you write: this shadow ought to be outshone by light and transform him completely. That alone would be a decision for our family life. Please believe me, I know all too well how difficult it will be for the children and also for us if a separation were to be necessary. I am fully cognizant of the significance and weight [of this decision]. Otherwise this would have happened much earlier, if I had not hung onto a thread for the sake of the children. I hope with you that God will give him the strength to transform and in so doing make our life bearable.[67]

Margaret Stark put divorce on the table as a means to put pressure on her husband. In a way, she renegotiated the theological conflict over the conditionality of love in marital relationship. What should come first? Unconditional love and grace, or repentance, change, and "works"? Schlingensiepen advised Margaret Stark to remain steadfast and promised her that her faithfulness would touch her husband's heart. Margaret Stark, on the other hand, maintained that it was his responsibility to change and that she could only resume married life if he was willing to change his ways. She agreed with Schlingensiepen that "this shadow could be overcome by a light from above if it pierced his heart and transformed it"[68] but also insisted that he had to "show measurable regret [spürbare Reue]; otherwise it would be even more unbearable for me."[69] For her, unlike for the pastor, her husband's remorse became a precondition for the return to normal family life. She insisted on love as a mutual process of negotiation that would require her husband to take a leap of faith. Schlingensiepen was more old-fashioned. He thought that

> God may think differently, and he may intend to bless your fidelity, once you decide in its favor, through entreaty and understanding [über Bitten und Verstehen]. The other way would entail great inner risks, particularly for your children. Their father happens to remain their father, and one half of their being is from him. Can you really

imagine that you will be able to separate from him without suffering an internal injury? Of course, neither you nor your children can pretend that there is no *irremovable shadow* on the life and image of your husband and of their father. But even this shadow could be overcome by a light from above if it pierced his heart and transformed it. (Emphasis added)[70]

Schlingensiepen's suggestion of an "irremovable shadow" (*nicht wegzuwischender Schatten*) raises the specter of the mark of Cain. This was an unusual formulation for Schlingensiepen, who otherwise firmly proclaimed that God's forgiveness was able to "wipe away" the stains of past trespasses.[71] Although he believed that "the blood of Christ cries louder than the blood of Abel"[72] and repeatedly suggested that the "blood of Christ" could overcome the misery (*Not*) of perpetrators, he seemed to have realized that Auschwitz leaves a remainder, a shadow that cannot be removed. Schlingensiepen comes close to acknowledging that atrocities committed in Auschwitz cannot be "outshone" or cleansed away. Instead, they have to be borne with dignity and in the full light of day. In other words, Hans Stark was forced to learn to endure the moral burden of his actions in Auschwitz in light of the suffering of his victims. The repair of his human dignity depended upon his courage to speak truthfully about his descent into inhumanity. He was the only defendant who came close to an expression of regret in his concluding remarks before the court:

I have participated in the murder of many human beings. I have often asked myself after the war whether I have become a criminal. I have not been able to find an answer. I have believed in the führer wanted to serve my *Volk*, and was convinced of the rightness of my actions. Today I know that these ideas were false. I regret my error [*Irrweg*] but I cannot make it undone.[73]

His comportment during the trial was contradictory. He admitted to performing executions and to assisting in the gassings, which he considered "unmanly and cowardly."[74] He was seen leading one Jewish woman with one or two children and shooting them. He ordered prisoners to drown family members for sport and beat inmates to death. A Polish educator who worked for him as a translator was intrigued and interested in Stark "from a pedagogical perspective. He was young, he looked nice, and I could not understand, why he was so cruel.... It appeared to me that he came too early under the influence of an evil ideology. Above his desk he pinned a saying that read: 'Compassion is Weakness.'"[75] He was convicted as a juvenile because he turned twenty-one in the midst of this paroxysm of violence in June 1942.[76]

Listening to the court testimony would make it hard to be married to such a man. But his wife did not recoil primarily out of moral revulsion, but because she found herself unable to breech the wall surrounding him. She seemed willing to love a man who could cry bitter tears of remorse, but she could not accept closure and concealment of the past. Her insistence on her husband's moral transformation is a sign of her moral integrity. In contrast to most other wives, she did not collude in defense and denial but demanded open accountability. She rightly pointed out that this was important not only for her own sake, but also for the well-being of her children, as well as for the human regeneration of her husband.

Hans Stark never answered Schlingensiepen's letters. By 1971, Schlingensiepen contacted him one last time and begged him to show "more genuine remorse" in order to increase public support for amnesty appeals. Once again, he did not respond. There are no further records, and I have no information about the date of his release or the future of his family life. He died in 1991.

There are two lessons that emerge from these historical documents. First, marriages based on the principles of uncritical love divorced from justice did not contribute to the moral recovery of perpetrators. Love without demand is complicit, care without condition is powerless. It is love that challenges, cajoles, threatens, and seduces a broken life into the fullness of human dignity that is praiseworthy and life-affirming. Women's love and nurture can only be considered virtuous or redemptive if their acts of care are embedded within larger frameworks of justice and opposition to oppression and genocide. Among all the wives, only Margaret Stark seemed to feel the enormity of what had happened in Auschwitz. She alone had enough critical distance from SS ideology to issue an unambiguous call for transformation. She wanted her husband to express regret and to reach a different perspective on the dehumanization he had been recruited into as a youthful member of the SS. Her threat of separation was a moral response that was more than a flight from responsibility. She did not want to get away from him but to proceed on the basis of open acknowledgment and contrition over the wasteland of Auschwitz.

8

Absolved from the Guilt of the Past?

MEMORY AS BURDEN AND AS GRACE

*Forgiveness that involves the mark of Cain is not total
forgetting.*[1]

IN EVERY DECADE since 1945, there have been calls for a final *Schlussstrich*
and closure. But the strategy of burying the past[2] has not worked. Despite
strenuous efforts to establish *Unbefangenheit*, or a normal, unburdened,
and relaxed approach to history, the compulsion to escape the guilt of the
past required complicated constructions of biographies and institutional
histories that jumped from the Weimar Republic into the Hour Zero of
postwar East and West Germany. Faith in these fabrications came at considerable personal and political cost. Complicity in the genocide of the
Jews remained a live wire in Germany's political culture, a raw nerve that
would regularly trigger recriminations, erupt in scandalous revelations,
and require shamefaced denials.

This book has argued that the path toward redemption for perpetrators
does not entail burying guilt, lifting its burden, or washing away its stain.
The renewal of moral integrity depends on a perpetrator's ability to recognize the suffering of victims and to bear the truthful memory of his or her
violation. Such recognition requires profound ideological change and
political transformation as well as personal strength and moral courage. It
is not an easy path, and it is not a well-trodden one. In fact, in my research
I found only one example where a Nazi perpetrator moved along the
course of open recognition and remorse.

It may be coincidental that he was a religious man and spoke of engaging
in penitence in an effort to "make good" (*wiedergutmachen*) the harm doing
he had participated in. But I want to suggest that the Christian tradition of
penitential practices may provide clues for a more activist approach to guilt
that enriches current thinking about overcoming legacies of atrocity.

Guilt and Penance

What in the religious tradition of penance may be relevant and worth rehabilitating in secular social contexts of transitional justice and state crimes? At first glance, the concept of penance conjures up the Middle Ages, when people engaged in strange rituals of self-flagellation, hair shirts, and indulgences. Penance, like the wooden confessionals in most Roman Catholic churches, has not been especially popular lately. What makes penance intriguing for contemporary, postgenocidal societies is its activist approach to the problem of guilt. Penance transforms guilt into a challenge. Penitential practices externalize culpability and turn internal feelings of shame into specific actions that require courage, discipline, and perseverance. Penance translates shameful secrets into symbolic acts and engages perpetrators in constructive activities that rebuild self-respect. It prescribes specific tasks that break the isolation of denial and delusion and draws perpetrators out of their self-centered denials into moral agency. Penance does not replace punishment. Perpetrators must be removed from positions of power and authority, especially over victims. But the concept of penance develops a transformative agenda that pulls individuals and communities into restorative action that rebuilds ruined relations and regenerates the human dignity of victims and perpetrators.

By contrast, the more common strategy of forgiveness and reconciliation leaves perpetrators passive, mere recipients of magnanimity (which they just as often have not requested and are not willing to accept). The road to reconciliation built upon forgiveness also involves the temptation to pressure and manipulate victims and their representatives into gestures of goodwill. When victims refuse, they can be shamed for their inability and unwillingness to overcome resentment and grievance. Forgiveness suggests that the past should be left behind, which often involves subtle and explicit exhortations to remain silent and suppress painful memories. We tend to assume that such forgiveness is in the interest of perpetrators, who stand to gain when victims relinquish resentment. But, as I have argued, such forgiveness is not beneficial to perpetrators of atrocity because it misdiagnoses their moral dis-ease: they don't feel guilty, they don't want forgiveness, and they won't change unless confronted with the human dignity and worth of victims. Their moral restoration requires truth, transparency, and critical engagement. The emergence of contrition is emotionally traumatic and demands enormous courage and personal strength. We should understand penance as an exercise program that practices the emotional skills and develops the social competence required to endure the full or even the partial realization of culpable wrongdoing. The tradition of penance, then, provides a different role to perpetrators of atrocities that involves more than passive acceptance of either punishment or forgiveness and proposes that individuals and communities become active bearers of culpability.

Guilt is wrongly conceived as a burden that can be lifted. Instead, it should be seen as a weight that ought to be carried—well or not so well. Seen as a crushing load, guilt ought to be removed, but seen as a demanding assignment, it can become the source of renewal. Secular feminist and analytic philosopher Claudia Card argues in *The Atrocity Paradigm* that "we tend to think of burdens as, naturally, burdensome, to be got rid of as soon as possible, as they are heavy and weigh upon us. But burdens need not just pull us down. Carrying a burden well builds strength, which can help to gain or regain others' respect and develop and recover self-esteem."[3] Guilt understood as penance does not simply weigh a person down, but challenges her to brace and to bear up under it.

Both Judaism and Christianity provide metaphors that speak to the benefits of carrying burdens. In Judaism, the people of Israel accept the yoke of the Torah and agree to carry out its precepts as part of the covenantal obligation. The disciples of Jesus are exhorted to "take my yoke upon you...for my yoke is easy, and my burden is light" (Matt. 11:29–30). The metaphors of carrying the Torah and of bearing the cross are tinged with some ambivalence, since neither task is necessarily easy or entirely pleasurable. Nevertheless, both religions convey in their central symbols a vision of carrying a burden as an ennobling and redemptive task. In the Christian tradition, the one who bears the cross is exalted, while those who carry the yoke of the Torah are praised as members of a holy nation. The religious traditions, then, offer ways to think of carrying a burden of guilt as an inherently dignifying task that rebuilds integrity and revitalizes the soul.

As we have seen in the previous chapters, the flight from responsibility strongly defines the experience of Nazi perpetrators. In their denial of guilt, they assumed a defensive and passive stance in order to abdicate moral agency. In their escape from the past, they were forever afraid of being detected, exposed, accused, and condemned. They felt haunted. They could not ask for forgiveness because they could not face the possibility of acknowledging wrongdoing. Instead, they craved a magical release from culpability that would erase the past and obliterate their guilt. They shrank in their humanity as they retreated into fortified walls of half-truths and outright lies that were designed to hide the secrets and the truths of their lives. Whenever the topic of "the past" was brought up they felt threatened, and they lived in constant fear of being asked to account for their lives. By erasing the truth of their lives, they fell ever more deeply into the clutches of guilt. The suppression of memory cannot generate redemption. Release is found in transparency and truthfulness. Penance is a training program that exercises the faculties necessary to carry the burden of guilt; it resists the temptation of denial, evasion, and willful forgetfulness and affirms responsible agency.

In this final chapter, we will meet two German clergymen who had different perspectives on penance. One embraced it and became a truthful witness, while the other rejected calls for symbolic action and was caught in defensive postures and evasive denials. Their denominational affiliations are coincidental and counterintuitive, since penitential practices are more deeply embedded in Roman Catholic piety than in the Protestant ethos. More than their religious practices, it was their social and political contexts that accounted for their different commitments to penitence. Matthias Defregger (1915–1995) became a Roman Catholic auxiliary bishop in Bavaria and retreated into apologetic assertions that Christian forgiveness of sins should "cover up" the memory of the offense. He fought the legal charges brought against him and won a dubious victory in a Munich courtroom. But he lost the battle to regain respect and failed to set an example of moral leadership. Otto Zakis was born in 1925 and became a Lutheran pastor in France, where he framed his life choices as a form of penance. He belongs to the very youngest cohort of perpetrators. He resolved to testify truthfully and without regard for the legal consequences and regained a measure of respect from witnesses and observers of the Majdanek trial, where he acknowledged that "no one…can ever free himself from such an experience."[4] His path, though, was far from straight and narrow and provides insight into the components of a successful moral transformation. Their biographies exemplify divergent Christian models for the role of memory in redemption. They also reflect the profound cultural and political changes that occurred in postwar Germany, which increasingly embraced the memory of the Holocaust as an ethical and political mandate.

Forgive and Forget: Auxiliary Bishop Matthias Defregger

Auxiliary Bishop Matthias Defregger (1915–1995) was thrust into the public limelight in 1969 when his participation in reprisal killings of civilians was exposed by the journal *Der Spiegel*. As captain of an intelligence unit of the 114th Anti-Partisan Division, Hauptmann Defregger had ordered the execution of Italian civilians in a reprisal action for the death of four German soldiers. After the war Defregger entered Roman Catholic seminary and was ordained a priest on June 29, 1949. He argued that he had truthfully confessed his involvement in this reprisal action and that he was, as a Protestant commentator put it, "absolved from the guilt of the past."[5] At the same time, Defregger steadfastly denied all "guilt, legal or moral."[6] "I feel myself legally and, above all, morally not guilty," he was quoted as saying in an article that summarized Defregger's interview for the German TV show *Report*. At the same time, Defregger asserted that "the memory of the execution [is] a heavy burden that I carry with me and of which no confessor and no public can relieve me."[7] As in so many other cases, Defregger's public exposure became a national and international media scandal, which forced him to articulate his perspective on the mass killings in the past.

He was shockingly unprepared, as was his confessor and supporter, Cardinal Döpfner of Munich, who had apparently failed to notify the Vatican of Defregger's military history.[8] Döpfner moved to defend Defregger's installation as auxiliary bishop with reference to the general principle of Christian forgiveness: "We as Christians know that the community of the church lives only through mutual forgiveness, because self-righteousness obstructs the path toward each other, to the world, and finally to God."[9] The term "self-righteousness" applied to anyone who felt inclined to question, expose, or judge someone's past. This code invoked the solidarity of guilt. Only the self-righteous person would condemn the straw in his brother's eye and ignore the beam in his own. As a church of sinners, the community of Christians can never be "wholly holy, totally pure, entirely without flaw," argued a Catholic commentator.[10] Since we are all guilty sinners, we are obligated to grant absolution and should be willing to forgive each other in order to allow new beginnings. We should, argued Cardinal Döpfner, "consider Defregger's decision with humane empathy" (*menschliches Verständnis*) and appreciate the "deep ethical dilemma" (*schwere Gewissensnot*) into which "he was thrust," and which caused him "great suffering."[11] The solidarity of human guilt and empathy for the sinner put a soothing blanket over the past. This was standard fare during the 1960s and was intended to placate the public in discussions of the legacy of mass violence.

Matthias Defregger caught himself in contradictions. On the one hand, he vigorously defended himself and proclaimed his blamelessness. On the other hand, like Wilke, he wanted to appear transformed and emphasized the great internal strain caused by the commission of violence. But his carefully scripted TV interview was "a catastrophe."[12] He "poured oil on the fire," judged the *Tagesanzeiger*, because he was unwilling and unable to express regret and acknowledge responsibility. Instead, he attacked the media and defended himself by painting himself as an obedient servant of the state and of the church. "The bishop threw a stone against the TV screen, and his self-defense caused an avalanche," commented the Italian newspaper *Il Messaggero*. Defregger had apparently not anticipated that his denial of responsibility would undermine the credibility of his assertion of an inner burden. As a theologically trained man, he should have realized that he was still stuck in the paralysis of guilt. According to the Catholic understanding of the sacrament, oral confession and cordial contrition are necessary steps in the sacrament of reconciliation. While a TV interview is no confessional, Defregger's inability to articulate a sense of wrongdoing and to demonstrate contrition aggravated the public outcry. Unfortunately, his confessor and mentor, Cardinal Döpfner, shared Defregger's incomprehension and failed to denounce the mass executions unequivocally.[13]

Both defended the legality of reprisal killings as a legitimate military tool against partisans. And the judges in the Munich court agreed with him when they dismissed the charges against him one year later, on September 17, 1970. Their verdict was aptly summarized in the headlines of the *Süddeutsche Zeitung* on the next day: "The Deed Confirmed—the Guilt Rejected."[14] The court's apparent endorsement of reprisal killings of noncombatants as a matter of legitimate military strategy shows the lingering presence of dehumanizing ideologies in the judicial system. Defregger was exonerated. But his evasive maneuvers and deceptive language had revealed the limits of his postwar conversion. His assurance that he had tried to help the civilians and attempted to avoid enforcing the execution order sounded hollow. "I tried to save what I could. But I saw no possibility to prevent the awful killings altogether" he wrote in his "Letter to the Priests and Congregations in the Diocese of Munich and Freising," published in Munich newspapers in July 1969. Defregger claimed to have tried to abrogate the severity of this reprisal order and chastised himself for not resisting "to the last…and without consideration of personal consequences."[15] With this formulation, the commanding officer Defregger tried to style himself into a near martyr. He never used the term "guilt" in this public letter. At most, Defregger was willing to fault himself for "unsuccessful resistance" and reluctance to sacrifice his life.

His former subordinates contested his recollection that he had been reluctant to enforce the order.[16] They recalled a heated discussion among "other officers, who challenged the execution of this order. One of these comrades asked, 'How could you do such a thing so close to the end?'"[17] In fact, American troops occupied the village of Filetto di Camarda only a week later, and Defregger's unit surrendered two weeks thereafter. Surely, with the end so close, the prudence of implementing such an order was debatable. With American artillery already in earshot, what had Defregger tried to save "by passing on and hence...implementing the execution order?"[18] Seventeen civilian men were shot. But by 1969, Defregger could still not get himself to acknowledge that he had failed "the test" imposed by God: "I cannot say whether I passed it. I can only trust in the judgment of God."[19] His inability to admit failure indicted him. The more he tried to appease the public and to placate critical voices within the church, the deeper he was bound into contradictory denials. He could not project moral integrity by affirming the "heavy load in his life" while at the same time insisting on his "judicial guiltlessness."[20] His inability to recognize the victims of this reprisal action was the most damning part of his public performance and was understood as a sign of his ongoing commitment to the militarist nationalism of his youth.

His lawyer, Catholic activist Marianne Thora, bluntly demanded that the media be silenced and threatened to counterexpose anyone who dared to continue raising questions: "If *Der Spiegel* and other comparable magazines don't keep quiet soon and stop their attacks on our cardinal, then these writers should be scrutinized for their own political and human histories, one after the other."[21] The web of collective guilt and Christian solidarity was invoked to manage memorial politics and to control the media. Defregger and his supporters testily denounced media outlets for investigating his past and deplored their revelations as anti-Catholic smear campaigns. Defregger claimed that the weekly journal *Der Spiegel* had "jumped on him," made him the target of a "hunt,"[22] and tried to "hit the bishop to strike the church."[23]

Of course, one can sympathize with Bishop Defregger's fear of being dishonored, stigmatized, and punished. Catholics called for his resignation from the bishop's seat,[24] and the Vatican (re)examined his eligibility for the priesthood and suitability for the episcopal office. German prosecutors reopened their criminal investigation, which had been discontinued. Italian prosecutors threatened Defregger with arrest should he attempt to cross the border, and they opened their own investigation into murder charges.[25] The village council of Filetto di Camarda demanded his extradition to face charges in Italy. Multiple dangers beleaguered Defregger, who fled his offices in Munich and went into hiding in his East Tyrolian home village. Exposed, Defregger felt threatened by loss of professional status and pressured by legal, social, and political sanctions. For many Germans, these threats to Defregger's status and respectability constituted "revenge."[26] Letters to the editors denounced his exposure and prosecution as an exercise of "perverse self-righteousness,"[27] "Pharisaic self-righteousness,"[28] and "vengeance."

His defenders could not see that Defregger's inability to signal contrition escalated demands for legal sanction. If Defregger had embraced, as Harvey Cox suggested in his commentary in *Christianity and Crisis,* "a painful act of penitence and personal reparations,"[29] the scandal could have turned into a lesson of Christian faith, humility, and obedience. Curiously, it was secular voices in the German press that suggested models for penitential practice. They imagined Defregger on the "path of penance to Filetto,"[30] in "the monk's cloak ... barefoot and bent under the burden of the cross,"[31] asking for forgiveness. This evoked cultural memories of the Way to Canossa, when Henry IV of the Holy Roman Empire walked from Speyer to the fortress in Canossa in Emilia Romagna and crossed the Alps barefoot in a hair shirt, humbly asking for forgiveness of Pope Gregory VII in January 1077. The German Roman Catholic hierarchy rejected any such proposition and refused requests to visit the survivors and relatives of victims in Filetto. Even after the dismissal of criminal charges, by the end of 1971, neither Defregger nor Cardinal Döpfner dared to cross the Alps to honor the victims or speak with survivors of the execution order.[32] As one journalist wrote: "As far as Christian forgiveness is concerned, the bishop should, even if only some of the charges against him are true, ask for forgiveness of the relatives as a penitential monk but not in the robes of the bishop."[33] The timidity of the church hierarchy's response to the Italian villagers was even more remarkable since they were fellow Roman Catholics, and not Jews or "godless Bolshevists."

Meanwhile, the victims were exhorted to forgive. Defregger's public declaration was titled "Solidarity with the Victims," but survivors and relatives of victims in Filetto di Camarda heard of its publication in Munich newspapers through TV, radio, and the newspapers.[34] Defregger had never posted the letter to the village itself, although the text asked villagers for "understanding and forgiveness for not being able to help you more."[35] This oversight and lack of concern did not deter the Italian village priest Don Demetrio Gianfrancesco from initiating a campaign to "move the affected families towards Christian forgiveness."[36] He maintained that "one not only forgives those who deserve it, but also those who are evil."[37] In a village referendum, this Christian position received seven signatures, while the Communist petition "Demand Justice Now" gathered eighty. Despite intense pressure on the part of Don Demetrio, who declared in an interview with *Der Spiegel*, "If they want to be Christians, they must all sign," the village majority rejected the notion that they should extend forgiveness in the absence of a direct request. Subsequently, Fr. Don Demetrio sent a letter to Bishop Defregger in Munich and assured him that the signatories had granted him the "most conceivably wide and magnanimous forgiveness."[38] Defregger's reaction to this offer is not known. On September 18, 1970, Defregger resigned from the public position of auxiliary bishop, against the wishes of Cardinal Döpfner, as the *New York Times* reported.[39] He assumed a less visible post in the pastoral supervision of religious orders in the archdiocese of Munich and Freising.

Scandals such as this provided opportunities to process the moral remainders. Along with Defregger, thousands of German men and women like him were faced with the reality of long-forgotten victims who might demand consideration of the legacy of violence. Defregger refused to meet the victims face to face. And he failed to ask for their forgiveness. This makes the Italian priest's extension of forgiveness problematic. As a verbal gesture it remained hollow because it did not initiate a repair of the relation between victims and perpetrator. Defregger remained as disconnected from the victims as on the day the executions were performed. It is possible that the village priest's unconditional act of magnanimity moved him. As far as we know, he was not able to respond meaningfully to this extension of forgiveness, and he never met with the survivors. Defregger could not cease the moment to show moral leadership by moving toward reconciliation on the basis of contrition.

Time, itself, does not heal all wounds. Even twenty-five years after the war, neither victims nor perpetrators "had moved on." Generally, it is the quality of critical engagement with suffering and guilt that contains the seeds of repair and restoration. Moral healing needs effort; it rarely occurs by itself. For perpetrators, such transformation required external interventions in the form of criminal proceedings and public exposures. In was in the court of law that perpetrators were forced to listen to the testimony of survivors and witnesses. They were coerced by the media and in the court of public opinion to confront the historical record. It was in these moments, painful and excruciating as they were for the individuals involved, that actual moral and political change occurred. The mere forgetfulness and repression of memories could not dismantle the ideological power of nationalism and militarism, or the legacy of dehumanization.

These public debates created the conditions for moral and political transformation. Without the threat of sanctions in the public limelight, Defregger might have continued to discount the lives of these villagers. Their deaths remained trivial to him until they became critically important to his own well-being and future. If he had embraced the path of penance, he could have become world-renowned like Willie Brandt, whose Warsaw Genuflection (*Warschauer Kniefall*) on December 7, 1970, earned him the Nobel Peace Prize in 1971. Unlike Defregger, who could not liberate himself from the controlling grip of complicity, Willie Brandt had spent the war in Sweden and Norway opposing National Socialism. When he visited the Warsaw Ghetto as chancellor of Germany, he fell to his knees and bowed his head in an expression of contrition and respect for the victims of the Holocaust. His symbolic act was followed by the signing ceremony of the peace treaty, which acknowledged the Oder-Neiße line as legitimate border between Germany and Poland, thereby accepting the expulsion of Germans from their ancestral lands and the loss of Eastern territories of Germany. Brandt may have been able to understand the symbolic power of an act of penance, because he himself had avoided the complicity of guilt. He could freely express grief and mourn the victims of the Warsaw Ghetto, while Defregger could not.[40] Defregger had staked his career on the invisibility and silence of the victims. When they spoke out and were validated by the media, he had no idea how to react with integrity.

Defregger's strategy of consigning the victims to oblivion finds support among those Christian theologians who understand forgiveness as a release from the burden of guilt rather than a call to responsibility for the victims. Uwe Dittmer, a Protestant theological commentator on Bishop Defregger, insisted that Christian forgiveness should be understood as a "relief and not as unbearable burden."[41] He explicitly rejected expectations that Defregger should have approached the victims with a request for forgiveness and defended his confessor's prerogative to dispense absolution. Dittmer maintained that the Christian priest has the authority and responsibility to release the sinner from the burden of guilt in the name of Christ, "who carried the sins of the world."[42] The penitential imposition of conditions that require perpetrators to approach their victims in humility is explicitly rejected by this conception of reconciliation between God and sinner.

> Therefore, anyone who calls for the performance of penance as a condition for forgiveness has not understood anything of the gospel. Forgiveness is intended as release and not as an imposition of an unbearable burden. This is true despite the call in the Sermon on the Mount that requires anyone who approaches the altar in the Temple to first go and reconcile with his brother (Matt. 5:23–24).[43]

The New Testament reflects the Jewish tradition's distinction between obligations incurred by offending God and the debt accrued by violating the rights of the neighbor. In the Jewish tradition God cannot release a contrite sinner from obligations that he or she acquired by harming the neighbor. Only the victim can release the wrongdoer from such debt. The Gospel of Matthew reflects this Jewish practice and requires that the debtor approach the victim with a verbal request of forgiveness. Only when God is the primary victim of the offense can God grant pardon. God cannot grant absolution in place of the victim. The Christian tradition has undercut the prerogative of the victim and eliminated the mandate to consider the willingness of the victim to grant release from ethical obligation in the liturgy and sacrament of reconciliation.

These theological and liturgical changes served to disempower victims, who now no longer played a role in rituals of reconciliation. As a consequence, prison chaplains could dispense absolution and reconciliation with God without giving any consideration to the Jewish, Communist, and homosexual neighbors whose human dignity had been willfully violated and with whose denigration most Christian clergy heartily agreed. No profound contrition could emerge as a result of such practices. Without recognition of the human rights of victims, genuine reconciliation could not come into reach. The promise of quick relief from the burden of guilt not only aggravated the disempowerment of victims but also deprived perpetrators of genuine transformation. Public vigilance, the empowerment of victims, international pressure, threats of criminal prosecution, and legal sanctions, on the other hand, did contribute to lasting political and ethical changes. We therefore need to find a theological language that validates memory and appreciates the exposure of painful truths as redemptive rather than as destructive.

Redemption as Oblivion: Theological Voices
against Memory

The desire to abolish repulsive and horrid memories as a means of release from the debts of the past is deeply entrenched in Christian theology.[44] Often reconciliation is conceived as liberation from the burden of guilt, as if forgetfulness could facilitate delivery from the bondage of past oppression.[45] Christ died to "take away" the sins of the world, and Christian pray in the "Our Father" that God may "forgive us our debt [or: trespasses], as we forgive our debtors [those who trespass against us]." While human beings deserve the chance to change, and are capable of new beginnings, such transformations do not happen by way of disconnection and disassociation from the past. Peace depends on justice, and reconciliation requires truth. Forgiveness that compromises the dignity and integrity of victims is a pretense. But for some Christian theologians, forgiveness holds preeminence over truth, and ultimate redemption entails the extinction of painful memories. For instance, Protestant theologian Miroslav Volf argues in *Exclusion and Embrace* that there cannot be, and should not be, any memory of Auschwitz in heaven.[46] Volf speaks as a Croatian Protestant theologian and torture survivor who is deeply suspicious of historical memory that forever seems to justify the renewal of hostilities in Balkan politics. He questions the possibility of forgiveness and redemption as long as the twin memories of victimization and perpetration are preserved. Only conscious setting aside of memory and the bliss of forgetfulness can secure lasting peace.

For Volf, heaven must be a place where the memory of pain, violence, and cruelty is pulled out by its roots. There cannot be former victims and former perpetrators in heaven since the very memory of atrocity would spoil it.[47] How can it be heaven, if we were to remember Auschwitz? The "final act" of redemption and the "most difficult grace....is the grace of nonremembering."[48] Volf concedes that in the political realm of history, memory serves as a "shield against inhumanity" and as a pedagogical lesson for the future. He also understands that we should commemorate the victims in order to honor their suffering.[49] Volf speaks as a victim of Balkan politics, where memories of victimization have been used to ignite the cycle of vengeance and violence.

But his teacher, Jürgen Moltmann, speaks from the political context and personal background of perpetration. When he formulates a similar understanding of justification as the elimination of memory, he enters into the discourses of denial that has defined the experience of perpetrators. Moltmann argues that the goal of justification entails the permission to stop thinking about the past: "Even in our lives it is not enough merely to atone for past guilt so as to be able to live with the past, important though that is. Something new has to be created, so that 'the old has passed away' (II Cor 7:17) and we do not have to think about it anymore."[50] He speaks as young recruit into Hitler's Wehrmacht, and we should be suspicious of his desire. He describes the "liberation of oppressors" as a lifting of the burden of guilt and asks: "Is this [i.e., the resurrection of Christ] God's answer to the dead of 'Auschwitz,' whose remembrance weighs so heavily on our souls?"[51] A theological vision that links the resurrection of Christ with the end of the memory of Auschwitz resonates with the compulsive desire of perpetrators to store the ashes of Auschwitz in the oblivion of history. The primary problem of perpetrators, as we have seen, is not that they are bent under the burden of memory, but that they desire to run from the truth of the reality of victims. They cannot *see* or *feel* the violation of victims as wrongful acts. This burden cannot be lifted because its weight cannot be perceived. Moltmann presupposes the presence of a moral burden and assumes that perpetrators feel a desire for liberation "from the injustice of oppression" because perpetrators "in their heart of hearts...know that they are acting unjustly."[52] However, the empirical evidence does not support this assumption. Nazi perpetrators did not feel morally and spiritually burdened, which is why their liberation is misconceived as the lifting of such a burden.

While we may wish it were true, as Jürgen Moltmann claims, that "guilt, whether it be individual or collective, weighs heavily on the guilty person and destroys his self-esteem,"[53] we cannot substantiate this from the historical evidence. In his study of Nazi perpetrators, Israeli psychologist Dan Bar-On concluded that, as a group, Nazi perpetrators were not symptomatic for psychological distress and displayed few indications of emotional or social dysfunction.[54] The vast majority did not require psychological help and did not seek therapeutic and spiritual counseling. Their mental health, professional integration, and social functioning surpassed that of their victims. Those Nazis who reconverted to Christianity consistently confused their desire to be liberated from the consequences of misconduct with a genuine liberation from the ideological deformation that had hardened their hearts and blighted their humanity. But without a life-threatening encounter with contrition, there could be no genuine redemption. One can imagine that the rekindling of feelings and the

reawakening of compassion would have deeply disturbing effects and create dangerous moments in the life of a perpetrator. But without the dread
of recognition, there can be no rebirth or humane regeneration. The
redemption from the debt of guilt also mandates external acts of satisfaction, including the restitution of ill-gotten profits and the renunciation the
privileges of oppression. Needless to say, very few were willing to go there.
It was so much easier to demand to be released from the memory of guilt
than to ask that the guilt of oppression itself be overcome.

As a member of the youngest German generation caught up in National
Socialism, Moltmann experienced regret. His generational cohort endured
the deepest and longest struggle with guilt in the postwar period. As one
born during the 1920s (cf. Günther Grass's revelation),[55] Jürgen Moltmann
spoke of suffering from guilt and "self-hate."[56] This teenage generation was
very vulnerable and receptive to indoctrination by skillful Nazi propagan-
dists and teachers. And they served in the trenches rather than the palaces
of power. By the time they were recruited and inducted into the Nazi programs of genocide and total war, there were few choices to be made. Of all
the perpetrators, the youngest cohort experienced the greatest level of
remorse. They were latecomers who were assigned into positions, places,
and situations designed by their elders. They did not plan, manage, and
implement Nazi extermination policies but served as its foot soldiers. Their
distance from the ideological and political center of power by virtue of their
youth may explain why they felt more guilt than those who had planned the
programs. In contrast to the ideological architects, political organizers, and
economic beneficiaries who never spoke openly of feeling guilty, these
younger men acknowledged suffering pangs of contrition.

The Grace of Memory: Otto Zakis

Otto Zakis belonged to this youngest cohort.[57] He was born in December
1925 in Riga as a member of the ethnic minority of Baltic Germans.[58] As
an "ethnic German" (Volksdeutscher), whose stepfather happened to be
caught on British soil when the war started and ended up serving in the
U.S. Army, Zakis felt vulnerable as a "second-class German," inferior to
genuine Reichsdeutsche. He volunteered for the SS at age sixteen in 1941.
He was sent to Buchenwald to an eight-week-long "SS boot camp" and
then to a succession of horrible concentration and death camps: Hinzert
in the Eifel, a satellite camp of Neuengamme in Wolfsburg, the Polish
Sonderlager Debica, and then Majdanek. He first came to Majdanek in

November 1942 and "was shocked." He "wanted to get away" and volunteered for further training as a canine leader in Schwabach toward the end of 1942. From there he was promptly dispatched back to Majdanek in May 1943, where he stayed until the camp's evacuation in 1944. After a short military stint, he ended his SS career in the Swabian concentration camp of Dautmergen before he was captured by French troops in Austria and handed over to a Soviet war crimes commission. He escaped from the train transport heading for Soviet captivity and subsequently registered as a DP (displaced person). He was twenty years old.

Otto Zakis was never tried as an SS guard. But he was interrogated and deposed several times by prosecutors in preparation for the Majdanek trial in Düsseldorf. In 1972 he declined his right to remain silent or to have an attorney present, although he was warned that his statements could be used against him and that he could be charged as an accomplice. He wanted to give a truthful account of an event that had haunted him for thirty years. It was his first *Waldkommando* (guard duty in the woods), and they had been instructed to shoot anyone trying to escape. "I did not know," he claimed, that "on the return the numbers of prisoners had to match those who had left; it did not matter whether they were dead or alive."[59] As newly arrived SS man, he was in charge of the Ukrainian guards, who, he was told, "knew what to do." They were drunk and ordered "a Jew" to run away before they shot him in the back.

> I was sixteen years old and afraid of the drunk Ukrainians. I walked over to the Ukrainians and stood next to them when the Jew was brought back by order of the Ukrainian *Unterscharführer*. He was laid down about four meters away from me and bled all over his body and gurgled. He looked in my direction.[60]

Zakis called this incident the "most awful experience that I have ever had."[61] It was after the retelling of this event that he was formally informed of his right to remain silent and given the opportunity to change his statement. He declined and declared: "I reiterate my previous statement as completely and absolutely accurate, even as an accused, and I do not want to talk to an attorney. I cannot say anything else.... When we returned to our quarters I was crying uncontrollably."[62] When it was pointed out to him that he was in command as *Wachführer* and invested with absolute authority [*absolute Befehlsgewalt*] and could have intervened immediately, he declared:

This was the first time that a human being was killed in my presence. Because of my youth the shock effect of these events was so great that I was helpless in confronting this situation. I have been carrying this thing with me for thirty years. This is the first time that I am talking about it.[63]

What makes Zakis's account unique is his mention of the eyes of the dying man. It was this eye contact with "the Jew" that humanized him and made this scene unbearable to Zakis. The intimacy of locking eyes with a dying person overwhelmed him emotionally. No other perpetrator in my sample spoke of making eye contact and such an intimate recognition of shared humanity. Instead, they steeled themselves against the vulnerability of victims and triumphed over human empathy, shielding themselves in the moment, but also in the years after. They were spared the tears of contrition because they did not allow themselves to look into the eyes of victims. Zakis, on the other hand, fell apart under the "oppressive burden" of his past. He wanted desperately to "get rid of it," a term he used twice. Two years after the first deposition, Zakis's statement was summarized thus:

Until 1972 my past occupied me tremendously. But then I got rid of those things [Dinge], especially those that affected me personally, and I turned away from these affairs [Sachen] even internally and concentrated fully on my profession. For instance, I held worship services in two prisons last Sunday, and I am increasingly in doubt, since I work with people who have come into conflict with themselves, whether we human beings can be [responsible] for affairs [Sachen] that lie far in the past—whether they really—whether these matters [Dinge] remain significant—for me this affair [Angelegenheit] came to an end in 1972. I have a profession and family.[64]

With its convoluted grammar and trailing half-sentences, Zakis's statement is reminiscent of the discourses of exoneration. He tried to remove the stain of guilt and wanted to be rid of the past. The more he attempted to disassociate himself, the more it recaptured him, as he veered into all-too-familiar defensiveness. The desire to "turn away from the past" drew him back into the twisted rhetoric of denial.

But Zakis's testimony was different for another reason. Already in his first deposition in 1972, he framed his life story in ways that were significantly different from that of other perpetrators. There seemed to be genuine flashes contrition, a sense of guilt and a desire to engage in pen-ance. After his escape from Soviet imprisonment, Zakis signed up as a coal miner in Belgium, a choice he explained as a "penance that I imposed on myself because of these experiences."[65] He worked in the coal mines in Belgium between 1947 and 1949 and volunteered for especially dangerous and unpleasant assignments, which would eventually earn him the nick-name "little Jesus."[66] In 1949, he decided to move to France and to study Protestant theology in Paris, a decision he explained as an attempt to "serve society" and to "prove to myself that I could make good [*wiedergut-machen*] the mistakes that I committed against society."[67] He was ordained a minister and called to Nice in southern France, where he served as city pastor for two years between 1953 and 1955. Once established in Nice, Zakis felt "so oppressed by the events that I witnessed that I reported myself to the police: I told them that I was an SS guard. The French justice system did not take this seriously. They evidently wanted to avoid a public scandal, because I was minister [*Seelsorger*], after all."[68] He had decided to turn himself him in after he attempted to commit suicide. But the French authorities merely sent him to a psychiatrist, who diagnosed him as "com-petent but a bit unstable."[69] By the time he was deposed in Düsseldorf in 1972, Zakis had struggled with the presence of guilt. He had launched himself on a penitential path that would eventually turn him into a truth-ful witness. Although he would never fully overcome the impulse to excul-pate, he tried to make reparations and to build his life on the basis of an open acknowledgment of culpable wrongdoing.

I was delighted when Zakis, who lives as a retired Lutheran minister in Bavaria, responded to my letter of inquiry within forty-eight hours and was willing to speak with me. Two telephone conversations in 2008 yielded important additional biographical information that helped me to better understand his life choices. One of my questions, for instance, was whether Zakis had gone into the coal mines as a form of penance, or as a way to escape detection and to stay under the radar of Allied military pros-ecutors. Speaking with him clarified this immediately. Zakis told me that his stepfather, from whom he had become separated during the war, was employed as a high-ranking "Commander of the U.S. War Shipping Administration,"[70] while his mother worked for the United Nations Refugee Agency. By 1946, the family lived very well and in relative privi-lege in a requisitioned villa in Bavaria. With such family connections, Zakis could have easily established himself in the American occupation zone of Bavaria. But he decided to spend two years in the coal mines because he wanted to do penance. It was in Belgium that he befriended a Belgian pastor who engaged him in conversations about religion and ethics. "I found my Christian faith because of my sense of guilt [*Schuldempfinden*],"[71] Zakis said in our phone conversation. His decision to study theology in France further distanced him from the politics of complicity and rehabilitation that characterized postwar Germany. France had a very different memorial politics.[72] On the other hand, Zakis generally avoided drawing attention to his wartime history. When I queried him about pervasive anti-German sentiments in France while he was in seminary, he said: "Of course, they hated the Germans, but I was Otto, and Otto was different." He did not disabuse his French fellow students of their naive assumptions about him.

The desire to deny the guilt, to suppress the memory, and to "turn away from the past" would never entirely go away. In 1972, he claimed that "this event has come to an end" and that he successfully "turned away" from the past.[73] When we ended our telephone conversation in 2008, which had been generally frank and truthful, he affirmed that he did not feel guilty because he "had never shot at a person." "Today," he said, "I see myself as a victim and not as a perpetrator in connection with the events of 1941–1945." I was stunned to hear him invoke blamelessness and victimhood, just like all the others. Did his life follow a different path of penitential practice or not? Was he just like the others in his denial?

Truthfully nor not, Zakis had always maintained that his guard duties had only been along the outside perimeters and on the watch towers, and that he had sometimes accompanied prisoners on external trips. He claimed that he was never involved in the daily brutal humiliations and cruel violations that characterized camp life. He was never indicted for personally killing a human being. He was a young, impressionable, and vulnerable recruit, but his SS career had included stays in some of the most notorious concentration camps, including Buchenwald, Hinzert, Dachau, Majdanek, and Dautmergen. He had observed individual murders and patrolled mass killings as a canine leader who protected the perimeter and prevented people from fleeing the massacres.[74] Did he have a right to consider himself a victim more than a perpetrator?

When Eberhard Fechner made a four-and-a-half-hour documentary on the Majdanek trial in 1983, he introduced Otto Zakis as "the one SS man who made a deep impression," and as one who "never got over Majdanek."[75] Zakis, who is the only interviewee who is not introduced by name and shown only in a shadowy profile in front of a large cross, described his summons to testify at the trial in Düsseldorf as a "release" (*Erlösung*). His willingness to testify truthfully made him controversial and infuriated the defendants. Out of fifteen hundred SS guards in Majdanek, fifteen had been indicted. During the trial 314 witnesses were summoned. Apart from Zakis, only one other female SS warden was similarly prepared to speak openly about her experiences in Majdanek. All other SS witnesses had trouble recollecting the past and could not remember specific incidents or names of persons. The defendants were obviously forgetful because they feared punishment. And the SS witnesses were constrained by their SS oaths of loyalty and the webs of complicity. Zakis stood out because he no longer abided by this ethos. He affirmed that "no one who was in Majdanek, whether as guard or as prisoner, can ever free himself from such an experience—even those who pretended during this trial that they've forgotten it."[76]

He seemed to have rebuilt the necessary moral backbone to bear up under the strain of the burden of guilt. Zakis explained his choice to go into the coal mines as an act of penance. It is possible that his penitential approach contributed to strengthening his moral integrity, as it drew him out of self-reverential narcissism into reparative action and, eventually, public witnessing. He prescribed a path of action for himself that transformed his guilt from an internal emotional condition (syndrome) into external activity. He left Germany and rebuilt his life in Belgium and France, where he chose a career of service. Although his penitential time in the coal mines did not directly benefit Jews, the actual victims of Majdanek, it may have worked to exercise his moral agency, courage, and personal strength. The victims of atrocities are under no obligation to accept reparative acts, and they do not hold the power to prevent its practice. The performance of penitential action imposes no expectations of particular reactions on victims. It is performed irrespective of "rewards." A penitent does not say, "I am doing this because I want your forgiveness," but rather, "I am doing this out of my own sense of justice and as a contribution to rebuild righteousness." Penance is a perpetrator-centered pathway that aims to humanize and sensitize a self and a community that have been dehumanized by the commission of atrocities.

Zakis regained the respect of others to the extent that he was able to recount specific events and to testify publicly about them. This does not make him a saint, and it does not cancel his complicity. And he could have gone further. When I asked him whether he ever spoke to German schoolchildren about his experience as a sixteen-year-old recruit of the SS and his experiences in concentration camps, he said, "Nobody will be helped when these stories are brought into the public light." I do not think that he is right.

Now more than ever, communities need models of what it might mean to live with integrity in the aftermath of collective evil. We need exemplars who can show that it is possible to emerge from complicity in genocide with dignity. Clearly, this study has not been successful at identifying many examples. But it seems clear that transparency, openness, and truthfulness are key for banishing the destructive power of guilt. Truthful memory commits a person to a path of responsibility and self-respect. It does not humiliate and degrade but empowers an agent to strive for moral agency. There were moments when Zakis rose to the occasion and transformed himself from a perpetrator into a witness and there were times when he retreated into denial and exoneration.

Conclusion

In the aftermath of war and genocide, it is not enough to rebuild the physical infrastructures of cities and factories. One also must attend to the moral and psychological devastation left by mass violence. The destruction visited upon the victims is manifest. But the damage done to the perpetrators is hidden. Although perpetrators appear undaunted and even satisfied, because they get to enjoy the spoils of war and the profits of genocide, the hardening of the heart that is necessary to destroy human lives takes a toll. The willful blindness required to ignore the suffering of victims festers and grows over time.

This study presented Nazi perpetrators in their own words and followed the trail of their self-reflections and intimate conversations with chaplains, spouses, and children. The documentary record reveals that, almost without exception, they were unable to openly admit culpable wrongdoing. They could not bring themselves to articulate remorse and were devoid of contrition. Their texts were characterized by the same cold logic and dispassionate indifference toward victims that had overwritten feelings of compassion and empathy in the first place. They were driven by an obsessive need to minimize moral agency, and they strenuously avoided specific memories of doing harm. They could not speak truthfully about some of the most traumatic moments in their lives, and their convoluted explanations and deceptions oozed into many of their communications. Although outwardly they were successful in their professional and private home lives, they could never fully entrust their secrets to the postwar world. Their guilty secrets bound them into the past.

It was much easier to diagnose the disease than to prescribe the medicine. The material amply documents the sickness of twisted logic and misleading reasoning, but wherein lies the recovery? As a theologian, I wanted to find clues in the empirical evidence that would point toward the possibilities of redemption and release from guilt. What, I wondered, would individuals and communities have to do in order to rebuild moral integrity? Is it possible to emerge from the grip of guilt? This second step moved the study from the realm of objective history into subjective normative commentary.

There are no easy answers to the question of how individuals and communities find redemption from the legacy of guilt for atrocities. The process is anything but straightforward and can best be described as a dance that moves two steps forward and one step backward, with several evasive sidesteps in between. In other words, the moral repair of perpetrator cultures is complex and shifts back and forth between the two opposing poles of justice and mercy, punishment and amnesty, censure and lenience. As soon as the process is permanently tilted to one side, it can be derailed.

The path of justice is critical to putting an end to genocide. Without prosecution and punishment, the arrogance of power that would set itself over life and death of others cannot be broken. The instigators and agents of such outrages must be held accountable. Communities are obligated to sentence those who became complicit at the many layers of genocide. But in the end, there are too many agents who will get away. It is impossible to do justice by sending all of those who deserve it to the gallows and the prison cells. Justice cannot be meaningfully restored by penalizing individual perpetrators. Furthermore, the retribution that can be exacted can never be entirely commensurate with the extremity of genocidal destruction. No prison term and no execution can satisfy the thirst for justice. Therefore, the path of indictment, prosecution, and punishment cannot constitute the only way forward.

The path of forgiveness, mercy, and amnesty has been vigorously debunked in this book, because it was the rallying cry of the German churches. As obnoxious as the widespread reintegration and restoration of the old elites in church and state were in postwar Germany, it is also true that no society can afford to remove large segments of its people. These doctors, lawyers, teachers, policemen and businessmen, fathers and husbands were not going anywhere. Even those who went to prison eventually returned to their families, jobs, and communities. Hence, the question of pardon and reprieve remained an integral element in recovery of this post-genocidal society. While retributive justice with its regiment of trials and punishments is important, so are strategies of critical engagement and moral repair.

A restorative approach to justice focuses on ideological conversion and moral transformation. It calls for critical engagement with perpetrators not as an act of charity but as an act of justice. The prison chaplains, for all their flaws, confronted the perpetrators with questions of ideology, morality, and faith and nudged them along the path of change. Their work required patience, tolerance, and forbearance. The fruits of their labors were often negligible, and yet they added up. The cumulative effect of these conversations and confrontations changed individual and cultural perspectives on the crimes of National Socialism.

This is the lesson of the mark of Cain. The mark signifies a path of moral repair based on openness and transparency. The mark invites memory and facilitates mourning. It was the vigorous and continuous debates over the "guilt question" that changed the perspective of Germany on its history. Not one decade went by in which the topic of the Nazi past was not debated on the front pages of national and international newspapers. The result of these often painful reminders was the restoration of moral health and political conscience. By all accounts, contemporary Germany has developed a unique way of integrating its history of perpetration into its cultural and political identity.

Like Cain, the political culture of Germany has shifted its energies from hiding and whitewashing its past toward commemoration, reparation, and reconciliation. Since the Holocaust has become a universal symbol of modern collective evil, Germany has embraced its role as Cain. Its political legitimacy, economic success, and international integration are staked on moral responsibility and historical transparency. Like Cain, Germany finds itself under special obligation. Its postwar history demonstrates that its desperate attempts at closure and escape served to endow this history with uncanny power. But those willing to accept the obligations arising from the commission of collective evil experienced the liberating qualities of repair.

The path of reparative action is rooted in the past but committed to the future. Unlike blood money, which is paid to seal the cycle of violence, penitential action regenerates and renews relationships. The pace and extent of reparative activity in Germany has accelerated over time. There are more grassroots initiatives now that commemorate the victims, repair the sites of camps and cemeteries, and document the history of complicity than ever before. Clearly reparative action is a renewable resource that grows with time, critical distance, and open engagement. For those who have taken on the obligation of restorative action, a deep sense of satisfaction emerges as these initiatives establish friendships and renew trust among individuals and communities torn apart by the injustices of history.

Biographical Appendix

Ammon, Wilhelm von (1903–1992). A lawyer by profession, he joined the SA in 1933 and moved to Berlin in 1935 to work as a jurist in the Reichsjustizministerium. He remained active in the ministry until 1945 and was responsible for rewriting German citizenship law on a racial basis (Nuremberg Laws of 1935), the legalization of killing "life unworthy of life" in the euthanasia program. He helped draft the "Night and Fog" orders legalizing extrajudicial executions. He was convicted in the Nuremberg Jurist trials, released from Landsberg in 1951, and appointed as director of church law in the Bavarian Lutheran Church, 1957–1970.

Blei, August (1894–1946). Blei was sentenced to death in the Dachau trials as an SS guard in the Mauthausen concentration camp.

Blobel, Paul (1894–1951). He joined the NSdAP in 1931 and the SS in 1932 and commanded Sonderkommando 4a between 1941 and 1942, a period that included the massacre at Babi Yar, where 33,771 Jews were killed. He was known as an alcoholic and supervised the task of unearthing and burning corpses with Sonderkommando 1005. He was sentenced to death in the Einsatzgruppen Trial and executed on June 7, 1951.

Bradfisch, Otto, Dr. (1903–1994). He studied law and economics and received a doctorate in political science. He entered civil service in Bavaria, becoming a member of the NSdAP in 1931, the SS, and then the Gestapo in 1937. He became a leader of Einsatzkommando 8, a subunit of Einsatzgruppe B that was responsible for mass killings of Jews in Belarus. In 1961, he was sentenced to ten years by the Regional Court of Munich. In 1963, he was convicted by the Regional Court in Hannover of overseeing the deportation of thousands of Jews from Lodz to the Chelmno death camp as head of the Gestapo office in Lodz and as the head of department IIB.

Brandt, Karl, Prof. Dr. (1904–1948). Brandt joined the Nazi party in 1932 and advanced to the rank *Generalleutnant* of the Waffen-SS as a medical doctor. He oversaw the euthanasia program that killed so-called "life unworthy of life." He was also responsible for performing medical experiments on prisoners in concentration camps and served as Adolf Hitler's personal physician from October 1944 until his death. He was sentenced to death on August 20, 1947, in the IMT Nuremberg and was executed June 2, 1948.

Braune, Werner, Dr. (1909–1951). After receiving his doctorate in law, Braune abandoned private practice and joined the Nazi party in 1931, the SS, and the SD in 1934. He became head of Einsatzgruppe 11b, which operated in the southern region of Russia in 1941 and 1942. He was shortly appointed as head of the German Academic Exchange Service (DAAD) and became commander of the Security Police and SD in Oslo, Norway. He was convicted in the Nuremberg Einsatzgruppen Trial and hanged on June 7, 1951.

Defregger, Matthias (1915–1995). He served as an officer in the Wehrmacht before his ordination as a Roman Catholic priest in June 1949. He was responsible for enforcing an order to execute Italian civilians in a reprisal action, which led to his exposure in 1968, legal prosecution, and acquittal.

Eichmann, Adolf (1906–1962). SS Hauptsturmbannführer Eichmann served as the head of the Central Office for Jewish Emigration (Zentralstelle für jüdische Auswanderung) beginning in 1938. Eichmann attended the Wannsee Conference in January 1941 and became director of Jewish Affairs (Judenreferat) in the RSHA. He played a central role in the deportation of over 1.5 million Jews from all over Europe to killing centers.

Frank, Hans (1900–1946). An early supporter of Hitler, he graduated with a law degree and became the legal advisor of the Nazi party and of Adolf Hitler. He was appointed as governor-general of Poland in October 1939 and oversaw the establishment of ghettos to facilitate the exploitation and eventually deportation of Polish and Jewish civilians. He was found guilty at the IMT Nuremberg in 1946 and executed on October 16, 1946.

Göbbels, Joseph (1897–1945). He graduated with a doctorate in literature before he joined the NSdAP in 1924 and became its chief propagandist. He called for "total war" and became plenipotentiary for total war in 1944. He committed suicide in the führer's bunker on May 1, 1945, with his wife Magda and their six children.

Göring, Hermann (1893–1946). Göring was an early supporter of Hitler in Munich and the highest-ranking Nazi government official to be tried at the IMT in Nuremberg. He was sentenced to death as commander in chief of the Luftwaffe (German air force) and as Hitler's acknowledged successor. He committed suicide in his prison cell while awaiting execution in Landsberg.

Greiffenberger, Wilhelm (b. 1900). Sentenced to three years in prison by the regional court in Berlin, he was deputy chief of Einsatzkommando 9, which was responsible for mass killings of Jews in Grodno, Lida, Molodeczno, Newel, Surash, Wilejka, Wilna, and Witebsk.

Greil, Michael (b. 1908). Greil joined the Waffen-SS in 1940 and was sentenced to four years imprisonment in Landsberg in the Dachau trials prosecuting SS guards at the Dachau concentration camp.

Hans, Kurt (b. 1911). SS-Hauptsturmbannführer Hans joined the Kripo and led Sonderkommando 4a during the mass execution of Jews in Babi Yar in 1941. He was sentenced to death for killing American pilots in Dachau and released from Landsberg in 1954. He was sentenced to eleven years in prison by the Regional Court of Darmstadt in 1968.

Hegenscheidt, Hans (1904–1946). He was sentenced to death in the Dachau trials in 1946 as an SS guard in the Mauthausen camp, and for cruel treatment of prisoners in detention camps and during evacuation marches.

Heim, Albert (1892–1946). His membership in the Nazi party was unknown when he was sentenced to death in the Dachau trials for ordering, as a member of the Wehrmacht, the execution of three American airmen who had been taken prisoner.

Heydrich, Reinhard (1904–1942). Heydrich was in charge of the Security Service (Sicherheitsdienst; SD) from 1931 until 1942; the Gestapo from 1934 to 1936; the German Security Police (Sicherheitspolizei; SiPo), which consisted of the Gestapo and the criminal police detective forces (Kriminalpolizei; Kripo), from 1936 until 1942; and the Reich Security Main Office (Reichssicherheitshauptamt; RSHA). After September 1939, the Security Police and SD were formally unified under Heydrich's command in the RSHA. The RSHA was the police agency most directly concerned with implementing the Nazi plan to murder the European Jews during World War II. He was assassinated in Prague on June 4, 1942.

Himmler, Heinrich (1900–1945). An early supporter of Hitler, beginning with the Beer Hall Putsch in 1923, he became chief of police in Munich in 1933 and leader of the Gestapo in 1934. He coordinated the rise of the SS as a paramilitary force and built the concentration camp system, including the implementation of the Final Solution of the Jewish Question in Europe. He committed suicide while in British custody on May 23, 1945.

Hitler, Adolf (1889–1945). Chancellor, führer, and chief of the Wehrmacht.

Höß, Rudolf (1900–1947). Höß joined the Nazi party in 1922 and the SS in 1934 and moved up the ranks to *SS-Obersturmbannführer* (lieutenant colonel). He was the first commandant of the death and concentration camp of Auschwitz between May 4, 1940, and November 1943, while more than a million people were murdered. He was hanged in 1947 following his trial in Warsaw, Poland.

Imort, Irene (b. 1921). She was trained as SS associate and guard in Ravensbrück before being transferred to Bergen Belsen. She was sentenced in the French Rastatt trials.

Kaltenbrunner, Ernst (1903–1946). He received his law degree in 1926 and joined the Austrian Nazi party in 1932, becoming leader of the Austrian SS. He replaced Reinhard Heydrich as chief of the Reich Security Main Office (RSHA) and later became chief of the Security Police. In this position Kaltenbrunner controlled the Gestapo, Criminal Police, and Security Service (SD). He was a prime figure in the Final Solution in the last years of the war. He was found guilty by the IMT in Nuremberg on counts 3 and 4 (war crimes and crimes against humanity), sentenced to death, and hanged on October 16, 1946.

Klehr, Joseph (1894–1988). As *SS-Oberscharführer*, he trained as a nurse in 1934 and deployed to Auschwitz in October 1941, where he was responsible for killing thousands of inmates by injection. He was convicted to life in prison in the Auschwitz trial. He died eight months after his release for medical reasons.

Koch, Ilse, born Köhler (1906–1967). She was the widow of Buchenwald commander Karl Koch, who was executed on corruption charges by the SS in April 1945. She was sentenced to four years in prison in the Dachau trials. Upon her release from Landsberg, she was convicted to life in prison by Regional Court of Augsburg in 1951 for random acts of brutality and denunciations of prisoners. Her sentence was commuted and she was released.

Kroeger, Erhard, Dr. (1905–1987). Kroeger completed his law degree in 1928 and in 1933 became a Nazi propagandist in Latvia, where he oversaw the resettlement of ethnic Germans after the Soviet-German nonaggression pact of 1939. In 1941 he supervised mass executions of Jews in Drobomil by Einsatzkommando 6. He was sentenced to three years and four months in 1969 by the regional court in Tübingen.

Kunze, Herbert (1923–1946). A member of the Wehrmacht, he was sentenced to death in the Dachau trials for shooting three American airmen who had been taken prisoner in Wollmatingen (a district of Constance), Germany.

Ley, Robert (1890–1945). Ley joined the NSdAP in 1925 and established the Deutsche Arbeitsfront (DAF; German Labor Front) as soon as the German trade unions were dissolved in 1933. He became the head of the DAF, whose membership totaled 25 million; Ley was known as the "undisputed dictator of labor" in Germany. He also was also in charge of recruiting and training Nazi leadership corps in schools and *Ordensburgen*. Ley was indicted at the IMT in Nuremberg on charges of conspiracy, war crimes, and crimes against humanity and committed suicide before the trial began.

Lucas, Franz, Dr. (1911–1994). An *SS-Obersturmbannführer*, Lucas was a medical doctor at Auschwitz between 1943 and 1944, where he performed selections. He transferred to Mauthausen and then by late 1944 to Ravensbrück, where he performed sterilizations on female inmates. By 1945, he was appointed chief gynecologist at Elmshorst. He was sentenced to three years and three months by regional court in Frankfurt 1965. His conviction was overturned on appeal.

Ludolf, Julius (1893–1947). Sentenced to death in the Dachau trials as commander of subcamps of Mauthausen (Loiblpaß, then Groß-Raming, then Melk), he was executed May 28, 1947, in Landsberg.

Mengele, Rolf, Dr. (1911–1979). He completed philosophical and medical doctorates before joining the SS in 1938. He moved from the immigration office in Lodz to Auschwitz, Birkenau, in May 1943, where he supervised selections and conducted medical experiments until January 1945. He lived in Brazil until 1979 under assumed names and married the widow of his brother after his divorce in 1954.

Miesel, Johannes (b. 1913). Miesel joined the SS in 1933 while studying theology and law; he completed his law degree. He was first acquitted of enforcing an execution order of returning slave laborers in March 1945 by the regional court in Hagen. The sentence was overturned in the revision, and he was sentenced to four years in prison in 1961.

Mulka, Robert (1895–1969). He joined the SS in 1941 because his officer's career in the Wehrmacht was blocked by a prior felony conviction. Because of stomach ailments, he was transferred to Auschwitz to supervise SS guards. By May 1942, he was serving as *Adjutant* (deputy) of the camp commander. His tasks included training female SS associates in Auschwitz. He was sentenced to fourteen years in prison by the Regional Court of Frankfurt am Main for killing 750 people during his time as deputy commander of the death camp between 1942 and 1943. His sentence was suspended for ill health.

Ohlendorf, Otto (1907–1951). An *SS-Brigadeführer*, he joined the Nazi party in 1925 before entering university to study law and political economy. He was recruited to lead Abteilung II of the security police (SD), which trained the *Einsatzgruppen*. As head of Einsatzgruppe D, which operated at the southern end of the Soviet Union, he frankly discussed the murder of 90,000 Jews between June 1941 and June 1942. He was sentenced in the IMT Einsatzgruppen Trial and was executed on June 7, 1951.

Ott, Adolf (b. 1904). SS-Obersturmbannführer Ott became a member of the Nazi party in 1922 and joined the SS in 1931 and the Security Police (SD) in 1935. Between February 1942 and January 1943, he commanded Sonderkommado 7b, a unit of Einsatzgruppe B that engaged in mass executions of partisans and Jews. He was sentenced to death in the IMT Einsatzgruppen Trial. His sentence was commuted to life, and he was released from Landsberg on May 9, 1958.

Pförtsch, Klara (b. 1906). Pförtsch joined the Communist party in 1924 and was arrested in 1936 for high treason. Upon completing her prison sentence she was transferred to Ravensbrück camp. She was recruited as prisoner functionary and became *Lagerälteste* in Auschwitz. She was interned and sentenced to death in the French military trials at Rastatt in 1949. Her sentence was commuted in 1953, and she was released from prison in 1957.

Piorkowski, Alex (1904–1948). He joined the SS in 1931 and reached the rank of *SS-Sturmbannführer*. He served as commander of the Dachau concentration camp between 1940 and 1942, when he was dismissed on corruption charges. In May 1943, he was dishonorably discharged from the SS. He was hanged on October 22, 1948, in Landsberg.

Pohl, Oswald (1892–1951). Pohl joined the NSdAP in 1926 and the SS in 1934. He oversaw the economic and business side of the SS, which included the exploitation of concentration camp inmates in factories. In 1942 he became chief of the SS Economic Main Administration (WVHA) in Berlin. He was convicted by the U.S. Military Government in 1947 and executed June 8, 1951.

Raabe, Werner (1922–1949). Raabe completed a degree in dentistry after his service in the Wehrmacht and opened a dental practice in Berlin. He was arrested in 1947 for killing an American GI during a black market deal, for which he was executed in Landsberg on January 7, 1949.

Schallermair, Georg (1894–1951). Sentenced to death as an SS guard and supervisor in the Dachau satellite camp Mühldorf, he was executed June 7, 1951, in Landsberg.

Schmidt, Hans Hermann (1899–1951). Known for cruelty in the concentration camp of Hinzert, Schmidt was transferred to Buchenwald and appointed as deputy camp commander. He was convicted in the Buchenwald trial and executed in Landsberg on June 7, 1951.

Schubert, Heinz (1914–197?). *SS-Obersturmbannführer* and deputy of Ohlendorf, Schubert was sentenced to death in the IMT Einsatzgruppen Trial and released from Landsberg/Lech in 1951. He was not retried.

Sorge, Gustav (b. 1911). An *SS-Hauptscharführer* who joined the SS in 1931 and made a career in various concentration camps, he received a life sentence for excessive brutality in Sachsenhausen from a Soviet military court in 1947. Upon his release in 1956, he was retried and sentenced to life in prison in 1959 by the regional court in Bonn.

Stark, Hans (1921–1991). He joined the SS in 1937 and was trained as an SS guard in Sachsenhausen, Buchenwald, and Dachau, transferring to Auschwitz in December 1940 as a member of the Gestapo. He was sentenced to ten years by the Regional Court of Frankfurt am Main in 1965 for the gassing death of Jewish men, women, and children, as well as the execution of individual prisoners (especially Jewish women), Polish hostages, and Polish civilians.

Streicher, Julius (1885–1946). He joined the NSdAP in 1921 and founded the rabidly antisemitic propaganda tabloid *Der Stürmer* in 1923. He organized the boycott of Jewish businesses on April 1, 1933, and published numerous antisemitic books. He was captured by U.S. forces in May 1945 and convicted on the charge of crimes against humanity at the IMT Nuremberg. He was executed October 16, 1946.

Wentzel, Erich (1901–1948). A merchant in civilian life, Naval Lieutenant Wentzel was implicated in the killings of downed U.S. pilots on the island of Borkum in the Dachau trials and executed in Landsberg on December 3, 1948.

Wetzling, Wolfgang (b. 1909). An *SS-Obersturmbannführer* who completed his law degree in 1931 and joined the SS in 1933, by 1940 he was an SS judge in Berlin. He was convicted by the Regional Court of Hagen in 1959 for the mass execution of 151 Russian foreign laborers in Langenbachtal (Sauerland) because they posed a risk to the German population after the withdrawal of the German troops in the so-called Final Phase Crimes.

Wilke, Artur Fritz (b. 1910). Wilke was sentenced by the Regional Court of Koblenz to ten years for mass executions of Jews in Belarus as a member of the SiPo police Minsk and of Sonderkommando 1005. The killings during the years 1941–1944 included shootings, "gas vans," and the burning alive of thousands of Soviet and west European Jews who had been deported to Minsk, Gypsies, the mentally disabled, and other Soviet civilians and Soviet agents.

Zakis, Otto (1927–). Born in Riga as an ethnic German, Zakis joined the SS at age sixteen and trained as an SS guard in the canine unit in Buchenwald before being transferred to the extermination camp of Majdanek. He was never charged but was called as a witness in the Majdanek trial in Düsseldorf.

PRISON CHAPLAINS

Eckardt, August (b. 1912). Eckardt worked in Landsberg from June 16, 1948, until his dismissal over violations of prison rules on May 30, 1949. Transferred to congregational ministry in Garmisch Partenkirchen, he established a secret bank account, code name *Konto Gustav*, to funnel money into the secretive Nazi solidarity movement Hilfswerk der Helfenden Hande, later renamed Stille Hilfe.

Ermann, Karl (b. 1911). Ermann was an Evangelical Lutheran prison chaplain in WCP 1 Landsberg/Lech from July 7, 1949, until his dismissal following his memorial sermon on June 10, 1951. He transferred to a congregational ministry in Kufstein, Bavaria.

Hess, Werner (b. 1915). He was sentenced to six months in prison in the Dachau trials for transmitting an order that resulted in the vicious beating of a downed American flyer. He engaged in pastoral counseling while in Landsberg, then as congregational minister in Hesse, and later became the director (*Intendant*) of the Hessischer Rundfunk.

Hull, William Lovell (1897–1992). Hull was a Canadian Pentecostal pastor and Christian Zionist who founded the Jerusalem Cornerstone Church in 1936 as part of the Zion Apostolic Mission in Jerusalem and volunteered to serve as chaplain to Adolf Eichmann. His exchanges with Eichmann were subsequently published as *Struggle for a Soul.*

Meiser, Hans (1991–1956). Meisner was bishop of the Evangelical Lutheran Church of Bavaria, one of three regional churches that did not split into a Confessing and a state-controlled Nazi church. Under the leadership of Bishop Meiser, the Bavarian church negotiated with the National Socialist state and remained "intact," not split into an illegal wing of the Confessing Church and a legally sanctioned National Socialist wing. A staunch conservative, Meiser avoided open confrontation and relied on quiet diplomacy to retain church autonomy. In 1945, he emerged as a spokesman on behalf of the defeated Germany for the Allied victors in the name of the "good" Germans who had resisted National Socialism.

Morgenschweis, Karl (1891–1968). He served as Roman Catholic prison chaplain in Landsberg/Lech prison from 1932. In 1952 he received the Bundesverdienstkreuz, and in 1959 was promoted to monsignor by Pope John XXIII.

Müller, Johann Heinrich Ludwig (1883–1945). He joined the NSdAP in 1931 and founded the Deutsche Christen (DC), the National Socialist movement among Protestant Christians in 1932. In 1933 he was appointed to the newly created position of *Reichsbischof* of the Deutschen Evangelischen Kirche (DEK), which intended to integrate the church into the Nazi state (*Gleichschaltung*). He committed suicide July 31, 1945.

Niemöller, Martin (1892–1984). A veteran of World War I, Niemöller voted for the NSdAP from 1924 but became a vocal opponent once he became pastor of the congregation in Berlin/Dahlem. In 1933 he founded the Pastor's Emergency League (Pfarrernotbund) and organized the Confessing Church. He was arrested July 1, 1937, and sentenced to seven months in prison, a period that was extended indefinitely, and he was moved to the concentration camps of Sachsenshausen and Dachau. Upon his liberation, he traveled through southern Germany to lecture and preach sermons about guilt. He also opposed the denazification programs in the U.S. zone.

Poelchau, Harald (1903–1972). He completed his dissertation with Paul Tillich and entered prison ministry on April 1, 1933, in Berlin-Tegel. He supported the political prisoners of National Socialism during torture, trial, and execution. He attended more than one thousand executions, including those of prominent resisters such as James Graf von Moltke, Pater Alfred Delp, Adolf Reichwein, and others involved in resistance to Hitler. He became a member of the Confessing Church in 1934 and participated in resistance activities of the Kreisau Circle as well as in underground networks to hide Jews in Berlin. In 1945, he participated in the synod of Treysa to reconstruct the Evangelical Church in Germany (EKD), but he subsequently moved into prison ministry in the Soviet sector and the GDR. In 1951 Poelchau led the Amt für Industrie- und Sozialarbeit, with offices in East and West Berlin.

Rott, Wilhelm (1908–1967). Trained in the Confessing Church underground seminary Finkenwald by Dietrich Bonhoeffer, he joined the Abwehr. He was interned in the American internment camp Moosburg, where he built the congregation. He later became superintendent in the Evangelical Church in the Rhineland.

Sachsse, Karl (1889–1966). He served as congregational minister beginning in 1920 and as superintendent beginning in 1941. He participated in the Barmen Synod and was an active member of the Confessing Church. In October 1945, he was appointed as the Rheinish plenipotentiary for political prisoners in French zone, a position he held until he retired in 1959.

Schlingensiepen, Hermann (1896–1980). Professor of practical theology in Kiel before the war, he became the director of the Kirchlichen Auslandsseminars in Ilsenburg/Harz, which trained ministers for congregations in Latin America. He was arrested by the Gestapo, and his permission to teach was rescinded. He worked in parish ministry until he was recalled into academia as professor of practical theology in Bonn in 1945. In 1952 he served as dean of the Kirchliche Hochschule in Wuppertal until his early retirement for a injury sustained in World War I that confined him to a wheelchair. He began contacting Nazi defendants and visiting them in prisons, beginning with Adolf Eichmann.

Stempel, Hans (1894–1970). Stempel completed his theological degree in 1921 and served as director of a practical and preaching seminary until it was closed in 1933. He was affiliated with the Confessing C hurch and served in congregational ministry. In 1947, he became bishop of the church in Pfalz and in 1949 he was appointed as plenipotentiary of the German Evangelical Church War Convicts in the Custody of Western Powers. He remained active in chaplaincy and advocacy for Nazi convicts until his retirement.

Notes

FM

1. Katharina von Kellenbach, Björn Krondorfer, and Norbert Reck, *Von Gott Reden im Land der Täter: Theologische Stimmen der dritten Generation nach der Shoah* (Darmstadt: Wissenschaftliche Buchgesellschaft, 2001); Björn Krondorfer, Norbert Reck, and Katharina von Kellenbach, *Mit Blick auf die Täter* (Gütersloh: Gütersloher Verlagshaus, 2006).

INTRODUCTION
Abbreviations

AEKIR   Archiv der Evangelischen Landeskirche im Rheinland, Düsseldorf
BAK   Bundesarchiv, Koblenz
BAL   Bundesarchiv, Ludwigsburg
EZAB   Evangelisches Zentral Archiv, Berlin
HSTA   Hauptstaatsarchiv, Düsseldorf
IFZ   Institut für Zeitgeschichte, Munich
LKAN   Landeskirchliches Archiv, Nürnberg
NACP   National Archives, College Park, MD

1. Regional Court Braunschweig, 1964, against members of SS Cavalry Regiment 2, C. F. Rüters, Fritz Bauer, et al., eds., *Justiz und NS-Verbrechen. Sammlung deutscher Strafurteile wegen nationalsozialistischer Tötungsverbrechen* (Amsterdam: Amsterdam University Press, 1968–1981), vol. 20, no. 570; Regional Court Hamburg, 1967, against members of Sonderkommando 1005, *Justiz und NS-Verbrechen*, vol. 27, no. 662; Regional Court Frankfurt am Main, 1973, against members of Police Battalion 306, *Justiz und NS-Verbrechen*, vol. 38, no. 787.
2. Azriel Shohet, *The Jews of Pinsk, 1881 to 1941*, ed. Mark Jay Mirsky and Moshe Rosman, trans. Faigie Tropper and Moshe Rosman (Stanford, CA: Stanford University Press, 2012).

3. Patrick Desbois, *The Holocaust by Bullets: A Priest's Journey to Uncover the Truth behind the Murder of 1.5 Million Jews* (New York: Palgrave Macmillan, 2009).

4. Numerous memoirs by descendants of high-ranking Nazis have appeared over the course of the last decades. A recent excellent documentary is by Malte Ludin, *2 or 3 Things I Know about Him*, 2005.

5. Howard Ball, *Prosecuting War Crimes and Genocide: The Twentieth-Century Experience* (Lawrence: University Press of Kansas, 1999), 222.

6. Cf. Erin McGlothlin, *Second Generation Holocaust Literature: Legacies of Survival and Perpetration* (Rochester, NY: Camden House, 2006); Peter Sichrovsky, *Born Guilty: Children of Nazi Families* (New York: Basic Books, 1988); Dörte von Westernhagen, *Die Kinder der Täter: Das Dritte Reich und die Generation danach* (Munich: Kösel Verlag, 1987); Barbara B. Heimannsberg and C. J. Schmidt, eds., *The Collective Silence: German Identity and the Legacy of Shame* (San Francisco: Jossey-Bass, 1993); M. S. Bergmann and M. E. Jucovy, eds., *Generations of the Holocaust* (New York: Columbia University Press, 1982); Björn Krondorfer, *Remembrance and Reconciliation: Encounters between Young Jews and Germans* (New Haven: Yale University Press, 1995); Brigitte Rommelspacher, *Schuldlos-Schuldig? Wie sich junge Frauen mit Antisemitismus auseinandersetzen* (Hamburg: Konkret, 1995); Ulla Roberts, *Spuren der NS-Zeit im Leben der Kinder und Enkel: Drei Generationen im Gespräch* (Munich: Kösel, 1998); Dan Bar-On, *Legacy of Silence: Encounters with Children of the Third Reich* (Cambridge: Harvard University Press, 1989); Gabriele Rosenthal, "Nationalsozialismus und Antisemitismus im intergenerationellen Dialog," in *Der Holocaust im Leben von drei Generation: Familien von Überlebenden der Shoah und von Nazi-Tätern*, ed. Gabriele Rosenthal (Hamburg: Edition psychosozial, 1997).

7. Eleonore Stump, *Wandering in Darkness: Narrative and the Problem of Suffering* (New York: Oxford University Press, 2010).

8. Maria Pia Lara, "Narrating Evil: A Postmetaphysical Theory of Reflective Judgment," in *Rethinking Evil: Contemporary Perspectives*, ed. Maria Pia Lara (Berkeley: University of California Press, 2001), 239.

9. Lara, "Narrating Evil," 242.

CHAPTER I

1. Dan Pagis, *The Selected Poems of Dan Pagis*, trans. B Stephen Mitchell (Berkeley: University of California Press, 1989), 29.

2. Ellen van Wolde, "The Story of Cain and Abel: A Narrative Study," *Journal for the Study of the Old Testament* 52 (1991): 25–41, 29.

3. *New Interpreter's Bible: A Commentary in Twelve Volumes* (Nashville: Abingdon Press, 1994), vol. 1, 375: " 'Keeping' is not something human beings do to one another in the OT; only God keeps human beings (see Num. 6:24; Ps. 121:3–8); hence *God* should know the answer to the question."

4. Claire Elise Katz, "Raising Cain: The Problem of Evil and the Question of Responsibility," *Cross Currents*, Summer 2005, 215–233, 216.

5. Dik Van Arkel, *The Drawing of the Mark of Cain: A Social-Historical Analysis of the Growth of Anti-Jewish Stereotypes* (Chicago: University of Chicago Press, 2010).

6. David Nirenberg, "The Birth of the Pariah: Jews, Christian Dualism, and Social Science," *Social Research* 70 (Spring 2003): 201–236; Stephen D. Benin, "Sacrifice as Education in Augustine and Chrysostom," *Church History* 52 (March 1983): 7–20; Christopher M. Leighton, "Religious Intolerance, Bach, St. John's Passion," http://www.icjs.org/scholars/bachcml.htm.

7. Ruther Mellinkoff, *The Mark of Cain* (Berkeley: University of California Press, 1981). Mellinkoff concludes her history of the mark of Cain: "There has been no consensus about the mark of Cain. We have seen now how interpretations frequently ranged and changed in the early period depending upon whether it was believed to be a symbol of God's pardon or a symbol of condemnation. It could denote divine forgiveness, thus suggesting that the mark was a positive and protective device. But most often the mark, though protective, also denoted punishment. It functioned simultaneously as condemnation-curse and taboo-protection. Yet another category of interpretations presented viewpoints where Cain's mark had lost all of its protective qualities and had become only and wholly the shameful stigmatic identification of a criminal—the viewpoint that has remained commonplace to today" (101).

8. Despite the Torah's endorsement of capital punishment (Ex. 21:12) the narrative of Cain allows for alternatives to the death penalty. Forgiveness, repentance, and the "openness of human futures," as Hannah Arendt put it, have been vital principles in the Jewish and Christian tradition that critique the administration of the death penalty. Hannah Arendt, *Vita Activa oder Vom tätigen Leben* (Stuttgart: Kohlhammer, 1960), 235; *The Human Condition* (Chicago: University of Chicago Press, 1989).

9. Arne Johan Vetlesen, *Evil and Human Agency: Understanding Collective Evildoing* (Cambridge: Cambridge University Press, 2005), 171.

10. Vetlesen, *Evil and Human Agency*, 172.

11. Vetlesen, *Evil and Human Agency*, 173–174.

12. AEKIR, Düsseldorf, 7 NL 016, letter, Gertrud Schneider to Schlingensiepen, September 11, 1965.

13. Hannah Arendt, "'Eichmann in Jerusalem': An Exchange of Letters between Gershom Scholem and Hannah Arendt," *Encounter* 22 (1964), 51–56; cf. Susan Neimann, *Evil in Modern Thought: An Alternative History of the Philosophy* (Princeton, NJ: Princeton University Press), 301.

14. Dietrich Bonhoeffer, "After Ten Years," in *Letters and Papers from Prison*, ed. Christian Gremmels, Eberhard Bethge, et al., trans. Barbara and Martin Rumscheidt (Minneapolis: Fortress Press, 2010), 43.

15. Bonhoeffer, *Letter and Papers from Prison*, 43.

16. Bonhoeffer, *Letter and Papers from Prison*, 43.

17. Neimann, *Evil in Modern Thought*, 273. She continues: "In contemporary evil, individuals' intentions rarely correspond to the magnitude of evil individuals are able to cause."
18. Bonhoeffer, *Letter and Papers from Prison*, 43.
19. Bonhoeffer, *Letter and Papers from Prison*, 44.
20. CF. Helmut Thielicke and Hans Diem, *Die Schuld der Anderen* (Göttingen: Vandenhoeck & Rupert, 1948).
21. Cf. the comment of Dr. Brandt, who was sentenced to death for his administrative role in the euthanasia program: "The nation that is eternally branded with the mark of Cain [*Kainszeichen*] of Hiroshima and Nagasaki...tries to hide behind moral superlatives. Power dictates." Quote in eulogy delivered at his funeral June 2, 1948, and published in *Deutsche Hochschullehrerzeitung* 11.1 (1963): 8.
22. Miesel conceded that he might be "standing before God with bloody hands like Cain," but attributed his guilt to his participation in aerial attacks on the city of Antwerp and not to the mass shooting of civilians for which he was convicted. His conflation of Pilate and of Cain served to implicate American and British pilots who flew bombing raids on German cities. AEKIR, Düsseldorf, 7 NL 016, letter, Johannes Miesel to Schlingensiepen, August 5, 1965.
23. Hans Herlin, *Kain, wo ist dein Bruder Abel? Die Flieger von Hiroshima und Nagasaki* (Hamburg: Nannen 1960). Hans Herlin was born in 1925 and defected to Switzerland in 1944 at the age of nineteen.
24. Herlin, *Kain*, 222.
25. Obituary, *Süddeutsche Zeitung*, November 3, 2007, 10.
26. Killy-Literaturlexikon, http://www.lwl.org/literaturkommission/alex/index.php?id=00000004&layout=2&letter=&place_id=00000633&author_id=1219&SID.
27. Donald B. Kraybill, Steven M. Nolt, and David L. Weaver-Zercher, *Amish Grace: How Forgiveness Transcended Tragedy* (San Francisco: Jossey-Bass, 2012).
28. Gregory Jones, *Embodying Forgiveness: A Theological Analysis* (Grand Rapids, MI: Erdmans Publishing Company, 1995), 102.
29. Jones, *Embodying Forgiveness*, 102.
30. Martin Luther King, *Strength to Love* (Philadelphia: Fortress Press, 1981), 19.
31. King, *Strength to Love*, 46.
32. King, *Strength to Love*, 46.
33. Claudia Brunner and Uwe von Seltmann, *Schweigen die Täter reden die Enkel* (Frankfurt am Main: Edition Büchergilde, 2004); Ulla Robert, *Spuren der NS-Zeit im Leben der Kinder und Enkel: Drei Generationen im Gespräch* (Munich: Kösel, 1998).
34. Memorandum of the Evangelical Church in Germany on the Question of War Crimes Trials before American Military Courts (hereafter cited as "EKD Memorandum"), NACP, Reg. 338, United States Army Europe, JAG War Crimes Branch, General Administrative Records 1942–1957, Box 12–14, 22.
35. Ronald Webster, "Opposing 'Victors' Justice': German Protestant Churchmen and Convicted Criminals in Western Europe after 1945." *Holocaust and Genocide Studies* 15.1 (2001): 47–50.

36. Oswald Pohl, *Credo: Mein Weg zu Gott* (Landshut: Alois Girnth Verlag, 1950).

37. Gudrun Schwarz, *Eine Frau an seiner Seite: Ehefrauen in der SS-Sippengemeinschaft* (Hamburg: Hamburger edition, 1997).

38. Some of these materials have been published as "God's Love and Women's Love: Prison Chaplain Counsel Wives of Nazi Perpetrators," *Journal of Feminist Studies in Religion* 20.2 (2004): 7–24.

CHAPTER 2

1. "Wort des Rates der EKD an die evangelischen Pfarrer in Deutschland, February 10, 1947," in *Im Zeichen der Schuld. 40 Jahre Stuttgarter Schuldbekenntnis*, ed. Martin Greschat (Neukirchen- Vluyn: Neukirchener Verlag 1985), 77.

2. Cf. Yale Law School Avalon Project, http://avalon.law.yale.edu/imt/nsdappro.asp.

3. Victoria J. Barnett, *Bystanders: Conscience and Complicity during the Holocaust* (Westport, CT: Praeger, 1999).

4. Christopher Browning, *Ordinary Men: Reserve Police Battalion 101 and the Final Solution in Poland* (New York: Harper Perennial, 1992).

5. Lucy Dawidowicz, *The War against the Jews: 1933–1945* (New York: Bantam, 1986).

6. Harold Marcuse, *Legacies of Dachau: The Uses and Abuses of a Concentration Camp, 1933–2001* (Cambridge: Cambridge University Press, 2001).

7. Michael R. Marrus, *The Nuremberg War Crimes Trial, 1945–1946: A Documentary History* (Boston: Bedford Book, 1997), 51–57.

8. Donald Bloxham, *Genocide on Trial: War Crimes Trials and the Formation of Holocaust History and Memory* (New York: Oxford University Press, 2001), 229.

9. For a helpful historical overview, cf. Hilary Earl, *The Nuremberg SS-Einsatzgruppen Trial, 1945–1958: Atrocity, Law, and History* (Cambridge: Cambridge University Press, 2009), 19–46.

10. These proceedings and verdicts of these trials are accessible and can be searched online: http://www1.jur.uva.nl/junsv/junsveng/DTRR/Dachau%20Trials%20start.htm and http://www.uni-marburg.de/icwc/forschung/2weltkrieg/usadachau.

11. Heinz Boberach, "Nachkriegsprozesse," *Enzyklopädie des Nationalsozialismus*, ed. W. Benz (Stuttgart: Klett-Cotta, 1997); Robert Sigel, *Im Interesse der Gerechtigkeit: Die Dachauer Kriegsverbrecherprozesse 1945–1948* (Frankfurt am Main: Campus Verlag 1992); Heinz Boberach, "Nürnberger Prozess," *Enzyklopädie des Holocausts: Die Verfolgung und Ermordung der europäischen Juden*, ed. I. Gutmann et al., 3 vols. (Berlin: Argon. 1993).

12. Earl, *Nuremberg Einsatzgruppen Trial*, 77.

13. Quoted in EKD Memorandum, 156.

14. Bloxham, *Genocide on Trial*, 159.

15. This controversy has been reopened by recent laws justifying the indefinite detention of so-called "enemy combatants" and the use of "enhanced interrogation techniques," aka torture, in various U.S. military detention centers, such as Guantánamo Bay (Cuba), Abu Ghraib (Iraq), and Bagram (Afganisthan).

16. Kathrin Meyer, *Entnazifizierung von Frauen: Die Internierungslager der US-Zone Deutschlands 1945–1952* (Berlin: Metropol 2004), 52–54.

17. Robert P. Ericksen and Susannah Heschel, *Betrayal: German Churches and the Holocaust* (Minneapolis: Fortress Press, 1999), 10.

18. Richard Steigmann-Gall, *The Holy Reich: Nazi Conceptions of Christianity, 1919–1945* (Cambridge: Cambridge University Press, 2003), 219.

19. Rainer Bucher, *Hitler's Theology: A Study in Political Religion,* trans. Rebecca Pohl (New York: Continuum, 2011).

20. Ericksen and Heschel, *Betrayal,* 10.

21. Steigmann-Gall, *The Holy Reich,* 233.

22. NACP, RG 549.2 USAEUR JAG Division, War Crimes Branch, Records of War Criminal Prison No. 1 Relating to Executed Prisoners ("Executee Files"), Box 1–14.

23. NACP, RG 549.2 "Executee Files," Box 5, Albert Ferdinand Hammer.

24. NACP, RG 549.2 "Executee Files," Box 3, Eichberger.

25. NACP, RG 549.2 "Executee Files," Box 3, Heinrich Eisenhofer.

26. NACP, RG 549.2 "Executee Files," Box 2, Hans Diehl.

27. Heiner Wember, *Umerziehung im Lager: Internierung und Bestrafung von Nationalsozialisten in der britischen Besatzungzone Deutschlands* (Düsseldorf: Klartext, 1992), 212. He cites a report from a local pastor of the British internment camp Eselheide (November 17, 1946) with 41.0 percent Protestant, 15.3 percent Catholic, and 43.2 percent *gottgläubige* inmates. Wember quotes an estimate of people appearing before *Spruchkammerverfahren* (denazification boards): 40.1 percent Protestants, 9.2 percent Roman Catholics, 40.5 percent *gottgläubig*, 10.2 percent "no religion" (Wember, 212). As of May 31, 1948, the American internment camp in Darmstadt listed the following denominational breakdown: "195 Protestant, 36 Catholic, 338 *gottgläubig*, 5 atheists and 9 other" (EZAB 2/255). By December 1951, U.S. military prison officials in Landsberg listed the following statistics: 43.6 percent Protestant, 34.7 percent Catholic, 2.3 percent no religion, and 13.1 percent *gottgläubig* (NACP, RG 549.2 USAEUR, Judge Advocate Division, War Crimes Branch: Records Relating to War Criminal Prison No. 1 Landsberg, 1947–1957, Box 3).

28. Klaus von Eickstedt, *Christus unter den Internierten* (Neuendettelsau: Freimundverlag, 1948), available online: http://moosburg.org/info/stalag/christus.html.

29. von Eickstedt, *Christus* 11.

30. Walther Künneth, *Der große Abfall: Eine geschichtstheologische Untersuchung der Begegnung zwischen Nationalsozialismus und Christentum* (Hamburg: F. Wittig, 1947).

31. On complicity and collaboration among Protestant church leaders, cf. Victoria J. Barnett, *Bystanders: Conscience and Complicity during the Holocaust* (Westport, CT: Praeger, 1999); Christopher Probst, *Demonizing the Jews: Luther and the Protestant Church in Nazi Germany* (Bloomington: Indiana University Press, 2012); Robert P. Ericksen, *Complicity in the Holocaust: Churches and Universities in Nazi Germany* (Cambridge: Cambridge University Press, 2012); Doris

L. Bergen, *The German Christian Movement in the Third Reich* (Chapel Hill: University of North Carolina Press, 1996). Manfred Gailus and Armin Nolzen, eds., *Zerstrittene Volksgemeinschaft: Glaube, Konfession und Religion im Nationalsozialismus* (Göttingen: Vandenhoeck & Ruprecht, 2011); Björn Mensing, *Pfarrer und Nationalsozialismus: Geschichte einer Verstrickung am Beispiel der Evangelisch-Lutherischen Kirche in Bayern* (Göttingen: Vandenhoeck & Ruprecht, 1998); Clemens Vollnhals, *Evangelische Kirche und Entnazifizierung 1945–1949: Die Last der nationalsozialistischen Vergangenheit. Studien zur Zeitgeschichte* (Munich: Oldenbourg, 1989). For the Roman Catholic church, cf. Michael Phayer, *The Catholic Church and the Holocaust: 1930–1965* (Bloomington: Indiana University Press, 2000); Kevin Spicer, *Hitler's Priests: Catholic Clergy and National Socialism* (Dekalb: Northern Illinois University Press, 2008) and *Resisting the Third Reich: The Catholic Clergy in Hitler's Berlin* (Dekalb: Northern Illinois University Press, 2004); Kevin Spicer, ed., *Antisemitism, Christian Ambivalence, and the Holocaust* (Bloomington: Indiana University Press, 2007); Wolfgang Gerlach, *And the Witnesses Were Silent: The Confessing Church and the Persecution of Jews*, trans. Victoria J. Barnett (Lincoln: University of Nebraska Press, 2000).

32. Anneliese Hochmuth, *Spurensuche: Eugenik, Sterilisation, Patientenmorde und die von Bodelschwinghschen Anstalten Bethel 1929–1945* (Bethel: Bethel-Verlag, 1997).

33. Antonia Leugers, *Jesuiten in Hitlers Wehrmacht: Kriegslegitimation und Kriegserfahrung* (Paderborn: Schöningh, 2009).

34. Gerlach, *And the Witnesses Were Silent*; Manfred Gailus, ed., *Kirchliche Amtshilfe: Die Kirche und die Judenverfolgung im Dritten Reich* (Göttingen: Vandenhoeck & Ruprecht, 2008).

35. LKAN, LKR 2451 Report, "Seelsorge in den Zivil-Interniertenlagern 1945–1946."

36. LKAN, LKR 2449 Report by Adolf Dresler, "Erfahrungen." August 27, 1947.

37. von Eickstedt, *Christus* 3.

38. In Italy and Austria, Roman Catholic priests began to "rebaptize" escaping Nazi functionaries and SS men as a condition for their assistance in leaving for South American exile. Cf. Gerald Steinacher, *Nazis auf der Flucht: Wie Kriegsverbrecher über Italien nach Übersee entkamen* (Innsbruck: StudienVerlag, 2008).

39. von Eickstedt, *Christus* 4.

40. von Eickstedt, *Christus* 15.

41. LKAN, LKR 2449 Adolf Dresler, "Erfahrungen," August 27, 1947.

42. EZAB 2/256, Kirchenrat Ernst Schieber, "Besprechung der Lagerpfarrer in Ludwigsburg," January 13, 1947.

43. Heiner Wember, *Umerziehung im Lager: Internierung und Betrafung von Nationalsozialisten in der britischen Besatzungzone Deutschlands* (Düsseldorf: Klartext, 1992), 213.

44. Gerhard Besier, "Die politische Rolle des Protestantismus in der Nachkriegszeit," *Beilage zu Das Parlament: Aus Politik und Zeitgeschichte* 50 (2000): 29–38, 33.

45. EZAB 2/256, Schieber, "Besprechung der Lagerpfarrer in Ludwigsburg," January 13, 1947.

46. von Eickstedt, *Christus* 1.

47. von Eickstedt, *Christus* 2.

48. von Eickstedt, *Christus* 4.

49. von Eickstedt, *Christus* 9.

50. Hans Asmussen, ed., *Agende für den Dienst der Lagerpfarrer in Kriegsgefangenen und Interniertenlagern* (Stuttgart: Quell Verlag, 1947).

51. von Eickstedt, *Christus* 8.

52. von Eickstedt, *Christus* 1.

53. von Eickstedt, *Christus* 14.

54. von Eickstedt, *Christus* 14.

55. von Eickstedt, *Christus* 14.

56. von Eickstedt, *Christus* 14.

57. Martin Niemöller, *From U-Boat to Pulpit*, trans. D. Hastie Smith (Chicago: Willett, Clark, 1937).

58. For an excellent discussion of the historical origin and sequence of this quote, see Harold Marcuse's website: http://www.history.ucsb.edu/faculty/marcuse/ niem.htm#discsources (March 9, 2006) and the website of the Martin Niemöller Stiftung: http://www.martin-niemoeller-stiftung.de/4/daszitat/a46. The poetic rendition of his sermons has been reproduced in several versions. Martin Niemöller, *Der Mann in der Brandung: Ein Bildbuch um Martin Niemöller* (Frankfurt am Main: Stimme Verlag 1962), 43.

59. Martin Niemöller, *Über die deutsche Schuld, Not und Hoffnung* (Zurich: Zollikon 1946); *Ach Gott vom Himmel sieh darein: Sechs Predigten* (Munich: Kaiser, 1946); *Zur gegenwärtigen Lage der evangelischen Christenheit* (Tübingen, Stuttgart: Furche Verlag, 1946); *Die Erneuerung unserer Kirche* (Munich: Neubau, 1946).

60. EZAB 2/255, M. Niemöller, sermon in Camp 77 (July 1, 1946).

61. Niemöller, Sermon, Camp 77; cf. Hans Joachim Oeffler, Hans Prolingheuer, Martin Schuck, Heinrich Werner, and Rolf Wischnath, eds., *Martin Niemöller: Ein Lesebuch* (Cologne: Pahl Rugenstein, 1987), 128.

62. Oeffler et al., *Lesebuch*, 128.

63. EZAB 2/255, "Anonyme Stellungnahme," Camp 77, July 1, 1946.

64. EZAB 2/255, "Anonyme Stellungnahme."

65. EZAB 2/255, "Kurze Stellungnahme—auf Grund von Urteilen," July 1, 1946.

66. EZAB 2/255, "Kurze Stellungnahme."

67. EZAB 2/255, "Einige Urteile aus dem Lager über den Vortrag," July 1, 1946.

68. Camp chaplains Huene (different spelling Hühn) and Dr. Joachim Müller submitted the women's comments along with an eleven-page, single-spaced reconstruction of his sermon "from several incomplete notes" to Hans Asmussen in the Church Chancellary on November 29, 1948.

69. EZAB 2/255, R. L. Fürst, response to Niemöller's sermon, Camp 77, July 1, 1946.

70. EZAB 2/255, Lina Weigand.

71. EZAB 2/255, R. L. Fürst.

72. EZAB 2/256, Kirchenrat Ernst Schieber, "Lage im Frauenlager Camp 77 Ludwigs-burg gemäß Besprechung des Lagerkirchengemeinderats am 27.1.1947."

73. EZAB 2/256, Schieber, "Lage im Frauenlager Camp 77."

74. Kathrin Meyer. *Entnazifizierung von Frauen: Die Internierungslager der US-Zone Deutschlands 1945–1952* (Berlin: Metropol, 2004), 212.

75. EZAB 2/255, "Einige Urteile."

76. EZAB 2/255, Anna Maria Flügzig.

77. EZAB 2/255, Runke.

78. EZAB 2/255, "Einige Urteile."

79. EZAB 2/255, "Einige Urteile."

80. EZAB 2/255, "Einige Urteile."

81. EZAB 2/255, "Einige Urteile."

82. I follow Marcuse's translation with some revisions. http://www.history.ucsb.edu/faculty/marcuse/projects/niem/StuttgartDeclaration.htm.

83. von Eickstedt, *Christus*, 14.

84. von Eickstedt, *Christus*, 14.

85. Gerhard Besier, "Zur Geschichte der Stuttgarter Schulderklärung vom 18./19. Oktober 1945," in *Wie Christen ihre Schuld bekennen*, ed. Gerhard Besier and Gerhard Sauter (Göttingen: Vandenhoeck Ruprecht, 1985), 9–63; Gerhard Sauter, "Vergib uns unsere Schuld: Eine theologische Besinnung auf das Stutt-garter Schuldbekenntnis," in *Wie Christen ihre Schuld bekennen: Die Stuttgarter Erklärung 1945*, ed. Gerhard Besier and Gerhard Sauter (Göttingen: Vanden-hoeck & Ruprecht, 1985), 63–129; Martin Greschat and Christiane Bastert, eds., *Die Schuld der Kirche: Dokumente und Reflexionen zur Stuttgarter Schulderklärung vom 18./19. Oktober 1945* (Munich: Kaiser, 1982); Martin Greschat, "Verweigertes Schuldbekenntnis," in *Erinnern. Bekennen, Verantworten: 50 Jahre Stuttgarter Schuldbekenntnis. Eine Dokumentation*, ed. EKD (Wendlingen: EKD Dokumenta-tion, 1995); Martin Greschat, ed., *Im Zeichen der Schuld: 40 Jahre Stuttgarter Schuldbekenntnis* (Neukirchen-Vluyn: Neukirchener Verlag, 1985); Gerhard Sauter, "Verhängnis der Theologie: Schuldwahrnehmung und Geschichtsan-schauung im deutschen Protestantismus," *Kirchliche Zeitgeschichte* 4 (1991): 475–492; Gerhard Sauter, *Versöhnung als Thema der Theologie* (Gütersloh: Güt-ersloher Verlagshaus, 1997).

86. The Stuttgart Declaration of Guilt, by the Council of the Protestant Church of Germany October 19, 1945, http://www.history.ucsb.edu/faculty/marcuse/projects/niem/StuttgartDeclaration.htm.

87. Stuttgart Declaration of Guilt, translation modified. Signatories were Theophil Wurm (bishop of Protestant Church in Wurttemberg), Hans Asmussen (president of Church Chancellery of the EKD), Hans Meiser (bishop in Bavaria), Heinrich Held (later *Praeses* of the Rhineland Church), Hanns Lilje (secretary general of the Lutheran World Federation, later bishop in Hanover), Hugo Hahn (minister, later bishop of a church in Saxony), Lic. Drizzle (minister, theology professor), Rudolf

Notes

Smend (theology professor), Gustav Heinemann (attorney, later president of the Federal Republic of Germany), Otto Dibelius (bishop in Berlin-Brandenburg), Martin Niemoeller (later church president of Hessen Nassau).

88. Norbert Frei, *Vergangenheitspolitik: Die Anfänge der Bundesrepublik und die NS-Vergangenheit* (Munich: dtv Verlag, 1999), 166–194; Clemens Vollnhals, *Evangelische Kirche und Entnazifizierung 1945–1949: Die Last der nationalsozialistischen Vergangenheit. Studien zur Zeitgeschichte* (Munich: Oldenbourg, 1989); Matthew Hockenos, *A Church Divided: German Protestants Confront the Nazi Past* (Bloomington: Indiana University Press, 2004); Marcuse, *Legacies of Dachau*; Ernst Klee, *Persilscheine und falsche Pässe* (Frankfurt am Main: Fischer Verlag, 1991); Gerald Steinacher, *Nazis auf der Flucht*.

89. Ronald Webster, "Opposing 'Victors' Justice:' German Protestant Churchmen and Convicted Criminals in Western Europe after 1945," *Holocaust and Genocide Studies* 15 (Spring 2001): 47–50.

90. Steinacher, *Nazis auf der Flucht*, 119–178.

91. Clemens Vollnhals, *Entnazifizierung und Selbstreinigung im Urteil der evangelischen Kirche: Dokumente und Reflexionen 1945–1949* (Munich: Kaiser, 1989).

92. NACP, RG 338, United States Army Europe, JAG War Crimes Branch General Administrative Records 1942–1957, Box 6. Cf. Norbert Frei, *Vergangenheitspolitik: Die Anfänge der Bundesrepublik und die NS-Vergangenheit* (Munich: dtv Verlag, 1999), 168.

93. The preparation for the Memorandum began in summer of 1948 and was overseen by church lawyer Hansjürgen Ranke; cf. Frei, *Vergangenheitspolitik*, 166.

94. This was a particular problem in the Protestant Church of Hesse under the presidency of Martin Niemöller. Cf. Rainer Lächele, "Vom Reichssicherheitshauptamt in ein evangelisches Gymnasium—Die Geschichte des Eugen Steimle," in *Das evangelische Württemberg zwischen Weltkrieg und Wiederaufbau,* ed. Rainer Lächele and Jörg Thierfelder (Stuttgart: Calwer Verlag, 1995), 260–288.

95. Wolfgang Stegemann, "Schwierigkeiten mit der Erinnerungskultur: Gedenkjahr für Landesbischof Meiser gerät zur kritischen Auseinandersetzung," *Kirche und Israel* 21.2 (2006): 120–144.

96. EKD Memorandum, 40.

97. Translation based on RSV Bible.

98. Bloxham, *Genocide on Trial*, 158.

99. EKD Memorandum, 51.

CHAPTER 3

1. LKAN Pfarreien III/17, no. 4a, Pastor August Eckardt, Nachdenklicher Rückblick, Christmas 1985.

2. Richard J. Evans, *Rituals of Retribution: Capital Punishment in Germany, 1600–1987* (New York: Oxford University Press, 1996), 805.

3. Norbert Frei, *Adenauer's Germany and the Nazi Past*, trans. Joel Golb (New York: Columbia University Press, 2002), 346 n. 24.

4. Anton Posset, "Der Priester und der SS-General. Die Bekehrungsgeschichte des Oswald Pohl," in *Landsberg im 20. Jahrhundert: Themenheft Landsberger Zeitgeschichte* 2 (1993), 20–24, 21.

5. LKAN Pfarreien III/17, no. 4a. Eckardt was appointed to the prison on June 16, 1948, and relieved of his duties on May 5, 1949. He was reassigned to congregational ministry in Garmisch-Partenkirchen on June 1, 1949.

6. LKAN Pfarreien III/17, no. 12. Ermann's first day in office was July 7, 1949, although his employment contract was dated September 24, 1949.

7. LKAN Pfarreien III/17, no. 4a, Eckardt Entnazifizierungsurkunde.

8. NACP, RG 549.2 USAREU/JAG Division, War Crimes Branch, Records Relating to Post-Trial Activities 1945–1957, General Clemency File 1951, Box 4, "Report by Headquarters European Command, Provost Marshall Division APO 757 US Army Proceedings of the Board of Officers appointed by General Order 127 (April 14, 1949)," 6.

9. LKAN Pfarreien III, 17, no. 3. Eckardt recounts numerous conflicts with the prison director over rules regarding confidentiality, visiting rights, and controlled media access.

10. LKAN Pfarreien III/17, no. 12. He notes an explicit change in prison regulations on August 14, 1950: "No minister or priest serving as prison chaplain will submit any releases for publication to any publishing agent until he has first submitted same to the prison Director for examination and received his written approval."

11. For instance the solidarity committee Gefangenenhilfe Landsberg was founded in close consultation with the chaplains. Its president was Catholic bishop Johannes Neuhäusler and its vice president Oberkirchenrat D. Daumiller; board members included Kirchenrat Rusam, a representative of the Caritasverband and of the Innere Mission. Its executive director was notorious Nazi attorney Rudolf Aschenauer. NACP, RG 549.2 USAREU/JAG Division, War Crimes Branch, General Administrative Records, 1942–1957, Box 6.

12. Ernst Klee, *Persilscheine und falsche Pässe* (Frankfurt am Main: Fischer, 1992); Oliver Schröm and Andrea Röpkem, *Stille Hilfe für braune Kameraden: Das geheime Netzwerk der Alt- und Neonazis* (Berlin: Chr. Links Verlag, 2001).

13. NACP, RG 549.2 USAREU/JAG Division, War Crimes Branch, Records of War Criminal Prison No. 1 Relating to Executed Prisoners ("Executee Files"), January 2, 1946–June 7, 1951, Box 1-14.

14. LKAN Pfarreien III/17, no. 4a, Eckardt, Nachdenklicher Rückblick, Christmas 1985.

15. Roy A. Martin, *Inside Nürnberg: Military Justice for Nazi War Criminals* (Shippensburg, PA: White Mane Book, 2000), 68–94. He recalls that convicts "would

be allowed approximately one minute for any statement he should desire to make" (70) and that "there were exactly thirteen steps leading up to the platform of the gallows."

16. Martin, *Inside Nürnberg*, 70.

17. Martin remembers that "a board would be nearby to strap a prisoner should he become hysterical or refuse to follow instructions." Martin, *Inside Nürnberg*, 68.

18. LKAN Pfarreien III/17, no. 3, Eckardt, Diary, 15.

19. NACP, RG 549.2, "Executee Files," Box 8, Herbert Kunze: "Prison Direktor, Herbert Kunze, 1st Lieutenant of the German Army, reports for execution. Tell your General, I am not guilty. I am not ready." And Hans Merbach: "Prison Director: Because I was obedient I carried out the order of the Camp commander. Long live my magnificent Fatherland an [*sic*] my beloved ones. I am ready."

20. NACP, RG 549.2, "Executee Files," Box 8, Christian Menrath.

21. NACP, RG 549.2, "Executee Files," Box 1, Stefan Barczay stated: "The Lord may forgive me." Stefan Barczay was a Slovak member of the Waffen-SS. His statement could be counted as an expression of remorse, but it also could be a liturgical recitation of a prayer before death.

22. Werner Hess was convicted on November 10, 1947, to six months in Landsberg for the abuse of a downed American pilot who was threatened by an angry mob after the bombing of a train and nearby farmers in the fields. Hess was convicted for transmitting an order to form a gauntlet through which Major James Cheney was forced to run. In the end, Hess probably saved the American pilot's life by closing the gates on the crowd and driving him off to a safe location. http://www.online.uni-marburg.de/icwc/dachau/000-012-1292.pdf; Cf. Klee, *Persilscheine und falsche Pässe*, 167 n. 179.

23. LKAN Pfarreien III/17, no. 1, letter, Pastor Werner Hess to Pastor Eckardt, July 7, 1948.

24. LKAN Pfarreien III/17, no. 1, letter, Hess to Eckardt, July 7, 1948.

25. LKAN Pfarreien III/17, no. 1, letter, Hess to Eckardt, July 7, 1948.

26. LKAN Pfarreien III/17, no. 3, Eckardt, diary, 85.

27. Hilary Earl, *The Nuremberg Einsatzgruppen Trial, 1945–1958: Atrocity, Law, and History* (Cambridge: Cambridge University Press, 2009), 209.

28. Earl, *Nuremberg Einsatzgruppen Trial*, 210.

29. LKAN Pfarreien III/17, no. 3, Eckardt, diary, 51.

30. LKAN Pfarreien III/17, no. 3, Eckardt, diary, 51.

31. LKAN Pfarreien III/17, no. 3, Eckardt, diary, 52.

32. LKAN Pfarreien III/17, no. 15, letter, Ermann to Pastor Anke, June 7, 1951.

33. LKAN Pfarreien III/17, no. 3, Eckardt, diary, 54.

34. LKAN Pfarreien III/17, no. 3, Eckardt, diary, 54.

35. Cf, Earl, *Nuremberg Einsatzgruppen Trial*, 46–96.

36. Earl, *Nuremberg Einsatzgruppen Trial*, 58.

37. LKAN Pfarreien III/17, no. 3, Eckardt, diary, 54.

38. Wolfgang Gerlach, *And the Witnesses Were Silent: The Confessing Church and the Persecution of the Jew*, trans. Victoria Barnett (Lincoln: University of Nebraska Press, 2000).

39. LKAN Pfarreien III/17, no. 11, letter, Eckardt to Miss Bertha Rupp (fiancee of Hermann Sturm) November 7, 1948.

40. LKAN Pfarreien III/17, no. 9, letter, Eckardt to Ms. Dr. Nopitsch, Bayrischer Mütterdienst, January 6, 1949. Eckardt attended mostly to the men, although he was aware of the seven women incarcerated in Landsberg.

41. LKAN Pfarreien III/17, no. 8, letter, Eckardt to Ms. Franke, October 29, 1948.

42. LKAN Pfarreien III/17, no. 9, letter, Eckardt to Ms. Hunsicker, October 29, 1948.

43. LKAN Pfarreien III/17, no. 8, letter, Eckardt to Ms. Vetter, February 5, 1949.

44. LKAN Pfarreien III/17, no. 10, letter, Eckardt to Miss Epstude (fiancee of Mr. Petrat), November 20, 1948.

45. LKAN Pfarreien III/17, no. 10, letter, Eckardt to Ms. Piorkowski, October 22, 1948.

46. LKAN Pfarreien III/17, no. 9, letter, Eckardt to Evang. Luth. Dekanat Wassertrüdingen (on funeral arrangements for Ernst Ittameier), November 8, 1948.

47. LKAN Pfarreien III/17, no. 11, letter, Eckardt to Mr. Hans Ertel (on the death of Karl Schröger), February 5, 1949.

48. LKAN Pfarreien III/17, no. 3, Eckardt diary.

49. LKAN Pfarreien III/17, no. 3, Eckardt, diary, 46.

50. Dagmar Herzog, ed., *Sexuality and German Fascism* (Brooklyn, NY: Berghahn, 2004); Dagmar Herzog, *Sex after Fascism: Memory and Morality in Twentieth-Century Germany* (Princeton, NJ: Princeton University Press, 2007).

51. He died after Oswald Pohl (head of the Economic and Administrative Main Office of the SS), Paul Blobel (Sonderkommando 4a), Otto Ohlendorf (Einsatzgruppe D), Erich Naumann (Einsatzgruppe B), Dr. Werner Braune (Einsatzgruppe 11b), and Georg Schallermair (Dachau trials).

52. NACP, Deputy Judge Advocate's Office 7708 War Crimes Group European Command; United States against Josias Prince zu Waldeck, November 16, 1947, 15.

53. NACP, M 1217 Roll 4, Reviews of US Army War Crimes Trials in Europe 1945–1948, 82.

54. NACP, RG 549.2, "Executee Files," Box 11.

55. NACP, RG 549.2, "Executee Files," Box 11. Hans Hermann Schmidt's statement was recorded by American witnesses: "Colonel, I will take the last words to protest emphatically against the completing of the executions. All documentary evidence which was gathered by my lawyer during the last four years and also in the fact that ¾ of the time of my trial was spent in the hospital undergoing operations did not help to prove my innocence. All this rebounded off the iron

walls of Heidelberg. Once again I protest emphatically, I am innocent of all the charges brought against me by the German newspapers, for all these articles were dictated by Heidelberg. I am dying here as the last of the Landsberger."

56. LKAN Pfarreien III/17, no. 15, sermon, Ermann, June 10, 1951.

57. LKAN Pfarreien III/17, no. 15, sermon, Ermann, June 10, 1951.

58. LKAN Pfarreien III/17, no. 15, sermon, Ermann, June 10, 1951.

59. LKAN Pfarreien III/17, no. 12, letter, Ermann to Mr. Rektor, August 17, 1951.

60. LKAN Pfarreien III/17, no 12, letter, Ermann to Mr. Rektor, August 17, 1951.

61. NACP, M1217 Roll 4, Reviews of U.S. Army War Crimes Trials in Europe 1945–1948, Buchenwald Review, Case # 000-50-0, 82.

62. LKAN Pfarreien III/17, no. 15, letter, Ermann to Pastor Schloemann, June 7, 1951.

63. NACP, M1217 Roll 4, Reviews of U.S. Army War Crimes Trials in Europe 1945–1948, Reviews and Recommendations for Cases # 000-50-2-41 to 000-50-5-20, p. 832.

64. Cited in Robert Sigel, *Im Interesse der Gerechtigkeit: Die Dachauer Kriegsverbrecherprozesse 1945–1948* (Frankfurt am Main: Campus Verlag, 1992), 180.

65. NACP, M1217 Roll 4, Reviews of U.S. Army War Crimes Trials in Europe 1945–1948, Deputy Judge Advocate Office 7708 War Crimes Group European Command, November 15, 1947, 83.

66. Cf. Thomas Alan Schwartz, "Die Begnadigung deutscher Kriegsverbrecher: John J. McCloy und die Häftlinge von Landsberg," *Vierteljahrshefte für Zeitgeschichte* 38 (1990): 375–414; Robert Sigel, "Gnadengesuche und Gnadenerlasse: Kriegsverbrecher in der amerikanischen Besatzungszone," *Dachauer Hefte* 10 (November 1994): 214–225.

67. LKAN Pfarreien III/17, no. 15, sermon, Ermann, June 10, 1951.

68. NACP, RG 549.2 "Executee Files," Box 11. Hans Hermann Schmidt claimed in his autobiographical statement that "camp employees were forbidden from abusing or mistreating prisoners. That was an order" (December 18, 1945), 10.

69. In postwar West Germany, the claim that "those who weren't there, can't judge" turned into a moral principle that categorically prohibited moral questioning by anyone who "had not been there." Cf. Reemtsma *Wie hätte ich mich verhalten? Und andere nicht nur deutsche Fragen. Reden und Aufsätze* (Munich: Beck Verlag, 2001), 9–30.

70. LKAN Pfarreien III/17, no. 10, letter, Eckardt to Waldemar Raabe, January 15, 1949.

71. LKAN Pfarreien III/17, no. 10, letter, Pastor Harald Poelchau to Eckardt, February 6, 1949.

72. Article XII, The Augsburg Confession, in J. Gordon Melton, *American Religious Creeds*, vol. 1 (New York: Triumph Books, 1991), 41.

73. Martin Niemöller *Die Erneuerung unserer Kirche* (Munich: Neubau-Verlag 1946), 7.

74. NACP, RG 549.2 "Executee Files," Box 11.

75. LKAN Pfarreien III/17, no. 10, letter, Eckardt to Waldemar Raabe, January 15, 1949.

76. NACP, RG 549.2 "Executee Files," Box 11.

77. "German Gets Death for Slaying of GI," *New York Times*, February 12, 1948.

78. NACP, RG 549.2 "Executee Files," Box 11. Paul Ruebsamen was hanged on July 15, 1947.

79. Dachau trial no. 12, May 12, 1947. http://www.online.uni-marburg.de/icwc/dachau/000-012-1915.pdf.

80. Dachau trial no. 12, May 12, 1947. http://www.online.uni-marburg.de/icwc/dachau/000-012-1915.pdf. 3.

81. NACP, RG 549.2 "Executee Files," Box 14. Jaroslaw Werbinski was shot on May 27, 1947.

82. NACP, RG 549.2 Records Relating to War Criminal Prison No. 1 Landsberg, 1947–1957, Inspection Records, Box 4.

83. LKAN Pfarreien III/17, no. 1, letter, Pastor Hess to Eckardt, July 7, 1948, 2.

84. Evans, *Rituals of Retribution*, 753–754.

85. Evans, *Rituals of Retribution*, 749.

86. NACP, RG 549.2 "Executee Files," Box 8. Metschislaw Kowalczyck was shot on March 18, 1948.

87. NACP, RG 549.2 "Executee Files," Box 8. Dimitrios Kosturos was shot on February 14, 1947.

88. NACP, RG 549.2 "Executee Files," Box 13. Julius Straub was hanged on October 29, 1948.

89. NACP, RG 549.2 "Executee Files," Box 6. Karl Horcicka was hanged on November 12, 1948.

90. NACP, RG 549.2 "Executee Files," Box 4. Rudolf Fiegel was hanged on May 27, 1947.

91. Idith Zertal, *Israel's Holocaust and the Politics of Nationhood* (Cambridge: Cambridge University Press, 2005), 52–91.

92. Primo Levi, *The Drowned and the Saved*, trans. Raymond Rosenthal (New York City: Simon and Schuster, 1986); Jonathan Petropoulos and John Roth, *Gray Zones: Ambiguity and Compromise in the Holocaust and Its Aftermath* (Brooklyn, NY: Berghahn Books, 2006).

93. Levi, *The Drowned and the Saved*, 81.

94. NACP, RG 549.2 Records Relating to War Criminal Prison No. 1 Landsberg, Records from 1951, Box 3.

95. NACP, RG 549.2 "Executee Files," Box 12; Johann Schneider was hanged on November 19, 1948. The sentence is available online, http://www.online.uni-marburg.de/icwc/dachau/000-012-2036.pdf.

96. NACP, RG 549.2 "Executee Files," Box 11. Johann Schmitz was hanged on October 15, 1948.

97. NACP, RG 549.2 "Executee Files," Box 8; Christian Menrath was hanged on December 5, 1947. As NSdAP *Ortsgruppenleiter* he led an American pilot from police detention to an execution site outside town on the morning after his arrest. See the trial documents: http://www.online.uni-marburg.de/icwc/dachau/000-012-0765.pdf.

98. NACP, RG 549.2 "Executee Files," Box 4. Richard Fritz Girke was hanged on October 15, 1948, for killing downed American pilots. LKAN Pfarreien III/17 Gefängnisseelsorge Landsberg/Lech no. 8, letter, Lucie Girke to Eckardt, October 27, 1948.

99. Evans *Rituals of Retribution*, 771-773. For instance, Johann Reichart "claimed to have executed 3,165 people altogether during the Third Reich, including the students Hans and Sophie Scholl... [and] was also employed by the American military authorities as an executioner, responsible both for guillotining common murderers and for hanging SS men and other war criminals." Evans, *Rituals of Retribution*, 772.

100. Martin, *Inside Nürnberg*, 71.

101. LKAN Pfarreien III/17, no. 1, letter, Hess to Eckardt, July 7, 1948.

102. LKAN Pfarreien III/17, no. 3, Eckardt, diary, 98.

103. LKAN Pfarreien III/17, no. 15, sermon, Ermann, June 10, 1951.

104. Charles Duff, *A Handbook on Hanging* (London: Putnam, 1955). Duff's history of hangings was originally published in 1928 and updated in 1934, 1938, 1948, 1954, and 1955 in various editions.

105. Evans, *Rituals of Retribution*, 759.

106. Renate Wald, *Mein Vater Robert Ley: Meine Erinnerungen und Vaters Geschichte* (Nürmbrecht: Martine Galunder-Verlag 2004), 144.

107. William L. Hull, *Struggle for a Soul: The Untold Story of a Minister's Final Effort to Convert Adolf Eichmann* (Garden City, NJ: Doubleday, 1963), 157.

108. Hull, *Struggle for a Soul*, 160.

CHAPTER 4

1. Oswald Pohl, *Credo: Mein Weg zu Gott* (Landshut: Alois Girnth Verlag, 1950), 57.

2. Michel Foucault, *Discipline and Punish: The Birth of the Prison* (New York: Random House, 1975).

3. Jan Erik Schulte, *Zwangsarbeit und Vernichtung: Das Wirtschaftsimperium der SS. Oswald Pohl und das SS-Wirtschafts-Verwaltungshauptamt 1933–1945* (Paderborn: Ferdinand Schöningh, 2001), 46.

4. Quoted in Schulte, *Zwangsarbeit und Vernichtung*, 41.

5. Christa Paul, *Zwangsprostitution: Staatlich errichtete Bordelle im Nationalsozialismus* (Berlin: Edition Hentrich, 1994); Robert Sommer, *Das KZ-Bordell: Sexuelle*

Zwangsarbeit in nationalsozialistischen Konzentrationslagern (Paderborn: Ferdinand Schöningh, 2009).

6. Michael Allen, "Oswald Pohl: Chef der SS-Wirtschaftsunternehmen," in *Die SS: Elite unter dem Totenkopf,* ed. Ronald Smelser and Enrico Syring (Paderborn: Ferdinand Schöningh, 2000), 394–407.

7. Robert M. W. Kempner, *Die SS im Kreuzverhör: Die Elite, die Europa in Scherben schlug* (Hamburg: Volksblatt Verlag, 1987), 106–130.

8. Karl Morgenschweis, foreword to Pohl, *Credo,* 10.

9. Morgenschweis, foreword, 10–11.

10. Morgenschweis, foreword, 13.

11. The first edition was produced in 9,000 copies. Cf. Anton Posset, "Der Priester und der SS-General. Die Bekehrungsgeschichte des Oswald Pohl," *Landsberg im 20. Jahrhundert: Themenheft Landsberger Zeitgeschichte* 2 (1993): 24.

12. Morgenschweis, foreword, 9.

13. Cf. Björn Krondorfer, *Male Confessions: Intimate Revelations and the Religious Imagination* (Stanford, CA: Stanford University Press, 2010), 100–132.

14. Morgenschweis, foreword, 9.

15. Gerald Steinacher, *Nazis auf der Flucht: Wie Kriegsverbrecher über Italien nach Übersee entkamen* (Innsbruck: StudienVerlag, 2008), 166–178; for a history of the sacrament of baptism cf. *The Oxford Dictionary of the Christian Church,* 3rd ed., ed. F. L. Cross and E. A. Livingstone (New York: Oxford University Press 2005), s.v. "Baptism."

16. Pohl, *Credo,* 34.

17. Pohl, *Credo,* 34.

18. Morgenschweis, foreword, 12.

19. Pohl, *Credo,* 43.

20. Pohl, *Credo,* 43.

21. Pohl, *Credo,* 44.

22. Pohl, *Credo,* 45.

23. Pohl, *Credo,* 45.

24. Pohl, *Credo,* 46.

25. Pohl, *Credo,* 42.

26. Pohl, *Credo,* 40.

27. Pohl, *Credo,* 40.

28. Pohl, *Credo,* 40.

29. Pohl, *Credo,* 66.

30. Pohl, *Credo,* 49.

31. Pohl, *Credo,* 53.

32. Pohl, *Credo,* 58.

33. Pohl, *Credo,* 67.

34. Pohl, *Credo,* 67.

35. Pohl, *Credo*, 68.
36. Pohl, *Credo*, 69.
37. Pohl, *Credo*, 60.
38. Pohl, *Credo*, 42.
39. NACP, RG 549.2, "Executee Files," Box 13.
40. Peter-Ferdinand Koch, *Himmler's graue Eminenz—Oswald Pohl—und das Wirtschafts- und Verwaltungshauptamt der SS* (Hamburg: Verlag Facta Oblita, 1988), 172–173. Reference to a papal telegram is also made by Kathrin Himmler, who cites a letter by Oswald Pohl circulated among family and friends in January 1951 announcing the pope's "Gruß und Segen." Kathrin Himmler, *Die Brüder Himmler: Eine deutsche Familie* (Frankfurt am Main: Fischer Verlag, 2005), 272.
41. Jan Heiner Tück, "Unforgivable Forgiveness? Jankélévitch, Derrida and a Hope against All Hope," trans. David C. Schindler, *International Catholic Review Communio* 31 (2004): 522–539; Tück, "Inkarnierte Feindesliebe: Der Messias Israels und die Hoffnung auf Versöhnung," in *Streitfall Christologie: Vergewisserungen nach der Shoah,* ed. Helmut Hoping, Jan Heiner Tück (Freiburg: Herder, 2005), 258.
42. Tück, "Inkarnierte Feindesliebe," 258.
43. Tück, "Inkarnierte Feindesliebe," 258.
44. Tück, "Inkarnierte Feindesliebe," 258.
45. Tück, "Inkarnierte Feindesliebe," 245.
46. Morgenschweis, foreword, 14.
47. Margarete Buber-Neumann describes how camp commander Redwitz picked Pförtsch out of a lineup because he recognized her as the woman who had hit him during a street fight between Communists and Nazis in 1933. This incident recommended her to him. Buber-Neumann characterized Pförtsch thus: "Mit Leo hatte der Schutzhaftlagerführer eine vorzügliche Wahl getroffen. Sie prügelte, brüllte, drohte mit Meldungen, war schlechthin für das anvertraute Amt wie geschaffen." Margarete Buber- Neumann, *Als Gefangene bei Stalin und Hitler: Eine Welt im Dunkel* (Stuttgart: Seewald Verlag, 1985), 279.
48. Primo Levi, *The Drowned and the Saved*, trans. Raymond Rosenthal (New York: Simon and Schuster: 1986), 75.
49. Martin Nimöller, *Die Erneuerung unserer Kirche* (Munich: Neubau Verlag 1946), 7.
50. Ronald Webster, "'Opposing Victors' Justice:' German Protestant Churchmen and Convicted War Criminals in Western Europe after 1945," *Holocaust and Genocide Studies* 15 (2001): 547.
51. Webster, "Opposing Victors' Justice," 547.
52. AEKIR, Düsseldorf, 1OB 004-47, letter, Lic. Carl Sachsse to Landesverband Pfalz der Inneren Mission, June 4, 1952.
53. "qu'il n'éxiste en sa faveur aucune circonstance atténuant." Ministère des Affaires Etrangère, Bureau des Archives de l'Occupation Française en Alle-

magne et en Autriche, Colmar, CD-ROM "Jugements du Tribunal Supérieur de Rastatt," Verdict no. 6/578, CD-No. 19, 4, 5.

54. 1OB 004-47, AEKIR, Düsseldorf, letter, Carl Sachsse to Landesverband Pfalz der Inneren Mission, June 4, 1952.

55. AEKIR, Düsseldorf, 1OB 004-47, letter, Sachsse to Dekan Lic. Gross, August 13, 1953.

56. AEKIR, Düsseldorf, 1OB 004-47, letter, Sachsse to Gross.

57. AEKIR, Düsseldorf, 1OB 004-47, letter, Sachsse to Landesverband Pfalz.

58. AEKIR, Düsseldorf, 1OB 004-47, letter, Sachsse to Landesverband Pfalz.

59. Dana M. Britton, *The Gender of Crime* (Lanham, MD: Rowman and Littlefield, 2011), 23–53.

60. Helga Schubert, *Judas Frauen: Zehn Fallgeschichten weiblicher Denunziation im Dritten Reich* (Frankfurt am Main: Luchterhand Literaturverlag, 1990).

61. Michael S. Bryant, *Confronting the Good Death: Nazi Euthanasia on Trial* (Boulder: University of Colorado Press, 2005).

62. http://www1.jur.uva.nl/junsv/. *Nazi Crimes on Trial: German Trials Concerning National Socialist Homicidal Crimes* compiled at the Institute of Criminal Law of the University of Amsterdam by C. F. Rüter and D. W. de Mildt.

63. Simone Erpel, ed., *Im Gefolge der SS-Aufseherinnen des Frauen KZ-Ravensbrück* (Berlin: Metropol Verlag, 2007); Gisela Bock, "Ordinary Women in Nazi Germany: Perpetrators, Victims, Followers, and Bystanders," in *Women in the Holocaust*, ed. Dalia Ofer and Lenore J. Weitzman (New Haven: Yale University Press, 1998), 89.

64. Elissa Mailänder Koslov, *Gewalt im Dienstalltag: Die SS-Aufseherinnen des Konzentrations- und Vernichtungslagers Majdanek* (Hamburg: Hamburger Edition, 2009).

65. This is known as the "sex role hypothesis" in criminal justice, according to Michael Bryant: "On this theory, women are indeed treated more leniently than men, but only for crimes consistent with their gendered role. Female defendants who commit crimes in violation of these roles, however, are punished more harshly." Michael Bryant, "Hitler's Henchwomen: The West German Trials of Female Perpetrators and Accomplices of 'Mercy Killings,' 1945–1965," paper presented at the German Studies Association, 2004, 10.

66. Konrad Kwiet, "'Hitler's Willing Executioners'" and 'Ordinary Germans': Some Comments on Goldhagen's Ideas," www.ceu.hu/jewishstudies/pdf/01_kwiet.pdf (accessed May 21, 2012).

67. Ulrike Weckel and Edgar Wolfrum, eds., *Bestien and Befehlsempfänger: Frauen und Männer in NS-Prozessen nach 1945* (Göttingen: Vandenhoeck & Ruprecht, 2003).

68. Simone Erpel, introduction to *Im Gefolge der SS-Aufseherinnen*, 22.

69. Kathrin Meyer, *Entnazifizierung von Frauen: Die Internierungslager der US-Zone Deutschlands 1945–1952* (Berlin: Metropol, 2004), 238ff.

70. Britton, *The Gender of Crime*, 78.

71. Daniel Patrick Brown, *The Beautiful Beast: The Life and Crimes of SS-Aufseherin Irma Grese* (Ventura, CA: Golden West Historical Publication, 1996); Weckel and Wolfrum, *Bestien und Befehlsempfänger*; Constance Jaiser, "Irma Greese: Zur Rezeption einer KZ-Aufseherin," in Erpel, *Im Gefolge der SS-Aufseherinnen*; Julia Duesterberg, "Von der Umkehr aller Weiblichkeit: Charakterbilder einer KZ-Aufseherin," in *Gedächtnis und Geschlecht: Deutungsmuster in Darstellungen des Nationalsozialistischen Genozids*, ed. Insa Eschenbach, Sigrid Jacobeit, and Silke Wenk (Frankfurt am Main: Campus, 2002), 237–243, 241.

72. Arthur L. Smith Jr., *Die Hexe von Buchenwald: Der Fall Ilse Koch* (Cologne: Böhlau Verlag, 1983).

73. Alexandra Pryzrembel, "Der Bann eines Bildes: Ilse Koch, die 'Kommandeuse von Buchenwald,'" in Eschenbach, Jacobeit, and Wenk, *Gedächtnis und Geschlecht*, 245–268. She was sentenced to life in prison by the regional court in Augsburg in 1951, where the judges explained their choice to impose the maximum penalty for all charges: "Strafschärfend waren folgende Umstände zu werten: Die Koch hat sich jeglicher besseren Einsicht und jeglicher Ausrichtung ihres Verhaltens nach dieser eigenwillig verschlossen, obwohl hier Regungen des Mitleids und des Mitgefühls für jede Frau besonders nahe lagen. Sie war in Buchenwald als Ehefrau des Lagerführers und als Mutter ihrer Kinder und hatte dort keinerlei dienstliche Funktionen. Während das Aufsichtspersonal beruflich in die Führung des KL eingegliedert war und bei seinem Zusammensein mit den Häftlingen auch mit dienstlichen Belagen auseinandersetzen musste, wäre es für die Koch Pflicht und für sie als Frau auch ein leichtes gewesen, sich aus dem KL Geschehen völlig fernzuhalten und gleich den anderen Frauen nur ihrer Familie zu leben. Die Koch aber fühlte sich nicht nur als Frau und Mutter, sondern als Kommandeuse. Sie machte es sich zur Aufgabe, in das eigentliche KL-Geschehen einzugreifen. Sie empfand es als innere Befriedigung, wenn sie einen fühlbaren Beitrag zu der möglichst linientreuen Verwirklichung des im Lager herrschenden Systems leisten konnte." *Justiz und NS-Verbrechen*, vol. 8, 127.

74. Brown, *The Beautiful Beast*; Constance Jaiser, "Irma Greese: Zur Rezeption einer KZ-Aufseherin," in Erpel, *Im Gefolge der SS-Aufseherinnen*.

75. Alexandra Przyrembel, "Transfixed by an Image: Ilse Koch, the 'Kommandeuse of Buchenwald,'" *German History* 19.3 (2001): 369–400; Claudia Koonz, *Mothers in the Fatherland: Women, the Family, and Nazi Politics* (New York: St. Martin's Press, 1987), 404ff.; Insa Eschebach, "NS-Prozesse in der sowjetischen Besatzungszone und der DDR: Einige Überlegungen zu den Strafverfahrensakten ehemaliger SS-Aufseherinnen des Frauenkonzentrationslagers Ravensbrück,"

in *Die frühen Nachkriegsprozesse: Beiträge zur Geschichte der nationalsozialistischen Verfolgung in Norddeutschland,* ed. Kurt Buck (Bremen: Edition Temmen, 1997), vol. 3, 65–74; Sybil Milton, "Women and the Holocaust: The Case of German and German-Jewish Women," in *Different Voices: Women and the Holocaust,* ed. Carol Rittner and John K. Roth (New York: Paragon, 1993), 225.

76. Survivor testimony that women were "more malicious and mean, more hateful and petty than men," is cited by Gisela Bock, "Ordinary Women in Nazi Germany: Perpetrators, Victims, Followers, and Bystanders," in Ofer and Weitzman, *Women in the Holocaust,* 90; Koonz, *Mothers in the Fatherland,* 404–405; Daniel Patrick Brown, *The Camp Women: The Female Auxiliaries Who Assisted the SS in Running the Nazi Concentration Camp System* (Atglen, PA: Schiffer, 2002).

77. Mailaender Koslov, "Täterinnenbilder im Düsseldorfer Majdanek Prozess 1975–1981," in Erpel, *Im Gefolge der SS-Aufseherinnen,* 219.

78. Britton, *The Gender of Crime,* 78.

79. Sachsse also hesitated in the cases of two female SS associates, Hedwig Koch and Ms. Thomae, convicted in the French Neubremme trial. He feared jeopardizing the prospects of clemency appeals for male convicts: "Ich darf natürlich wegen dieser 2 Fälle mich nicht der Gefahr aussetzen, dass meine gesamten Gnadengesuche in Zukunft keinen Erfolg mehr haben, weil ich mich für Personen einsetze, welche man im Hohen Kommissariat als wirklich schlimme und grausame Verbrecher ansieht." AEKIR, Düsseldorf, 1OB 004-47, letter, Sachsse to Landesverband Pfalz der Inneren Mission, October 21, 1950.

80. Irene Imort was trained in Ravensbrück and assigned to Bergen-Belsen and its satellite camps Merzdorf, Zittat, Braunschweig, and Beendorf. SS associates were listed as "Reichsangestellte" (employees of the state) and "Aufseherin im weiblichen Gefolge der Waffen-SS" (guard as female associate of the Waffen-SS). They were not regular members of the SS but subject to SS jurisdiction. Johannes Schwartz, "Handlungsoptionen von KZ-Aufseherinnen. Drei alltags- und geschlechtergeschichtliche Fallstudien," in *NS-Täter aus interdisziplinärer Perspektive,* ed. Helgard Kramer (Munich: Martin Meidenbauer Verlag, 2006), 349.

81. AEKIR, Düsseldorf, 1OB 004-47, letter, Sachsse to Evangelische Gemeinde Löhne/Westfalen, June 27, 1951.

82. AEKIR, Düsseldorf, 1OB 004-47, letter, Sachsse to Evang. Gem. Löhne.

83. AEKIR, Düsseldorf, 1OB 004-47, letter, Sachsse to Evang. Gem. Löhne.

84. Annette Neumann, "Funktionshäftlinge im Konzentrationslager Ravensbrück," in *Tod oder Überleben: Neue Forschungen zur Geschichte des Konzentrationslager Ravensbück,* vol. 1 of *Faschismus und Weltkriegsforschung Beiheft,* ed. Werner Röhr and Brigitte Berlekamp (Berlin: Organon, 2001), 45.

85. "Jugements du Tribunal Supérieur de Rastatt," no. 6/578, 3.

86. "Jugements du Tribunal Supérieur de Rastatt," no. 6/578, 8.

87. BAL, B162/4346, deposition of Klara Pförtsch, Stadtpolizeiamt Hof, October 1, 1968; BAL B162/9809, deposition of Klara Pförtsch, Staatsanwaltschaft Frankfurt am Main, May 9, 1974; Neumann, "Funktionshäftlinge im Frauen-Konzentrationslager Ravensbrück," 47; Bernd Steger and Peter Wald, *Hinter der grünen Pappe: Orli Wald im Schatten von Auschwitz* (Hamburg: VSA Verlag Hamburg, 2008), 224.

88. Information by Peter Gohle, Bundesarchiv Außenstelle Ludwigsburg, June 13, 2012; reference to this lawsuit is made in a letter of Sachsse to Dr. Gawlik, January 6, 1962, AEKIR, Düsseldorf, 1OB 004-47.

89. Claudia Card, *The Atrocity Paradigm: A Theory of Evil* (Oxford: Oxford University Press, 2002), 212.

90. Cf. Neumann, "Funktionshäftlinge Ravensbrück," 36.

91. Johannes Schwartz, "Die französischen Militärgerichtsprozesse gegen KZ-Aufseherinnen," in Erpel, *Im Gefolge der SS-Aufseherinnen*, 129–141; esp. helpful is his overview on pp. 140–141.

92. Jugements du Tribunal Supérieur de Rastatt," no. 6/578, 4.

93. Jugements du Tribunal Supérieur de Rastatt, no. 6/578, 10, attests: "ces actes revêtent un character de gravité aussi criminelle."

94. Jugements du Tribunal Supérieur de Rastatt, no. 6/578, 10.

95. Jugements du Tribunal Supérieur de Rastatt," no. 6/578, 10: "son absence totale de pitié a l'occasion des selections qui ont eu lieu au camp."

96. AEKIR, Düsseldorf, 1OB 004-47, letter, Herta Gotthelf to High Commissioner Francois-Poncet, November 21, 1949.

97. Andrea Steffek, *Rosa Jochmann: Nie Zusehen, wenn Unrecht geschieht. Ihr Leben und Wirken 1901–1945 als Grundlage für ihre stetige Mahnung gegen Faschismus, Nationalsozialismus und das Vergessen* (Vienna: OBG Östereicherischer Gewerksschaftsbund, 1999).

98. AEKIR, Düsseldorf, 1OB 004-47, letter, Rosl Jochmann to Dr. Jur. Göhrig, November 30, 1949.

99. "Rosl" and "Rosa" refer to the same woman. Jochmann cited the fate of Else Krug; cf. Neumann, "Funktionshäftlinge Ravensbrück," 45.

100. AEKIR, Düsseldorf, 1OB 004-47, letter, Gotthelf to François-Poncet, November 21, 1949.

101. Annette Neumann concluded that "das sowjetische Militärtribunal [hat] zwischen dem Funktionshäftling Kaiser und den SS-Aufseherinnnen in keiner Weise differenziert." "Funktionshäftlinge Ravensbrück," 38.

102. Atina Grossmann, *Jews, Germans, and Allies: Close Encounters in Occupied Germany* (Princeton, NJ: Princeton University Press, 2007).

103. LKAN Pfarreien III/37, Seelsorge im Interniertenlager Dachau no. 2, Minutes of Meeting with Oberkirchenrat Daumiller of May 14, 1947. He com-

plained that "among the 4,300 inmates, of whom approximately 80–90 percent served as former camp guards, are also a number of former KZ prisoners. Some of them, especially the political prisoners, have integrated well into the internment camp community and help in the self-administration. But others who were transferred to concentration camps as professional criminals [*Berufsverbrecher*] and became kapos there—which is why they are interned today—constitute a severe burden on the new community, which cannot get rid of them in the usual ways. Every human community has its laws to penalize such criminals, but our community is only protected by American disciplinary procedures, which impose a mere 30 days of solitary confinement on a homosexual who has seduced several young men into unnatural behavior. . . . what is even worse, once their political record has been examined, such people are released just like the decent men [*anständige Männer*], since their criminal records from the concentration camp were burned when Dachau was conquered. They then become members of the German *Volk*, which has no power to get rid of them [*das keinerlei Handhabe besitzt, sich ihrer zu entledigen*]."

104. EZAB 2/256, Kirchenrat Ernst Schieber, "Lage im Frauenlager Camp 77," January 27, 1947.

105. EZAB 2/256, Schieber, "Lage im Frauenlager."

106. EZAB 2/256, Schieber, "Lage im Frauenlager."

107. Jugements du Tribunal Supérieur de Rastatt, no. 6/578, p. 7.

108. AEKIR, Düsseldorf, 1OB 004-47, letter, Orli Wald to High Commissioner François-Poncet, April 2, 1951.

109. Lawrence Langer, "The Dilemma of Choice in the Deathcamps," in *Holocaust: Religious and Philosophical Implications,* ed. John K. Roth and Michael Berenbaum (New York: Paragon House, 1989), 222–232.

110. Her name is spelled differently as Fela Drexler in the Yad Vashem photo archive, which identifies her as a former inmate of Auschwitz who was tried as a kapo. http://collections.yadvashem.org/photosarchive/en-us/52712.html. Bernd Steger and Peter Wald, her stepson, have collected her published writings and letters in *Hinter der grünen Pappe,* 226–230.

111. Steger and Wald, *Hinter der grünen Pappe,* 226–230.

112. AEKIR, Düsseldorf, 1OB 004-47, letter, Rosl Jochmann to Göhrig, November 30, 1949.

113. AEKIR, Düsseldorf, 1OB 004-47, letter, Jochmann to Göhrig, November 30, 1949.

114. Primo Levi, *The Drowned and the Saved,* 49.

115. Primo Levi, *The Drowned and the Saved,* 59.

116. Primo Levi, *The Drowned and the Saved,* 60.

117. Primo Levi, *The Drowned and the Saved,* 53.

118. Primo Levi, *The Drowned and the Saved,* 49.

119. Idith Zertal, *Israel's Holocaust and the Politics of Nationhood* (Cambridge: Cambridge University Press, 2005).

120. BALB 162/9809 deposition Pförtsch, Staatsanwaltschaft Frankfurt am Main, May 9, 1974.

121. BAL B162/2831, deposition Pförtsch, Regional Court Frankfurt am Main, August 18, 1963.

122. BAL, B162/2831, deposition Pförtsch, Frankfurt am Main, August 18, 1963.

123. BAL, B162/4346, deposition Pförtsch, Stadtpolizeiamt Hof, October 1, 1968.

124. BAL B162, deposition Pförtsch, Frankfurt am Main, August 18, 1963.

125. BAL B162/2831, deposition Pförtsch, Frankfurt am Main, August 18, 1963.

126. BAL, B162/4346, deposition Pförtsch, Stadtpolizeiamt Hof, October 1, 1968.

127. Card, *Atrocity Paradigm*, 220.

CHAPTER 5

1. Images of the crucifixion were also prominently displayed by the antisemitic propaganda magazine *Der Stürmer*, which showed a personified Germania nailed to the cross while an evil-looking Jew looked on. The inscription above the naked female body reads: *Ecce Germania*. *Der Stürmer* 15 (April 1927) (http://churchesandtheholocaust.ushmm.org/page/historical-documents).

2. Hans Frank, *Im Angesicht des Galgens* (Munich: Beck Verlag, 1954), 431.

3. Hans Frank, "Schlußwort des Angeklagten," in *Im Angesicht des Galgens*, 458.

4. Hans Frank, "Schlußwort des Angeklagten," 457.

5. Letter of Hans Frank to Brigitte Frank, Easter Sunday 1946, in Niklas Frank, *Meine deutsche Mutter* (Munich: Bertelsmann, 2005), 356.

6. LKAN Kleine Bestände III/17 Gefängnisseelsorge Landsberg/Lech no. 11, letter, Eckardt to Wera Wentzel, December 4, 1948: "'I was born on Good Friday 1901,' he told me, when I sat with him on the evening before his death day for a longer conversation in his small cell.... Good Friday and the cross of Christ were more for him than a symbol from then on, but a God-given fact that would complete his life." Erich F. Wentzel was convicted to death for executing seven American pilots on the island Borkum.

7. LKAN Pfarreien III/17 Gefängnisseelsorge Landsberg/Lech no. 8, letter, Lucie Girke to Eckardt, October 27, 1948, on the execution of her husband Richard Fritz Girke, October 15, 1948.

8. The apostle Paul describes bodily resurrection in 1 Corinthians with a seed metaphor: "So is it with the resurrection of the dead. What is sown is perishable, what is raised is imperishable. It is sown in dishonor, it is raised in glory. It is sown in weakness, it is raised in power. It is sown a physical body, it is raised a spiritual body" (1 Cor. 15: 42–44).

9. Ulf Schmidt, *Karl Brandt: Medicine and Power in the Third Reich* (New York: Continuum, 2007).

10. Letter of Prof. Dr. Karl Brandt to his son, April 6, 1947, in *Deutsche Hochschullehrer-Zeitung* 10 (1962): 5.

11. Last words of Prof. Dr. Karl Brandt, quoted by Pastor Lonitzer in his eulogy, in *Deutsche Hochschullehrer-Zeitung* 10 (1962): 8; Oscar Friedrich, *Über Galgen wächst kein Gras: Die fragwürdige Kulisse der Kriegsverbrecherprozesse im Spiegel unbekannter Dokumente* (Braunschweig: Erasmus Verlag, 1950), 12.

12. Last words of Prof. Dr. Karl Brandt, 8; cf. Friedrich, *Über Galgen wächst kein Gras*, 12.

13. LKAN Pfarreien III/17 Gefängnisseelsorge Landsberg, no 11, letter, Eckardt to Miss Meier (niece of Dr. Josef Schmidt), November 30, 1948: "He saw spiritual fruit growing from the sacrifice of his life."

14. LKAN Pfarreien III/17 Gefängnisseelsorge Landsberg, no. 8. Fritz Dietrich was hanged October 22, 1948.

15. LKAN Pfarreien III/17 Gefängnisseelsorge Landsberg, no. 8, letter, Eckardt to Luise Dietrich, October 22, 1948.

16. NACP, RG 549.2 "Executee Files," Box 8. Julius Ludolph was hanged May 28, 1947. His sentence from the Mauthausen trial is available online, http://www.online.uni-marburg.de/icwc/dachau/000-050-0005.pdf.

17. LKAN Pfarreien III/17 Gefängnisseelsorge, Landsberg 4a. "Nachdenklicher Rückblick, Christmas 1985." Herbert Kunze was hanged November 22, 1948, for executing downed American pilots in Konstanz. NACP, RG 549.2 "Executee Files," Box 8. His sentence is available online, http://www.online.uni-marburg. de/icwc/dachau/000-012-0045.pdf.

18. LKAN Pfarreien III/17, Gefängnisseelsorge Landsberg/Lech, no. 9, letter, Eckardt to Ms. Heim, February 5, 1949; NACP, RG 549.2 "Executee Files," Box 5.

19. NACP, RG 549.2 "Executee Files," Box 1. August Blei was hanged June 13, 1946.

20. NACP, RG 549.2 "Executee Files," Box 5. Hans Hegenscheidt was the SS official responsible for food distribution in the concentration camp of Mauthausen. His sentence is available online, http://www.online.uni-marburg.de/icwc/dachau/000-050-0005.pdf.

21. For Protestant and Catholic reactions to the Eichmann trials, cf. Peter Krause, *Der Eichmann-Prozeß in der deutschen Presse* (Frankfurt am Main: Campus Verlag, 2002), 115–125.

22. Devin O. Pendas, *The Frankfurt Auschwitz Trial: Genocide, History and the Limits of Law* (Cambridge: Cambridge University Press, 2006).

23. Reinhard Henkys, *Die nationalsozialistischen Gewaltverbrechen: Geschichte und Gericht* (Stuttgart: Kreuz Verlag, 1965), 196.

24. EZAB 2/2488, "Seelsorgerliche Handreichung für die Pfarrer in Sachen der NS-Verbrecherprozesse," 2.

25. EZAB 2/2488, "Seelsorgerliche Handreichung für die Pfarrer," 2.

26. Barbara Just-Dahlmann and Helmut Just, *Die Gehilfen: NS-Verbrechen und die Justiz nach 1945* (Frankfurt am Main: Athenäum, 1988).

27. AEKIR, 7 NL 016-51, letter, Just-Dahlmann to Schlingensiepen, January 10, 1963.

28. Annette Weinke, *Die Verfolgung von NS-Tätern im geteilten Deutschland: Vergangenheitsbewältigung 1949–1969 oder eine deutsch-deutsche Beziehungsgeschichte im kalten Krieg* (Paderborn: Ferdinand Schöningh, 2002), 160.

29. "Wort des Rates der EKD zu den NS Verbrecherprozessen vom 13. März 1963," in Henkys, *Die nationalsozialistischen Gewaltverbrechen*, 339–342, 340 . The biblical citation is incorrect and should be Prov. 14:34. The translation is from the NRSV.

30. Henkys, *Die nationalsozialistischen Gewaltverbrechen*, 339.

31. Schlingensiepen repeatedly requested permission to serve time in prison alongside Nazi convicts. His applications to join Nazi convicts were declined because of his severe disabilities. "Pfarrer will freiwillig ins Zuchthaus, aber das Justizministerium lehnt ab," *Süddeutsche Zeitung*, August 14, 1965. He also appealed to Pastor Lothar Kreyssig, who founded Action Reconciliation in 1958, to call on older volunteers of Action Reconciliation to serve in prisons as a way to show "solidarity of guilt." AEKIR, 7 NL 016-58, letter, Pastor Lothar Kreyssig to multiple recipients, March 17, 1966.

32. AEKIR, 7 NL 016, undated draft, "Die Unverjährbarkeit von Mord und Völkermord und die Menschlichkeit für die Unmenschen."

33. AEKIR, 7 NL 016-65, letter, Johannes Miesel to Schlingensiepen, August 5, 1965. Cf. SS medical doctor Werner Scheu, who wrote: "It is not easy to be a criminal if one does not feel like one; this requires more than readiness to repent [*Bußfertigkeit*]." AEKIR, 7 NL 016, letter, Werner Scheu to Schlingensiepen, July 4, 1966.

34. 3 Ks1/57, Regional Court Hagen, Verdict, November 17, 1959, C. F. Rüters, Fritz Bauer, et al., eds., *Justiz und NS-Verbrechen: Sammlung deutscher Strafurteile wegen nationalsozialistischer Tötungsverbrechen* (Amsterdam: Amsterdam University Press, 1968–1981), vol. 16, 167–248, 218. On May 5, 1961, he was sentenced on appeal to four years an as accomplice. Rüters et al., *Justiz und NS-Verbrechen*, vol. 17, 279–310.

35. Rüters et al., *Justiz und NS-Verbrechen*, vol. 16, 218; cf. vol. 17, 279–310.

36. AEKIR, 7 NL 016-65, letter, Miesel to Schlingensiepen, August 5, 1965.

37. AEKIR, 7 NL 016-65, letter, Miesel to Schlingensiepen, August 5, 1965.

38. His codefendant Wolfgang Wetzling argued similarly: "ich habe zwar der SS angehört, aber nicht irgendeiner KZ Wachmannschaft oder einem Judenvernichtungs-kommando, sondern…ausschliesslich als Truppenrichter…Dadurch bin ich in die Lage gekommen, am 20. März 1945 an einer Erschießung von

sowjetrussischen Fremdarbeitern beiderlei Geschlechts mitwirken zu müssen.... Die Fremdarbeitermassierung stellte eine schwerwiegende Bedrohung der allgemeinen Sicherheit dar..." AEKIR 7 NL 016-114, letter, Wetzling to Schlingensiepen, July 19, 1970.

39. AEKIR, 7 NL 016-65, letter, Miesel to Schlingensiepen, August 5, 1965.

40. AEKIR, 7 NL 016, Anonymous, "Uns wird geschrieben: Ein Brief aus dem Zuchthaus," *Sonntagsblatt* 26 (1965).

41. AEKIR, 7 NL 016-65, letter, Miesel to Schlingensiepen, August 5, 1965.

42. AEKIR, 7 NL 016-17, letter, Otto Bradfisch to Schlingensiepen, January 1, 1967. See also Peter Klein, "Der Mordgehilfe: Schuld und Sühne des Dr. Otto Bradfisch," in *Die Gestapo nach 1945: Karrieren, Konflikten, Konstruktionen,* ed. Klaus-Michael Mallmann and Andrej Angrick (Darmstadt: Wissenschaftliche Buchgesellschaft, 2009), 221–234.

43. 22 Ks 1/61, Regional Court Munich, Verdict, in Rüters et al., *Justiz und NS-Verbrechen,* vol. 17, 658–708.

44. Schlingensiepen challenged Bradfisch's opinion that God would automatically grant forgiveness and "painlessly store" away his sins "which you resist steadfastly to name concretely.... Forgive me... if I should do you an injustice, but for a chaplain who really wants to help another, everything depends on maintaining his love and his commitment to truth mercilessly on this issue. Otherwise he would sell make-believe grace, which in truth is no grace." AEKIR, 7 NL 016-17, letter, Schlingensiepen to Bradfisch, July 16, 1965. Schlingensiepen supported his parole applications citing health reasons (letter, October 16, 1970).

45. Rudolf Aschenauer, ed., *Ich, Adolf Eichmann: Ein historischer Zeugenbericht* (Leoni am Starnberger See: Druffel Verlag 1980), 15.

46. AEKIR, 7 NL 016, Protokoll der Konferenz der Evangelischen Strafanstaltspfarrer Deutschlands, March 29–April 3, 1965.

47. "Brief der Arbeitsgemeinschaft der Bergischen Gefängnisgemeinde an den Rat der EKD, September 7, 1963," in Henkys, *Die nationalsoziaistischen Gewaltverbrechen,* 342–345.

48. AEKIR, 7 NL 016, Dr. Weber, Antwort der Redaktion, *Juristenzeitung,* June 12, 1967.

49. See the coffee drink dubbed *Pharisäer,* which covers the smell of rum with a generous topping of whipped cream.

50. AEKIR, 7 NL 016-17, letter, Otto Bradfisch to Schlingensiepen, July 11, 1965.

51. This term was introduced by Daniel Goldhagen to distinguish German genocidal antisemitism. *Hitler's Willing Executioners: Ordinary Germans and the Holocaust* (New York: Knopf, 1996).

52. Paragraph 130 made *Volksverhetzung* punishable with prison sentences up to five years. http://bundesrecht.juris.de/stgb/BJNR001270871BJNE028206377.html.

53. Peter Krause, *Der Eichmann Prozeß in der deutschen Presse* (Frankfurt am Main: Campus, 2002), 115.

54. Declaration of the Kirchentag 1961, Krause, *Der Eichmann Prozeß*, 119.

55. AEKIR, 7 NL 016-57, letter, Dr. Erhard Kroeger to Schlingensiepen, May 1, 1966, 2.

56. Verdict, Regional Court Tübingen, Rüters et al., *Justiz und NS-Verbrechen*, vol. 32, 705–734.

57. AEKIR, 7 NL 016-57, letter, Dr. Erhard Kroeger to Schlingensiepen, May 1, 1966, 19.

58. AEKIR, 7 NL 016-57, letter, Kroeger, 19.

59. AEKIR, 7 NL 016-57, letter, Kroeger, 18.

60. AEKIR, 7 NL 016-57, letter, Kroeger, 8–9.

61. AEKIR, 7 NL 016-57, letter, Kroeger, 4.

62. AEKIR, 7 NL 016-57, letter, Kroeger, 3.

63. AEKIR, 7 NL 016-67, letter, Robert Mulka to Schlingensiepen, June 16, 1965.

64. AEKIR, 7 NL 016-67, letter, Mulka, June 16, 1965.

65. AEKIR, 7 NL 016-67, letter, Mulka, June 16, 1965.

66. Mulka lied about his party membership. The court was in possession of his file that dated his Nazi party membership to February 1, 1940. Rüters et al., *Justiz und NS-Verbrechen*, vol. 21, 362–887, 426.

67. Irmtrud Wojak, *Eichmanns Memoiren: Ein kritischer Essay* (Frankfurt am Main: Campus Verlag, 2001).

68. David Cesarani, *Eichmann: His Life and Crimes* (London: William Heinemann, 2004), 219.

69. Cesarani, *Eichmann*, 219.

70. Aschenauer, *Ich, Adolf Eichmann*, 501.

71. Aschenauer, *Ich, Adolf Eichmann*, 496.

72. Less W. Avner introduction to *Eichmann Interrogated: Transcripts from the Archives of the Israeli Police*, ed. Jochen von Lang and Claus Sybill (New York: Vintage Books, 1983), vi.

73. Hannah Arendt, *Eichmann in Jerusalem: A Report on the Banality of Evil* (New York: Penguin, 1963), 248.

74. Arendt, *Eichmann in Jerusalem*, 278.

75. Cf. the misleading translation in William L. Hull, *Struggle for a Soul: The Untold Story of a Minister's Final Effort to Convert Adolf Eichmann* (Garden City, NJ: Doubleday, 1963), 159.

CHAPTER 6

1. In general, the Hebrew Bible opposes the punishment of children for the sins of their fathers. There are some exceptions, e.g. King David's rape/adultery with Bathsheba, the wife of Uriah, which results in the death of the child

(2 Sam. 12:14). Bathsheba's second son, however, is King Solomon (2 Sam. 12:24).

2. Lars Rensmann, "Collective Guilt, National Identity, and Political Processes in Contemporary Germany," in *Collective Guilt: International Perspectives*, ed. Nyla Branscombe and Bertjan Doosje (Cambridge: Cambridge University Press, 2004), 169–189.

3. Dan Bar-On, in *Legacy of Silence: Encounters with Children of the Third Reich* (Cambridge: Harvard University Press, 1989), broke a virtual taboo when he interviewed children of perpetrators about their family lives and intergenerational communication in the 1980s. "Silence" became the catchphrase that described the lack of conversation in German families after 1945. Bar-On diagnosed the existence of a "double wall phenomenon" that served to reinforce pervasive ignorance and "postwar silence about the Nazi years" (328). Parents didn't want to share their involvement, and the children were not prepared to listen. The title of an anthology edited by Barbara B. Heimannsberg and C. J. Schmidt, *The Collective Silence: German Identity and the Legacy of Shame* (San Francisco: Jossey-Bass, 1993), similarly articulates the problem in intergenerational dynamics. The generally accepted hypothesis of an "unspeakable" past was first challenged by Robert Moeller in *War Stories* (2001) wherein he argued that Germans were not silent about the past but rather remembered it selectively: "West Germans remembered key parts of the first half of the 1940s with extraordinary passion and emotion...remembering selectively was not the same as forgetting." Robert G. Moeller, *War Stories: The Search for a Usable Past in the Federal Republic of Germany* (Berkeley: University of California Press, 2001), 16. Recent scholarship has moved beyond the either/or of either forgetting or remembering to trace the convoluted constructions of biographical memory that served to induct subsequent generations into the guilty legacy of genocidal perpetration.

4. AEKIR, 7 NL 016-117-67, letter of Artur Wilke to his son, undated.

5. Cf. Erin McGlothlin, *Second Generation Holocaust Literature: Legacies of Survival and Perpetration* (Rochester, NY: Camden House, 2006); Peter Sichrovsky, *Born Guilty: Children of Nazi Families* (New York: Basic Books, 1988); Dörte von Westernhagen, *Die Kinder der Täter: Das Dritte Reich und die Generation danach* (Munich: Kösel Verlag, 1987); Barbara B. Heimannsberg and C. J. Schmidt, eds., *The Collective Silence: German Identity and the Legacy of Shame* (San Francisco: Jossey-Bass, 1993); M. S. Bergmann and M. E. Jucovy, eds., *Generations of the Holocaust* (New York: Columbia University Press, 1982); Björn Krondorfer, *Remembrance and Reconciliation: Encounters between Young Jews and Germans* (New Haven: Yale University Press, 1995); Brigitte Rommelspacher, *Schuldlos-Schuldig? Wie sich junge Frauen mit Antisemitismus auseinandersetzen* (Hamburg: Konkret, 1995); Ulla Roberts, *Spuren der NS-Zeit im Leben der Kinder und Enkel: Drei Generationen im Gespräch* (Munich: Kösel, 1998); Bar-On, *Legacy of Silence*; Gabriele Rosenthal, "Nationalsozialismus und Antisemitismus im

intergenerationellen Dialog," in *Der Holocaust im Leben von drei Generation: Familien von Überlebenden der Shoah und von Nazi-Tätern*, ed. Gabriele Rosenthal (Hamburg: Edition psychosozial, 1997).

6. AEKIR, 7 NL 016-117-67, letter of Artur Wilke to his son, undated, 72.

7. James E. McNutt, "Adolf Schlatter and the Jews," *German Studies Review* 26 (May 2003): 353–370; James E. McNutt, "Vessels of Wrath Prepared to Perish: Adolf Schlatter and the Spiritual Extermination of the Jews," *Theology Today* 63 (2006): 176–190; Anders Gerdmar, *Roots of Theological Anti-semitism: German Biblical Interpretation and the Jews, from Herder and Semmler to Kittel and Bultmann* (Leiden: Brill, 2008); Leonore Siegele Wenschkewitz, "Adolf Schlatters Sicht des Judentums im politischen Kontext: Die Schrift *Wird der Jude über uns siegen?*" in *Christlicher Antijudaismus und Antisemitismus: Theologische und kirchliche Programme deutscher Christen*, ed. Leonore Siegele Wenschkewitz (Frankfurt am Main: Haag + Herrchen, 1994), 95–111.

8. After several promotions, he reached the rank of *SS-Haupsturmbannführer* on April 20, 1942. C. F. Rüters, Fritz Bauer, et al., eds., *Justiz und NS-Verbrechen: Sammlung deutscher Strafurteile wegen nationalsozialistischer Tötungsverbrechen* (Amsterdam: Amsterdam University Press, 1968–1981), vol. 19, 178.

9. AEKIR, 7 NL 016-117, letter, Artur Wilke to Pastor Müller, April 25, 1964, 8.

10. Rüters et al., *Justiz und NS-Verbrechen*, vol. 19, 158–315.

11. Rüters et al., *Justiz und NS-Verbrechen*, vol. 19, 313.

12. AEKIR, 7 NL 016-117, letter, Artur Wilke to Pastor Müller, April 25, 1964, 13.

13. AEKIR, 7 NL 016-117, letter, Artur Wilke to Müller, April 25, 1964, 14.

14. They married in 1940 and produced four children, one of whom died. Rüters et al., *Justiz und NS-Verbrechen*, vol. 19, 178.

15. Rüters et al., *Justiz und NS-Verbrechen*, vol. 19, 178.

16. Wilke faced two additional indictments, namely bigamy and fraud for the falsification of documents (his birth certificates, teacher qualifications, adoption proceedings). His *Verbeamtung* (tenure) was revoked.

17. AEKIR, 7 NL 016-117, letter, Dr. med. Ursula Wilke to Schlingensiepen, May 31, 1964. Schlingensiepen confirmed the mother's concern in a letter to state's attorney Barbara Just-Dahlmann: "am meisten leidet ein eben konfimierter Junge, der an dem Vater offenbar besonders hängt, und um den er sich in besonderer Weise bekümmert haben muss." BAK, NL 415 Just 000004, Letter Schlingensiepen to Just-Dahlmann, June 16, 1964.

18. AEKIR, 7 NL 016-117, letter, Wilke to Schlingensiepen, June 12, 1965; he used the English term "problem child."

19. In a phone conversation, Dr. Ferdinand Schlingensiepen, son of Hermann Schlingensiepen, confirmed that Wolfdietrich Wilke joined the family during vacations. Hermann Schlingensiepen mentioned that Wilke's "splendid son"

stayed with the family for Pentecost. AEKIR 7 NL 016-67, letter, Schlingen-siepen to Pastor Hans Georg Müller, June 25, 1966.

20. Letter, Wilke, 77.

21. Bischof Stempel, *EKD Beauftragter für Kriegsverurteilte*, visited Wilke on August 23, 1966, and presented him with a Vulgate Latin Bible.

22. Letter, Wilke, 46.

23. Letter, Wilke, 46.

24. AEKIR, 7 NL 016-117, Letter, Wilke to Pastor Müller, April 25, 1964.

25. Letter, Wilke, 5.

26. Letter, Wilke, 14–15.

27. Letter, Wilke, 46.

28. Letter, Wilke, 27–28.

29. Letter, Wilke, 46.

30. Claus-Dieter Krohn, "Studentenbewegung und das 'andere Deutschland,'" in *Dynamische Zeiten*, ed. Axel Schild, Detlef Siegfried, and Karl Christian Lammers (Hamburg: Hans Christians Verlag, 2000), 702ff.

31. A. S. Markovits and R. S. Hayden, "Holocaust before and after the Event: Reactions in Germany and Austria," in *Germans and Jews since the Holocaust*, ed. Anson Rabinbach and Jack Zipes (New York: Holmes and Meier, 1986), 234–257.

32. Letter, Wilke, 50.

33. Letter, Wilke, 43. Given his indictment on bigamy, Wilke's stance on sexual morality confirms Dagmar Herzog's analysis of conservatism in the 1950s as a reaction to the sexual libertinism of National Socialism. "The Sexual Revolution and the Legacies of the Nazi Past," in *Coping with the Nazi Past: West German Debates on Nazism and Generational Conflict 1955–1975*, ed. Phillip Gassert and Alan Steinweis (New York: Berghahn, 2006), 161–176.

34. Letter, Wilke, 43.

35. Letter, Wilke, 32.

36. Letter, Wilke, 10.

37. Hannah Schissler, ed., *Miracle Years: A Cultural History of West Germany, 1949–1968* (Princeton, NJ: Princeton University Press, 2001).

38. Letter, Wilke, 50.

39. Ernst Klee, Willi Dressen, and Volker Riess, eds., *The Good Old Days: The Holocaust as Seen by Its Perpetrators and Bystanders*, trans. Deborah Burnstone (New York: Konecky and Konecky, 1996).

40. Letter, Wilke, 11–12.

41. Letter, Wilke, 71.

42. Letter, Wilke, 50.

43. Letter, Wilke, 44.

44. Letter, Wilke, 44.

45. Eichmann considered himself an "honorary member" of the Roman Catholic Church out of gratitude for the assistance of Catholic priests in his flight, but he said, "In reality I belonged to no church." Quoted in Gerald Steinacher, *Nazis auf der Flucht: Wie Kriegsverbrecher über Italien nach Übersee entkamen* (Innsbruck: StudienVerlag, 2008), 167. He affirmed his commitment to Nazi *Gottglaube* in his last words.

46. Letter, Wilke, 37.

47. Letter, Wilke, 7.

48. Letter, Wilke, 45.

49. Letter, Wilke, 61.

50. Letter, Wilke, 45.

51. AEKIR, 7 NL 016-117, letter, Wilke to Pastor Müller, April 25, 1964, 7.

52. The EKD office to provide pastoral care and assistance to Nazi defendants and convicts, staffed by Bishop Stempel, was called "Plenipotentiary for War Convicts."

53. Barbara Just-Dahlmann, *Die Gehilfen: NS-Verbrechen und die Justiz nach 1945* (Frankfurt am Main: Athenäum, 1989).

54. Reinhard Henkys, *Die nationalsozialistischen Gewaltverbrechen: Geschichte und Gericht* (Stuttgart: Kreuz Verlag, 1964).

55. Wilke piggybacked on the Wehrmacht's postwar strategy of presenting itself as military force untainted by Nazi atrocities. The Wehrmacht strived to defend its "clean" record as a military force, especially after West Germany's remilitarization and integration into the Western military alliance NATO. This narrative remained largely unchallenged until the *Wehrmachtsaustellung* in the 1990s. Hannes Heer, *Vom Verschwinden der Täter: Der Vernichtungskrieg fand statt, aber keiner war dabei* (Berlin: Aufbau Verlag, 2004).

56. Letter, Wilke, 41.

57. Letter, Wilke, 30.

58. Letter, Wilke, 30–31.

59. Letter, Wilke, 30–31.

60. AEKIR, 7 NL 016-117, letter, Wilke to Schlingensiepen, June 12, 1965.

61. Michael Geyer, "Cold War Angst: The Case of West German Opposition to Rearmament and Nuclear Weapons," in Schissler, *The Miracle Years*, 385.

62. Geyer, "Cold War Angst," 385–6.

63. Letter, Wilke, 44.

64. Letter, Wilke, 33.

65. Geyer, "Cold War Angst," 397.

66. Letter, Wilke, 48.

67. Letter, Wilke, 68.

68. AEKIR, 7 NL 016-117, letter, Wilke to Pastor Müller, April 25 1964, 14. He failed to mention that two children of his first marriage had immigrated to the United States. His son was serving in the U.S. Army in Missouri.

69. Letter, Wilke, 29.

70. Letter, Wilke, 56.

71. Letter, Wilke, 37, 74.

72. Letter, Wilke, 37.

73. His reference to Uriel ben Nathan Blau presumably refers to an Ultra-Orthodox, anti-Zionist rabbi from the Jerusalem neighborhood of Mea Shearim who gained media notoriety after he was ostracized for marrying a French convert from Catholicism in 1965.

74. Bernd-A. Rusinek, "Von der Entdeckung der NS-Vergangenheit zum generellen Faschismusverdacht - akademische Diskurse in der Bundesrepublik der 60er Jahre," in *Dynamische Zeiten: Die 60er Jahre in den beiden deutschen Gesellschaften*, ed. Axel Schild and Detlef Siegfried (Hamburg: Hans Christians Verlag, 2000), 114–148; Detlef Siegfried, "Don't Look Back in Anger: Youth Pop Culture, and the Nazi Past," in Gassert and Steinweis, *Coping with the Nazi Past*, 144–161.

75. Wolfgang Kraushaar, *Die Bombe in Jüdischen Gemeindehaus* (Hamburg: Hamburger Edition: 2005).

76. Andrei Markovits, *Uncouth Nation: Why Europe Hates America* (Princeton, NJ: Princeton University Press, 2007); Wolfgang Kraushaar, "Philosemitismus und Antisemitismus: Zum Konflikt zwischen Horkheimer, Adorno und der Studentenbewegung," in *Das Echo des Holocaust: Pädagogische Aspekte des Erinnern*, ed. Helmut Schreier and Mattias Heyl (Hamburg: Kraemer, 1994), 71–97, 93.

77. Katharina von Kellenbach, *Anti-Judaism in Feminist Religious Writings* (Atlanta: Scholars Press, 1994).

78. http://www.freiburger-rundbrief.de/de/.

79. http://www.iccj.org.

80. http://www.deutscher-koordinierungsrat.de.

81. http://www.jcrelations.net/Der_ungek__ndigte_Bund.1297.0.html?L=2.

82. http://www.asf-ev.de/en.

83. http://www.vatican.va/archive/hist_councils/ii_vatican_council/documents/vat-ii_decl_19651028_nostra-aetate_en.html.

84. Christian Hoffmann, "Christlicher Antijudaismus und moderner Antisemitismus: Zusammenhänge und Differenzen als Problem der historischen Antisemitismusforschung," in *Christlicher Antijudaismus und Antisemitismus: theologische und kirchliche Programme deutscher Christen*, ed. Leonore Siegele Wenschkewitz (Frankfurt am Main: Haag + Herrchen, 1994), 293–319.

85. Letter, Wilke, 31–32.

86. Letter, Wilke, 31.

87. Letter, Wilke to Schlingensiepen, June 12, 1965.

88. Ralph Giordano, *Die zweite Schuld oder von der Last ein Deutscher zu sein* (Munich: Knaur, 1990).

89. Letter, Wilke, 70.

90. AEKIR, 7 NL 016-117, letter, Schlingensiepen to Pastor Müller, June 25, 1966, 1.

91. Letter, Schlingensiepen to Müller.

92. Letter, Schlingensiepen to Müller, 2.

93. Letter, Schlingensiepen to Müller, 2.

94. Gabriele Rosenthal argues that "separation from the parents, which is often accompanied by self-hatred, can also be interpreted as attachment to the parents." *Der Holocaust im Leben von drei Generationen*, 22.

95. Children whose last names were identifiable were forced to develop a response to questions. Cf. Norbert Lebert and Stephan Lebert, *Denn Du trägst meinen Namen* (Munich: Goldmann Verlag 2002).

96. Renate Wald, *Mein Vater Robert Ley: Meine Erinnerungen und Vaters Geschichte* (Nürmbrecht: Martine Galunder-Verlag, 2004), 142.

97. Gerald L. Posner, *Hitler's Children: Sons and Daughters of Leaders of the Third Reich Talk about their Fathers and Themselves* (New York: Random House, 1991), 217.

98. Gudrun Himmler took a distinctly different path from her great niece Kathrin Himmler, who published *Die Brüder Himmler: Eine deutsche Familie* (Frankfurt am Main: Fischer Verlag, 2005). In her portrait of a German family, Kathrin Himmler explores the milieu in which her great-uncle Heinrich Himmler grew up "with a horrifying inability to feel empathy" and the drive to turn the SS into a powerful machine of destruction and annihilation. She self-consciously reflects on "this stickiness that consisted of vague half-truths, belittlement, misinterpretation, even falsifications, like a thick fog. Its 'befuddling' effect always held something seductive and turned everyone into accomplices of varying degrees in the maintenance of family myths" (293). Midway through the book project, her Israeli boyfriend and grandson of Polish Jews becomes the father of her son. Her moral extrication becomes the basis for the future of her son. Other second-generation accounts include Richard von Schirach, *Der Schatten meines Vaters* (Munich: Carl Hanser Verlag 2005), Martin Bormann, *Leben gegen Schatten: Gelebte Zeit—geschenkte Zeit. Begegnungen—Erfahrungen—Folgerungen* (Paderborn: Bonifatius Druckerei, 1996); Wiebke Bruns, *Meines Vaters Land: Geschichte einer deutschen Familie* (Munich: Econ Verlag, 2004); Lebert and Lebert, *Denn Du trägst meinen Namen*; Wolf-Rüdiger Heß, *Rudolf Heß: "Ich bereue nichts"* (Graz: Leopold Stocker Verlag, 1998).

99. Oliver Schröm and Anrea Röpke, *Stille Hilfe für braune Kameraden: Das geheime Netzwerk der Alt- und Neonazis* (Berlin: Christoph Links Verlag, 2001); cf. the neo-Nazi website White Pride World Wide, http://www.stormfront.org/forum/t687600/(June 13, 2010).

100. Niklas Frank, *In the Shadow of the Reich*, trans. Arthur Wensinger and Carole Clew-Hoey (New York: Knopf, 1991), 371.

101. Niklas Frank, *Meine deutsche Mutter* (Munich: Bertelsmann Verlag, 2005).

102. Frank, *In the Shadow of the Reich*; Frank, *Vater: Eine Abrechnung* (Munich: Bertelsman Verlag, 1987); Frank, *Meine deutsche Mutter.*

103. McGlothlin, *Second Generation Holocaust Literature,* 182.

104. McGlothlin, *Second Generation Holocaust Literature,* 182.

105. He specifically criticizes Martin Bormann and Richard von Schirach; Niklas Frank, "Keine Versöhnung—Niemals," *Die Welt online,* November 5, 2005, http://www.welt.de/print-welt/article175601/Keine_Versoehnung_niemals. html.

106. Posner, *Hitler's Children,* 216.

107. Quoted in McGlothlin, *Second Generation Holocaust Literature,* 155.

108. Quoted in McGlothlin, *Second Generation Holocaust Literature,* 155.

109. Schirach, *Der Schatten meines Vaters.*

110. Beate Niemann, *Mein guter Vater: Mein Leben mit seiner Vergangenheit* (Berlin: Hentrich & Hentrich, 2005), 190.

111. Niemann, *Mein guter Vater,* 121–128.

112. Martin Pollack, *Dead Man in the Bunker: Discovering My Father,* trans. William Hobson (London: Faber, 2008).

113. Martin Pollack, *Der Tote im Bunker: Bericht über meinen Vater* (Vienna: Paul Zsolnay Verlag, 2004), 174.

114. Pollack, *Der Tote im Bunker,* 172–73.

115. Michael Wildt, afterword to Himmler, *Die Brüder Himmler,* 299.

CHAPTER 7

1. Hitler wrote: "The German girl is State subject and only becomes a State citizen when she marries." Adolf Hitler, *Mein Kampf,* trans. John Chamberlain et al. (New York: Reynal & Hitchcock, 1940), 659. Cf. Andrea Bieler, "Aspekte nationalsozialistischer Frauenpolitik in ihrer Bedeutung für die Theologinnen," in *Darum wagt es Schwestern,* ed. Göttinger Frauenforschungsprojekt zur Geschichte der Theologinnen (Neukirchen-Vluyn: Neukirchener Verlag, 1994), 249.

2. Jill Stephenson, *Women and Nazi Society* (New York: Barnes and Noble, 1975), 178.

3. Gisela Bock, *Zwangssterilisation im Nationalsozialismus: Studien zur Rassenpolitik und Frauenpolitik* (Opladen: Westdeutscher Verlag, 1986).

4. As Gudrun Schwarz pointed out, Heinrich Himmler was quite aware of the emotional toll of mass murder on his men, and he encouraged the presence of wives and families close to concentration camp sites and execution sites, frequent visits by women to deployment sites, and home vacations in order to normalize and stabilize the gruesome work of the men. Women fulfilled an important role in the extermination business—and continued to do so after the war. By upholding the normalcy of family life and reassuring the men of

the ordinariness of everyday life, they served a vital stabilizing function in the successful execution of genocide. Gudrun Schwarz, *Eine Frau an seiner Seite: Ehefrauen in der SS-Sippengemeinschaft* (Hamburg: Hamburger edition, 1997), 112–169.

5. These files were captured by U.S. military forces and are accessible in NACP, RG 242: BDC Microfilm Publications A 3343, Series RS, RusHA files.

6. Leonie Wagner, "Totalitäre Projektionen: Zum Verhältnis von Weiblichkeit und Politik im Nationalsozialismus," in *Gebrochene Kontinuitäten? Zur Rolle und Bedeutung des Geschlechterverhältnisses in der Entwicklung des Nationalsozialismus*, ed. Ilse Korotin and Barbara Serloth (Innsbruck: StudienVerlag, 2000), 131–151.

7. Daniel Goldhagen was among the first to describe the presence of wives and girlfriends at killing sites. He was especially disturbed by the pregnant Vera Wohlauf. *Hitler's Willing Executioners: Ordinary Germans and the Holocaust* (New York: Knopf, 1996), 241–244; Cf. Silke Wenk, "Rhetoriken der Pornografisierung," in *Gedächtnis und Geschlecht: Deutungsmuser in Darstellungen des nationalsozialistischen Genozids*, ed. Insa Eschenbach (Frankfurt am Main: Campus Verlag, 2002), 269–291; Schwarz, *Eine Frau an seiner Seite*, 99–200.

8. Gudrun Schwarz, "Frauen in der SS: Sippenverband und Frauenkorps," in *Zwischen Karriere und Verfolgung: Handlungsräume von Frauen im nationalsozialistischen Deutschland*, ed. Kristen Heinsohn (New York: Campus Verlag, 1997), 239.

9. My ethical and theological questions build on the work of feminist historians, especially Schwarz, *Eine Frau an seiner Seite*; Claudia Koonz, *Mothers in the Fatherland: Women, the Family, and Nazi Politics* (New York: St. Martin's, 1987); Sigrid Weigel, *Bilder des kulturellen Gedächtnisses: Beiträge zur Gegenwartsliteratur* (Dülmen-Hidingsel: Tende, 1994), 198–231; Lerke Gravenhorst and Carmen Tatschmurat, eds., *Töchter-Fragen NS-Frauen-Geschichte* (Freiburg im Breisgau: Kore, 1990).

10. Anna Maria Sigmund, *Frauen der Nazis*, translated as *Women of the Third Reich* (Richmond Hill, ON: NDE, 2000), 52. Sigmund describes the grandiose wedding, planned according to the couple's desires, including the stipulation that the sermon was not to exceed five minutes.

11. Emmy Göring, *An der Seite meines Mannes: Begebenheiten und Bekenntnisse* (Göttingen: Verlag K. W. Schütz, 1967), 117. Biblical quotations are from the NRSV.

12. Schwarz, "Frauen in der SS," 224.

13. LKAN Pfarreien Kleine Bestände III/17, no. 11, letter, Clara Schubert to General Lucius D. Clay, August 4, 1948. Heinz Hermann Schubert was convicted in the Ohlendorf trial in Nuremberg, released, and twice rearrested. Clara Schubert became politically active in the solidarity network Stille Hilfe. Cf. Oliver Schröm and Andrea Röpke, *Stille Hilfe für braune Kameraden: Das geheime Netzwerk der Alt- und Neonazis* (Berlin: Links Verlag, 2001).

14. AEKIR, 7 NL 016-30, letter, Schlingensiepen to chaplain Hans Guther, October 1, 1969. In a lecture on pastoral care for Nazi perpetrators, Schlingensiepen affirmed that "Die Familien der Verurteilten sind meist intakt, oft sogar kirchlich." "Jahrestagung der evangelischen Gefängnispfarrer in Freudenstadt," April 25, 1966, quoted in Pastor Hans Freitag, "Erfahrungen mit NS-Verurteilten," unpublished memoir, 126.

15. LKAN Pfarreien Kleine Bestände III/17, no. 10, letter, Ms. Klüttgen to Eckardt, November 3, 1948.

16. Ludwig Kluettgen was convicted in the Dachau trials for the execution of two American pilots in September 1944. http://www.online.uni-marburg.de/icwc/dachau/000-012-1502.pdf.

17. LKAN Pfarreien Kleine Bestände III/17, no. 10, letter, Berta Piorkowski to Eckardt, December 17, 1948.

18. LKAN Pfarreien Kleine Bestände III/17, no. 10, letter, Eckardt to Berta Piorkowski, October 22, 1948.

19. NACP, RG 549.2 "Executee Files," Box 10.

20. Koonz, *Mothers in the Fatherland*, 418.

21. AEKIR, 7 NL 016-42, letter, Adelheid Hans to Schlingensiepen, August 16, 1966.

22. Hermann Langbein, *Der Auschwitz-Prozeß: Eine Dokumentation*, vol. 2 (Frankfurt am Main: Verlag Neue Kritik), 616–618.

23. AEKIR, 7 NL 016-62, letter, Susanne Lucas to Schlingensiepen, April 15, 1967.

24. AEKIR, 7 NL 016-62, letter, Lucas to Schlingensiepen.

25. Langbein, *Der Auschwitz-Prozeß*, 642.

26. Devin O. Pendas, *The Frankfurt Auschwitz Trial, 1963–1965* (Cambridge: Cambridge University Press, 2006), 227.

27. AEKIR, 7 NL 016, Hermann Schlingensiepen, "Unverjährbarkeit von Mord und Völkermord—aber mehr Menschlichkeit auch für Mörder," 2.

28. AEKIR, 7 NL 016-41, letter, Helene Greiffenberger to Schlingensiepen, June 6, 1962. He was convicted by Regional Court Berlin Moabit, June 22, 1962, C. F. C.Rüters, Fritz Bauer, et al., eds., *Justiz und NS-Verbrechen: Sammlung deutscher Strafurteile wegen nationalsozialistischer Tötungsverbrechen* (Amsterdam: Amsterdam University Press, 1968–1981), vol. 18, 603–645. Schlingensiepen supported him enthusiastically because Greiffenberger had expressed remorse and affirmed a religious conversion to Christianity. But neither his remorse nor his return to Christianity is entirely credible. When Schlingensiepen requested that the Protestant bishop of Bavaria, Hermann Dietzfelbinger, show his support, Dietzfelbinger responded that several attempts for a visit were rebuffed: "At the time he politely but resolutely rejected any church assistance. The resident Catholic priest attempted to visit the remaining family but could never encounter them at home." AEKIR, 7 NL 016-41, letter, Dietzfelbinger to Schlingensiepen, May 15, 1964.

29. EZAB, LKR 2451, Seelsorge in den Zivil-Interniertenlager 1945–1946, Memorandum des Lagerkirchenrats der evang. Gemeinde des Arbeits- und Internierungslagers Regensburg 9 an den Rat der EKD, November 1946.

30. For the Jewish observer Shalom ben Chorin, Eichmann's inability to acknowledge his crimes sealed his condemnation. In a letter to Schlingensiepen, he wrote: "I had occasion to observe the man for a long time during the trial. He remained entirely untouched and in the unshakable conviction to have done his duty as a recipient of orders [*Befehlsempfänger*]. The imperviousness of such a creature seems unimaginable to you" (November 28, 1963). For Shalom ben Chorin, "denial can close the gates to tshuvah/repentance . . . and hence all hope had to be abandoned" (January 18, 1964). AEKIR, 7 NL 016-84. Schlingensiepen countered that it is up to God whether "a heart is closed, as in the case of Pharaoh before Moses, or opened, as in the case of the king of Niniveh under the impression of the sermon of repentance by the prophet Jonah" (AEKIR, 7 NL 016-81, letter, Schlingensiepen to Robert Servatius, Eichmann's defense attorney, June 15, 1962).

31. Letter, Eichmann to Hull, May 15, 1962, appendix to William L. Hull, *Struggle for a Soul: The Untold Story of a Minister's Final Effort to Convert Adolf Eichmann* (Garden City, NJ: Doubleday, 1963), 149.

32. Hull, *Struggle for a Soul*, 86; also 133: "He believes that God is not a God of judgment and punishment but only of love."

33. Hull, *Struggle for a Soul*, 83, 133.

34. Koonz, *Mothers in the Fatherland*, 418.

35. Hull, *Struggle for a Soul*, 156.

36. Hull, *Struggle for a Soul*, 143.

37. Hull, *Struggle for a Soul*, 143.

38. Hull, *Struggle for a Soul*, 58.

39. Hull, *Struggle for a Soul*, 157.

40. The "love of enemies" that underlies theories of nonviolent resistance does not condone evil, but practices strategies of confrontation that eschew antagonism and violence and arouse an enemy's humanity and intrinsic morality.

41. Alan Torrance, "The Theological Grounds for Advocating Forgiveness and Reconciliation in the Sociopolitical Realm," in *The Politics of Past Evil: Religion, Reconciliation and the Dilemmas of Transitional Justice*, ed. Daniel Philpott (Notre Dame, In: University of Notre Dame Press, 2006), 45–87, 51.

42. Torrance "Theological Grounds," 51.

43. Schlingensiepen's conservatism is evident in his suggestion that murder and adultery carry equal weight in the Ten Commandments and warned that "the postwar world replaced one set of evil (murder) with another set (adultery, sexual lust, lack of discipline)." AEKIR 7 NL 016-64, letter, Schlingensiepen to prison chaplains Merkt, Müller, Knepper, June 3, 1965.

44. LKAN Pfarreien Kleine Bestände III/17, no. 12, Court decision, Marital Case E.W. Bielefeld, April 2, 1948.

45. LKAN Pfarreien Kleine Bestände III/17, no. 12, Ruling Bielefeld, April 2, 1948.

46. LKAN Pfarreien Kleine Bestände III/17, no. 12, Ruling Bielefeld, April 2, 1948.

47. LKAN Pfarreien Kleine Bestände III/17, no. 12, Ruling Bielefeld, April 2, 1948.

48. LKAN Pfarreien Kleine Bestände III/17, no. 9, letter, Pastor Eckardt to Rosa Greil, July 7, 1948. Michael Greil, born 1908, joined the Waffen-SS in 1940 and was sentenced to four years as an SS guard in Dachau. http://www.online.uni-marburg.de/icwc/dachau/000-050-0002-084.pdf.

49. http://www.online.uni-marburg.de/icwc/dachau/000-050-0002-084.pdf.

50. LKAN Pfarreien Kleine Bestände III/17, no. 9, letter, Eckardt to Pastor Waldhausen, re: Alfred Hofmann, November 1948.

51. LKAN Pfarreien Kleine Bestände III/17, no. 5, letter, Ermann to Ms. Heitmann-Ascher, re: the marital situation of Erwin Schienkewitz, November 30, 1950; cf. AEKIR, 7 NL 016-92, in which Gustav Sorge complained to Schlingensiepen on March 3, 1965, that his wife lived in "wilder Ehe" with a former member of the SA because his incarceration had permitted her to divorce him: "For these two my conviction meant that they could feel morally superior; they had only been party members and made a mere mistake in their choice of party." Sorge was notorious for "excess violence" and known as "Iron Gustav."

52. AEKiR, 10B 004-46, letter, Pastor Sachsse to Ms. Brenda, February 18, 1954.

53. AEKiR, 10B 004-34, letter, Sachsse to Parole Supervisor Gernert, February 17, 1954. Sachsse supported parole for Jakob Seiler so that his divorced wife would repent and "undo the injustice of the divorce" and allow Seiler to "return to an orderly family life." He claimed that the wife only divorced because Seiler received a death sentences and she "had to assume that she would never see him again." Seiler was convicted in the Dachau trials for killing seven American POWs; his sentence was first commuted, then reduced, and then he was released. "But," Sachsse continues, "she has—as far as I know—kept herself from any relations with other men and seems to regret the preliminary divorce." He hoped that "in the long run a closer relationship can be initiated between the divorced spouses and that the marriage can be restored."

54. EZAB 2/2488, "Seelsorgerliche Handreichungen für die Pfarrer in Sachen der NS-Verbrecherprozesse," June 21, 1963.

55. "Seelsorgerliche Handreichungen," 6.

56. AEKIR, 7 NL 016-96, letter, Schlingensiepen to Hans Stark, August 10, 1965; letter, Margaret Stark to Schlingensiepen, September 18, 1965.

57. AEKIR, 7 NL 016-96, letter, Margaret Stark to Schlingensiepen, October 18, 1965.

58. AEKIR, 7 NL 016-64, letter, Pastor Konrad Merkt to Schlingensiepen, June 7, 1968. Cf. also the letter of Pastor Yonker to Schlingensiepen July 1, 1966. Yonker

was contacted by Kroeger's divorced first wife. She complained because her ex-husband was offended by Schlingensiepen's suggestion that he should show repentance for his participation in executions in Latvia. AEKIR, 7 NL 016-57.

59. AEKIR, 7 NL 016-96, letter, Margaret Stark to Schlingensiepen, October 18, 1965.

60. AEKIR, 7 NL 016-96, letter, Schlingensiepen to Margaret Stark, November 20, 1965.

61. AEKIR, 7 NL 016, Interview with Schlingensiepen, "Friede auch den Menschen, die bösen Willens sind," *Westdeutsche Rundschau*, August 13, 1966. Schlingensiepen notes the prevalence of heathy families and lauds the fidelity of wives: "Dabei machte ich die ermutigende Erfahrung, daß es sich bei einigen von ihrer Familien um heile Familien im schönsten Sinne des Wortes handelt—um Ehefrauen, die in großer Treue an ihren Männern hingen; um Kinder die sich aus Dankbarkeit und Liebe, so nahe das liegen könnte, ihrer Väter nicht schämen."

62. AEKIR, 7 NL 016-54, letter, Schlingensiepen to Josef Klehr, undated.

63. Langbein, *Der Auschwitz-Prozeß*, 759; Robert Jay Lifton, *The Nazi Doctors: Medical Killing and the Psychology of Genocide* (New York: Basic Books, 1986), 266; Bernard Naumann, *Auschwitz: A Report on the Proceedings against Robert Karl Ludwig Mulka and Others before the Court at Frankfurt* (New York: Praeger, 1966), 263–264.

64. Lifton, *The Nazi Doctors*, 266.

65. Langbein, *Der Auschwitz-Prozeß*, 759; Lifton, *The Nazi Doctors*, 266.

66. Emmy Göring, *An der Seite meines Mannes: Begebenheiten und Bekenntnisse* (Göttingen: Verlag K. W. Schütz, 1967); Ilse Heß, *England, Nürnberg, Spandau: Ein Schicksal in Briefen* (Leoni am Starnberger See: Druffel-Verlag, 1955); Lina Heydrich, *Leben mit einem Kriegsverbrecher* (Pfaffenhofen: Ludwig Verlag, 1976); Anna Maria Sigmund, *Frauen der Nazis* (Vienna: Carl Ueberreiter, 1990), trans. *Women of the Third Reich* (Richmond Hill, ON: NDE, 2000).

67. AEKIR, 7 NL 016-96, letter, Margaret Stark to Schlingensiepen, February 20, 1966.

68. AEKIR, 7 NL 016-96, letter, Schlingensiepen to Margaret Stark, January 8, 1966.

69. AEKIR, 7 NL 016-96, letter, Margaret Stark to Schlingensiepen, September 18, 1965.

70. AEKIR, 7 NL 016-96, letter, Schlingensiepen to Margaret Stark, January 8, 1966.

71. AEKIR, 7 NL 016-67, letter, Schlingensiepen to Pastor Hans-Georg Müller, June 25, 1966. This idea appeared in letters to Josef Klehr and Adolf Eichmann, to whom he wrote that "there is more joy in heaven over the return of a sinner than over 99 just men who do not need to repent."

72. Interview, Hermann Schlingensiepen, "Friede auch den Menschen, die bösen Willens sind," *Westdeutsche Rundschau*, August 13, 1966.

73. Langbein, *Der Auschwitz-Prozeß*, 470.

74. Langbein, *Der Auschwitz-Prozeß*, 440.

75. Langbein, *Der Auschwitz-Prozeß*, 466.

76. 4 Ks 2/63 Regional Court Frankfurt am Main, Rüters et al., *Justiz und National-sozialismus*, vol. 21, 842; Ernst Klee, *Das Personallexikon zum Dritten Reich: Wer war was vor und nach 1945* (Frankfurt am Main: Fischer Verlag, 2003), 596.

CHAPTER 8

1. Avishai Margalit, *The Ethics of Memory* (Cambridge: Harvard University Press, 2002), 199.

2. Nigel Biggar, ed., *Burying the Past: Making Peace and Doing Justice after Civil Conflict* (Washington, DC: Georgetown University Press, 2001).

3. Claudia Card, *The Atrocity Paradigm: A Theory of Evil* (Oxford: Oxford University Press, 2002), 188.

4. Eberhard Fechner, *Der Prozess: Eine Darstellung des Majdanekverfahrens in Düsseldorf* (NDR Production, Waltham, MS: The National Jewish Center for Jewish Film, 1984).

5. Uwe Dittmer, *Im Blickpunkt: Sünde und Vergebung* (Berlin: Evangelische Verlagsanstalt, 1981), 54; Carl Amery, "Defreggers Flucht zu alten Kameraden," *Die Zeit*, August 29, 1969; "Der Fall Döpfner," *Neues Deutschland*, August 2, 1969; Klaus Stiller, *Tagebuch eines Weihbischofs* (Berlin: Klaus Wagenbach, 1972).

6. "Bishop Defregger Denies Guilt, Legal or Moral in '44 Killings," *New York Times*, August 5, 1969; TV interview with Auxiliary Bishop Defregger, *ARD Report*, August 4, 1969.

7. "Bishop Defregger Denies Guilt, Legal or Moral in '44 Killings," *New York Times*, August 5, 1969.

8. "Bischof Defregger: Druck aus Rom," *Der Spiegel*, August 8, 1969.

9. Döpfner quoted in "Bischof Defregger: Herde gemieden," *Der Spiegel*, July 21, 1969.

10. Dr. Hans Wagner, "Des Spiegels Spiegel," *Münchner Katholische Kirchenzeitung*, July 1969, IFZ Munich, Defregger news collection.

11. "Kardinal Döpfner stellt sich vor Defregger," *Münchner Katholische Kirchenzeitung*, Sonderdruck, July 1969. Döpfner concluded: "Einem Mann, der, wie Weihbischof Defregger, in schwere Gewissensnot gedrängt, eine Entscheidung traf, an der er immer gelitten hat, kann man menschliches Verständnis nicht verweigern."

12. So the commentary in the *Frankfurter Rundschau*. *Der Spiegel* assembled seven media commentaries on the TV broadcast under the heading "Hauptmann im Priesterrock: *Pressestimmen zu Defregger's Fernsehauftritt*," August 8, 1969.

13. "Kardinal Döpfner stellt sich vor Defregger," *Münchner Katholische Kirchenzeitung*, Sonderdruck, July 1969. Döpfner declared: Vor der Ernennung zum

Weihbischof habe ich den Fragekomplex gründlich untersucht und bin zu der Überzeugung gekommen, dass nach dem für Kriegshandlungen geltenden Völkerrecht kein schuldhafter Tatbestand vorlag."

14. "Die Tat bestätigt—die Schuld bestritten" *Süddeutsche Zeitung*, September 18, 1970.

15. Matthias Defregger, "Solidarität mit den Opfern: Brief an die Priester und Gemeinden im Erzbistum München und Freising," *Münchner Katholische Kirchenzeitung*, Sonderdruck, July 1969.

16. Friedrich Meichsner, "Für einen getöteten Soldaten starben 17 Italiener," *Die Welt*, July 26, 1969.

17. "Bischof Defregger: Herde gemieden," *Der Spiegel*, July 21, 1969.

18. Defregger, "Solidarität mit den Opfern."

19. Defregger, "Solidarität mit den Opfern."

20. Marianne Thora, "Gibt es so viel Dumme?" *Münchner Katholische Kirchenzeitung*, Sonderdruck, July 1969: "Die Vorgänge in Filetto waren dem Hauptmann Defregger und sind dem Bischof Defregger offensichtlich trotz aller juristischen Schuldlosigkeit eine schwere Lebenslast. Es ist gut, daß wir das jetzt wissen und zeigen können, daß es uns Ernst ist mit der christlichen Liebe, die des anderen Last mitträgt" (4).

21. Thora, "Gibt es so viel Dumme?"

22. "Des Spiegels Spiegel," *Münchner Katholische Kirchenzeitung*, Sonderdruck, July 1969.

23. "Bishop Defregger Denies Guilt, Legal or Moral in '44 Killings," *New York Times*, August 5, 1969.

24. "Innerkirchliche Spannungen wegen Defregger: Rücktritt von Diözesanpräses Nieberle," *Frankfurter Allgemeine Zeitung*, July 17, 1969.

25. "Italien ermittelt gegen Defregger," *Frankfurter Allgemeine Zeitung*, July 24, 1969. "Defregger wird nicht einreisen: Spiegel-Interview mit dem leitenden Oberstaatsanwalt von L'Aquila, Dr. Armando Troise," *Der Spiegel*, March 23, 1970.

26. "Zwischen Rache und Versöhnung," July 1969, newspaper clipping, IFZ Munich, Defregger News Collection.

27. "Vergebung für Defregger," *Frankfurter Allgemeine Zeitung*, July 16, 1969.

28. Erwin Wilkens, "Verpasste Gelegenheit," *Wiesbadener Tageblatt*, August 9, 1969.

29. Harvey Cox, "Beyond Discreet Silence," *Christianity and Crisis* 29.15 (September 15, 1969): 226.

30. Gerhard Mauz, "Franziskus nahm den Purpur nicht," *Der Spiegel*, August 4, 1969.

31. Mauz, "Franziskus nahm den Purpur nicht."

32. "Filetto-Reise verschoben. Döpfner: Versöhnungsgeste zur falschen Zeit," *Spandauer Volksblatt*, October 17, 1971.

33. Meichsner, "Für einen getöteten Soldaten."

34. Mauz, "Franziskus nahm den Purpur nicht."

35. Defregger, "Solidarität mit den Opfern."

36. Meichsner, "Für einen getöteten Soldaten."

37. "Bischof Defregger: Bis auf Weiteres," *Der Spiegel*, July 14, 1969.

38. "Bischof Defregger: Die Stunde kommt," *Der Spiegel*, July 28, 1969.

39. "Munich Bishop Resigns," *New York Times*, September 18, 1970.

40. Cox, "Beyond Discreet Silence."

41. Dittmer, *Im Blickpunkt*, 54, emph. in original.

42. Dittmer, *Im Blickpunkt*, 54.

43. Dittmer, *Im Blickpunkt*, 54.

44. Cf. Elsa Tamez, *The Amnesty of Grace: The Doctrine of Justification from a Latin American Perspective* (Nashville: Abingdon Press, 1993); Miroslav Volf, *Free of Charge: Giving and Forgiving in a World Stripped of Grace* (Grand Rapids, MI: Zondervan Publishing House, 2006).

45. Scottish Episcopal Richard Holloway, the former bishop of Edinburgh, maintains that "we are exiled in the horror of the past" since neither September 11, nor the Africa slave trade nor the Holocaust of the Jews "can be undone...or appropriately avenged." Therefore "only unconditional impossible forgiveness can switch off the engine of madness and revenge and invite us, with infinite gentleness, to move into the future." Richard Holloway, *On Forgiveness: How Can We Forgive the Unforgivable?* (Edinburgh: Canongate, 2002), 86.

46. Miroslav Volf, *Exclusion and Embrace* (Nashville: Abingdon Press, 1996).

47. This is also the position of Jan Heiner Tück, "Das Unverzeihbar verzeihen? Jankélévitch, Derrida und eine offen zu haltende Frage," *Communio* 33 (2004): 2:14.

48. Volf, *Exclusion and Embrace*, 138.

49. Volf, *Exclusion and Embrace*, 137.

50. Jürgen Moltmann, *Spirit of Life: The Holy Spirit and the Theology of Life* (Minneapolis: Fortress Press, 1997), 138.

51. Moltmann, *Spirit of Life*, 138.

52. Moltmann, *Spirit of Life*, 132.

53. Moltmann, *Spirit of Life*, 133.

54. Dan Bar-On, "Holocaust Perpetrators and Their Children," *Journal of Humanistic Psychology* 29 (Fall 1989): 424–443.

55. "Günther Grass under Siege after Revealing SS Past," *New York Times*, August 17, 2006.

56. Moltmann, *Spirit of Life*, 133.

57. Björn Krondorfer, "Nationalsozialismus und Holocaust in Autobiographien protestantischer Theologen," in *Mit Blick auf die Täter: Fragen an die deutsche Theologie nach 1945*, ed. Björn Krondorfer, Katharina von Kellenbach, and Norbert Reck (Gütersloh: Gütersloher Verlagshaus, 2006), 23–61.

58. Telephone conversation with Zakis, April 14, 2008.

59. HSTA (Hauptstaatsarchiv Düsseldorf), Gerichte Republik 432, no. 204/7278, Zakis interrogation, March 8, 1972.

60. HSTA Düsseldorf, Ger. Rep. 432, no. 204/7278.

61. HSTA Düsseldorf, Ger. Rep. 432, no. 204/7277.

62. HSTA Düsseldorf, Ger. Rep. 432, no. 204/7279.

63. HSTA Düsseldorf, Ger. Rep. 432, no. 204/7279.

64. HSTA Düsseldorf Ger. Rep. 432, no. 204, 138, Zakis interrogation, May 28, 1974.

65. HSTA Düsseldorf, Ger. Rep. 432, no. 204/7280.

66. Telephone conversation, April 14, 2008.

67. HSTA Düsseldorf, Ger. Rep. 432, no. 204/7280.

68. HSTA Düsseldorf, Ger. Rep. 432, no. 204/7279.

69. HSTA Düsseldorf, Ger. Rep. 432, no. 204/7280.

70. HSTA Düsseldorf, Ger. Rep. 432, no. 204/7280.

71. Telephone conversation, April 14, 2008.

72. Michael Rothberg, *Multidirectional Memory: Remembering the Holocaust in the Age of Decolonization* (Stanford, CA: Stanford University Press, 2009).

73. HSTA Düsseldorf, Ger. Rep. 432, no. 204/7278.

74. http://www.dradio.de/dkultur/sendungen/zeitreisen/515002/, February 6, 2008; Aussage des Zeugen Zakis, Hundeführer der Wachkompanie: "Am Morgen des 3.11.1943 kam jemand und sagte, es gebe eine Sonderaktion und zwei Liter Schnaps und 200 oder 400 Zigaretten für den, der mitmachen wolle. Als damals von der Teilnahme an einer Sonderaktion die Rede war, wußte ich, daß damit Erschießungen gemeint waren. An dem Tag wurde das Lager in Alarm versetzt. Ein Teil der Hundestaffel wurde auf Außenposten geschickt. Man konnte das Heranbringen der auswärtigen Juden sehen. Das Schießen war auch von meinem Posten zu hören. Das Schießen ging bis zum Einbruch der Dunkelheit."

75. Fechner, *Der Prozess.*

76. Fechner, *Der Prozess.*

Bibliography

Allen, Michael. "Oswald Pohl: Chef der SS-Wirtschaftsunternehmen." In *Die SS: Elite unter dem Totenkopf,* ed. Ronald Smelser and Enrico Syring, 394–407. Paderborn: Ferdinand Schöningh, 2000.

Alt, Karl. *Todeskandidaten: Erlebnisse eines Seelsorgers im Gefängnis München-Stadelheim mit zahlreichen im Hitlerreich zum Tode verurteilten Männern und Frauen.* Munich: Neubau-Verlag Adolf Gross, 1946.

Aly, Götz. *Bilanz der Verfolgung von NS-Straftaten.* Cologne: Bundesanzeiger, 1998.

Amstutz, Mark. *The Healing of Nations: The Promise and Limits of Political Forgiveness.* Lanham, MD: Rowman and Littlefield, 2005.

Arendt, Hannah. *Eichmann in Jerusalem: A Report on the Banality of Evil.* New York: Penguin, 1963.

———. *The Human Condition.* Chicago: University of Chicago Press, 1989.

———. *Vita Activa oder Vom tätigen Leben.* Stuttgart: Kohlhammer, 1960.

Arkel, Dik Van. *The Drawing of the Mark of Cain: A Social-Historical Analysis of the Growth of Anti-Jewish Stereotypes.* Chicago: University of Chicago Press, 2010.

Aschenauer, Rudolf, ed. *Ich, Adolf Eichmann: Ein historischer Zeugenbericht.* Leoni am Starnberger See: Druffel-Verlag, 1980.

Asmussen, Hans, ed. *Agende für den Dienst der Lagerpfarrer in Kriegsgefangenen und Interniertenlagern.* Stuttgart: Quell Verlag, 1947.

Ball, Howard. *Prosecuting War Crimes and Genocide: The Twentieth-Century Experience.* Lawrence: University Press of Kansas, 1999.

Barnett, Victoria J. *Bystanders: Conscience and Complicity during the Holocaust.* Westport, CT: Praeger, 1999.

Bar-On, Dan. "Holocaust Perpetrators and Their Children." *Journal of Humanistic Psychology* 29 (Fall 1989): 424–443.

———. *Legacy of Silence: Encounters with Children of the Third Reich.* Cambridge: Harvard University Press, 1989.

————. "Will the Parties Conciliate or Refuse? The Triangle of Jews, Germans, and Palestinians." In *From Conflict Resolution to Reconciliation*, ed. Yaacov Bar-Simon-Tov, 239–255. Oxford: Oxford University Press, 2004.

Bendel-Maidl, Lydia. "Katholische Tradition des Schuldbekenntnisses und der Vergebung vor neuen Herausforderungen: Die Notwendigkeit einer historischen Tiefenschärfung." In *Die katholische Schuld?* ed. Rainer Bendel, 345–358. Münster: LIT Verlag, 2002.

Benz, Wolfgang, Hermann Graml, Hermann Weiß, eds. *Enzyklopädie des National-sozialismus.* Stuttgart: Klett-Cotta, 1997.

Bergen, Doris L., *Twisted Cross: The German Christian Movement in the Third Reich.* Chapel Hill: University of North Carolina Press, 1996.

Bergmann, M. S., and M. E. Jucovye, eds. *Generations of the Holocaust.* New York: Columbia University Press, 1982.

Besier, Gerhard. "Zur Geschichte der Stuttgarter Schulderklärung vom 18./19. Oktober 1945." In *Wie Christen ihre Schuld bekennen*, ed. Gerhard Besier and Gerhard Sauter, 9–63. Göttingen: Vandenhoeck Ruprecht, 1985.

————. "Die politische Rolle des Protestantismus in der Nachkriegszeit." *Beilage zu Das Parlament: Aus Politik und Zeitgeschichte* 50 (2000): 29–38.

Bieler, Andrea. "Aspekte nationalsozialistischer Frauenpolitik in ihrer Bedeutung für die Theologinnen." In *Darum wagt es Schwestern*, ed. Göttinger Frauenforschungsprojekt zur Geschichte der Theologinnen. 243–271. Neukirchen-Vluyn: Neukirchener Verlag.

Biess, Frank. "Survivors of Totalitarianism." In *The Miracle Years: A Cultural History of West Germany, 1949–1968*, ed. Hanna Schissler, 57–82. Princeton, NJ: Princeton University Press, 2001.

Biggar, Nigel, ed. *Burying the Past: Making Peace and Doing Justice after Civil Conflict.* Washington, DC: Georgetown University Press, 2001.

Bloxham, Donald. *Genocide on Trial: War Crimes and the Formation of History and Memory.* Oxford: Oxford University Press, 2001.

Bock, Gisela. "Ordinary Women in Nazi Germany: Perpetrators, Victims, Followers, and Bystanders." In *Women in the Holocaust*, ed. Dalia Ofer and Lenore J. Weitzman, 85–100. New Haven: Yale University Press, 1998.

————. *Zwangssterilisation im Nationalsozialismus: Studien zur Rassenpolitik und Frauenpolitik.* Opladen: Westdeutscher Verlag, 1986.

Bonhoeffer, Dietrich. *The Cost of Discipleship.* Trans. R. H. Fuller. New York: Macmillan, 1963.

————. *Letters and Papers from Prison.* Ed. John W. De Gruchy and Victoria Barnett, trans. Barbara Rumscheidt and Martin Rumscheidt. Minneapolis: Fortress Press, 2010.

Bormann, Martin. *Leben gegen den Schatten: Gelebte Zeit, Geschenkte Zeit, Begegnungen, Erfahrungen, Folgerungen.* Paderborn: Bonifatius, 1998.

Brandt, Karl. "Selbstbildnis eines 'Kriegsverbrechers.'" *Deutsche Hochschulzeitung* 10.1 (1962): 5–9.

Branscome, Nyla R., and Bertjanm Doosje, eds. *Collective Guilt: International Perspectives*. Cambridge: Cambridge University Press, 2004.

Britton, Dana M. *The Gender of Crime*. Lanham, MD: Rowman and Littlefield, 2011.

Brown, Daniel Patrick. *The Beautiful Beast: The Life and Crimes of SS-Aufseherin Irma Grese*. Ventura, CA: Golden West Historical Publication, 1996.

―――. *The Camp Women: The Female Auxiliaries Who Assisted the SS in Running the Nazi Concentration Camp System*. Atglen, PA: Schiffer, 2002.

Browning, Christopher. *Ordinary Men: Reserve Police Battalion 101 and the Final Solution in Poland*. New York: Harper Perennial, 1992.

Brunner Claudia, and Uwe von Seltmann. *Schweigen die Täter reden die Enkel*. Frankfurt am Main: Edition Büchergilde, 2004.

Bruns, Wiebke. *Meines Vaters Land: Geschichte einer deutschen Familie*. Munich: Econ Verlag, 2004.

Bryant, Michael S. *Confronting the Good Death: Nazi Euthanasia on Trial*. Boulder: University of Colorado Press, 2005.

Buber-Neumann, Margarete. *Als Gefangene bei Stalin und Hitler: Eine Welt im Dunkel*. Stutrgart: Seewald Verlag, 1985.

Bucher, Rainer. *Hitlers Theologie*. Würzburg: Echter Verlag, 2008. Trans. Rebecca Pohl as *Hitler's Theology: A Study in Political Religion* (New York: Continuum, 2011).

Buscher, Frank. *The U.S. War Crimes Trial Program in Germany, 1946–1955*. New York: Greenwood Press, 1989.

Buscher, Frank M., and Michael Phayer. "German Catholic Bishops and the Holocaust, 1940–1952." *German Studies Review* 11.3 (1988): 463–485.

Buttner, Ursula, and Martin Greschat. *Die verlassenen Kinder der Kirche: Der Umgang mit Christen jüdischer Herkunft im Dritten Reich*. Göttingen: Vandenhoeck & Ruprecht, 1998.

Card, Claudia. *The Atrocity Paradigm: A Theory of Evil*. Oxford: Oxford University Press, 2002.

Cesarani, David. *Eichmann: His Life and Crimes*. London: William Heinemann, 2004.

de Mildt, Dick Welmoed. *In the Name of the People: Perpetrators of Genocide in the Reflection of Their Postwar Prosecutions in West Germany. The Euthanasia and Aktion Reinhard Trial Cases*. The Hague: Martinus Nijhoff, 1996.

Desbois, Patrick Father. *The Holocaust by Bullets: A Priest's Journey to Uncover the Truth behind the Murder of 1.5 Million Jews*. New York: Palgrave Macmillan, 2009.

Deselaers, Manfred. *Und sie hatten nie Gewissensbisse? Die Biografie von Rudolf Höß, Kommdandant von Auschwitz und die Frage nach seiner Verantwortung vor Gott und den Menschen*. Leipzig: benno Verlag, 1997.

Diephouse, David J. "Wanderer zwischen zwei Welten? Theophil Wurm und die Konstruktion eines protestantischen Geschichtsbildes nach 1945." In *Das evan-*

gelische Württemberg zwischen Weltkrieg und Wiederaufbau, ed. Rainer Lächele and Jörg Thierfelder, 49–70. Stuttgart: Calwer Verlag, 1995.

Dittmer, Uwe. *Im Blickpunkt: Sünde und Vergebung*. Berlin: Evangelische Verlagsanstalt, 1981.

Duff, Charles. *A Handbook on Hanging*. London: Putnam, 1955.

Earl, Hilary. *The Nuremberg SS-Einsatzgruppen Trial, 1945–1958: Atrocity, Law, and History*. Cambridge: Cambridge University Press, 2009.

Eickstedt, Klaus von. *Christus unter den Internierten*. Neuendettelsau: Freimundverlag, 1948.

Ericksen, Robert P., and Susannah Heschel. *Betrayal: German Churches and the Holocaust*. Minneapolis: Fortress Press, 1999.

———. *Complicity in the Holocaust: Churches and Universities in Nazi Germany*. Cambridge: Cambridge University Press, 2012.

Erpel, Simone. *Im Gefolge der SS-Aufseherinnen des Frauen KZ-Ravensbrück*. Berlin: Metropol, 2007.

Eschebach, Insa. "NS-Prozesse in der sowjetischen Besatzungszone und der DDR: Einige Überlegungen zu den Strafverfahrensakten ehemaliger SS-Aufseherinnen des Frauenkonzentrationslagers Ravensbrück." In *Die frühen Nachkriegsprozesse: Beiträge zur Geschichte der nationalsozialistischen Verfolgung in Norddeutschland*, ed. Kurt Buck, vol. 3, 65–74. Bremen: Edition Temmen, 1997.

Eschebach, Insa, Sigrid Jacobeit, and Silke Wenk, eds. *Gedächtnis und Geschlecht: Deutungsmuster in Darstellungen des nationalsozialistischen Genozids*. Frankfurt am Main: Campus, 2002.

Evans, Richard J. *Rituals of Retribution: Capital Punishment in Germany, 1600–1987*. New York: Oxford University Press, 1996.

Fechner, Eberhard. *Der Prozess: Eine Darstellung des Majdanek Verfahrens in Düsseldorf.* VHS. NDR Production. Waltham, MS: National Jewish Center for Jewish Film, 1984.

Foucault, Michel. *Discipline and Punish: The Birth of the Prison*. New York: Random House, 1975.

Frank, Hans. *Im Angesicht des Galgens: Deutung Hitlers aufgrund eigener Erlebnisse und Erkenntnisse*. Munich: F.A. Beck, 1953.

Frank, Niklas. *In the Shadow of the Reich*. Trans. Arthur Wensinger and Varole Clew-Hoey. New York: Knopf, 1991.

———. "Keine Versöhnung—Niemals." *Die Welt online*. November 5, 2005. http://www.welt.de/print-welt/article175601/Keine_Versoehnung_niemals.html (accessed November 20, 2012).

———. *Meine deutsche Mutter.* Munich: Bertelsmann Verlag, 2005.

———. *Vater: Eine Abrechnung*. Munich: Bertelsman Verlag, 1987.

Frei, Norbert. *Vergangenheitspolitik: Die Anfänge der Bundesrepublik und die NS Vergangenheit*. Munich: dtv Verlag, 1999.

Freitag, Hans. "Erfahrungen mit NS Verurteilten." Unpublished manuscript, June 2001.

Friedrich, Jörg. *Die kalte Amnestie: NS-Täter in der Bundesrepublik.* Frankfurt am Main: Fischer Verlag, 1984.

Friedrich, Oscar. *Über Galgen wächst kein Gras: Die fragwürdige Kulisse der Kriegsverbrecherprozesse im Spiegel unbekannter Dokumente.* Braunschweig: Erasmus Verlag, 1950.

Gailus, Manfred, ed. *Kirchliche Amtshilfe: Die Kirche und die Judenverfolgung im Dritten Reich.* Göttingen: Vandenhoeck & Ruprecht, 2008.

———. "Vom 'gottgläubigen' Kirchenkämpfer Rosenbergs zum 'christgläubigen' Pfarrer Niemöllers." *Zeitschrift für Geschichtswissenschaft* 11 (2006). http://www. xn--martin-niemöller-stiftung-voc.de/4/zumnachlesen/a104.

Gailus, Manfred, and Armin Nolzen, eds. *Zerstrittene Volksgemeinschaft: Glaube, Konfession und Religion im Nationalsozialismus.* Göttingen: Vandenhoeck & Ruprecht, 2011.

Geertz, Clifford. *The Interpretation of Cultures: Selected Essays.* New York: Basic Books, 1973.

Geis, Jael. *Übrig sein—Leben danach: Juden deutscher Herkunft in der britischen und amerikanischen Zone Deutschlands 1945–1949.* Berlin: Philo, 2000.

Gerdmar, Anders. *Roots of Theological Antisemitism: German Biblical Interpretation and the Jews, from Herder and Semmler to Kittel and Bultmann.* Leiden: Brill, 2008.

Gerlach, Christian. *Kalkulierte Morde: Die deutsche Wirtschafts- und Vernichtungspolitik in Weißrußland 1941–1944.* Hamburg: Hamburg Edition, 1999.

Gerlach, Wolfgang. *And the Witnesses Were Silent: The Confessing Church and the Persecution of Jews.* Trans. Victoria J. Barnett. Lincoln: University of Nebraska Press, 2000.

Giardano, Ralph. *Die zweite Schuld oder von der Last ein Deutscher zu sein.* Munich: Knaur, 1990.

Girard, René. *Violence and the Sacred.* Trans. Patrick Gregory. Baltimore: Johns Hopkins University Press, 1977.

Goldhagen, Daniel. *Hitler's Willing Executioners: Ordinary Germans and the Holocaust.* New York: Knopf, 1996.

Göring, Emmy. *An der Seite meines Mannes: Begebenheiten und Bekenntnisse.* Göttingen: Verlag K. W. Schütz, 1967.

Goschler, Constantin. "Der Fall Philipp Auerbach: Wiedergutmachung in Bayern." In *Wiedergutmachung in der Bundesrepublik,* ed. Ludolf Herbst and Constantin Goschler, 77–98. Munich: R. Oldenbourg, 1989.

———. *Wiedergutmachung: Westdeutschland und die Verfolgten des Nationalsozialismus 1945–1954.* Munich: Oldenbourg, 1992.

Gravenhorst, Lerke, and Carmen Tatschmurat, eds. *Töchter-Fragen: NS-Frauen-Geschichte.* Freiburg im Breisgau: Kore Verlag, 1990.

Greschat, Martin, ed. *Im Zeichen der Schuld: 40 Jahre Stuttgarter Schuldbekenntnis.* Neukirchen-Vluyn: Neukirchener Verlag, 1985.

———. *"Verweigertes Schuldbekenntnis."* In *Erinnern. Bekennen, Verantworten: 50 Jahre Stuttgarter Schuldbekenntnis. Eine Dokumentation.* Wendlingen: EKD Dokumentation, 1995.

———. *"*'Er ist ein Feind dieses Staates!' Martin Niemöllers Aktivitäten in den Anfangsjahren der Bundesrepublik Deutschland." *Zeitschrift für Kirchengeschichte* 114 (2003): 333–356.

Greschat, Martin, ed., with Christiane Bastert. *Die Schuld der Kirche. Dokumente und Reflexionen zur Stuttgarter Schulderklärung vom 18./19. Oktober 1945.* Munich: Kaiser Verlag, 1982.

Grossman, Atina. "Victims, Villains, and Survivors: Gendered Perceptions and Self-Perceptions of Jewish Displaced Persons in Occupied Post-war Germany." *History of Sexuality* 11 (2002): 291–319.

———. *Victims, Victors, Allies and Jews in Occupied Germany, 1945–1949.* Princeton, NJ: Princeton University Press, 2006.

Gutmann, Israel, Eberhard Jäckel, Peter Longerich, and Julius H. Schoeps, eds. *Enzyklopädie des Holocaust: Die Verfolgung und Ermordung der europäischen Juden.* 3 vols. Berlin: Argon, 1993.

Heer, Hannes. *Vom Verschwinden der Täter: Der Vernichtungskrieg fand statt, aber keiner war dabei.* Berlin: Aufbau Verlag, 2004.

Heimannsberg, Barbara B., and C. J. Schmidt, eds. *The Collective Silence: German Identity and the Legacy of Shame.* San Francisco: Jossey-Bass, 1993.

Heinz, Hanspeter. "Feier der Versöhnung: Einführung in die christliche Bußliturgie." In *Versöhnung in der jüdischen und christlichen Liturgie*, ed. David Ellenson and Hanspeter Heinz, 11–31. Freiburg im Breisgau: Herder Verlag, 1990.

Helmick, Raymond G, S.J., and Rodney Petersen, eds. *Forgiveness and Reconciliation: Religion, Public Policy and Conflict Transformation.* Philadelphia: Templeton Foundation, 2002.

Henkys, Reinhard. *Die nationalsozialistischen Gewaltverbrechen: Geschichte und Gericht.* Stuttgart: Kreuz Verlag, 1965.

Herbst, Ludolf, and Constantin Goschler. *Wiedergutmachung in der Bundesrepublik.* Munich: R. Oldenbourg, 1989.

Herlin, Hans. *Kain, Wo ist dein Bruder Abel?* Hamburg: Nannen, 1960.

Herzog, Dagmar. *Sex after Fascism: Memory and Morality in Twentieth-Century Germany.* Princeton, NJ: Princeton University Press, 2007.

———, ed. *Sexuality and German Fascism.* Brooklyn, NY: Berghahn, 2004.

Heschel, Susanna. *The Aryan Jesus: Christian Theologians and the Bible in Nazi Germany.* Princeton, NJ: Princeton University Press, 2008.

Heß, Ilse. *England, Nürnberg, Spandau: Ein Schicksal in Briefen.* Leoni amd Starnberger See: Druffel-Verlag, 1955.

Heß, Wolf-Rüdiger. *Rudolf Heß: Ich bereue nichts.* Graz: Leopold Stocker Verlag, 1998.

Heydrich, Lina. *Leben mit einem Kriegsverbrecher.* Pfaffenhofen: Ludwig Verlag, 1976.

Himmler, Kathrin. *Die Brüder Himmler: Eine deutsche Familie.* Frankfurt am Main: Fischer Verlag, 2005.

Hitler, Adolf. *Mein Kampf.* Trans. John Chamberlain et al. New York: Reynal & Hitchcock, 1940.

Hockenos, Matthew D. *A Church Divided: German Protestants Confront the Nazi Past.* Bloomington: Indiana University Press, 2004.

Hölscher, Christoph. *NS-Verfolgte im "antifaschistischen Staat": Vereinnahmung und Ausgrenzung in der ostdeutschen Wiedergutmachung (1945–1989).* Berlin: Metropol, 2002.

Höss, Rudolph. *Death Dealer: The Memoirs of the SS Kommandant at Auschwitz.* Trans. Andrew Pollinger. New York: Da Capo Press, 1996.

Hourihan, William. "U.S. Army Chaplain Ministry to German War Criminals at Nuremberg 1945–1946." *Army Chaplaincy: Professional Bulletin of the Unit Ministry Team,* Winter–Spring 2000, 86–94.

Hull, William L. *The Struggle for a Soul: The Untold Story of a Minister's Final Effort to Convert Adolf Eichmann.* Garden City, NJ: Doubleday, 1963.

Isaac, Jules. *The Teaching of Contempt: Christian Roots of Antisemitism.* Trans. Helen Weaver. New York: McGraw-Hill, 1965.

Jones, Gregory L. *Embodying Forgiveness: A Theological Analysis.* Grand Rapids, MI: Eerdmans, 1995.

Judt, Tony. *Postwar: A History of Europe since 1945.* New York: Penguin, 2005.

Just-Dahlmann, Barbara, and Helmut Just. *Die Gehilfen: NS-Verbrechen und die Justiz nach 1945.* Frankfurt am Main: Athenâum, 1988.

Karlin, Wayne. *Wandering Souls: Journeys with the Dead and the Living in Viet Nam.* New York: Nation Books, 2009.

Katz, Claire Elise. "Raising Cain: The Problem of Evil and the Question of Responsibility." *Cross Currents,* Summer 2005, 215–233.

Kellenbach, Katharina von. *Anti-Judaism in Feminist Religious Writings.* Atlanta: Scholars Press, 1994.

———. "Christian Discourses of Forgiveness and the Perpetrators." In *Remembering for the Future: The Holocaust in an Age of Genocides,* ed. John K. Roth and Elisabeth Maxwell, 725–731. Basingstoke, UK: Palgrave, 2001.

———. "Theologische Rede von Schuld und Vergebung als Täterschutz." In *Von Gott Reden im Land der Täter: Theologische Stimmen der dritten Generation nach der Shoah,* ed. Katharina von Kellenbach, Björn Krondorfer, and Norbert Reck, 48–72. Darmstadt: Wissenschaftliche Buchgesellschaft, 2001.

———. "Vanishing Acts: Perpetrators in Postwar Germany." *Journal of Holocaust and Genocide Studies* 17.2 (2003): 305–329.

Kempner, Robert M. W. *Die SS im Kreuzverhör: Die Elite, die Europa in Scherben schlug.* Hamburg: Volksblatt Verlag, 1987.

King, Martin Luther. *Strength to Love.* Philadelphia: Fortress Press, 1981.

Klee, Ernst. *Persilscheine und falsche Pässe: Wie die Kirchen den Nazis halfen.* 3rd ed. Frankfurt am Main: Fischer Verlag, 1992.

———. *Das Personenlexikon zum Dritten Reich: Wer war was vor und nach 1945.* Frankfurt am Main: Fischer Verlag, 2003.

———. "Der Umgang der Kirche mit dem Holocaust nach 1945." In *Der Umgang mit dem Holocaust: Europa—USA—Israel,* ed. R. u. I. B. Steininger, 119–137. Vienna: Böhlau Verlag, 1994.

Klee, Ernst, Willi Dressen, and Volker Riess, eds. *The Good Old Days: The Holocaust as Seen by Its Perpetrators and Bystanders.* New York: Konecki and Konecki, 1991.

Klein, Peter. "Der Mordgehilfe: Schuld und Sühne des Dr. Otto Bradfisch." In *Die Gestapo nach 1945: Karrieren, Konflikte, Konstruktionen,* ed. Klaus-Michael Mallmann and Andrej Angrick, 221–234. Darmstadt: Wissenschaftliche Buchgesellschaft, 2009.

Kloke, Martin W. *Israel und die deutsche Linke: Zur Geschichte eines schwierigen Verhältnisses.* Frankfurt am Main: Haag und Herrchen, 1990.

Klüger, Ruth. *Weiterleben: Eine Jugend.* Göttingen: Wallstein Verlag, 1992.

Koch, Peter-Ferdinand. *Himmler's graue Eminenz—Oswald Pohl—und das Wirtschafts- und Verwaltungshauptamt der SS.* Hamburg: Verlag Facta Oblita, 1988.

Koonz, Claudia. *Mothers in the Fatherland: Women, the Family, and Nazi Politics.* New York: St. Martin's Press, 1987.

———. *The Nazi Conscience.* Cambridge: Harvard University Press, 2003.

Krause, Peter. *Der Eichmann-Prozeß in der deutschen Presse.* Frankfurt am Main: Campus Verlag, 2002.

Kraushaar, Wolfgang. *Die Bombe im Jüdischen Gemeindehaus.* Hamburg: Hamburger Edition, 2005.

———. "Philosemitismus und Antisemitismus: Zum Konflikt zwischen Horkheimer, Adorno und der Studentenbewegung." In *Das Echo des Holocaust: Pädagogische Aspekte des Erinnern,* ed. Helmut Schreier and Mattias Heyl, 71–97. Hamburg: Kraemer, 1994.

Kraybill, Donald B., Steven M. Nolt, and David L. Weaver-Zercher. *Amish Grace: How Forgiveness Transcended Tragedy.* San Francisco: Jossey-Bass, 2012.

Kritz, Neil L., ed. *Transitional Justice: How Emerging Democracies Reckon with Former Regimes.* Washington, DC: U.S. Institute of Peace, 1995.

Krohn, Claus-Dieter. "Studentenbewegung und das 'andere Deutschland.'" In *Dynamische Zeiten,* ed. Axel Schild, Detlef Siegfried, and Karl Christian Lammers. 695–719. Hamburg: Hans Christians Verlag, 2000.

Krondorfer, Björn. *Remembrance and Reconciliation: Encounters between Young Jews and Germans.* New Haven: Yale University Press, 1995.

Kwiet, Konrad. "'Hitler's Willing Executioners'" and 'Ordinary Germans': Some Comments on Goldhagen's Ideas." http://www.ceu.hu/jewishstudies/pdf/01_kwiet.pdf (accessed May 21, 2007).

Lächele, Rainer. "Vom Reichssicherheitshauptamt in ein evangelisches Gymnasium—Die Geschichte des Eugen Steimle." In *Das evangelische Württemberg zwischen Weltkrieg und Wiederaufbau*, ed. Rainer Lächele and Jörg Thierfelder, 260–288. Stuttgart: Calwer Verlag, 1995.

Lang, Jochen von, and Claus Sybill, eds. *Eichmann Interrogated: Transcripts from the Archives of the Israeli Police*. New York: Vintage Books, 1983.

Langbein, Hermann. *Der Auschwitz-Prozeß: Eine Dokumentation*. 2 vols. Frankfurt am Main: Verlag Neue Kritik, 1995.

Langer, Lawrence, "The Dilemma of Choice in the Deathcamps." In *Holocaust: Religious and Philosophical Implications*, ed. John K. Roth and Michael Berenbaum, 222–232. New York: Paragon House, 1989.

Lara, Maria Pia. "Narrating Evil: A Postmetaphysical Theory of Reflective Judgment." In *Rethinking Evil: Contemporary Perspectives*, ed. Maria Pia Lara, 239–259. Berkeley: University of California Press, 2001.

Lebert, Norbert, and Stephan Lebert. *Denn Du trägst meinen Namen*. Munich: Goldmann Verlag, 2002.

Levi, Primo. *The Drowned and the Saved*. Trans. Raymond Rosenthal. New York: Simon and Schuster, 1986.

Lifton, Robert Jay. *The Nazi Doctors: Medical Killing and the Psychology of Genocide*. New York: Basic Books, 1986.

Ludwig, Andrea. *Neue oder Deutsche Linke? Nation und Nationalismus im Denken von Linken und Grünen*. Opladen: Westdeutscher Verlag, 1995.

Mailänder Koslov, Elissa. *Gewalt im Dienstalltag: Die SS-Aufseherinnen des Konzentrations- und Vernichtungslagers Majdanek*. Hamburg: Hamburger Edition, 2009.

———. Täterinnenbilder im Düsseldorfer Majdanek Prozess 1975–1981." In *Im Gefolge der SS-Aufseherinnen des Frauen KZ-Ravensbrück*, ed. Simone Erpel, 211–230. Berlin: Metropol, 2007.

Marcuse, Harold. *Legacies of Dachau: The Uses and Abuses of a Concentration Camp*. Cambridge: Cambridge University Press, 2001.

Margalit, Avishai. *The Ethics of Memory*. Cambridge: Harvard University Press, 2002.

Markovits, A. S., and R. S. Hayden. "Holocaust before and after the Event: Reactions in Germany and Austria." In *Germans and Jews since the Holocaust*, ed. Anson Rabinbach and Jack Zipes, 234–257. New York: Holmes and Meier, 1986.

Marrus, Michael R. *The Nuremberg War Crimes Trial, 1945–1946: A Documentary History*. Boston: Bedford Book, 2007.

Martin, Roy A. *Inside Nürnberg: Military Justice for Nazi War Criminals*. Shippensburg, PA: White Mane Books, 2000.

McGargee, Geoffrey. *War of Annihilation: Combat and Genocide on the Eastern Front, 1941*. Lanham, MD: Rowman and Littlefield, 2007.

McGlothlin, Erin. *Second Generation Holocaust Literature: Legacies of Survival and Perpetration*. Rochester, NY: Camden House, 2006.

McNutt, James E. "Adolf Schlatter and the Jews." *German Studies Review* 26 (May 2003): 353–370.

———. "Vessels of Wrath Prepared to Perish: Adolf Schlatter and the Spiritual Extermination of the Jews." *Theology Today* 63 (July 2006): 176–190.

Melton, J. Gordon. *American Religious Creeds: An Essential Compendium of More Than 450 Statements of Belief and Doctrine.* 3 vols. New York: Triumph Books, 1991.

Mensing, Björn. *Pfarrer und Nationalsozialismus: Geschichte einer Verstrickung am Beispiel der Evangelisch-Lutherischen Kirche in Bayern.* Göttingen: Vandenhoeck & Ruprecht, 1998.

Meyer, Kathrin. *Entnazifizierung von Frauen: Die Internierungslager der US-Zone Deutschlands 1945–1952.* Berlin: Metropol, 2004.

Miller, Basil. *Martin Niemöller: Hero of the Concentration Camps.* Grand Rapids, MI: Zondervan Publishers, 1942.

Milton, Sybil. "Women and the Holocaust: The Case of German and German-Jewish Women." In *Different Voices: Women and the Holocaust,* ed. Carol Rittner and John K. Roth, 213–250. New York: Paragon, 1993.

Minow, Martha. *Between Vengeance and Forgiveness: Facing History after Genocide and Mass Violence.* Boston: Beacon Press, 1998.

Mochalski, Herbert, Werner Jaspert, Erich Roether, and Dietmar Schmidt, eds. *Der Mann in der Brandung: Ein Bildbuch um Martin Niemöller.* Frankfurt am Main: Stimme Verlag, 1962.

Moeller, Robert G. *War Stories: The Search for a Usable Past in the Federal Republic of Germany.* Berkeley: University of California Press, 2001.

Moltmann, Jürgen. "Political Reconciliation." In *Religion, Politics, and Peace,* ed. Leroy Rouner, 17–32. Notre Dame, IN: University of Notre Dame Press, 1999.

———. *Spirit of Life: The Holy Spirit and the Theology of Life.* Minneapolis: Fortress Press, 1997.

Moser, Tilman. *Dabei war ich doch sein liebstes Kind: Eine Psychotherapie mit der Tochter eines SS-Mannes.* Munich: Kösel, 1997.

Müller, Gerhard, et al., eds. *Theologische Realenzyklopädie.* 36 vols. Berlin: De Gruyter, 1981.

Müller-Fahrenholz, Geiko. *The Art of Forgiveness: Theological Reflections on Healing and Reconciliation.* Geneva: WCC Publications, 1997.

Naumann, Bernd. *Auschwitz: A Report on the Proceedings against Robert Karl Ludwig Mulka and Others before the Court at Frankfurt.* New York: Frederick A. Praeger, 1966.

Neimann, Susan. *Evil in Modern Thought: An Alternative History of Philosophy.* Princeton, NJ: Princeton University Press, 2002.

Neumann, Annette. "Funktionshäftlinge im Frauen-Konzentrationslager Ravensbrück." In *Tod oder Überleben? Neue Forschungen zur Geschichte des Konzentrationslagers Ravensbrück.* Vol. 1 of *Faschismus und Weltkriegsforschung Beiheft,* ed. Werner Röhr and Brigitte Berlekamp, 25–87. Berlin: Organon, 2001.

Niemann, Beate. *Mein guter Vater: Mein Leben mit seiner Vergangenheit.* Berlin: Hentrich & Hentrich, 2005.

Niemöller, Martin. *Ach Gott vom Himmel sieh darein: Sechs Predigten.* Munich: Chr. Kaiser, 1946.

———. *Die Erneuerung unserer Kirche.* Munich: Neubau-Verlag, 1946.

———. *From U-Boat to Pulpit.* Trans. Hastie Smith and Henry Smith Leiper. Chicago: Willett Clark, 1937.

———. *Über die deutsche Schuld, Not und Hoffnung.* Zurich: Evangelischer Verlag, 1946.

———. *Zur gegenwärtigen Lage der evangelischen Christenheit.* Tübingen: Furcheverlag, 1946.

Nirenberg, David. "The Birth of the Pariah: Jews, Christian Dualism, and Social Science." *Social Research* 70.1 (2003): 201–236.

Oeffler, Hans Joachim, Hans Prolingheuer, Martin Schuck, Heinrich Werner, and Rolf Wischnath, eds. *Martin Niemöller: Ein Lesebuch.* Cologne: Pahl Rugenstein, 1987.

Padover, Saul K. *Psychologist in Germany: The Story of an American Intelligence Officer.* London: Phoenix House, 1946.

Pagis, Dan. *The Selected Poems of Dan Pagis.* Trans. B. Stephen Mitchell. Berkeley: University of California Press, 1989.

Patterson, David, and John Roth, eds. *After-words: Post-Holocaust Struggles with Forgiveness, Reconciliation and Justice.* Seattle: University of Washington Press, 2004.

Paul, Christa. *Zwangsprostitution: Staatlich errichtete Bordelle im Nationalsozialismus.* Berlin: Edition Hentrich, 1994.

Phayer, Michael. *The Catholic Church and the Holocaust: 1930–1965.* Bloomington: Indiana University Press, 2000.

Poelchau, Harald. *Autobiographisches und Zeitgeschichtliches seit den zwanziger Jahren.* Berlin: K. Vogt, 1963.

———. *Die letzten Stunden: Erinnerungen eines Gefängnispfarrers.* Berlin: Volk und Welt, 1949.

Pohl, Oswald. *Credo: Mein Weg zu Gott.* Landshut: Alois Girnth Verlag, 1950.

Pollack, Martin. *Der Tote im Bunker: Bericht über meinen Vater.* Vienna: Paul Zsolnay Verlag, 2004. Trans. William Hobson as *Dead Man in the Bunker: Discovering My Father* (London: Faber, 2008).

Posner, Gerald L. *Hitler's Children: Sons and Daughters of Leaders of the Third Reich Talk about their Fathers and Themselves.* New York: Random House, 1991.

Posset, Anton. "Der Priester und der SS-General: Die Bekehrungsgeschichte des Oswald Pohl." *Landsberg im 20. Jahrhundert: Themenheft Landsberger Zeitgeschichte* 2 (1993): 20–24.

Probst, Christopher. *Demonizing the Jews: Luther and the Protestant Church in Nazi Germany.* Bloomington: Indiana University Press, 2012.

Prolingheuer, Hans. *Wir sind in die Irre gegangen: Die Schuld der Kirche unterm Hakenkreuz.* Cologne: Pahl Rugenstein Verlag, 1987.

Pross, Christian. *Wiedergutmachung: Kleinkrieg gegen die Opfer.* Frankfurt am Main: Athenäum, 1988.

Przyrembel, Alexandra. "Transfixed by an Image: Ilse Koch, the 'Kommandeuse of Buchenwald.'" *German History* 19.3 (2001): 369–400.

Railton, Nicholas. "Henry Gerecke and the Saints of Nuremberg." *Kirchliche Zeitgeschichte* 13.1 (2000): 112–138.

Reemtsma, Jan Phillip. *Das Recht des Opfers auf Bestrafung des Täter—als Problem.* Munich: Beck, 1999.

———. "Über den Begriff 'Handlungsspielräume.'" *Mittelweg* 36.6 (2002): 5–23.

———. *Wie hätte ich mich verhalten? Und andere nicht nur deutsche Fragen. Reden und Aufsätze.* Munich: Beck, 2001.

Reiser, Konrad. "Schuld und Versöhnung: Erinnerung an eine bleibende Aufgabe der deutschen Kirchen." *Kirchliche Zeitgeschichte* 4 (1991): 512–522.

Rensmann, Lars. "Collective Guilt, National Identity, and Political Processes in Contemporary Germany." In *Collective Guilt: International Perspectives*, ed. Nyla R. Branscombe and Bertjan Doosje, 169–190. Cambridge: Cambridge University Press, 2004.

Renz, Ulrich. "Zum Schutz der Mörder: NS Verbrecher waren keine Kriegsverbrecher." In *Täter-Opfer-Folgen: Der Holocaust in Geschichte und Gegenwart*, ed. Heiner Lichtenstein and Otto R. Romberg. Bonn: Bundeszentrale für politische Bildung, 1997.

Roberts, Ulla. *Spuren der NS-Zeit im Leben der Kinder und Enkel: Drei Generationen im Gespräch.* Munich: Kösel, 1998.

Rommelspacher, Brigitte. *Schuldlos-Schuldig? Wie sich junge Frauen mit Antisemitismus auseinandersetzen.* Hamburg: Konkret, 1995.

Rosenthal, Gabriele. "Nationalsozialismus und Antisemitismus im intergenerationellen Dialog." In *Der Holocaust im Leben von drei Generation: Familien von Überlebenden der Shoah und von Nazi-Tätern*, ed. Gabriele Rosenthal, 345–357. Hamburg: Edition psychosozial, 1997.

Rothberg, Michael. *Multidirectional Memory: Remembering the Holocaust in the Age of Decolonization.* Stanford: Stanford University Press, 2009.

Rückerl, Adalbert. *The Investigation of Nazi Crimes, 1945–1978.* Hamden, CT: Müller, 1980.

Rüters, C. F., Fritz Bauer, et al., eds. *Justiz und NS-Verbrechen: Sammlung deutscher Strafurteile wegen nationalsozialistischer Tötungsverbrechen.* 49 vols. to date Amsterdam: Amsterdam University Press, 1968–.

Sacken, Peter Osten, ed. *Das mißbrauchte Evangelium: Studien zu Theologie und Praxis der Thüringer Deutschen Christen.* Berlin: Institut Kirche und Judentum, 2002.

Sauser, Ekkart. "Defregger, Matthias." *Biographisch-Bibliographisches Kirchenlexikon.* http://www.bautz.de/bbkl/d/Defregger.shtml (accessed November 20, 2012).

Sauter, Gerhard. "Vergib uns unsere Schuld: Eine theologische Besinnung auf das Stuttgarter Schuldbekenntnis." In *Wie Christen ihre Schuld bekennen: Die Stuttgarter Erklärung 1945*, ed. Gerhard Besier and Gerhard Sauter, 63–129. Göttingen: Vandenhoeck & Ruprecht, 1985.

———. "Verhängnis der Theologie: Schuldwahrnehmung und Geschichtsanschauung im deutschen Protestantismus." *Kirchliche Zeitgeschichte* 4 (1991): 475–492.

———. *Versöhnung als Thema der Theologie*. Gütersloh: Gütersloher Verlagshaus, 1997.

Schäfer, Ingeborg, and Susanne Klockmann. *Mutter mochte Himmler nie: Die Geschichte einer SS-Familie*. Hamburg: Rowohlt, 1999.

Schimmel, Solomon. *Wounds Not Healed by Time: The Power of Repentance and Forgiveness*. Oxford: Oxford University Press, 2002.

Schirach, Richard von. *Der Schatten meines Vaters*. Munich: Carl Hanser Verlag, 2005.

Schmidt, Ulf. *Karl Brandt: Medicine and Power in the Third Reich*. New York: Continuum, 2007.

Schreiber, Matthias. *Martin Niemöller*. Hamburg: Rowohlt, 1977.

Shriver, Donald W., Jr. *An Ethic for Enemies: Forgiveness in Politics*. New York: Oxford University Press, 1995.

———. "Where and When in Political Life Is Justice Served by Forgiveness." In *Burying the Past: Making Peace and Doing Justice after Civil Conflict*, ed. Nigel Biggar, 23–40. Washington, DC: Georgetown University Press, 2001.

Schröm, Oliver, and Andrea Röpke. *Stille Hilfe für braune Kameraden: Das geheime Netzwerk der Alt- und Neonazis. Ein Inside Report*. Berlin: Links, 2001.

Schubert, Helga. *Judas Frauen: Zehn Fallgeschichten weiblicher Denunziation im Dritten Reich*. Frankfurt am Main: Luchterhand Literaturverlag, 1990.

Schulte, Jan Erik. *Zwangsarbeit und Vernichtung: Das Wirtschaftsimperium der SS. Oswald Pohl und das SS-Wirtschafts-Verwaltungshauptamt 1933–1945*. Paderborn: Ferdinand Schöningh, 2001.

Schwarz, Gudrun. *Eine Frau an seiner Seite: Ehefrauen in der SS-Sippengemeinschaft*. Hamburg: Hamburger edition, 1997.

———. "Frauen in der SS: Sippenverband und Frauenkorps." In *Zwischen Karriere und Verfolgung: Handlungsräume von Frauen im nationalsozialistischen Deutschland*, ed. Kristen Heinsohn, 223–245. Frankfurt am Main: Campus Verlag, 1997.

Schwartz, Johannes. "Die französischen Militärgerichtsprozesse gegen KZ-Aufseherinnen." In *Im Gefolge der SS-Aufseherinnen des Frauen KZ-Ravensbrück*, ed. Simone Erpel, 129–141. Berlin: Metropol, 2007.

Sichrovsky, Peter. *Born Guilty: Children of Nazi Families*. New York: Basic Books, 1988.

Sigel, Robert. *Im Interesse der Gerechtigkeit: Die Dachauer Kriegsverbrecherprozesse 1945–1948*. Frankfurt am Main: Campus Verlag, 1992.

Sigmund, Anna Maria. *Women of the Third Reich*. Richmond Hill, ON: NDE, 2000.

Smith, Arthur L., Jr. *Die Hexe von Buchenwald: Der Fall Ilse Koch*. Cologne: Böhlau Verlag, 1983.

Sommer, Robert. *Das KZ-Bordell: Sexuelle Zwangsarbeit in nationalsozialistischen Konzentrationslagern*. Paderborn: Ferdinand Schöningh, 2009.

Speer, Albert. *Spandauer Tagebücher*. Frankfurt am Main: Ullstein Verlag, 1977.

Spicer, Kevin P. *Hitler's Priests: Catholic Clergy and National Socialism*. Dekalb: Northern Illinois University Press, 2008.

————. *Resisting the Third Reich: The Catholic Clergy in Hitler's Berlin*. Dekalb: Northern Illinois University Press, 2004.

————, ed. *Antisemitism, Christian Ambivalence, and the Holocaust*. Bloomington: Indiana University Press, 2007.

Steffek, Andrea. *Rosa Jochmann: Nie Zusehen, wenn Unrecht geschieht. Ihr Leben und Wirken 1901–1945 als Grundlage für ihre stetige Mahnung gegen Faschismus, Nationalsozialismus und das Vergessen*. Vienna: OBG Östereicherischer Gewerksschaftsbund, 1999.

Steger, Bernd, and Peter Wald. *Hinter der grünen Pappe: Orli Wald im Schatten von Auschwitz*. Hamburg: VSA Verlag Hamburg, 2008.

Steigmann-Gall, Richard. *The Holy Reich: Nazi Conceptions of Christianity, 1919–1945*. Cambridge: Cambridge University Press, 2003.

Steinacher, Gerald. *Nazis auf der Flucht: Wie Kriegsverbrecher über Italien nach Übersee entkamen*. Innsbruck: StudienVerlag, 2008.

Stephenson, Jill. *Women and Nazi Society*. New York: Barnes and Noble, 1975.

Stiller, Klaus. *Tagebuch eines Weihbischofs*. Berlin: K. Wagenbach, 1972.

Stump, Eleonore. *Wandering in Darkness: Narrative and the Problem of Suffering*. Oxford: Oxford University Press, 2010.

Tamez, Elsa. *The Amnesty of Grace: The Doctrine of Justification from a Latin American Perspective*. Nashville: Abingdon Press, 1993.

Thielicke, Helmut, and Hans Diem. *Die Schuld der Anderen*. Göttingen: Vandenhoeck & Ruprecht, 1948.

Torrance, Alan. "The Theological Grounds for Advocating Forgiveness and Reconciliation in the Sociopolitical Realm." In *The Politics of Past Evil: Religion, Reconciliation and the Dilemmas of Transitional Justice*, ed. Daniel Philpott, 45–87. Notre Dame, IN: University of Notre Dame Press, 2006.

Tück, Jan-Heiner. "Das Unzeihliche Verzeihen: Jankélévitch, Derrida and eine offen zu haltende Frage." *Internationale Katholische Zeitschrift Communio* 33 (2004): 174–188.

————. "Inkarnierte Feindesliebe: Der Messias Israels und die Hoffnung auf Versöhnung." In *Streitfall Christologie: Vergewisserungen nach der Shoah*, ed. Helmut Hoping and Jan Heiner Tück, 216–258. Freiburg im Breisgau: Herder Verlag, 2005.

Tutu, Desmond. *No Future without Forgiveness*. New York: Doubleday, 1999.

Verkamp, Bernhard. *The Moral Treatment of Returning Warriors in Early Medieval and Modern Times.* Scranton: Scranton University Press, 1993.

Vetlesen, Johan Arne. *Evil and Human Agency: Understanding Collective Evildoing.* Cambridge: Cambridge University Press, 2005.

Volf, Miroslav. *Exclusion and Embrace.* Nashville: Abingdon Press, 1996.

———. *Free of Charge: Giving and Forgiving in a Culture Stripped of Grace.* Grand Rapids, MI: Zondervan, 2005.

Vollnhals, Clemens. "Die Hypothek des Nationalprotestantismus. Entnazifizierung und Strafverfolgung von NS-Verbrechen nach 1945." *Geschichte und Gesellschaft* 18 (1992): 51–69.

———. *Entnazifizierung und Selbstreinigung im Urteil der evangelischen Kirche. Dokumente und Reflexionen 1945–1949.* Munich: Kaiser, 1989.

———. *Evangelische Kirche und Entnazifizierung 1945–1949: Die Last der nationalsozialistischen Vergangenheit. Studien zur Zeitgeschichte.* Munich: Oldenbourg, 1989.

Wagner, Georg. "Sühne im Strafrecht und im Strafvollzug." In *Sühne und Versöhnung,* ed. Josef Blank and Jürgen Werbick, 43–172. Düsseldorf: Patmos Verlag, 1986.

Wagner, Leonie. "Totalitäre Projektionen: Zum Verhältnis von Weiblichkeit und Politik im Nationalsozialismus." In *Gebrochene Kontinuitäten? Zur Rolle und Bedeutung des Geschlechterverhältnisses in der Entwicklung des Nationalsozialismus,* ed. Ilse Korotin and Barbara Serloth, 131–151. Innsbruck: StudienVerlag, 2000.

Wald, Renate. *Mein Vater Robert Ley: Meine Erinnerungen und Vaters Geschichte.* Nürmbrecht: Martine Galunder-Verlag, 2004.

Webster, Ronald. "Opposing Victors' Justice: German Protestant Churchmen and Convicted War Criminals in Western Europe after 1945." *Holocaust and Genocide Studies* 15 (Spring 2001): 47–70.

Weckel, Ulrike, and Edgar Wolfrum, eds. *Bestien und Befehlsempfänger: Frauen und Männer in NS-Prozessen nach 1945.* Göttingen: Vandenhoeck & Ruprecht, 2003.

Weigel, Sigrid. *Bilder des kulturellen Gedächtnisses: Beiträge zur Gegenwartsliteratur.* Dülmen-Hidingsel: Tende, 1994.

Weinke, Annette. *Die Verfolgung von NS-Tätern im geteilten Deutschland: Vergangenheitsbewältigung 1949–1969 oder eine deutsch-deutsche Beziehungsgeschichte im kalten Krieg.* Paderborn: Ferdinand Schöningh, 2002.

Weiß, Konrad. *Lothar Kreyssig: Prophet der Versöhnung.* Gerlingen: Bleicher Verlag, 1998.

Welzer, Harald. *Opa war kein Nazi: Nationalsozialismus und Holocaust im Familiengedächtnis.* Frankfurt am Main: Fischer Verlag, 2002.

———. *Täter: Wie aus ganz normalen Menschen Massenmörder wurden.* Frankfurt am Main: Fischer Verlag, 2005.

Wember, Heiner. *Umerziehung im Lager: Internierung und Bestrafung von Nationalsozialisten in der britischen Besatzungzone Deutschlands.* Düsseldorf: Klartext, 1992.

Westernhagen, Dörte von. *Die Kinder der Täter: Das Dritte Reich und die Generation danach*. Munich: Kösel Verlag, 1987.

Wetzel, Juliane. "An Uneasy Existence: Jewish Survivors in Germany after 1945." In *The Miracle Years: A Cultural History of West Germany*, ed. Hanna Schissler, 131–145. Princeton, NJ: Princeton University Press, 1999.

Wilkens, Erwin. *NS-Verbrechen: Strafjustiz, deutsche Selbstbestimmung*. Berlin: Lutherisches Verlagshaus, 1964.

Wiesenthal, Simon. *The Sunflower*. New York: Schocken, 1969.

———. *The Sunflower*. Rev. ed. New York: Schocken, 1997.

Wojak, Irmtrud. *Eichmanns Memoiren: Ein kritischer Essay*. Frankfurt am Main: Campus Verlag, 2001.

Wolde, Ellen van. "The Story of Cain and Abel: A Narrative Study." *Journal for the Study of the Old Testament* 52 (1992): 25–41.

Zertal, Idith. *Israel's Holocaust and the Politics of Nationhood*. Trans. Chaya Galai. Cambridge: Cambridge University Press, 2005.

Index